COYOTE'S SWING

COYOTE'S SWING

A MEMOIR AND CRITIQUE
OF MENTAL HYGIENE
IN NATIVE AMERICA

David Edward Walker

WSU
PRESS

Washington State University Press
Pullman, Washington

WASHINGTON STATE UNIVERSITY
WSU PRESS

DISCLAIMER

Coyote's Swing recounts the author's experiences and opinions while he was employed as a psychologist by the US Indian Health Service (IHS). A former Tribal Council member of the Confederated Tribes and Bands of the Yakama Nation has reviewed the manuscript and provided feedback. The work does not reflect an official position or opinion of the Yakama Nation or the IHS.

Washington State University Press
PO Box 645910
Pullman, Washington 99164-5910
Phone: 800-354-7360
Email: wsupress@wsu.edu
Website: wsupress.wsu.edu

Author's website: davidedwardwalker.com

Library of Congress Cataloging-in-Publication Data

Names: Walker, David Edward, 1956– author.
Title: Coyote's swing : a memoir and critique of mental hygiene in native
    America / David Edward Walker.
Description: Pullman, Washington : Washington State University Press,
    [2022]. | Includes bibliographical references and index.
Identifiers: LCCN 2022033510 | ISBN 9780874224207 (paperback)
Subjects: LCSH: Walker, David Edward, 1956– | Yakama Indians—Mental
    health services. | Indians of North America—Mental health services—
    Washington (State) | Psychologists—Washington (State)—Biography.
Classification: LCC E99.Y2 W35 2022 | DDC 979.7004/974127019—
    dc23/eng/20220823
LC record available at https://lccn.loc.gov/2022033510

The Washington State University Pullman campus is located on the homelands of the Niimíipuu (Nez Perce) Tribe and the Palus people. We acknowledge their presence here since time immemorial and recognize their continuing connection to the land, to the water, and to their ancestors. WSU Press is committed to publishing works that foster a deeper understanding of the Pacific Northwest and the contributions of its Native peoples.

Cover design: Patrick Brommer

To the Seven Generations . . .

Praise for *Coyote's Swing*

"In the IHS, dissension is often suppressed as blasphemy and whistleblowers are rarely tolerated. Walker is to be commended for his thorough research and timely recommendations for reform of the agency's delivery of mental health services in Indian County ... I join him in praying that this period of tribal history comes to an end."

—Toobshudud Jack Fiander (Yakama), attorney

"A great piece of work ... I can't emphasize that enough. As a community how do we begin to dialogue with each other and encourage our people to speak up, especially given the power imbalance between 'professionals' and 'clients' as to who knows what is best? ... Incorporating his personal experiences of adversity and willingness to acclimate into our community was greatly appreciated."

—Lucy Smartlowit, MSW (Yakama/Mexican),
Interim Executive Director, Peacekeeper Society

"David Walker's Coyote's Swing *is a tour de force. It is an extraordinary work of heart, spirit, incisive intelligence, and unflinching truth telling. I highly recommend it."*

—Steven Newcomb (Shawnee/Lenape),
author of *Pagans in the Promised Land* and
co-producer of the documentary *The Doctrine of Discovery*

"An engaging and highly informative read that expertly weaves a much-needed counterpoint to the prevailing narratives of the mental health profession. Walker brings his story to life with the unheard voices and stories of those marginalized by the mental health system ... [yet] it is also a story of survivorship, resilience, and, at the end, a humble and heartfelt hope."

—Dr. Amber Logan, psychologist, public health professional,
Indigenous historian, and traditional Kahungunu Maori wahine

"A comprehensive account of how Native Americans, first assaulted by the U.S. government, continue to be re-traumatized by a U.S. mental health profession that has exacerbated rather than reduced violence, suicide, and substance abuse. Original and compelling, Coyote's Swing *is Walker's personal and professional odyssey to becoming a dissident psychologist."*

—Bruce E. Levine, author of *A Profession Without Reason*

"To medicalize human suffering through psychiatric language is to strip it of political and historical meaning ... Walker's book is at once a humble, heartfelt personal tale and a rigorously researched, incisively academic critique of the consequences of the 'mental health'-ization of Indigenous people in the United States. While Coyote's Swing *carefully catalogues the harms that have been done, it is also a clarion call of hope."*

—Laura Delano, Executive Director,
Inner Compass Initiative, author of *UNSHRUNK*

"This is a story that must be told ... This vivid, personal and very moving account has much to teach us all."

—Lucy Johnstone, PsyD, consultant clinical psychologist (UK)
and a lead author of *The Power Threat Meaning Framework*

CONTENTS

ACKNOWLEDGMENTS

I can't adequately express my gratitude to the circle of people who've helped, encouraged, and supported me through the completion of *Coyote's Swing*. I realize as well that I'm doomed to fail to recall many who deserve to be remembered. I begin, therefore, with an apology to whomever I'm about to neglect.

One morning during a very troubled time in my life in 1970, Mrs. Rennels stroked my hair as I wept in her ninth-grade English class. Eventually she taught me how to write a five-paragraph essay and haiku, which might be at the heart of all creative nonfiction. In 1972, Dr. C. Robert Maxfield, founder of the Galileo Institute for Teacher Leadership, was only my social studies teacher when he caught me skipping class. He told me he expected more of me and then walked right past me, letting his words plant their seed. In 1985, Dr. Virginia Blankenship at Oakland University sponsored my undergraduate thesis, helped me write my first journal article, and made me primary author, all to help me enter graduate school.

That fall, Dr. Patrick Kavanaugh, Dr. Marvin Hyman, and many other talented teachers challenged my new cohort to think much more critically about applied psychology. As I faced off with my dissertation project, Dr. Mimi LaDriere exuded Jesuit *Magis*, driving me to prove my commitment to interculturalism. During my early encounters with cultures of poverty and race at the Detroit Psychiatric Institute, Dr. Cheryl Munday, Dr. Linda Young, and thoughtful students brought many important and differing ideologies for me to consider.

Soon after starting my work at Yakama Nation in 2000, I met a wonderful educator (and human being) named Dr. Apanakhi Jeri Buckley at Heritage University. Our valuable conversations over tea continued until her tragic passing in 2021. Early on in our friendship, she introduced me to her then husband, Long Standing Bear Chief, a Piikáni Blackfoot elder, Sun Dancer, and pipe carrier. A fellow troublemaker, Bear Chief made numerous strong cups of coffee for me. We had many councils and sweats together in our preoccupations regarding "how to help the youth." Concurrently, Buck and Vicki Ghosthorse hosted my family at a feast far out in the country in Goldendale, Washington. Buck was a Lakota spiritual leader and good friends with Bear Chief, and they'd both reportedly been involved in the American Indian Movement (AIM). Their conversations often included Lavina Washines (Ḵ'mílpam), the first female chair of the Yakama Nation Tribal Council. I was a plebe, a novice, somehow permitted to sit and learn from powerful minds and razor-like senses of humor about lived realities of historical oppression, particularly along the Columbia River.

Everyone in this last paragraph has since walked on, but memories of our times together still bring me inspiration. I feel entirely accountable to them all, and I long for the time we might meet again somehow.

In 2000, Verna Smith Yallup (Blackfoot, Pitá-aki, "Eagle Woman") was a counselor at Yakama Nation Tribal School when she took my wife, Susan, and me into a sweat together in the Blackfoot way. Therein, her prayerful apology to the Creator for "speaking in the borrowed language" became a phrase that influenced my emerging critical writing. We pioneered our Pathways talking circles together at tribal school while teachers like Marilyn Goudy (Yakama) and Mary Looney (Yakama) graciously helped us build bridges toward their students.

My friend Victor Wilson (Yakama) brought me into many sweats, taught me about Yakama traditions, and—together with his wife, Carrie (Blackfoot), and their sons—welcomed my family into their home. Sometimes Victor, his sons, and I would sweat in the Yakama way at the home of Julian, JoJay, and other members of the Pinkham family, and I'm grateful for those spiritual times. Native friends like Eleanor White, Cynthia Mills, Lindin, Norene, and many others at the Yakama Nation Youth Treatment Center taught me more about local youth than I'd ever have learned on my own. Raymond Qualchan Olney (Yakama) and the Nak Nu We Sha ("We Care") staff were invaluable toward learning about the land around me and the struggles of Native foster youth and their families. Ray and his wife also welcomed us into their home and immersed us in Indian Shaker beliefs and practices. Although we suffered through some difficult interpersonal predicaments, I'll always be grateful to them.

Oscar Olney, Sharon John, Connie Jim, Diane Pebeahsy, Toni White-grass, Joanne Walker, Lorintha Umtuch, Helen and Patti Zack, Berta Norton, Stella Washines, Ruth Tahkeal, Joanne and Margaret Strong and the Strong family, Lucy Smartlowit, Adam and Henry Strom, Frank Mesplie, and RoAnna Wahpat all contributed in their own way to my growth as I struggled with the Yakama Indian Health Service (IHS) Clinic. There were many more to name here than I can adequately remember.

Dr. Joseph Stone, elder and pipe carrier, first taught me how to build fire for the sweat lodge in the Blackfoot way. We had many conversations about working as psychologists both during and after leaving IHS. I'm grateful we stayed in touch after Joe and his partner, psychologist Dr. Amber Logan (Maori), moved to New Zealand. I'm also thankful for the insightful work of Dr. Eduardo Duran (Apache/Tewa), who joined Joe, me, and several others back then in the iconic sweat lodge ceremony in 2001 at the first "Healing Our Wounded Spirits" Conference on the sacred lands of the Confederated Tribes of Grand Ronde. Dr. Duran also very graciously supported my novels.

Ellie Carrithers was an excellent assistant clinical director and therapist while we worked together to launch and stabilize Níix Ttáwaxt ("Good Growth to Maturity") Residential Program with EPIC Youth Services in 2004. Our mutual friend and colleague Scott Hinton cleared the path, coaxed youth into forgiving our faults, and kept us all grounded. House parents Josh and Rebecca Rousculp served through hard times at Níix Ttáwaxt with personal sacrifice and a relentless love and regard for the youth in their care. Dr. Jeff Thompson reunited recovering mothers with abused children while we began our ongoing consultations about the human condition. Ken Nichols, retired Children's Services regional administrator, made good things happen at EPIC by massaging a dysfunctional system from the inside.

I owe so much to my *kála* (my friend and adopted grandma) Kussamwhy Levina Wilkins (Yakama/Winátchapam) and can hardly depict the intangible and inestimable gifts she's given me. Through my *kála*'s lived example, I've learned the more visceral features of Yakama survival and resiliency. We've helped youth together on many occasions, seen one another's lives go in and out of turmoil, and continued to communicate for over twenty years now. Without her support and guidance, Níix Ttáwaxt could not have been designed and launched. Although the program itself was short-lived, her Níix Ttáwaxt teachings were its centerpiece and live on through those she's taught. She told me to sing this song called "Coyote's Swing" and to not give up until I'd finished. *Kwaa'la.* My deep thanks go out also to esteemed educator and leader Patsy Whitefoot (Yakama/Diné), *kála*'s niece, who as Yakama tribal administrator challenged me to do all I could to serve the community.

I also hold much gratitude to and esteem for former Yakama Nation councilman and tribal attorney Jack Fiander (Yakama) for carefully combing through my manuscript draft and offering invaluable feedback and guidance. His encouragement and insights improved my draft tremendously. The many long talks I've had with good friend and journalist Steven Newcomb (Shawnee/Lenape) widened the aspirations of *Coyote's Swing*, while his wife, Paige, and great friend Pila have offered continual moral support. Jon Claymore (Lakota), past director of Native education for the Washington State Office of the Superintendent of Public Instruction, has continually supported my work and helped fortify my approach to this project. My deep thanks extend also to Dr. Bonnie Duran (Opelousas/Coushatta descendent), director of the Indigenous Wellness Research Institute, Center for Indigenous Health Research, at the University of Washington, for arranging digital library access at the University for several years at a time. Without this help, *Coyote's Swing* could never have been completed. Similarly, the staff members at Yakama Nation Cultural Center and its Tribal Library made available to me unique resources that greatly enhanced my research.

Fellow anti-authoritarian, liberation psychologist, and writer Dr. Bruce Levine and his wife, Bonnie, have been revolutionary collaborators and supporters since my earliest days at Yakama Nation when they visited and joined Sue and me in a sweat lodge with Long Standing Bear Chief. I met Bruce and Bonnie through the International Society for Ethical Psychology and Psychiatry (ISEPP). We have many important allies there, too—so many, it would be hard to mention them all. However, I'll tip my hat to Drs. Albert Galves, Dominic Riccio, Tony Stanton, Chuck Ruby, Jacqueline Sparks, Grace Jackson, Gina Nikkel, and David Cohen, each of whom helped me survive the turmoil of my IHS tenure in both real-time and its echoes. I also feel much gratitude to fellow ISEPPers Rick Winking, guitarist extraordinaire; my childhood friend, psychiatric survivor, and counselor Elizabeth McCarthy; and Dr. David Clark, who is doing inspiring work alongside Aboriginal people through Sharing Culture and the Carrolup Story in New South Wales, Australia.

Dr. Paula Caplan, a leading feminist psychologist, psychiatric critic, author, playwright, and Harvard professor, somehow took an interest in my Medicine Valley novels (*Tessa's Dance* and *Signal Peak*), helped to promote them, and even recommended them to her literary agent. Before she died of cancer in 2021—a complete shock to many friends and followers—we communicated about her ongoing efforts on behalf of a feminist deconstruction of psychiatric systems and my own efforts toward decolonizing the U.S. mental health system in Native America. I know she'd support *Coyote's Swing* fiercely and unreservedly while taking me to task for all I've missed. I'm forever grateful to have had access to her cheerleading and challenging, spirited intellect.

The spirit of collaboration is no more evident than when one researcher shares an abundance of resources with another. Dr. Susan Burch, associate professor of American Studies at Middlebury College, did just that with me when she sent me multiple DVDs of thousands of records for the Hiawatha Asylum for Insane Indians in Canton, South Dakota, gathered from the National Archives and Records Administration (NARA) during her Regional Residency Fellowship. Each of these disks is worth a volume of books on Hiawatha, and I immediately forwarded a second set to Bonnie Duran at the Indigenous Wellness Research Institute. I can never repay this favor, so I must try to pay it forward. I want to also mention how grateful I am to Jungian analyst and psychologist Dr. Frances Parks, who was my boss when she signed the paperwork for a mini-grant so I could visit Fort Worth on my own NARA reconnaissance in 2007.

I'm indebted to Laura Delano for introducing me to investigative journalist Robert Whitaker, author of the best-selling psychiatric drug exposé *Anatomy of an Epidemic: Magic Bullets, Psychiatric Drugs and the Astonishing Rise of Mental Illness* (New York: Crown, 2010) and other crucial books on our corrupt mental health system. Laura's own story of psychiatric survival was featured in the *New Yorker* in 2019, and I'm very thankful to this very busy person for continually linking Twitter followers of her Inner Compass Initiative to my articles for *Indian Country Today*. Thanks as well to both Robert Whitaker and Dr. Lucy Johnstone, leader of the Power Threat Meaning Framework initiative at the British Psychological Society, for supplying supportive comments for the book proposal for *Coyote's Swing*. To journalist Rob Wipond, who is highly concerned about First Nations mental health coercion in the United States and Canada: thank you for being a fellow advocate throughout the years.

Through the many helpers I've mentioned thus far, I became visible to writer, feminist, and healer Deena Metzger, who invited me into a new kind of circle in 2017. I'm as indebted to her for personal healing as for the support and encouragement she's offered to my work. I've learned important lessons from Deena about our urgent duty to make many more circles in our immediate, local vicinity for the healing of Mother Earth and the future of humanity. We must unite now to end the global corporate feudalism and national and cultural hegemony damaging our home planet, to educate and disempower ignorance, oppose hatred and war, surrender empty consumerist lifestyles, and begin to live deliberately, simply, and conscientiously with careful regard for all our relatives, on the land and in the sea, be they human, animal, or plant. This is the path of the heart.

After my family and I moved to Seattle, my travels over the mountains to visit and work at Yakama Nation almost always included staying with fellow Bahá'ís and spiritual sister and brother, Drs. Randie and Steve Gottlieb. Our many conversations about serving social justice and the future promise of unity and peace toward which we are all inextricably tied form the bone marrow of this work. There are not adequate words for my abiding gratitude to them.

My long-distance and long-lasting friendship with Thomas Barrie, professor, writer, fellow questioner, and a notable authority on sacred architecture, is another true brotherhood. Without Tom's advice and support, I'm not sure I could have held on emotionally for the long ride to final publication. It is my editor, Linda Bathgate, and her team at Washington State University Press who've maintained faith in *Coyote's Swing* and worked so hard to shepherd this project through peer review and editorial approval. Thank you, Linda, and everyone at WSU Press for believing in this book. Thanks also to copy editor David Chesanow for his careful attention to detail, scrupulous fact-checking, advice, and improvements to the manuscript.

I come finally to the close friends in my writing circle: Ben Dennis, Jan Meredith, and Fredric and Susan Matteson, and of course, my dear wife, Sue. I'm so grateful to know all of you and to have shared the synchronicities and metaphors within the deeper substrata of this book.

My father and fellow writer, George Lee Walker, visits me in dreams, and I feel his pat on my back as he congratulates me. I apologize if I leave readers puzzled when I write here in my father's memory that I "saw the windchime swing, and heard the coyote howl, and didn't understand at first, but now I do." My ninety-four-year-old mother, Edith, can still tell me directly that she's proud of me. My sisters, Cindy and Suzy, and their husbands stand behind my niece and nephews to wish me well. My gratitude to my in-laws, Dr. Helen Lieberman, Stan Lieberman and Joyce White, and Carole Fisher and Gary Smith, who have often cheered me on. My aunt Barbara, my aunt Jane, and my uncle Roger have offered me such encouragement over the years, and I know all my cousins greet me too. Together with their own cousins, my sons and their wives, Ben and Chaima, Seth and Hollie—the next generation—reach toward an uncertain future well beyond mine. Their example only pleases me and gives me hope. For all these loving people in my family circle, I am deeply grateful.

My beautiful wife, Susan, has lived and endured so much with me, never faltering in her commitment, encouragement, and love, supporting my creative absences and preoccupations for years at a time, unfaltering in her desire that I succeed in making this offering on behalf of justice for our Native sisters and brothers. And I do so thank her and all the people I've mentioned—as well as any I haven't—every single day.

INTRODUCTION

BRINGING THE SONG OUT

This book is like a song that arose out of grief. I remember saying, "I have to write something," as I walked out of a crisis residential center sometime in 2002 after trying to "evaluate" a Native young man so sedated by psychiatric drugs, he couldn't recall his own name.[1] A year or so later I felt the same imperative after watching a police officer tackle and handcuff a hysterical Native middle school boy for lobbing his backpack at him. The officer had just completed a combat-like foray through this boy's group home—his only refuge from horrendous violence in his life—and all the while clicked his Taser, loudly shouting, "Who's next?" He seemed to me like a scary monster right out of the dreams this boy had told me. Not long afterward I sat in my office, fighting back tears, after gently persuading a teenage Native girl to surrender her knife one day and then sitting down with her on the next to light some sage in an abalone shell and bless us both before telling her that her brother had just died. I was not a family member, but in the Native way I was the nearest relative.

A few days passed, and I was informed another young Native woman I'd visited in jail had died in an accident right after being released. She'd only just asked me about "getting therapy" for nightmares about physical and sexual abuse. Two days later, her shocked boyfriend ingested an overdose of drugs over this girl's death. By Friday I was meeting him by his hospital bed, and *he* was telling *me* he was sorry. He didn't want me to feel like a bad therapist because he'd tried to kill himself to be reunited with her.

These were the exigencies of a small slice of my work. I had some cancellations, and I needed something—anything—to do about all the sadness I felt. The crises moved so fast, I felt disoriented and numb. I simply wanted to understand who I was and what I was doing. I suppose typing free associations on my government desktop was outside my assigned duties as a federal civil service employee. Then again, the social worker down the hall was often seen lounging and reading John Grisham novels. No one was going to call me out, and if they did, I'd describe what I was doing as "continuing professional education."

I had no real collegial support, so I began consulting online with members of the International Society for Ethical Psychology and Psychiatry (ISEPP), publishers of the small critical psychology journal *Ethical Human Psychology and Psychiatry*, a "little mouse that roars" for which I've since served as an advisory editor. The people on the ISEPP Listserv became a lifeline, navigating me through my new work environment at the U.S. Indian Health Service (IHS), where I was charged with serving the community of the Confederated Tribes and Bands of the Yakama Nation in central Washington State.

I had a penchant for taking notes—sometimes merely to organize my thoughts or cope, but more often, as a response to an intuition about self-protection. I also wrote emails to friends, family members, and colleagues and kept copies. On my lunch break, of course. I printed off all the memos I sent in-house too. I knew then that I didn't want to forget anything, and I had few people with which to communicate to help me remember.

A sizable portion of the memoir parts of *Coyote's Swing* comes out of this collection of miscellaneous work notes from over eighteen years ago. Other portions are more recent, and I hope my reader can excuse my reluctance to distinguish between them. A linear chronology doesn't matter in depicting the powerful story I've been living. To me, everything in *Coyote's Swing* is about this very moment in the U.S. mental health system in Native America anyway.

As we go to press, I've recently reinstated my contract temporarily as a consultant to Yakama Nation[2] after a one-year lapse due to the pandemic. My relationship with the tribe now extends back twenty-two years. I've made friends with many Yakama people as well as members of other Original Nations living within this community. Among them are Blackfoot[3] tribal members; much like the Yakama, their ways have influenced me too. Blackfoot scholar Wendy Running Crane notes:

> Blackfoot learners are constantly striving to find ways to bring harmony and balance out of the chaos. That is why the meaning of "I know" in Blackfoot ways of thinking really means "I'm making

a mark right here and from here on this is my reference point."
Saying "I know" means that the Blackfoot person actually had some
relationship to the knowledge being sought, either through their
own personal experience, observation, or transfer of knowledge
through story, song, dream, or vision.[4]

Coyote's Swing is my own way of saying "This is what I know" and of trying
to draw sense and meaning out of chaos I've experienced. After numerous
attempts, the writing voice that's arrived through me has become a hybrid—
reaching out to my scholarly relatives in our shared thirst for numbers,
citations, and references while considering memories and vulnerabilities as
equally valid to the story I must tell. I feel that only in this synthesized way
might I properly open heart, mind, and spirit toward stimulating counsel
within the community of the U.S. mental health system in Native America.

I know I must offer the "data" of empiricism to be believed, but I also
want to challenge modes of argumentation where only that can matter and
that exclude Native perspectives on "truth telling." My writing is not a literature review or empirical analysis. It is as I have said: a story. I recently wrote
in other places:

> Psychology's inherent *positivistic naturalism* ... can be foreign to an
> Indigenous epistemology. We are taught within the mental health
> profession to consider the logical and systematic study of causal
> relationships as the *sin qua non* methodology for establishing the
> legitimacy of any Western mental health "healing" approach. This can
> cause us to miss the cultures of applied psychology and psychiatry
> themselves, which are very new human endeavors intimately tied to
> Western cultural values of individualism and materialistic philosophy,
> as well as potential servants to both conquest and colonization. With
> respect to Indigenous peoples, the dominance of such Western values
> already secularizes the place of the sacred, the spiritual, and the soul,
> away from consideration regarding human wellbeing.[5]

Ironically, psychological science itself, which suffers terribly from its own
crisis of replication,[6] clearly supports the adage "We believe what we want to
believe." As humans, we tend to seek information and data that confirms our
prejudices and presuppositions.[7] I doubt I'm any more immune than anyone
else from this tendency, but I do feel strongly allied with the idea that truth
seeking is very nearly a human instinct.

The specific gifts of European post-Enlightenment thought are skepticism, reasoning, careful observation, and the methodological detection of causal relationships between phenomena. An intrinsic bias deeply embedded within this same philosophy is its presumption that such ways don't feature in Indigenous science as well, making it somehow inferior. The blend of science and spiritual wisdom in the latter seems to antagonize those wedded to the European perspective, and Western positivism has only recently begun to make room for chaos, albeit grudgingly and ambivalently.

Nonetheless, Spotted Tail (Brulé Sioux) remarked back in 1877: "My friends, your people have both intellect and heart; you use these to consider in what way you can do the best to live. My people, who are here before you, are precisely the same."[8] We need to enter more forthrightly into cultural tensions and ways of knowing between two worlds and try to sort things out. As Robin Wall Kimmerer remarks in *Braiding Sweetgrass*, this involves going

> back to the questions that science does not ask, not because they aren't important, but because science as a way of knowing is too narrow for the task.[9]

I've sought to check my own potential biases, but *Coyote's Swing* remains a work of "informed" opinion. Please be aware that I've engaged in practices antithetical to the positions I take in this book. For instance, I recommended psychiatric drugs to Native clients early in my IHS career (to my abiding regret). Such professional actions, happening during chaos and uncertainty, set me on a path of "scientific inquiry" as to whether I should be doing so. Additionally, I've been fascinated with brain-behavior relationships since my earliest exposure to psychology, became a practicing neuropsychologist for the first decade of my career, taught graduate neuropsychology seminars, and have practiced periodically in this field until recently. Only gradually did I begin to suspect how the tremendous overreach of biological reductionism and biopsychiatry corrupts many facets of today's neuroscience into an elegant version of phrenology. My own clinical experience and emerging research began colliding, at first creating cognitive dissonance, then shaking me toward the realization that many mainstream assumptions in the U.S. mental health system in Native America and elsewhere are not only wrong but dangerous. *Coyote's Swing* is the fruit of years of questioning not only mainstream mental health assumptions but my own.

At first, I wanted to dismantle "IHS mental health psychobabble": the psychiatric labels, theories, cleverly named drugs, intake protocols, note formats, etc.—all the materials I saw inside Native patient charts. As I thought about the lives of certain Native people I knew and the near-constant stress they faced, I began considering how Western mental health practices and language obscure their lived experience of oppression. I thought this linguistic path might be interesting, even clever.

I completed four chapters of a book called *Speaking in the Borrowed Language* and disliked them. My friend Paula Joan Caplan referred me to her literary agent, Regina Ryan, and I don't think she liked them much either. She suggested I instead "fictionalize" my experiences. So began my first novel, *Tessa's Dance*, which continued into its sequel, *Signal Peak*. These novels arose out of my love and regard for the youth of Yakama Nation, but I felt insecure about writing them. I remember calling my *kála*, friend, and Yakama cultural specialist Levina Wilkins (Kussamwhy) and asking her whether as an outsider, I had any right to create them.

"In our way," she explained, "if you don't sing the song given to you, you'll get sick. You have to let your song come through. It's a gift to you from the Creator and not your choice." She continued, "I do have one request, however ... Please write this book so the *páshtin* will understand us. They don't. They don't know how it's been for us because they themselves have lost their way and don't understand themselves."[10]

The *páshtin* ("push'tin," with the *u* pronounced as in "up") are the "white" people or "EuroAmericans" as described in Western academia's racialized narrative. In *Coyote's Swing*, I've adopted this word *páshtin* instead of "white" out of respect for the Yakama viewpoint and language, Ichishkíin Sinwit. *Páshtin*, by the way, is rumored to come from the Yakama community's earliest encounters with foreign traders, miners, and speculators, primarily men, who declared themselves as from "Boston" or as "Bostonians." Rather than referring to skin color as in the Western academic narrative and as much of U.S. society has been taught to do, *páshtin* identifies these intruders with their stated place of origin, a tendency more in keeping with how many Native communities identify themselves. There will be moments in what I write where "white" and "EuroAmerican" work better, such as in more broadly applied ideas or when describing Western research statistics. But *páshtin* will be the rule rather than the exception when I'm discussing EuroAmericans.

I slowly realized my *káɬa* was asking me to deploy a kind of "intervention" among these *páshtin*. Colleague Michael Karlberg refers to this as *"discourse intervention*—an effort to change our social reality by altering discourses that help constitute that reality."[11] In sum, I believe I've been formally requested by a Yakama elder to help challenge an established narrative of Western culture.

Toward beginning this effort, I'll pause now to share the following poem gifted to me by a mid-teen Yakama client. It's composed on lined composition paper in loopy cursive pink ink and pertains to what being positively recognized and understood means to her:

Forever No More

No more invisible,
Speechless, deaf and blind child
With neglected pleasures
Being addicted to denial
Floating through time,
Gravitating toward a warm arm
For the emptiness
That promises no harm
No more relentless sifting
Through bodies seeking self-settling
Through competitive combat
For what's left on the shelf—
A mad melee of supply and demand
Driven by gullible pride
That leads to sedating the you
That suffocates inside.
Then the negative whispering subsided
And the panicking ceased
The undercurrent suppression
Of pent-up terror was released
As the mystery of the Unknown
Manifested pristine clear
A positive message of Truth
Entered my ear.[12]

Perhaps this poem may help inform you, my reader, about this young woman's spirit and potential in life. At the time she gave it to me, she'd just quit alcohol abuse but was still running with a youth gang. She had dropped out of school. Bullets literally flew through her life. The juxtaposition of her poem's power alongside the treacherous context of her life soars like a skyrocket above any known behavioral rating scale or achievement test. She and many gifted young people are out there, failed, miserably, by me and you.

MORE ON TIME

I draw inspiration from the Yakama traditional teaching of the "time ball" through which

> Time is a relationship between two events,
> Kept fresh in memory by selected objects on knotted hemp.
> Connection is as vital as Separation.[13]

In this Yakama practice, "cultural chronology is a way of measuring the separation of knots, a way of ordering, sometimes relatively and sometimes absolutely, what happened."[14]

I've tried to fashion *Coyote's Swing* as a time ball in written form, one that traces the string running through my own life and learning. Again, as Blackfoot traditions educate me:

> There is no dependence on a certain body (e.g., the Earth's rotation around the Sun) that determines when things will happen. Time is only a measurement; it is not a law. Time is also circular, rather than linear, which means it always happens again and again.[15]

I hope, after I'm dead and gone, certain knots made together with friends at Yakama Nation will remain within family memory. I still touch and feel knots tied with others on that land, and they affect how I think about my life now and what I've sought to do as a helper in this world. In my own spiritual view, the work of this book is a form of worship of the Creator and a concretization of a felt spiritual duty.

Coyote's Swing is divided into four parts. In part 1, "Cat Brings Coyote's Swing," I introduce myself in deference to the traditions of so many Original Nations who insist a story cannot be understood without first knowing the teller. I summarize my upbringing in the most open ways I can muster, including certain vulnerable disclosures, in my effort to meet standards set by my own clients in what they've bravely told me. By sharing who I am and where I come from, I may begin to address the question "Why are you here?" posed to me long ago in my first few weeks of work at Yakama Indian Health Service. I am mindful how this introduction is also "culturally nested," because it highlights numerous aspects of my EuroAmerican "individual self." I also mention certain events transpiring shortly after I arrived at Yakama Nation that set the stage regarding similar questions—that is, what is this system and why is it here?

Part 2, "Coyote Swings Back and Forth," offers sociohistorical analysis and critique of the current U.S. mental health system in Native America. I bring forth well- and lesser-known numbers, some of my own quantitative reasoning, and certain observations about "what I see happening." I ask whether IHS's *páshtin* notions about "depression" obscure reactions to ongoing oppression and genocide based upon United Nations criteria. I provide data challenging IHS and tribal grantees' reliance upon psychiatric labels and drugs as a strategy for preventing suicide. I construct the composite but realistically tumultuous case of "Tessa," her desire to "be PTSD," and the history and relevance of this popular label to the psychopharmaceutical "trauma industry." I contrast Pathways Circles and the power of youth helping to support and nurture one another. Principles of liberation psychology encourage a deeper investigation by today's mental health providers in Native America regarding what occurred before their "arrival." This is a mostly untold story that I believe everyone should know.

In part 3, "Building Coyote's Swing," I consider some possible philosophical and religious foundations to *páshtin* efforts to improve Native "mental hygiene." I locate my own family's Missouri Cherokee heritage within the factors leading up to the launch of the EuroAmerican mental hygiene movement. Under what conditions was the first lunatic asylum dedicated to American Indians built? What was an Indian Lunacy Determination? How have psychological tests and measures created robust stereotypes with which Native youth struggle today? I demonstrate how early mental "hygienists" helped to create specific difficulties that today's mental health system "treats." I also bring forth certain stories of Native people held as inmates, some all their lives, at the Hiawatha Asylum and other sordid places. Finally, I trace the time ball's string into today's U.S. jails and prisons overpopulated with Native American inmates.

The title of part 4, "Dismantling Coyote's Swing," refers to my own ideas for disrupting the current mental health paradigm dominating Indian Country. I contend that "prevention" should really mean preventing further abuses occurring within this approach. I question motives behind so-called community participatory research with its obligations and responsibilities to parties outside tribal sovereignty. I suggest a "community-driven" approach that emphasizes greater partnership with traditional values and ways of knowing before determining which methods, including those of Western academia, best serve the needs and desires of Original Nations. I summarize the British Psychological Society's Power Threat Meaning Framework as one rich and viable bridge away from the current IHS paradigm of labels, pills, and brief counseling. This section closes by describing my experience of a healing circle for mental health providers themselves called "Revisioning Mental Health."

Throughout *Coyote's Swing*, I demonstrate the colonial hierarchies and paternalism of Western medicine embedded within the U.S. mental health system in Indian Country. But I try to go about this more by implication than treating the topic directly or completely. I have only one story among many yet to be shared. It does seem important for me to advise my reader that this hierarchical system in certain ways inhabits me, and I need to watch out for the ways it does so. One of my personal motives for writing has to do with healing from cultural teachings in my own learning and socialization that I consider toxic. Despite whatever impressions may arise, I like being a psychologist. Unfortunately, this must mean that I remain among the anointed of a secular priesthood that has emerged alongside Western medicine to help Native well-being. If this analogy holds, I am also in many respects a heretic.

THE PANDEMIC

Much of *Coyote's Swing* was researched and completed prior to the COVID-19 pandemic. For much of the time during the pandemic, I served as a participant-volunteer in consultative meetings with leaders at State-Tribal Education Compact schools (STECs) in the state of Washington. My role was to help with social and emotional learning (SEL) during an extraordinary and unprecedented period.

Before I temporarily backed away from my contract work at the Yakama Nation Tribal School in late 2021, I witnessed massive change inflicted by the pandemic on the community. Many treasured staff members left; the school continued in only limited stop-start fashion; many students were jostled by circumstance further away from their own commitment to learning. Schools in Native communities are critical sources of nourishment, respite, connection, activity, resources, and support. Many students are from high-poverty backgrounds and many stressed families have caregivers working multiple jobs that are often considered "essential." Students' family members were being exposed to much higher COVID risks and fears than the general U.S. population, and this was happening across Native America.[16] Losing access to school, combined with long-standing marginalization in benefiting from digital and other solutions, resulted in a general lack of human contact, which exacerbated ongoing threats to basic emotional and physical well-being,[17] in addition to keeping up with one's education.

The Trump administration's secretary of education, Betsy DeVos, delayed releasing CARES Act funding targeted for U.S. tribal schools, and this meant literally no school at all for many Yakama youth during the spring of 2020. School administrators and teachers acted heroically by distributing school meals to hungry students, driving many miles across the large expanse of the Yakama reservation land to bring not just food but emotional sustenance as well. Teachers also stood outside in Yakama Nation Tribal School parking lot wearing masks and handing out "pass packets" in hopes that they'd partially support the education of youth stuck at home without internet connections or just to keep kids active.

After long delays and legislative advocacy, CARES funds were finally released in August 2020, allowing for the purchase of laptops and tablets. However, the release left inadequate time for administrators to apply it in planful ways before school started. Additionally, the local rural infrastructure for internet and remote learning already had many problems and challenges, and many Native young people remained without adequate access and became terribly demotivated. The team sports that brought everyone together and coalesced the community were completely disrupted. Powwows and longhouse gatherings are only now cautiously reemerging.

Culturally essential memorials and funeral ceremonies for the deceased could not be observed during the pandemic. For several weeks, Yakima County had one of the highest levels of incidence and mortality for COVID-19 in the United States. Many elders were lost, and in this time of unrelenting sorrow there wasn't an opportunity to hold the ceremonies considered necessary for their repose.

The appointment of Representative Deb Haaland (Laguna Pueblo) as the first Native American secretary of the interior has brought great hope for paradigmatic change in the entrenched systems she oversees. It's quite possible that the influence of her administration may bridge over to the Indian Health Service, which is an agency of the U.S. Department of Health and Human Services. At the very least, we can hope that, out of the adversity of the pandemic, we might witness renewed scrutiny on all systems intended to serve Native American communities, including those bearing upon "mental health."

PART I

Cat Brings

Coyote's Swing

ONE

Coyote Swings

THE STORY TOLD

Charley is one of many English language surnames likely imposed upon or assigned to families historically by *páshtin* church or government officials at the Confederated Tribes and Bands of the Yakama Nation in Central Washington, where more than a few storytellers reside. In the early 1920s, William Charley told my favorite Yakama story to Lucullus Virgil McWhorter, his *páshtin* friend. The two men hunted elk together and were close enough that William and his wife named their new baby daughter after Lucullus's deceased little girl.[1] Lucullus probably learned Ichishkíin Sinwit, the Yakama language, from William, who was a fluent speaker when there were still many such people.

William Charley was a dedicated advocate for the Yakama, a highly valued interpreter who grew up among the Klickitat, one of the confederated bands. I first learned about Lucullus McWhorter from my close friend and mentor, Long Standing Bear Chief, a Piikáni Blackfoot pipe carrier and educator who passed away too young.[2] He gifted me a reprint of an old pamphlet Lucullus authored in 1912 called *The Crime Against the Yakimas*.[3]

Lucullus funded this publication himself in an effort to defeat local *páshtin* legislative efforts to usurp Yakama water rights. He was eventually adopted by a Yakama family and given the name Hemene Ka-wan, "Old Wolf," a significant honor, "having mystical connections with the sky," and related to the story of wolf brothers from the oral tradition of the

3

Wasco-Wishram.[4] He likely had permission to share this story offered by his storyteller friend, William:

> The Cat belongs to the white man and goes ahead of his travels everywhere. The white man followed Cat to America which until that time belonged to the Red man.
>
> Coyote [Spilyáy] was preparing to bring the Indians to a higher stand in life, bring them to education and a written language. Cat did not want this, so he fixed to get rid of Coyote. So he fastened a great swing to the sky. It was a big swing, and the people could swing far out over the world and be brought back by the swing again to their own country.
>
> Coyote came along and wanted to swing. Cat let him get in the swing and began swinging him. He shoved the swing farther and still farther out, until finally Coyote saw the ocean. He liked this. He asked to be swung over the water, which was done. Then he asked to be sent still farther. That he might see what was on the other side of the ocean.
>
> Then Cat shoved him harder, and Coyote saw the land on the other side. He wanted to see still more, and Cat swung him far out over the land beyond the ocean. The swing came back empty, and Coyote was never again heard from. He is supposed to have grown dizzy and fallen from the swing. It is believed that he landed in Germany, for those people are the wisest of all nations, more inventive, more learned than any other country. Coyote is supposed to have continued his work over there, for he had no way of returning to the land of the Indians.[5]

William Charley shared this story with his *páshtin* friend only sixty years after the Yakama Nation reservation had been created by the Treaty of 1855 at the conclusion of three years of bitter war. At the time of his telling, the original tribal agency headquarters was still at Fort Simcoe near White Swan, where many Native people lived and still do—in a rural spot adjacent to Mool Mool Spring on the way to sacred Pahto.[6]

However, this agency locale was in the process of being shut down, one of its boarding schools was being closed—the Yakima Indian Christian School, often referred to locally as Methodist Mission Boarding School, remained open—and much controversy had erupted about creating a new agency near the reservation town of Toppenish.[7] Powerless over these undesired changes,

Yakama leaders went so far as to appeal for the support of sympathetic local *páshtin* women to help subvert the efforts of their husbands.[8] Ultimately they lost the contest, and the agency was shifted twenty-five miles east of the core Yakama population. Having been vehemently resisted by Yakama people, the change was successfully pushed through by local *páshtin* businessmen lobbying the Bureau of Indian Affairs.[9]

These *páshtin* men, who successfully dominated the Yakama community's wishes, wanted to expand economic opportunities for the fledgling reservation town of Toppenish. They were in charge. White supremacy was a common, openly embraced sensibility, fueling headlines and editorials in newspapers like the *Seattle Star*.[10] It was expressed through the firebombing of homes owned by Japanese farmers and laborers and their families,[11] who rented Yakama allotments parceled under the connivance of the Dawes Act and brought unfamiliar agriculture methods that competed with local white farmers. It was evident in the 1924 induction of seven hundred new members to the Ku Klux Klan before a crowd of 40,000 at the city of Yakima's Central Washington Fairgrounds.[12] This was a period of bold racist extremes not so dissimilar from the one in which we currently live. In 1927, for example, 150 *páshtin* descended upon Filipino migrant workers living in and around Toppenish and beat and forcibly "deported" them out of the Yakima Valley.[13]

William Charley told his story to his friend Lucullus at a moment when the white supremacist "Cat" was pushing on Native and many other non-white people very hard. This feline "civilizing force" was trying to ensnare Coyote, Spilyáy, trickster-hero of the Yakama people, and the story warned of swinging too close to European ways. William was teaching his friend about competing cultural worlds and ways of knowing, and the hazards through which voluntary assimilation may quickly become involuntary. (Coyote wants to swing, but once he volunteers, he is trapped.) His story ends in the greatest of calamities for a Yakama person: a permanent loss of connection to the sacred land. This is my own understanding of William's story, and there are certain to be others.

LEARNING TO INTRODUCE MYSELF

I arrived a little more than seventy years after William Charley shared Coyote's Swing and began my intimate work with the lives and concerns of people of Yakama Nation as a clinical psychologist, a Western version of "helper" or "healer." A recent hire by the Indian Health Service (IHS) in a brand-new millennia, I came at a tumultuous time. In an unprecedented test of tribal sovereignty, Yakama Nation Tribal Council had demanded only a few weeks before my arrival that United States attorney James Shively enforce Article Nine of the Treaty of 1855 forbidding the sale of alcohol on tribal land, infuriating many local non-Yakama people and the Washington State attorney general.[14]

Yakama leaders were fed up with local profiteering off alcohol addiction and vowed to do all they could to reduce a chronic scourge on their people, including improving substance abuse and mental health programming. My position as the first doctoral psychologist at Yakama IHS Clinic was created as one means of appeasing numerous complaints about poor mental health services.

From my first day, rumors of a budgetary crisis circulated around the clinic, including the possibility of an "RIF" (reduction in force). This was not at all reassuring after uprooting my family from Michigan, where we'd lived all our lives. Our new "adventure" seemed to be quickly morphing into a disaster. Our house back in Royal Oak was still on the market, and we were holding two mortgages with one paycheck while feeling uncertain whether we should just cut our losses and retreat. There were many other sources of tension I'll soon discuss, but what I really wanted then was to get involved with this community. I had an urgent need to know whether my new job was actually going to work out.

William Charley (right) poses with friend Lucullus Virgil McWhorter before a historical marker commemorating the killing of Indian Agent Andrew Bolon in 1918. *L.V. McWhorter Photographs Collection (pc085b05f73_36), Manuscripts, Archives, and Special Collections (MASC), Washington State University Libraries.*

Sharon John, a Yakama nurse-educator who soon became a friend, suggested I attend a weekly meeting of Nak-Nu-We-Sha (We Care),

Yakama Nation's child welfare program. She'd even called ahead and made sure the program's staff members expected me.

I'd been invited to offices in an old modular behind the only Chinese restaurant in the reservation town of Toppenish, about a mile from the clinic. This was my first "field" visit to meet people I was to serve, and I felt both nervous and excited. But I found the front door to the module locked, and when I squinted through the window on a hot and cloudless day, the front reception area appeared dark. Turning back toward the parking lot, I saw cars.

I made my way along a weathered wooden deck surrounding the structure toward a different door and stood outside pondering it. I could plainly hear voices, so I grabbed the handle, found it to be unlocked, pulled the door open, and stepped out of the bright sun into cavernous darkness. It took a moment for my eyes to adjust before I found myself standing at the head of a conference table, facing a room full of Native people. Everyone looked directly at me, and I had the sense I'd startled them.

A man began speaking to me in an authoritative tone in Ichishkíin Sinwit. Of course, I didn't have a clue what he was asking or telling me. He motioned for me to take a seat at the middle of the table, and everyone watched as I sat down. I smiled a bit, said "Hi," and several people greeted me or nodded. A long silence ensued until an older woman sitting directly across from me said, "Well ... why not go ahead and introduce yourself? Who are you, and why are you here?"

I stated my name and identified myself as the new psychologist with Yakama Indian Health Service Clinic. I explained I'd just moved from Michigan with my family and described my education, degrees, and places where I'd trained toward my professional licensure. I finished with a smile and a casual, friendly remark that I looked forward to working with everyone.

I felt awkward and my introduction was automatic. I failed to recognize I'd been dropped into an important intercultural encounter. I spoke from within my own cultural routine, a by-product of my academic and professional socialization. I filled the necessary blanks of a EuroAmerican "selfhood" with achievements and career credentials, offering my version of a "self" noted worldwide for its "remarkable absence of community, tradition, and shared meaning."[15]

No one responded, and I became embarrassed. I glanced down along one side of the table and up the other for reassurance. A couple of people nodded again, but they didn't smile. I felt as though people were waiting for me to say something more. Silence is highly valued in Indian Country, but I didn't know anything about this then. Nothing at all happened for several excruciating seconds, and I couldn't think of another word. The older Yakama woman sitting across from me watched me too.

Finally, she raised her eyebrows, and said in the "Indian English" vernacular I'd eventually come to recognize for its teasing friendliness, "Well ... seems the air's got awful hot in here, 'idn't it?"

This question was highly ambiguous for me. At the time, I took it to mean I was full of hot air. It makes me laugh now, but I flushed back then. I believe someone did open a door, and I may have been completely wrong about her intent. I was far too inhibited to ask what she meant. When it's hot in the Yakima Valley, it's very hot. In any case, this was the moment when a door opened inside of me to the realization that I was in a place where what I thought I knew about human relationships did not apply.

Several days later, I mentioned my embarrassment to a new friend, Verna Smith (Blackfoot, Pitá-aki, "Eagle Woman") at Yakama Nation Tribal School, where I'd also been approached to consult.

Verna explained, "Well, you'll be measured at the heart. So, when somebody asks you who you are, you need to describe your family: where you come from, who raised you, and who your people are. Don't worry about your degrees and book learning and all that. People might think you're saying you're better than them. Say who your family is; maybe tell about your dad and mom and grandma and grandpa. Then go ahead and speak whatever you want. That's the right way here and pretty much all over Indian Country."

Over the years, I've come to feel more natural describing who I am and who raised me as a means of introduction and to recognize the necessity of doing so before presuming to offer opinions to others about topics or issues in which I share common interest. Since Verna's early counsel, I've felt gifted with innumerable other instances of similar guidance, and I'm grateful to have been allowed, at least to a particular degree, "into" a community very different from the one in which I grew up. I'm also thankful to have been forgiven for my rudeness in not knowing how to behave and for being accepted anyway.

Looking back, I'm still amazed I never received any kind of "cultural orientation" from the Indian Health Service. In fact, my rapport and friendship with people in the Yakama Nation community grew in a kind of inverse relationship with my professional standing at Yakama IHS Clinic. As

I became more involved with the community, I became maligned by a small cabal of *páshtin* IHS detractors as having "gone Native" or having "left the fort," so to speak. I believe some of this resentment came about because my relationship with Native people mattered much more to me than conforming to the organizational culture of IHS.

From the beginning, I didn't get along with a predominantly "biological mental health ideology" held by my new coworkers. They'd been socialized over decades of working for the Indian Health Service into this strongly medical perspective that I considered anathema. And how can one hope to form new working relationships with distrusting, threatened, and close-knit coworkers with whom one fervently disagrees? I nonetheless tried to be a bridge builder. I assumed I must have much to learn from such experienced people. I also felt I might face down their resistance to me via some new ideas coming from a psychosocial and cultural viewpoint. But it became quickly evident that the kind of reciprocity I envisioned was never going to happen and then matters deteriorated immeasurably. We became like oil and water.

As I found stronger footing, I became more assertive about what I considered invalid and dangerous about the psychiatric labels and pills these workers so frequently dispensed. I'm sure this came across as arrogance and helped trigger the fury with which I was eventually met. But just as clearly, my new colleagues seemed completely closed to and disinterested in any ideas at variance with what they'd already been doing. There was no institutional expectation whatsoever that they should act any differently. Throughout my four years working for the agency, I saw no IHS initiatives fostering creative solutions, as I'd seen so often during a four-year term I'd just left behind as a clinically informed, organizational psychologist.

The health services model at IHS was quasi-military: hierarchical and command-control oriented. This was boldly symbolized by the blue U.S. Public Health Service Commissioned Corps and military-reserve uniforms some were compelled to wear while serving Native descendants of people who'd had to survive the assaults of *páshtin* in similar clothing. I also noticed how certain forms of speech and etiquette echoed military formalities, and this shocked me. The medical director was more of a commanding officer. My subordinate position felt like something akin to a frontline lieutenant. Pressures regarding "professional speech" inside the clinic, what things I said or didn't say, seemed quite affected by my civil service rank and "scope of medical authority." When I began to make trouble in this system, in-clinic medical bylaws were brought under review so that my own misbehaviors would become sanctionable. In retrospect, I might have considered that medical services first delivered to Native people by U.S. authorities would come via military medicine and that this system's generational descendent was what I was entering. But I didn't anticipate IHS organizational culture at all.

EuroAmerican allopathic medical culture also dominates IHS. There was no presence in-clinic of a traditional healing practitioner or any recognition of the holistic, traditional healing ways of Yakama people I was eventually permitted to learn something about.[16] Instead, a decidedly EuroAmerican medical culture of aggression toward disease and injury—of battle mounted through lab work, diagnosis, and surgical, pharmaceutical, or orthopedic rehabilitation—drove hard toward our Native patients. In her classic book *Medicine & Culture*,[17] medical journalist Lynn Payer highlights this distinctly EuroAmerican approach, one going all the way back to Benjamin Rush's influential caveat against "undo [*sic*] reliance upon the powers of nature in curing disease"[18] and readily distinguishable even from medical approaches across Europe. At Yakama IHS Clinic, the body was not to be relied upon to heal itself. It is instead like an automobile, a machine to be investigated and fixed. Nowhere was this more evident than in the emphasis upon psychopharmaceutical drugs in the provision of primary care "behavioral health."

An unflinching rigidity of Western psychiatric protocol and an overt lack of work ethic among some mental health coworkers combined to provoke me. In what my new colleagues did and didn't do, I saw an unnecessary barrier toward helping with the suffering and injustice I was just beginning to learn about in the community. I didn't want to have any part in what threatened my own efforts to establish credibility as a newly arrived helper. Additionally, the openly expressed unwelcome and lack of support of my colleagues didn't help matters.

I had to find ways to bypass this antipathy because I was simultaneously being observed by a beleaguered Native community taking a fierce stand with state and federal government authorities while dealing with intergenerational loss and trauma in their daily lives. I felt more immediately oriented to do whatever was expected of me and more by this community if I could. My coworkers' attitudes had alienated many tribal members prior to my arrival, and I knew I wanted to differentiate myself and be part of positive change. I wrote about my own fears and misgivings to a friend back in Michigan: "I am constantly being watched by the tribe. My ethics, consistency, trustworthiness are being evaluated. There are huge battles brewing in this community." This turned out to be inaccurate: I wasn't really under surveillance and evaluation but arriving in the midst of turmoil and a very real opportunity to help foment change. But I didn't know this yet.

The brewing battles were about tribal sovereignty and power, and for signaling my alliance with tribal sovereignty early on and so publicly with regard to this community's "mental health," I would experience enough heat from inside Yakama IHS Clinic and IHS regional administrators that I and my family almost packed up and moved back to Michigan our first year. The support of Yakama people themselves, however, made the real difference. I have many Native people to thank for committing themselves to making me a better helper, teaching me, and encouraging me to stay the course by including me in numerous sweat lodges, naming and healing ceremonies, traditional memorials, funerals, first foods feasts, powwows, family gatherings, Indian Shaker meetings, and longhouse events.

Yakama dancers at the Ellensburg Rodeo, circa September 1945, as published in the *Seattle Post Intelligencer. Museum of History and Industry, Seattle.*

In brief, I was shown, briefed, counseled, scolded, handed responsibility, lectured, hugged, and gradually transformed in how I think about myself, my relationships with other people and the world, and really how I behave as a human being. The unrelenting love and respect I experienced might be called a "resocialization experience" by some academic somewhere, but it felt like much more than that for me. As Verna suggested, I was found at the heart.

Ink atawi mash ("I love you").

This is one way I explain my deviance from a typical Euro form—that is, continuing my narrative with an introduction of my "self" in the Yakama way. I feel obliged to situate myself for you, my reader, contextually, emotionally, and spiritually before I share what I've learned about the U.S. mental health system present and past in Native America. I offer somewhat more than a "psychosocial profile," because I feel that only by knowing more about me, my family, how I was raised, and certain life trials I experienced will you be able to decide what to make of what I have to say.

As I've gone over what I'm about to describe many times, it often occurs to me that I've composed a rather detailed "individualized self" in the *páshtin* sense. But this turns out to be not entirely true. I am saying who I am from an experience of walking in two worlds. I am telling my own story first because it is proper manners in Native America.

TWO

"Who Are You, and Why Are You Here?"

THE SLOW SPIRAL

When I was six in rural East Lansing, Michigan, in the early 1960s, my mother had her hands full with my two younger sisters, and I ran free with a gang of mostly poor kids through the miles of woods, fields, and farms surrounding us. Such permissiveness is rare today, of course, but still evident in the rural Native America I've known. Our adventures were drawn from the land beneath our feet, whether climbing high up willow trees, chasing junk tires down into the steep crevasses of gravel pits, or whittling arrows from reeds and prickly pear thorns (which sent one buddy to the ER). Jumping out of a barn loft or into the wet basement of a demolished house, shearing moody sheep at sunrise, plucking feathers from beheaded chickens, feeding brown sugar to nipping horses, or poking an electric fence to see if it was live or a dead feral dog to learn if it was truly dead—these were among the limitless dares of an idealized time in my early days.

In 1965 my dad found a promising job as a feature writer for the *Detroit Free Press*, and by 1966, my mom returned to teaching high school English composition full-time. We'd moved away from East Lansing and into a yellow ranch house with a one-third-acre yard in the upper-middle-class Detroit suburb of Bloomfield Township.

I believe the shock of this move sparked a slow spiral inside me. I found no trees to climb and no wandering kids, only neighbors who yelled at me if I stepped on finely trimmed lawns stretching across miles of sameness. I quickly became very lonely, but any new kids I met seemed different from those I'd known. They were disappointed I didn't own the latest toys. They actually rode Schwinn Sting-Ray five-speeds my East Lansing buddies only dreamed about. I did not, and they didn't think much of my funky full-size clunker.

I began wanting "things" to help me fit in, but my parents clung to their Depression-era frugality. More pointedly, they worried about spoiling their kids if they indulged them, and I learned early on that if I wanted something, I'd have to work for it. I was raking leaves and mowing lawns by age ten and felt overjoyed to take over a five a.m. paper route by age twelve—at least until the Michigan winter set in.

I saved enough to buy a minibike, which was all the rage for suburban boys back then, but the kids I sought to impress considered it the sorriest and slowest they'd ever seen. Their white-collar dads, many employed by Detroit automakers, had both the time and know-how to soup up their minibikes into dangerous little speed machines. My dad had no such inclinations or interests.

My friends back in East Lansing had never treated me the way these new peers did. We'd shared our few possessions without thinking much about it. There would never have been any bragging about what one had or its quality or lack thereof. How strange it feels to consider our move to Bloomfield as a kind of childhood culture shock over clashing communitarian and individualistic sentiments. Back then I thought it just meant there was something wrong with me. I simply didn't fit.

By age thirteen I'd discovered kids living in the small-house neighborhoods a few miles to our south in working-class Birmingham. In 1969 these boys were into black leather, winklepickers, stainless steel combs, Brylcreem, and their fathers' or brothers' muscle cars. They had cute sisters who liked to "make out." My new "greaser" friends introduced me to sex, tobacco, cannabis, alcohol, and the adrenaline of delinquency. I learned to play Johnny Cash's "Folsom Prison Blues" on guitar, broke a few windows, engaged in BB gun wars (without padding), and took on a menacing blue-collar stare. At fourteen, however, I got so badly beaten up by a boy twice my size that I still sometimes have nightmares about him.

Seeking better friends, I gravitated toward a hippy crowd, dropped strawberry acid during homeroom class, and experimented with huffing spot remover. By my freshman year in high school I'd migrated to buying prescription "downers" like phenobarbital and Quaaludes from kids who stole them from their parents and grandparents. I developed a great appreciation for how drugs and alcohol kept me distant from emotional pain. I wasn't clear on why I wanted to be numb, and I wasn't aware of being unhappy so much as bored.

As a latchkey kid, I'd been unlocking the door for my sister and me after school since shortly after we'd first moved from East Lansing. We literally "drank the Kool-Aid" of modern white suburbia, sitting sedately in front of our Sony Trinitron color TV with glasses of lime sugar water and Fritos and waiting for our mom to come home from work with our baby sister, who'd been in full-time day care. Mom would check in, go take a nap, and then begin fixing dinner, an arduous routine for a busy teacher, which only became more complicated after my baby sister entered school and Mom entered after-school psychoanalysis five days a week.

As my sisters and I grew older, I'd often not even come home until close to suppertime. Instead, I'd hang out in the woods behind an elementary school with drug-involved buddies and get high. More often than not during my early teen years, I was stoned and trying not to appear so.

Dad arrived home not long before the 6:30 evening news, usually in time for Mom and him to pull down two or even three manhattans while visiting privately in the living room. Many years passed before I realized how much booze they consumed or how often our communications with one another took place in a shared, substance-altered state.

We were expected to avoid interrupting when they were drinking and visiting. The television was like a babysitter, and we were supported in our capacity to self-occupy. It wasn't that we were unwelcome if we had something to ask or say; our concerns would be dealt with and then we'd be asked to find something to do. The doors leading from the family room to the living room were kept closed during my parents' private time. I believe this sometimes intrigued my sisters and me. Perhaps we'd spy a bit, listening to complaints about work or other matters.

My parents would check in with us directly via the brief quasi-formal "reports" my sisters and I made during dinner. These were led by Dad, who was, after all, a journalist by profession. We were not allowed to interrupt reports unless our remark or question was pertinent to the subject at hand and the kid reporting.

There certainly was more contact between our family than this, but the remoteness I recollect during this time in my life takes up the most emotional space. Like many teenagers, I preferred my room. As the only boy, I had this privilege, and behind my closed door I would be either doing or pretending to do homework, reading books, or listening to music. My middle sister is nearly four years younger, and she and my youngest sister shared a room next door and a bond that I could not. They'd pilfer "Chex Mix" my mom made and have little parties of their own together in their room late at night. For me, my room was located emotionally between my longing for independence and my loneliness and solitude. Like the Beach Boys song, I did both crying and sighing as a teen "In My Room."

I often felt like the fifth wheel in my family. I tried to avoid this sense by going out somewhere unverifiable to get high with my peers. Whatever intimacy existed in our family felt unstable to me; I didn't trust it, and I know this had to do with Dad's volatility, which I'll soon say more about. Vacations, holidays, and birthdays were always an exception—real celebrations and full of joy. Sometimes on weekends we'd watch a movie together or muster ourselves for a game of Monopoly (which we called "Monotony") or play cards with Dad (Mom didn't like games).

I'd make my own efforts to connect with Dad by watching "Victory at Sea" documentaries or helping him out in his darkroom. He was an excellent amateur photographer, and I somehow understood that being close with him involved me joining in with what he wanted to do. I think the converse was difficult for him. He did once take me out to shoot off an Estes rocket his older brother, my uncle Ed, sent me for my birthday. However, I built it myself.

Beyond a short stint in the Cub Scouts, I didn't participate in school sports, clubs, or other peer group activities. If I expressed an interest, Dad would make sweeping statements like "Your mom and I were never good at sports. I doubt you'll have much luck with them." It became harder for me to express much overt interest in what I was presumed to not be good at, and it would have been impractical anyway for me to partake of any extracurricular or after-school events. My schools were miles away; my parents both worked and weren't available to transport me, and I learned to second-guess whatever might be fun or interesting for me along those lines.

When I was twelve a buddy persuaded me to join Little League for one season, but I can remember only the conspicuousness I felt when neither of my parents came to my games. I asked about it at the time, and Mom said she couldn't stand to watch my team lose. Dad tended to always be working or otherwise occupied. I was more likely to tell him how a game went than be asked. He'd always be celebratory if we won and supportive if we lost. But he never saw me play.

After meeting a couple of musical friends, I developed a terrible longing to learn guitar and worked hard to teach myself on the Teisco Del Rey electric my parents bought me at a drugstore for Christmas. I begged for lessons for several years, but they were worried I'd become a drugged-out rock star. I greatly resented this lack of support, especially when being asked to stop playing my guitar in my room so my middle sister could practice her piano lessons—which they did pay for and transported her to. The distinction set up years of rage and conflict for me.

I knew my parents loved me—and they often said so—but I think I gathered an implicit message that my direction in life would be primarily up to me. On the other hand, if I made a mistake or crossed a line in relation to their values, I'd be in big trouble. They seemed content with their socio-economic "arrival," focused upon many career demands and on their intense codependency too. In this way, I grew into a suburban white boy securely situated for his physical and material needs. But I felt mostly on my own emotionally and psychologically from about the age of ten, and I'm certain this sense of aloneness brought me closer to drugs and self-medicating.

A family tsunami arrived with my overdose on Nembutal and Seconal at age fifteen. I'd followed through on an inward vow to get very high if forced to comply with my parents' demand that I finish reading Albert Camus's *The Stranger*, the French absurdist classic, to shore up my shaky English grades. I detested this book's premise that life held no intrinsic meaning, and yet Camus and I were more on the same page than I'd have admitted. Granted a two-hour reprieve to attend a love interest's birthday with the promise I'd be home early and finish the book I found repulsive, I downed four aptly named "downers" with passive-suicidal disregard.

I have a photograph of myself that night with my young eyes at half-mast, taken by a young female friend who eventually killed herself. I was so doped up, my twenty-minute walk back home became a four-hour hiatus. I arrived in the early morning hours still in a stupor, and my shocked parents rushed me to St. Joseph's Mercy Hospital in Pontiac, where I was fed ipecac syrup and threw up until nearly passing out.

The author at age 15, refusing Camus and overdosed on sedatives. Photo by Gail Skurtu. *Author's collection.*

As I became a little more clearheaded, an ER doctor with a godlike demeanor pulled back the curtains around my gurney and announced to my parents with much gravitas, "This boy will be a heroin addict by the time he's seventeen."

I raised my middle finger to his face and said, "Fuck you." And that is my first memory of thinking critically about the U.S. mental health system.

I woke up late the next morning to both of my parents charging through my bedroom door. Dad threatened to cut off all my hair, toss out all my blue jeans, and keep me from seeing any of my friends. I responded with expletives, and he rushed forward and offered to sock me in the nose. Mom restrained his fist as he shook it in my face. Other than spankings, he'd never struck me or physically abused me, but my behavior had clearly pushed him to the limit. I'm sure I terrified both him and Mom, and they had no idea how to respond to my rebelliousness and drug abuse. Neither had ever misbehaved toward their own parents. There was some discussion of getting me into therapy with local child psychoanalyst Editha Sterba. This might've been a great idea, but it never happened.

Because of my deceptive drug abuse, trust between my father and me was broken, and his authoritarianism took on a new level of severity. Lying, to him, was a profound violation and betrayal. For me, it felt like survival. If I did speak truthfully, I wasn't going to be believed from that point forward. During various blowups, Dad called me a "loser," an "idiot," a "moron," and even "not much of a son." On several occasions I recall him saying I'd "never amount to anything or go anywhere." If I did poorly in school or dropped the ball on a chore he wanted done, I'd be confronted with shaming questions, like "What exactly is wrong with you?" I was expected to admit my defects, a near impossibility for many insecure teenage boys, and the hardest part was that I sometimes did so. Mostly, I'd just go mute and shut down to protect myself.

The protocol became a kind of pattern. I'd be called into the living room, "on the carpet" so to speak. Dad would begin flicking his hand dismissively at me as he began a tirade. I'd feel an intense desire to escape, my palms would sweat, my heart would race, and my mouth would go dry. I'd feel like less of a man if I broke down, but I sometimes did and then I'd be told, "Stop crying." I recall feeling astounded to have many of these same physiological reactions during a clash between us when I was in my forties.

On one occasion I unconsciously held my arm up, cocked somewhat effeminately across my chest, while he yelled at me.

"Put your arm down! You look like a faggot!" Dad shouted.

A final hand flick—perhaps he'd say, "You're dismissed"—and the protocol was completed. I'd go to my room and collapse on my bed. Such scenarios played out many times when I was between the ages of fourteen and seventeen. But I did have some sense that things could be worse. Dad had a close friend who worked at *Army* magazine. When we'd visit this man and his family, I was amazed at how his sons called him "sir" and stood at attention whenever he addressed them. Dad admired this man. If anything, he blamed my misbehavior on his own failure to be tough enough on me as a father.

Rarely but conspicuously during his meltdowns, Dad would call me "Ed" instead of "David," confusing me with his older brother, the favorite, the apple of his mother's eye, the son for whom his parents had sacrificed everything, even selling their home to pay for his college education. Dad had had to make his own way in the world, financing his college degree via four years in the Navy. Although I dimly sensed even then the deep wounds he must carry regarding this favoritism (and his brother's privilege), he never said anything directly to me about it.

After many years I came to better understand Dad, whom I loved very much, as terribly hurt by his own family of origin. I've also only recently realized how much alcohol played a role in his disinhibited rage. The two or three generous cocktails he consumed so quickly during family prime time would have made him legally drunk in most states. Shortly before Dad died, my mother confessed to me her feeling that he saw me as a competitor. This surprised me.

"You took the brunt of his anger," she observed, an admission that would have threatened their marriage if she'd said such a thing while he was alive. She told me that, not long after I was born, Dad began six years of psychoanalysis for chronic psychosomatic headaches.

"The analyst would always say, 'It all goes back to your brother, George,'" said Mom.

I never had such explanations as a teen, and so I had no help to undo a sense that I was entirely at fault for all that went wrong between us.

"Buddy, you're going to find out what 'tough' means!" he'd shout. "Buddy" was Uncle Ed's nickname growing up. Dad would often tell the story of a lead soldier crafting set he coveted as a boy. He spotted the kit hidden in the milk chute shortly before his birthday. But his parents decided it might be unsafe and returned it. When he excitedly opened his presents, it wasn't there. Years later, Uncle Ed took me on a long walk during a visit.

"I just want to tell you, Davy, that whatever your dad has ever told you about getting the short end of the stick while growing up is true. I've felt guilty about that all of my life."

He told me when they were really poor during the Great Depression, there wasn't always enough sugar to go around in the household. Their mother would secretly butter and sugar a slice of white bread for Uncle Ed but not for Dad. This story suggested many other such stories that would never be told. I try to remember these things when I recall how Dad would appear "possessed" by forces beyond both of us in his rages. Unfortunately, I often believed the things he shouted at me. When you come to believe yourself an errant and disappointing son, what your raging father says about you, no matter how seemingly irrational, must be true.

From a Yakama perspective, these are knots tied on my own time ball, difficult memories of my personal encounters with a generational pain that existed in my relationship with my father. Dad needed me to feel how hard the world had been for him, and he considered this good for me. Maybe I was his brother's proxy sometimes and an idealized version of himself that he wanted to make "tougher" at other points. Whatever the case, I wish I'd known then what I know now.

When my grades weren't up to par, I'd be grounded, isolated from my friends for an entire semester. My drugstore guitar would be hidden in my parents' bedroom closet, a constant temptation for me when my parents went out. I'd secretly steal change from Dad's overcoat pockets as a guilt-ridden act of retaliation, a manifestation of my longing to be more valued, I think. I got into trouble several times in ways that involved police officers pointing loaded pistols in my face. I was the classic acting-out, attention-seeking teenager.

Dad never could understand the underpinnings of all of this, and his rage and unhappiness left certain scars. He couldn't do much to fix what went wrong between us other than sustain a relationship with me, and doing so wasn't always easy for him. He was as unable to reflect on his outbursts as he was unable to avoid yielding to them, and he was incapable of apologizing. I became a difficult kid to parent, but I don't believe it had to be that way. I desperately needed a father who could be more positively involved with me. Dad's relationship with me came much too often from the opposite direction.

Coinciding with such teenage relational trauma at home was the horrible morning at age fourteen when I accidentally fully exposed myself in front of my entire swim class cohort and the girls' synchronized swim team, the Aquabelles. I recall how my entire body turned beet red. For quite a time, I was a laughingstock of my school over this event. Unfortunately, I found little solace for this social calamity at home. The "fool," the "moron," the "idiot," became more thoroughly reinforced, and I felt like an outsider basically everywhere.

Often immersed in depression or despair when I wasn't high, I'd sometimes climb out my bedroom window and run to a local crisis center called Common Ground to find someone to listen to me. At age sixteen I lay on my bed holding a serrated kitchen knife to my chest and calling myself a coward for not plunging it in. I still remember what it feels like to be very young and in suicidal anguish.

AIMLESS AND LOST

I stumbled on, graduating high school with middling grades, further diminished by headshaking criticisms for achieving far below my "potential." I so longed to attend Berklee College of Music in Boston, but my parents said there was no way they'd support such an endeavor. I began to carry a chip on my shoulder about it. If they wouldn't support my musical aspirations, I'd become the self-taught guitar legend who'd prove them and everyone else wrong. I moved in with friends at age eighteen to form an art rock band, which helped bring my guitar skills up several levels, and yet no marquee lights appeared.

In 1975, I followed my first real girlfriend to Thomas Jefferson College, an experimental school once housed within what is now Grand Valley State University in Allendale, Michigan. But we broke up over her infidelities, and I came home destroyed by this first serious romance, promising never to return. My parents had little patience and vowed I'd have no further support for college if I didn't return the following fall. My sisters finally had their own rooms, and if I didn't go back, I'd owe $20 a week to sleep on a cot in the family room where everyone watched TV. That's about $100 a week in today's money and seemed enormous to me.

I moved out for good a few weeks after my twentieth birthday. I was euphoric to find my first roommates, to feel nearly as free as I did in my East Lansing childhood, and to start work full-time in a record shop. Despite lackluster performance in school, I had a strong work ethic: by then I had already been a taxi driver and radio dispatcher, car wash and gas attendant, dishwasher and house painter.

A whirlwind romance led to a quick marriage at age twenty-two to a kind older woman who became a surrogate mother to me for four more years of questing for musical glory obscured by cannabis and alcohol. I eventually left her and the fourteen cats that displaced our affections and encouraged her toward an affair. By then I'd also been fired for the first time—from a promising assistant manager's job at the largest record store chain in Michigan. I became unemployed for a long while, sold insurance briefly and ineffectively, and soon lost all my money. My life shifted beyond losing momentum into total inertia.

A WALK IN THE WOODS

In September of 1983, I finally landed a minimum wage job as an order clerk for a flavor factory, Northville Laboratories (now Jogue, Inc.) in Northville, Michigan, and moved into a tiny rural apartment in Brighton, where I didn't know a soul. I was mostly cut off from family interaction; I'd "acquired poverty" and felt completely alone. I entered a new kind of struggle to simply gather enough money for gas and food. My music shop friends disappeared entirely, perhaps out of their own immaturity or embarrassment at my downfall and depression. I really had no one at all in my life, and my divorce was still pending. The few phone calls I had came from my estranged wife's parents, and I was glad they didn't call often.

I was fortunate enough to find work and have a roof over my head, but I felt an utter failure. Each day I came home to this sparse apartment, smoked cannabis, played my guitar, watched TV, and fell asleep. My life substantiated earlier predictions, and I became what I truly believed myself to be: a loser.

At Northville Labs, my role as an "order clerk" would now be called a "customer service representative." This job involved being screamed at for overdue shipments of strawberry variegate ice cream flavoring or going onto the plant floor and being harassed by food workers who viewed my inquiries as a constant irritation. One morning, after asking about a shipment, a bodybuilder mixing a giant vat of vanillin hoisted me upside down and shook all my change out of my pockets. I recall looking down and thinking I was going to need to pick up all that change to eat lunch. He only released me after I firmly grabbed his testicles.

I held on somehow. On days off I'd take long solo hikes. During one frozen outing I found myself standing in a dense Michigan forest, chagrined to discover rapidly falling snow had entirely covered my path in. I couldn't see my way back out. I tried to think of solutions, unable to recall if moss grew on the north sides of trees or even if that was actually true. I became disoriented and started walking around aimlessly. Dusk crept in and I started jogging around, looking for something, anything, that looked familiar. I thought about having read somewhere that humans tend to walk in circles when lost.

A half hour or more passed, and I now contemplated freezing to death. No one would know where I'd perished. Perhaps my bones would be found in the spring—or maybe never. The light became dimmer, although the white of the snow still helped. I began calling out for help. I'd never done anything like this before. It is an incredibly momentous and fearful prompting when it wells up inside you: to cry out boldly for help from anyone who might hear—to yell loudly and really mean it. No one answered.

At the top of a rise, I stopped in my tracks, sensing movement. About twenty yards directly in front of me, a buck with a huge rack of antlers eyed me in utter silence, motionless. Behind him were several does and a fawn. I became wary, but I wouldn't have realized he might be at the height of mating aggressiveness at that time of year. I knew nothing about deer and only felt a vague relief at encountering any living creature.

The buck began chewing a few shoots from a sapling next to him, and his harem followed suit. I continued to stand completely still. Eventually he turned his head slightly sideways and looked me over again, very directly. Then he slowly turned around and wandered off. The herd followed him and, keeping my distance, so did I. I found the highway about twenty minutes later and was home within an hour as moonless darkness descended completely.

This deer saved my life. The experience dazzled and inspired me. Having felt lost for so long, I'd been guided to safety by this beautiful animal. Having contemplated the ease by which my own death might occur, I wanted to begin really living. Having been uncertain of my own path, I wanted a new sense of direction. All these desires merged together as I sat alone that evening and stayed with me in the days that followed.

Only a few weeks later I met a new love with whom I'd stay for the rest of my life. My wife-to-be, Susan, saw something in me. On our early dates, she encouraged me to take a chance again on getting an education. Being lost and found by the buck and her belief in me were all I had to go on. I'd left college six years earlier with abysmal grades, and my relationship with my parents remained very strained. I was still finalizing my divorce, had little money, and worked at a terrible job. To say the least, any optimism rising in me felt quite fragile.

It seemed as though I placed my first completed college application in the mailbox one day and pulled the rejection letter out the next. I thought I must be crazy trying this education route while continuing to type bills of lading for barrels of "Towne Club Very Cherry." Then a brief note arrived from Oakland University in Rochester, Michigan, scheduling me for an on-campus interview. After glancing at my disastrous Grand Valley College transcript, the admissions counselor tentatively admitted me on academic probation for six months on the basis of something called "life experience." He warned that if I didn't maintain a grade point average of 3.0 or higher, I'd be expelled.

I needed a different job while in school and found work as a residential aide for people who'd suffered severe head injuries. I immediately discovered tremendous satisfaction in helping. Combining my below-poverty-level paycheck with student loans, I barely afforded a tiny basement apartment in a decrepit building on Detroit Avenue in Pontiac, unaware that the ample cockroaches and very low rent of $185 a month masked its status as an outplacement facility for Pontiac State Asylum (formerly Eastern Michigan Asylum). This was a lively building to live in.

I began classes and, unlike in my old Grand Valley days, fell in love with learning. After all, I'd just left behind a windowless office and being yelled at for not knowing the difference between *cherry* and *wild cherry* compote.

I did have to somehow cope with the deaf alcoholic living directly above me. He'd fall asleep nearly every night snoring loudly with his television at top volume. I'd hit the ceiling with a broom handle or even call the cops, neither of which had any effect. Finally, I walked down to the nearby gun store. I purchased a pair of shooter's ear protectors, stuffed them with tissue, and inserted wax earplugs into my ears. Then I turned my own TV to a nonexistent channel to make white noise. In this way, I studied for my first three terms back at school.

My grades were pretty good, which felt like personal redemption, but I still suffered from feelings of shame and worthlessness. I began visiting a psychologist on campus for $5 a session and finally began talking about what I carried around emotionally. A period of rapid and positive transformation ensued, and I felt drawn to wanting to help others as she was helping me.

My marriage to Sue was a profoundly joyous occasion in 1985. Good fortune in finding a loving and supportive partner melded with our mutual longing to create a family. I was still studying very hard, majoring in psychology and minoring in anthropology. Sue, who was further along in her graduate studies as a psychologist, was able to help us both financially. We both benefited from the support of her mother, a practicing psychiatrist, who bought me my first real suit. Even my parents began sending me what they called "book money." I also received better financial aid than students in the United States can find anywhere now. It's equally true, however, that I lacked many resources and barely financed my education through my day job, campus work, scholarships, and student loans. Life was a struggle, but at least it moved forward.

In 1986, the gracious mentorship of a psychology professor, Dr. Virginia Blankenship, supported my primary authorship on a research article about head injury rehabilitation.[1] It was a rare achievement for an undergraduate and became my golden ticket to being interviewed for the University of Detroit's graduate program in clinical psychology. I wore my new suit and prepared carefully. Amazed to be accepted, I entered a new world of intellectual challenges, competing ideologies, and academic rites of passage. The completion of this journey took six more years of full-time study.

My ascendancy from drug-abusing "moron" to "order clerk in a flavor factory" to "professional psychologist" culminated in 1992, just short of my thirty-sixth birthday.

LEARNING TO BE CONTRARY

Thus far, I've emphasized the knots on my own life's string reflecting dark times. What I've said about the painful complexities in my relationship with my parents belies other moments of fun, love, humor, and caring. Unbeknownst to them was their gift of anti-authoritarianism, a disposition to which my friend, fellow writer Bruce Levine, helped me become quite reconciled.[2]

Just before the COVID-19 pandemic took hold, Dad died after fourteen years of vascular dementia. Throughout most of this time, he no longer knew me or had any memories of our life together. He became charming and compliant, but of course his great intellect was destroyed. Most of my grief at losing him came before he died. I still recall our good times and miss him, despite the trouble we had. I'm still sometimes moved to tears over my empty wishes to make him happier with himself and with me, and the precious time anger and conflict wasted. I miss what might have been had it not been for dementia. Like many families, due to the pandemic, we couldn't inter his ashes until after more than a year of waiting.

He would likely say he was happiest working as a journalist analyzing and commenting on human rights. However, he spent most of his career putting persuasive words into the mouths of an elite he inherently distrusted: Michigan governors George Romney and William Milliken; several automotive CEOs, including Lee Iacocca; U.S. senator Robert P. Griffin (R-Mich.); and President Gerald Ford.

Frequently stressed as a speechwriter, he made his escape by retiring young (to Mom's dismay) and lashing out at corporatism through his black satire, *The Chronicles of Doodah*,[3] which was widely and positively reviewed. A rumor surfaced that the board of directors at his last "real job," American Motors Corporation, stole several galleys and illegally circulated them in order to plan for potentially negative publicity. Dad always liked this rumor. He was generally skeptical of whoever was in charge, and his numerous efforts at exposé and preoccupations with justice definitely had an influence on me.

Throughout the time we lived together during the 1950s, '60s, and early '70s, my parents strongly supported the U.S. civil rights movement. They had come to doubt the American dream, the legitimacy of the Vietnam War, and particularly the intentions of an entitled wealthy class they sometimes got to know personally. They immersed my sisters and me in progressive liberal values and thorny moral discussions at the dinner table. I don't exaggerate in saying that, other than manhattans and private chats, the evening news was the most important feature of their daily lives at a time when American society was in tremendous flux. Like many Americans, suspicions about a manipulated news media were inconceivable to them, and we all firmly believed in a free press as a safeguard against despotism and corruption.

Perhaps Dad's own hardships growing up in poverty, his exposure to race issues as a feature writer for the *Detroit Free Press* during the 1967 riot, and my parents' support of the civil rights movement provoked an acute awareness of privileges inherent in my whiteness from an early age. These privileges were often brought to my attention growing up. A much more visceral awareness emerged, however, after accompanying my mom at age sixteen to memorial services at a packed Grace (Baptist) Temple in downtown Detroit. We were attending the open-casket funeral of our beloved African American housekeeper's only son, Willie. He'd helped build my maternal grandfather's greenhouse and not long afterwards been shot three times in the head during an armed robbery after stopping along the John C. Lodge Freeway to help someone fix a flat tire. This was the first time I ever saw a dead body, and the mortician had done all he could to reconstruct Willie's forehead.

This tragedy caused a family crisis, because my maternal grandmother, an otherwise lovely person who adored Jesse, Willie's mother (who also cleaned her house), thought it inappropriate for her as a white woman to attend a "black funeral." My mother felt very angry about her mother's stance. My father had to work and couldn't attend, either. So Mom tugged me out of school and across the color line that day and directly into the path of a kind of pain neither of us had ever witnessed.

The screams and anguish I recall from that morning as I watched Jesse being nearly carried down the aisle by church deacons and seated before her only son's body remain burned into my heart and will always matter. Just a few months after Willie's funeral, I tried to visit a girlfriend who wasn't home and stood paralyzed as I stared over her back fence, watching several Birmingham, Michigan, police officers beat a black man with billy clubs.

"You're in the wrong neighborhood!" one of the officers yelled. I hurried home to report what I'd witnessed, but Dad told me nothing could be done. He'd been on scene during the Detroit riots. His fierce gray eyes shine brightly in my memory as he assures me the police will do nothing to "police" their own brutality.

Something began shifting in me. Willy's funeral and the police beating both happened in 1973, the same year the Wounded Knee occupation commenced—when about two hundred members of the American Indian Movement (AIM) took over the town and historic massacre site after a failed attempt to impeach the Lakota tribal dictator, Dick Wilson, at the Pine Ridge Reservation. In response to an effort to defend their community, they were surrounded by the FBI, police, soldiers and "fifteen armored personnel carriers . . . rifles, grenade launchers, flares, and 133,000 rounds of ammunition."[4]

My parents' obsession with the news kept me transfixed on the Wounded Knee story (echoes of which resounded during the Dakota Access Pipeline protests of 2016), but I'd already been riveted recently by an independent film called *Billy Jack* about a "vigilante character [who] defends a counter-culture 'Freedom School' from townspeople who harass and discriminate against the Native American students."[5]

I wanted to be him, and I bought a Billy Jack replica hat during a family vacation and wore it everywhere. I read Vine DeLoria's *Custer Died for Your Sins* and John G. Neihardt's *Black Elk Speaks*. In the world around me, the last gasp of 1960s social upheaval was set to collide with the emerging plutocracy of Reaganism. Cynicism about hippie values of love and peace was rising, and the uprooting of American exceptionalism was no longer a popular social project.

Floundering as I was up through my young adulthood, I nonetheless held on to a secret hope of playing some role in a Native civil rights struggle.

I came by such promptings honestly. My paternal grandmother, Donna Smouse Walker, had encouraged me from the time I was a little boy to honor our Missouri Cherokee heritage through our ancestors in the Barlow, Gibson, and Alexander families. Although I only saw them every year or so, she and Grandpa Verwin Walker often took us to Oconaluftee Indian Village in Cherokee, North Carolina, home of the Eastern Band of the Cherokee Nation, during summer visits. She called me her "Cherokee kid."

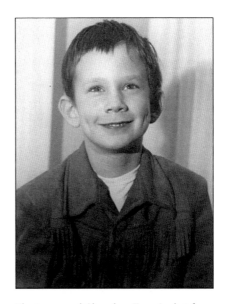

In 1963, though living frugally on Grandpa Verwin's postman's pension, Grandma Donna sent me a handmade Cherokee Togs fringe jacket from Pryor, Oklahoma, for my birthday. This expensive kernel of Indian-ness risked on a seven-year-old sprouted and took form. I was always the Indian in our cowboys-and-Indians games, and I wore that jacket until I could no longer get the sleeves on.

A decade later, I sat watching the Wounded Knee siege, longing to be with those protesters, wearing my Billy Jack hat. The outgrown, cherished regalia Grandma Donna had sent me, my old Cherokee Togs fringe, still hung in my bedroom closet. In 2005 and just before he started to become disoriented, Dad

The treasured Cherokee Togs jacket from Grandma Donna and Grandpa Verwin. Photo by George Lee Walker. *Author's collection.*

and I substantiated our Cherokee family story for ourselves, confirming a sense I'd always felt viscerally but only really signifying I'd never feel truly Native nor completely white.[6]

While working my way through graduate school in the late 1980s, I was offered the delight of singing for people stranded in run-down nursing homes around the Detroit area through a grant from the LeVine Institute on Aging. One afternoon I was stunned to silence by the beautiful, spontaneous chanting of an ancient Diné man. I put down my guitar and walked to the back of the small room to thank him, and he held my hand for a few moments but never spoke. The nurses said he was blind, and they hadn't heard him speak for years. Yet his chant arose in a way that seemed to answer my song. This felt like another sacred experience of "being found," an echo of the buck who'd led me home, and I paid attention. I wondered who this man was, what he'd been through, and how he'd ended up in this place of urine and linoleum.

By the time I'd driven home, a new song about this elder came through me called "Joshua Maiden." I began singing it at open mikes at coffeehouses around Detroit. A local audio engineer invited me to contribute it to a Dream Catchers recording project, a loose nonprofit organization of musicians benefiting the Bay Mills Indian Community (Sault Ste. Marie Band of Chippewa Indians) in Brimley, Michigan, and the American Indian College Fund.[7] "Joshua Maiden" was the first song I wrote that I ever heard on the radio.

Soon I was a Dream Catchers board member and contributing another song to the organization's follow-up recording. This success sparked other ambitions, including an interview for a psychology

The author performing for Dream Catchers in 1993. Photo by Joseph Taylor. *Author's collection.*

position at the Detroit American Indian Center while still taking graduate classes in 1989, a job for which I wasn't yet qualified.

By 1993, I was a half-time psychologist and half-time singer-songwriter, and my wife and I had two wonderful sons. The biggest challenge of both our lives soon arrived. As our youngest boy entered toddlerhood, he was diagnosed with a severe form of muscular dystrophy called spinal muscular atrophy, type 2. He has never walked and suffers from physical weakness and chronic pain to this day.

Grief and shock regarding our baby's physical challenges shattered us both. Everyone on both sides of our family had moved away from the Detroit area by then, and we had no one around us to help us. Strangely, close friends kept distant from our pain and more distant friends came closer. We began to enter a new and odd status as a family with a severely disabled family member. Retail clerks would see our son's tiny wheelchair and say, "I'm sorry, you can't bring a stroller in here." A strange woman ran up to us at an airport simply to ask, "Oh, tell me! Will he ever walk?" Physical and social barriers erupted around us in trying to be part of our community of friends. Sue and I dedicated ourselves to growing our all-inclusive family, which meant both our sons had to included wherever we all went together. Unfortunately, many people in our lives had difficulty recognizing or accepting our stance.

My naïve wonderment at feeling unstoppable collided with a brick wall. Music making lost its magic just as the *Detroit Free Press* panned all my hard work on my second, self-funded CD, the success of which was supposed to somehow make life better for everyone in my family. Embarrassed, humiliated, and bitter, I backed up from all musical pursuits and pulled back from musical friends, most of who couldn't possibly understand what I was going through.

MEETING UP WITH BARNEY

A moment of light emerged when my then brother-in-law visited us in Royal Oak, Michigan, in 1999 and brought his close friend, Barney. I was floored. I hadn't seen Barney in twenty-five years, and we'd been close in high school. He was a tough but intellectual kid who came from a large Irish-Catholic family. A fellow anti-authoritarian, we'd made forays into trouble together as teenagers on numerous occasions.

I'd once witnessed Barney respond to an egregious insult by putting his lit cigarette out in the middle of the offender's forehead. I'm not saying the fellow deserved it, but the insult was clearly preliminary to a fight, and Barney got the upper hand. Such behavior made him legendary. Shortly after we graduated, he left Michigan, moved to Homer, Alaska, and worked on fishing boats, using the money he earned to travel. I'd been sorry to have lost touch with him and was very glad to see him.

Barney was impressed that I'd earned an advanced degree in psychology, and he enthusiastically suggested, "Hey, let's reconnect regarding what you're doing. I'm going to a conference on the psychology of consciousness next spring in Scottsdale, Arizona, and you have got to meet me down there."

I immediately remembered how much I admired his adventurousness and felt glad about possibly rekindling our friendship. We exchanged email addresses and agreed to keep in touch about our future rendezvous.

A month later, Barney overdosed and died. Nobody even seemed to know he had had a drug problem. My brother-in-law and sister-in-law had sustained their friendship with him over the years, so the grief was much harder for them. But I, too, was stricken, and more than I would have expected, given that it had been years since we'd seen one another.

Periodically, I'd seek stillness to face down a growing powerlessness I felt in my life. My work as an organizational psychologist was feeling more and more meaningless, and I disliked working to help corporations make more money or obtain more efficiency from their employees. One night in early 2000, I sat in meditation, very moved, weeping and praying, pleading for a way to assuage my grief for my son's situation somewhat if only I could find some means of being more useful, perhaps by serving other people who suffered.

The following morning and with no prompting at all, a client suddenly asked me if I'd ever considered working as a psychologist in Indian Country. She looked at me very directly when she asserted, "I think you should work with Native people. I think that's where you belong. I think you should check into going in that direction."

After my anguished prayers of the previous evening, I was shocked by the synchronicity of her suggestion. She then told me about a conference on "healing American Indian communities" taking place the following weekend adjacent to the Pima Maricopa reservation in Arizona.

Although I'd played concerts at the Bay Mills Reservation with Dream Catchers, I'd never been to any event of the sort she described. I checked out the online link she provided and it seemed legitimate. I discussed with Sue the convergence of my prayers with this invitation. At a time when we were both grieving and searching intensely for meaning, we decided we had enough money for me to pursue this synchronicity.

In May of 2000, I'd no idea what I was doing as I stepped into a hall filled with Native people I didn't know. The entire first day was taken up with introductions. A wireless microphone was being passed around, and the one hundred or more people in attendance stood in a huge circle, listening to each participant share what brought them to this event. Many brought forth intense and tragic stories of multiple losses and trauma with a kind of openness that brought everyone to tears.

I greatly feared the microphone. Who was I to speak here? What did I have to share in such an open and vulnerable way before this room full of people I didn't know? I had my own deep pain in life, but I was not prepared to talk about it in this way. I tried to be present and listen, but I kept getting distracted as I tried to think of what to say.

Perhaps I should just decline the opportunity to speak—but this seemed dishonest, as though I were somehow immune to life's disasters. So many people spoke about losing loved ones to suicide and substance abuse: parents, grandparents, sisters, brothers, children, friends, leaders.

I stood inside this room solely because prayer had brought me there. What, if anything, could I say about myself? The Native woman standing next to me handed the microphone to me with both her hands—ceremonially, as though it were a talisman. It was my turn, and all eyes were upon me. There was the hush of very respectful attentiveness that had greeted every single speaker before me.

I started speaking with much hesitation, "Um, I, um . . ."

At that exact moment, I remembered Barney. I suddenly recalled the rendezvous we'd planned to have at the conference on the psychology of consciousness, right there where I stood, in Scottsdale, Arizona, that very same spring.

It felt as though he were tapping me on the shoulder. Slowly, I began to talk about who he was, what I knew of him, our friendship in high school, how we'd confided in one another about difficulties in our families, and how I thought I understood the roots of what made him often act so tough. I briefly recalled our drunken escapades and how I'd hoped to rekindle our friendship right there, right then. And in such a strange and meaningful way, we were doing so. My own tears began to flow as I became a part of the circle.

During a break, a Zuni tribal council member approached me and shook hands with me. My talk seemed to mean something to him, and we began a conversation. I told him I was a psychologist and asked him directly what might someone unfamiliar with Zuni ways, someone like me, do to be helpful to his people?

He gazed at me for a moment and then smiled.

"You'd have to be blackened," he said.

I had no idea what he meant, of course, and he explained that my mind was too cluttered with EuroAmerican ideas and theories. The blackening ceremony practiced by both Zuni and Diné (Navajo) people would cleanse and remake me into "the equivalent of a two-year-old child," he told me. Only then might I possibly be able to receive teachings so as to be of service to his community. I was both impressed and intimidated by the sophistication of his answer.

At lunch, I met several people who worked for the Indian Health Service (IHS). Until then, I wasn't familiar with IHS or its mission of providing the bulk of health care services to Native people in the United States. They told me there was a recruiting drive for psychologists, and I should apply. After I arrived back home, I did so, then flew out to interview with both the Colorado River Indian Tribes and the Navajo Nation.

My interview with several people at Yakama Indian Health Service Clinic, on the other hand, was conducted entirely over the phone, which might have given me pause had I known what was to come. They were in the Pacific Northwest, such a beautiful region of our country, and I thought I had little chance. In early June 2000, Yakama IHS Clinic's personnel director offered me a position along with moving expenses, and, with Sue's agreement, I accepted.

After spending over forty years of our lives in Michigan, we packed our kids into our two cars and left Detroit for Yakima, in central Washington State, on Labor Day, 2000, a journey of over 2,200 miles. As we left my parents' golden wedding anniversary party, we waved goodbye to relatives I'd known since I was a baby. The great physical distance between us and them has existed ever since. It was a very hard thing to do, and we were moving across the country to a place we'd never been or seen.

THREE

A Brief Swing Backwards

LOOKING BACK ON "GOOD GROWTH"

After four years of Byzantine intrigue, open conflict, and ostracism at Yakama Indian Health Service Clinic for my various contentions that the in-house approach to Native "behavioral health" is a potential danger to the Yakama or any Native community, I quit Yakama IHS Clinic in 2004. I was very lucky that the community met me at the door, hiring me on contract, and permitting me a role as community partner, co-designer, and manager of a short-lived program called Níix Ttáwaxt (neeK-tauwawKt).[1]

This project emerged out of community focus groups held at the Pathways to Hope and Healing Conference at Yakama Nation in late

Níix Ttáwaxt Receiving Home, Grand Opening, 2004. Photo by author.

June of 2002, which I had a hand in organizing and designing. Following two years of community consultation, Níix Ttáwaxt's first component,[2] a residential home for displaced Native youth, opened in November 2004, and I took over as program manager.[3] To my knowledge, Níix Ttáwaxt is still the only behavioral health program to receive official support through a formal resolution of Yakama Nation Tribal Council, which passed unanimously.[4]

From inception to launch, Yakama Indian Health Service Clinic and the Indian Health Service did nothing to support the Níix Ttáwaxt community initiative.[5] Instead, the clinic continued to emphasize psychiatric labeling and drugs, mostly providing "medication management" sessions while offering individual counseling of limited competence and scope. The focus upon psychiatric drugs became so intense that, in 2004 and just prior to my departure, a part-time contractual psychiatric nurse working two days a week was being compensated at a rate approximating my annual salary as a full-time civil service employee.

I eventually discerned the fiscal sense of clinic administrators who recognized that a psychiatric nurse could achieve a reimbursable Medicaid encounter every twenty minutes, whereas I could derive only a single encounter from a fifty-minute counseling session. The economic benefit of labeling Native patients and putting them on drugs for their troubles was a cash cow for an underfunded agency.

I encountered frustration about this approach throughout the Yakama community. While still trying to help solidly establish Níix Ttáwaxt, I was recruited by the lead tribal administrator to join a team developing a grant proposal to be submitted to IHS that would permit Yakama Nation to manage its own mental health programming. Public Law 93-638, the Indian Self-Determination and Education Assistance Act of 1975, authorizes the secretary of the interior, the secretary of health, education, and welfare, and several government agencies to make grants directly to federally recognized Indian tribes so that they can administer their own programs.

We had no such grant for Níix Ttáwaxt, and in spring 2005 the program collapsed under the weight of unanticipated resource issues. I had the unfortunate role of pulling the plug. However, the IHS grant proposal I'd helped the tribal administrator and others write was accepted, and the tribally managed Yakama Nation Behavioral Health Program (YNBHP) soon opened its doors. The Nine Virtues of Níix Ttáwaxt,[6] composed by my *káła*, Níix Ttáwaxt cultural specialist Levina Wilkins,[7] were integrated into YNBHP's first program manual.

Yet the Yakama traditional beliefs and ways that the *Virtues* reflected, and that Níix Ttáwaxt community partners were unanimous in supporting, became eviscerated by the Indian Health Service's contractual authority within Public Law 93-638. This meant that IHS officials were able to ignore the community's will and desire for a psychologically, culturally, and community-based program like Níix Ttáwaxt by applying grant-making policies mandating YNBHP's compliance with a centralized model built upon a pseudoscientific biological mental health ideology.[8] This was the same ideology with which I had clashed with my IHS coworkers and which reestablished the force-feeding and propagandizing of labels and drugs. I understand that both Yakama Indian Health Service Clinic and Yakama Nation Behavioral Health Program have since re-recruited psychiatric nursing staff members to serve the "biomedical model" we'd abhorred and rejected in designing our program.

It took some years for me to understand that IHS's disregard for the Níix Ttáwaxt initiative and the forced adoption by YNBHP of a medical model ideology are tied to generations of federal authority over the mental health system in Indian Country. Níix Ttáwaxt was a very new idea when first conceived in 2002—a community-driven program making the subversive claim that the "psychology" of Yakama people, particularly in protecting and supporting youth, survives and thrives within spiritual and cultural traditions. Níix Ttáwaxt was specifically created to elevate the Yakama community's cultural *sovereignty* in defining and designing what "mental health" means.

From the beginning, I saw my role as reflecting reverence and support for local cultural practices and ways, and I didn't fully realize that YNBHP could never assert such autonomy under PL93-638. The semantic abuse of terms like "sovereignty" and "self-determination" in this law was recently described by Choctaw professor Michael D. Wilson:

> The Act does not encourage self-determination in any sense of the term but instead offers tribes the option of taking a measure of ownership of programs designed by federal officials, not programs or initiatives imagined or constructed by tribal people. The simple fact is that self-determination is not achieved by government programs or grants, no matter how well intentioned or designed.[9]

The demise of Níix Ttáwaxt proved a bitter disappointment, but I came to realize that it was a federal doctrine—that is, the "biomedical doctrine" of IHS—with which we'd become entangled. And as I came to understand its history, I detected an intergenerational cycle, or historical recapitulation, of domination, oppression, coercion, stigmatization, stereotyping, and disempowerment for which I coined the term "Generational Carry."

On the afternoon of September 11, 2001, a day of massively escalated stress for all Americans, I had one of my stormiest encounters with estranged colleagues at Yakama IHS Clinic. During our exchange, a provider testily snapped at me: "IHS has *always* and *will always use* a medical model." My efforts to foment questioning and change regarding this model since then have often elicited a similar kind of psychiatric-religious zealotry.

Having shut down Níix Ttáwaxt, I held on to hopes that our advisory group would find additional funding. But Níix Ttáwaxt remained shuttered, primarily because of a poorly managed nonprofit youth agency with which we'd partnered, which soon shut down all its services for youth.[10] In the midst of an organizational crisis and having no place left to go, I felt very fortunate to accept a faculty position with the Washington School of Professional Psychology in Seattle.

We moved to the Puget Sound region in 2006, and I arrived feeling wounded, discouraged, and—not surprisingly—distrustful of organizations in general. I was fortunate to meet friendly colleagues and students who helped me gradually regain some sense of personal balance. With much to "work through" regarding what might've been, I was encouraged to embark on a research and writing project.

I was pleased to have a supportive boss who provided me with a tiny faculty development budget. Combining this with my own money, I traveled to the National Archives and Records Administration (NARA) in Fort Worth, Texas, in 2007, bringing with me a used scanner (purchased from a thrift store), which took up most of my suitcase. I hoped to gather as many records as I could find on the Hiawatha Asylum for Insane Indians, which had been shut down amid squalor and scandal in 1933.

I'd first learned about this place in 2001 through an article by Native activist and psychiatric survivor Pemina Yellow Bird[11] at the very moment when I'd started struggling with practices at Yakama IHS Clinic. I felt an incredible resonance between what I was encountering in the moment and what Ms. Yellow Bird's article revealed about unacknowledged coercion and oppressiveness in my own profession's past.

I drove my rental car past hundreds of FEMA trailers initially destined for Katrina survivors but rendered useless by the formaldehyde used in their construction. I found the correct building among a series of small warehouses that looked interchangeable, and I was soon provided a researcher's identification card by a dowdy, kind woman with possibly the last known pair of horn-rimmed glasses on a necklace. I requested that a large box containing records of the asylum be brought out.

"Do you want to see the Indian lunacy determinations too?" she asked me.

My quest to know more about the "generational carry" of oppressive mental health practices really began there. I soon procured a copy of Thomas Russell Garth's 1931 book, *Race Psychology: A Study of Racial Mental Differences*,[12] which featured numerous boarding-school-era studies attempting to demonstrate the intellectual and "constitutional" inferiority of American Indians, as well as Nathaniel D. Mttron Hirsch's 1926 *A Study of Natio-Racial Differences*.[13]

I dove into more research through my faculty role until the Washington School of Professional Psychology closed its doctoral program in 2012. Since then, I've felt fortunate for the support of the Indigenous Wellness Research Institute at University of Washington. I began a private practice and drove over the "hump," Snoqualmie Pass, to Yakama Nation Tribal School, which I continue to do now under a temporary contract after a short break enforced by the pandemic.

Along the way, I wrote two novels inspired by Yakama youth[14] as well as several articles for the *Indian Country Today* media (ICTM) network aimed at exposing the current mental health system's checkered and oppressive history. The latter were surprisingly widely disseminated.[15] My ICTM articles stimulated controversy among a small but highly committed cohort of peers working in Indian Country.

I am seeking not to attack or hurt any individual or group but only to assert a profound need for system change. It's been a long time since I was part of Indian Health Service's efforts to intervene in the "mental hygiene" of Native people, and I recognize there are bright, good-hearted, well-intentioned people there who are still trying to do so. I don't wish to deny or invalidate whatever benefits Native families may feel working with IHS or IHS-grant tribal program providers. Many might agree that the treaty-mandated government health care system supporting IHS and IHS-grant mental health programs is chronically under-resourced and underfunded. Some might even agree that aspects of IHS mental health programming are dysfunctional or misdirected. Yet I suspect few would see this system as actually complicit in the oppression of American Indians and Alaska Natives.

A thorough consideration of the U.S. mental health system in Indian Country will determine that its role in domination, oppression, and revisionism is undeniable. I hope that this will lead to wider discussions of this system's complicity in oppression in other places.

I offer no excuses or apologies for telling the truth.

Having shared my story and described who I am, I intend to disrupt a paradigm from which others necessarily derive satisfaction, security, and comfort. As a former IHS civilian employee and independent contractor, I, too, have paid my bills via the same system I critique. I am just one person, and if what I have to say seems without merit, no doubt it will be ignored or dismissed. (I'm sorry to say that it may be treated in such a way even if it *does* have merit.) I've sometimes described my novels as inspired by love. But this book, involving as it has the necessity of detailed research into brutal and oppressive events, came to completion as a felt moral duty.

As Senator Robert Kennedy once suggested, I believe systems change by chipping away until fractures form. The song I sing joins the winds and brushfires of our late Washington summers, where burning down brings new growth. I'm getting older, and it's time to build a fire.

PART II

Coyote Swings Back and Forth

FOUR

The Disordered Native

ILLUSIVE AND ESSENTIALLY "NATIVE"

The Confederated Tribes and Bands of the Yakama Nation emerged out of necessities imposed by a *páshtin* invasion, its violence and assault, and a treaty forced upon various families of Original People living around what is now central Washington. Although seldom thought about in quite this way, even the designation "Yakama" is actually a general term purposely applied in the Treaty of 1855 initiated by territorial governor Isaac Stevens to segregate Indians away from the colonizers. The many peoples to be confined away from areas they once seasonally hunted, gathered, fished, and camped actually "called themselves or were called by others the *Winátchapam, Pshwánwapam, Mámachatpam, Siláma*, and the like."[1] The suffix -*pam* denotes a place name—such as Mámachatpam for people *living in* what is now the lower Yakima[2] Valley, or Pshwánwapam referring to those *living in* the upper Yakima Valley, north of the natural landscape feature of Union Gap.[3] There were more bands from other places pushed and compressed by this treaty, such as the *K̲'mílpam* (people *living in* Rock Creek). By using "Yakama" in the treaty language, Stevens deliberately removed the context of place inherent in their *real* names, thereby dismantling future claims to land rights.

The word "Native" itself has similar insidious, homogenizing effects. Oneida journalist Mary Annette Pember recently noted that "labels meant to describe and distill more than 500 diverse federally recognized tribes into one monolithic group are mostly a white man's search for convenience."[4]

A complete biological fiction, the racial connotation of "Native" or "Indian" nonetheless holds profound cultural, historical, and sociopolitical meaning in American society.

"Indians" and "Natives" did not exist before Europeans arrived in North America. The term I've admittedly selected to rely upon myself—"Native"—has morphed over the years from its racist roots into more positive connotations of belonging, survival, and a shared political dilemma. I believe its proactive and unifying features evolved out of its racist roots from the Indian clubs, brass bands, football teams, and art programs that bolstered cultural resilience and covert resistance during the boarding school era of forced assimilation.[5]

Many Americans are not aware that Native people were denied United States citizenship—due to their perceived inferior racial status—until 1924. In some states, rights achieved by citizenship, including the right to vote, were not actually honored until 1962.[6] In the 2018 national midterm elections, efforts to disenfranchise Native voters in North Dakota, Montana, and Arizona continued through election restrictions, voter identification laws, and voter purges.[7]

Why has white American society sought to erect barriers to its Native citizens? We should remember that for many centuries being "Indian" or "Native" meant one was presumed to be an enemy of Europeans invading and colonizing North America. Given Native people's historically ambivalent status, it's unsurprising that their social power and influence in the U.S. have been kept greatly limited. Political and social power is still in the hands of white people, and their longstanding racial privilege was only made stronger through the post-Obama backlash of the Trumpian era. This was seen most readily, for example, in Donald Trump tipping his hat to the white supremacy of "America First"[8] and in his political exploitation of female Native stereotypes (U.S. Senator Elizabeth Warren portrayed as "Pocahontas") beneath a presidential portrait of notorious "Indian Killer" Andrew Jackson while esteemed Diné (Navajo) veterans were openly dishonored.[9]

White supremacy can also be demonstrated in the New Organizing Institute's findings that white men in the United States have four times the political power of women and people of color in governing the country.[10] Although the U.S. population is 37 percent people of color, white men hold 90 percent of elected public offices.[11] White people hold 88 percent of corporate directorships at Fortune 500 companies[12] as well as 87 percent of positions with the influential "Power Elite" of "the Business Roundtable (BR), the Business Council (BC), The Brookings Institution (BI) and the Council on Foreign Relations (CFR)."[13]

By contrast, Native people remain massively underrepresented within the U.S. power structure, holding only 0.33 percent (one-third of 1 percent) of elected offices while constituting 1.7 percent of the U.S. population.[14] Of course, this statistic shifted symbolically in 2021 as Congresswoman Deb Haaland (Laguna Pueblo) of New Mexico moved into her new position in the Biden administration as the nation's first Native American secretary of the interior. Additionally, U.S. Congresswoman Sharice Davids (Ho-Chunk) from Kansas took her seat in 2019.[15] These are encouraging signs, but one survey found as many as 1 million eligible Native voters still unregistered to vote in 2012, while Native voter turnout has consistently been the lowest of all U.S. ethnic groups.[16] Meanwhile, Native participation in the U.S. labor force is also the lowest of all ethnicities,[17] and according to the Bureau of Labor Statistics, Native people consistently experience the highest rates of unemployment.[18]

As mentioned, voter discrimination and limiting access are ongoing factors and remain tied to the efforts of political conservatives. A case in point is disgraced Montana chief U.S. district court judge Richard Cebull's 2012 interpretation of the Voting Rights Act, which was characterized as "completely incorrect" by the U.S. Department of Justice.[19] While he was scandalizing himself by posting racist emails about President Obama to his friends, Judge Cebull, a white man, nonetheless had time to apply his misinterpretation to dismissing a lawsuit initiated by disenfranchised Native voters living in the rural areas around Fort Belknap, the Crow Agency, and Lame Deer who sought satellite voting offices and in-person absentee voting.[20]

Instead of facilitating the access Cebull denied, the U.S. Supreme Court in 2013 compounded the blunder by nullifying provisions of the Voting Rights Act that compelled county and state jurisdictions with a history of discrimination to seek U.S. Department of Justice approval before making voting procedural changes.[21] From 1965 until the 2013 decision, 90 percent of voter discrimination lawsuits brought by Native people resulted in decisions in their favor, a telling series of court victories that demonstrates chronic, unchecked patterns of organized discrimination.[22] The Supreme Court's revisions to the Voting Rights Act, however, have now smoothed this litigious landscape, permitting an established pattern not only to continue but to expand, making it much more difficult to prove voter discrimination. This was the context behind Republican efforts to limit Native access through voter identification laws during the 2018 election, which led the Oglala and Rosebud Sioux tribal members, and the Lakota People's Law Project to successfully sue South Dakota secretary of state Steve Barnett in May 2022.[23] Similar efforts at voting suppression have been identified in Arizona and Montana.[24]

Herein lies a great irony. The same white supremacy that created a "Native" racial construct has developed judicial forums through which legal assertions regarding Native voting discrimination are mounted and now positioned to fail. White men founded the United States Census Bureau, invented the "Indian," and then arbitrated the original memberships of tribes, first through treaty negotiations and then through the deliberations of the U.S. commissioners for Indian affairs regarding claims to blood quantum (the formula for determining degree of ancestry) and lineal descent. According to family lore, my Gibson ancestors likely went through such a process before the U.S. commissioners in 1900 when they sought enrollment at Cherokee Nation, only to be told they didn't qualify because they were Creek, which they adamantly denied. Their own identity was not their own.

From a psychological standpoint, we might say that "Native" and "Indian" now represent identity internalizations symbolizing membership— those who "are" and those who "are not." On the one hand, "Native" depicts whether one is recognized by the federal or state government inside a Euro-constructed racial metaphor currently curated by tribal governments. On the other, "Native" denotes the passion and strength by which one identifies with a particular family's or community's traditions; its experience of domination, oppression, displacement, and genocide; and its unique experiences of resistance and survival.

People identify as Native in various ways, which makes the actual number of Native people in the United States somewhat hard to gauge. In the official U.S. census, self-identification is sufficient to claim to be "Native," and many people do so alongside other constructed racial identities (white, African American, Hispanic, etc.). The census numbers recently stretched to 6.6 million for people endorsing themselves as American Indian or Alaska Native along with another race.[25] The number of people self-identifying as American Indian or Alaska Native "alone"—that is, without claiming any additional racial identity—is roughly 4 million people.[26]

Specific to the U.S. mental health system in Indian Country, then, the majority of people identifying as Native in the census likely don't possess a federally recognized, enrolled status entitling them to access the services of the Indian Health Service or its tribal grantees. The IHS responds to a particular subset of those identifying as Native who have met federal standards and are also recognized by a particular federally recognized community, generally using guidelines tied to blood quantum and lineal descent.

Yet IHS policy in this regard is highly limited. It would be more consistent with federal recognition of tribal sovereignty if this federal agency permitted tribes to make their own determinations regarding eligibility for its services. If this were so, more Native people would be served, including children of parents who are eligible but who are themselves rendered ineligible under IHS criteria. The written Code of Law of the Confederated Tribes and Bands of the Yakama Nation, section 2.01.07, "Definition of an Indian," specifies:

(I) For purposes of this Code, an Indian shall be defined as follows:
   A. An enrolled member of the Yakama Nation; or,
   B. A member by enrollment or custom of any federally recognized tribe in the United States and its territories; or
   C. Any resident of the Reservation who is considered an Indian by the traditions, customs, culture and mores of the Yakama Nation.[27]

Based on its current definition of "Native," the IHS describes serving about 2.1 million federally recognized, tribally enrolled individuals each year, either directly through its facilities, or through the PL 93-638 tribal grants the agency oversees.[28] This figure compares closely with the U.S. Department of Interior, which is mandated to oversee certain shared material interests of enrolled Native people through the U.S. Bureau of Indian Affairs (BIA) and which estimated in 2013 a "total service population" of roughly 2 million people (as identified by tribal governmental entities) "living on or near its reservation or community during the 2010 calendar year."[29]

Thus, the U.S. census finds 6 million people claiming Native identity, with 4 million claiming it "alone," but only slightly over 2 million accessing health care through IHS and having interests managed by the BIA. The degree that these various statuses overlap as well as the legitimacy of identity claims can be a topic of hot debate, a state of affairs that was anticipated historically.

The contrivance of who is and who is not of "Indian race" and related fractures and factions (especially as they pertain to ownership of land) were initially mediated by U.S. commissioners with the overall goal of *shrinking* the entire Native population.[30] Instead, the Native population has grown, and now various nineteenth century federally-sanctioned racial formulae, especially that of blood quantum, exert intense pressure upon many of the recognized communities. Cherokee law professor Michael D. Oeser recently summarized the problems:

> Exclusive reliance on either minimum blood quantum or lineal descent has four known major flaws: (1) either approach will ultimately result in the extinction of tribes, either legally or practically; (2) use of either approach is inconsistent with the historic customs of most tribes; (3) both approaches lack a strong correlation to the subjective qualities that citizenship criteria are ideally designed to identify; and (4) both approaches have been used to justify the extension of state jurisdiction into Indian country by the United States Supreme Court.[31]

Blood quantum and lineal descent issues so affected the Confederated Salish and Kootenai Tribes of the Flathead Reservation, in Montana, that the tribal government narrowed enrollment criteria in 2002, "effectively splitting families in half of those siblings born before the enacted criteria who were enrolled and those born after the new rule who are not enrolled, creating mixed-status households."[32] Similar formulae were used in tribal efforts to deny Cherokee Freedman, including the descendants of African American Cherokee slaves who had walked the Trail of Tears, treaty-guaranteed rights to citizenship in the Cherokee Nation, which were effectively defended in federal court in August 2017.[33] Only three months later these formulae came to bear upon three hundred enrolled members of the Nooksack tribe (whose lands are just east of Bellingham, Washington) as they moved to the final stages of being "dis-enrolled" for being unable to prove their "tribal lineage."[34]

The formulae, derived from European notions about a concocted race, have become married historically to federal penalties, entitlements, and inducements aimed at compelling assimilation into white society. It is strange, then, that historical resistance to this process is juxtaposed with the idea that being enrolled in a federally recognized tribe somehow makes one "more" Native. In reality, federal and tribal benefits have continually been threatened over the years, most particularly during the years of attempted termination of tribal recognition in the 1950s. We should also remember that there have always been Native families and their descendants who for many unique and varied reasons had no desire to sign up for—that is, enroll in—the federalized definition of what it means to be Native.[35]

Those wishing to open the door to federal recognition have found it tightly locked for decades. Between 1978 and 2012, more than 350 American Indian or Alaska Native groups sought federal recognition, but only 87 succeeded in submitting completed petitions for the arduous vetting process. Only 17 of these applicant groups became officially recognized by the Bureau of Indian Affairs, while 19 more applications were recognized through an act of Congress or other channels, 33 groups were denied recognition, and the remaining 18 remain in various stages of negotiation.[36] Skeptics may presume the rejections were justified, but this would not be the view of the not-Native-enough people describing themselves as "Native alone" in the U.S. census. The success rate for Native groups seeking federal recognition was about 10 percent over the entire 34-year period.

The chaotic politics of Native identity leave people inside and outside a racial contrivance, and I've witnessed numerous microaggressions along the borders. I recall, for example, overhearing a fair-skinned, enrolled tribal leader at the Indian Health Service say to another of similar pigmentation, "Let's not have full-bloods involved in the position we're recruiting, okay?" I've worked with urban people who strongly identified as Native and who possessed degrees of blood quantum that made them enrollable in communities with which they'd lost any lineal familial ties. Some reported to me chronic shame about "not being Native enough," especially when interacting with "enrolled" people. A non-enrolled Native professor was publicly attacked as a "wannabe" by an enrolled Native student upset about the professor's academic policies. I've experienced similar shaming for asserting my own family's Missouri Cherokee heritage. In these ways and many more, racial identity markers of Native-ness continue to serve the original agenda of historical white supremacy: keeping its targets fighting with one another until they abandon their identity altogether.

THE "MENTALLY DISORDERED" NATIVE

Within the uncertain category of "Native," then, the primary arbiters of an allegedly "mentally disordered Native" are health care providers working for or under grants issued by the Indian Health Service. The IHS estimated in 2013 that the agency experienced 70,000 inpatient admissions[37] and more than 13.6 million outpatient visits.[38] Enrolled Natives entitled to IHS services are more than a decade younger than the median age of other Americans, while their population grows at twice the rate of other ethnic groups.[39] These are among the many youthful reasons for IHS outpatient visits[40] climbing 17 percent between 2009 and 2013.[41] In 2013, more than 851,000, or 6.5 percent, of outpatient visits to IHS[42] and its tribal grantees and nearly 5,000 inpatient discharges from the agency's small hospital system listed "mental disorder" as the *primary* reason for services.[43]

However, this statistic does not adequately represent the subset of Native youth within the IHS service population characterized in this manner. "Mental disorder" is listed by IHS as the third leading reason Native children aged five to fourteen years are brought to its facilities and the second leading reason for outpatient visits by and inpatient hospitalizations of Native youth and young adults aged fifteen to twenty-four.[44] In 2013, mental disorder was the *primary* reason for 10 percent of the agency's services to Native youth, aged five to twenty-four years.[45] Over $78 million was requested by the Obama administration for that fiscal year for IHS mental health services.[46]

What, precisely, constitutes the "mental disorders" afflicting these Native youth? The American Psychiatric Association's *Diagnostic and Statistical Manual of Mental Disorders, Fifth Edition* (*DSM-5*) is considered the main authority by the Indian Health Service and most public health agencies for such labels and applies the following definition:

A mental disorder is a syndrome characterized by clinically significant disturbance in an individual's cognition, emotion regulation, or behavior that reflects a dysfunction in the psycho- logical, biological, or developmental processes underlying mental functioning. Mental disorders are usually associated with signif- icant distress in social, occupational, or other important activities. An expectable or culturally approved response to a common stressor or loss, such as the death of a loved one, is not a mental disorder. *Socially deviant behavior (e.g., political, religious, or sexual) and conflicts that are primarily between the individual and society are not mental disorders unless the deviance or conflict results from a dysfunction in the individual, as described above.*[47]

This definition is multifaceted and complex. The IHS's Division of Behavioral Health is charged with partnering with tribes to design or offer programs for intervening in the problems of Natives labeled as "mentally disordered," including those related to emotional turmoil and suicide, alcohol and substance abuse, domestic violence, the health needs of violence survivors, and child and youth toxin exposure. The division produced IHS's *American Indian/Alaska Native Behavioral Health Briefing Book*, published in 2011, which states "it is critical that mental healthcare professionals understand the stress and anxiety associated with AI/AN [American Indian/Alaska Native] identity, the AI/AN acculturation and deculturation that trigger *mental health disorders*,[48] and the need for traditional and cultural practices as a part of the treatment and prevention process."[49]

"Acculturation" is defined by Merriam-Webster's online dictionary (Merriam-Webster.com) as the "cultural modification of an individual, group, or people by adapting to or borrowing traits from another culture," while "deculturation" refers to "the process of divesting a tribe or people of their indigenous traits." In its briefing book, IHS is offering an implicit theory in which sociopolitical stressors tied to forced assimilation impinge upon individual identity and "trigger mental health disorders" in Native people. Yet, how can forced assimilation pressures *not* be considered an inherent conflict between individual Native people and American society?

The IHS is directly contradicting the American Psychiatric Association's caveat that "socially deviant behavior" and conflicts between an "individual and society" tied to political, religious, and other social factors should *not* be considered mental disorders "unless the deviance or conflict results from a dysfunction in the individual."[50] In order for IHS to avoid violating the caveat, the agency should be able to demonstrate that the many Native youth and adults it labels as "mentally disordered" are either *not* experiencing conflicts with American society—which violates its own stated theory—or if they do experience such conflicts, they don't form part of the emotional or behavioral troubles that lead to labeling Natives as "disordered."

The IHS *Briefing Book*'s politically correct mention of Native traditional and cultural practices to "treat" mentally disordered Natives (as if treating the common cold) sees these approaches as add-ons to its Eurocentric mental health ideology—that is, a "part of a treatment and prevention process."[51] Although IHS formally integrates such practices in some of its facilities and tribal grant programs, they have considerably less status in relation to those of credentialed mental health professionals. This may be due to not being billable or reimbursed by Medicaid, although it seems equally true that they are not afforded the same respect as Western mental health practices because they don't derive from the dominant EuroAmerican allopathic model of military medicine.

The paternalism and tokenism with which traditional Native cultural healing practices are treated is yet another irony. I'm certain neither IHS nor any other U.S. government agency ever sought community permission to apply either its "mental disorder" labeling nor Eurocentric mental health "treatment" approaches to Native people in the first place. But cultural belief is central to the helpfulness of both types of practices. The IHS's Division of Behavioral Health evidently mediates to what degree Native cultural ways and understandings about well-being matter regarding mental health dealings in Indian Country. One way I've witnessed how this works is through eclipsing of and meddling with community initiatives like Níix Ttáwaxt in order to implant an IHS biomedical ideology within program design and grant oversight.

FIVE

Oppressive and Genocidal Realities

ENEMY NATIVE

Using its medical ideologies, IHS has recently set strategic goals related to detecting and intervening in Native *depression*. For example, IHS has stated its goal of widening use of the Patient Health Questionnaire-9 (PHQ-9).[1,2] This brief questionnaire asks Native patients to describe to what degree they feel discouraged, downhearted, tired, poor appetite, unable to sleep, slow-moving, easily distracted, or as though life is no longer worth living.

Is the "depressed" Native a misconstrual by IHS that softens and revises Native reality? Are Native people often reacting to broad discrimination, poverty, powerlessness, and marginalization experiences in their daily lives? Or are emotional turmoil, substance abuse problems, or behavioral troubles among people in Native American communities interchangeable with any encountered by those in "WEIRD" societies (Western, Educated, Industrialized, Rich, and Democratic)[3] from which the modern-day concepts of malaise and melancholy first emerged? Let's consider such questions by perusing what is occurring *now* in real time while keeping in mind the generations of violence, subjugation, and mayhem Native people have experienced historically at the hands of EuroAmericans.

Despite growing population numbers, tribally enrolled Native people in the United States currently face the shortest life expectancy and highest mortality rate of any ethnic or racial group described by the U.S. census. The life expectancy for Yakama women, for example, is currently 67.5 years, compared to 82.3 years for *páshtin* women in the state of Washington.[4] Yakama men live 61.6 years on average, compared to 77.8 years for their male *páshtin* counterparts in Washington.[5]

Historical information firmly substantiates the history of massacre and maltreatment of Native people in the United States as a chronic atrocity. Although it is not uncommon, calling the intense and horrific adversities Native people experience "genocide" remains somewhat controversial in academic circles. UCLA Distinguished Professor of Anthropology Russell Thornton, an enrolled Cherokee, notes how scholarly ideas about a Native American genocide vary widely.[6] Because colonial atrocities against Natives were not orchestrated by a central federal policy or strategy and were sometimes controversial even among white people of the time, they are thought to lack the deliberateness codified within the 1948 United Nations definition of genocide.[7] Dr. Thornton notes that the common contemporary tendency to portray historical assaults and massacres as genocide may represent an effort to bolster the credibility of concepts like "historical trauma." He also clarifies that a deliberate "mass killing" type of Native genocide may "conceivably not [be] the most important determinant of group destruction over a long span" anyway.[8] Rather than focusing exclusively upon past atrocities and the likely trickling down of emotional upheaval and pain through generations, we might instead ask: Does the limited life expectancy Native people face today reflect an *ongoing* genocide?

The protocol of the United Nations Office of the Special Adviser on the Prevention of Genocide (OSAPG) is useful because it originates from a body officially designated to decide whether the UN's 1948 definition of genocide applies to specific national situations. In particular, the OSAPG assesses whether *actions* or *inactions* of a government or dominating societal group are "deliberately inflicting on [a target] group conditions of life calculated to bring about its physical destruction in whole or in part."[9]

The OSAPG approach to analyzing the *deliberateness* of genocidal actions or inactions is complex and entails assessing eight critical factors. Below, I provide phrases lifted from the most salient aspects of seven of these factors, leaving out those pertaining to the last, which highlights future events as potential "triggers" for genocide. I ask the reader to keep these factors in mind in considering this chapter and the next.

OSAPG factors underlying the assessment of deliberate and ongoing genocide include:

- History of genocide or related serious and massive human rights violations against a particular group; denial by the perpetrators;
- Whether vulnerable groups have genuine access to the protection afforded by the [legislative, judicial, and human rights] structures;
- Whether there exists a capacity to perpetrate genocide—especially, but not exclusively, by killing;
- Underlying political, economic, military or other motivation to target a group and to separate it from the rest of the population;
- The use of exclusionary ideology and the construction of identities in terms of "us" and "them" to accentuate differences;
- Propaganda campaigns and fabrications about the targeted group used to justify acts against a targeted group by use of dominant, controlled media;
- Introduction of legislation derogating the rights of a targeted group;
- Imposition of emergency or extraordinary security laws and facilities that erode civil rights and liberties;
- *Less obvious methods of destruction*,[10] such as the deliberate deprivation of resources needed for the group's physical survival and which are available to the rest of the population, such as clean water, food and medical services;
- Creation of circumstances that could lead to a slow death, such as lack of proper housing, clothing and hygiene or excessive work or physical exertion;
- Programs intended to prevent procreation, including involuntary sterilization;
- Forcible transfer of children, imposed by direct force or through fear of violence, duress, detention, psychological oppression or other methods of coercion;
- In a non-conflict situation, widespread and/or systematic discriminatory and targeted practices culminating in gross violations of human rights of protected groups, such as extrajudicial killings, torture and displacement.[11]

I'll now survey some of the social and political barriers (and brutalities) currently faced by Native people in American society. Before I begin, I must mention another remark by Mary Annette Pember: "Overall, we remain defined by our 'plight' and our gold standard of despair."[12] What I'm about to detail is limited in just this unfortunate way, and I'm only doing so to link my reader back to these OSAPG points. I hope to avoid tarnishing the respect and regard in which I hold Native people, who continue to survive, grow, and thrive in the face of relentless adversity.

DEATH BY RADIATION AND CHEMICAL POISONING

Many Yakama people "live in areas having some of the Nation's highest levels of man-made radioactive and chemical contamination,"[13] due to the toxicity permeating *Nch'i-wána*, the Columbia River, and land around the Hanford nuclear reservation in south-central Washington. Extensive radioactive and chemical contamination has been detected throughout the Columbia River Basin, where the Yakama fish, hunt, and live off the land.

The validity of complaints about major health problems experienced by "downwinders" of all ethnicities living near Hanford has been repeatedly called into question or downplayed by outside experts.[14] For example, outside epidemiological research over the years has failed to support the idea that living near the official geographic boundaries of Hanford raises the risk of cancer over living anywhere else in the United States.[15] However, similar research conducted with older construction workers who had worked *inside* Hanford's official boundaries showed higher risks for "all cancers … COPD [chronic obstructive pulmonary disease] and asbestosis."[16] Since both asbestos fibers and radioactive elements are readily carried by wind and water, the findings inside and outside the Hanford boundaries seem markedly different and suspect.

Kate Brown, an award-winning investigative historian from the University of Maryland, visited the Hanford area in 2015 and tried to understand downwinder complaints about heightened disease susceptibility, deformed and adversely affected children, and crippled livestock. She noted that "in four decades of operation, the Hanford plutonium plant … issued at least 200 million curies of radioactivity—twice what Chernobyl emitted …"[17] She was critical of outside health studies she reviewed, concluding that, "to do a thorough epidemiological study, the scientists would have had to get to know the population on intimate terms, not just the people living there but also those who had moved or died."[18] Instead, she found research on health hazards generally confined to legally actionable issues around which "lawyers representing manufacturers had created a highly restrictive set of court rules dictating the evidence necessary to prove damages from environmental contamination."[19]

Fortunately, downwinders were eventually able to link arms with local doctors, scientists, and advocates in order to conduct more extensive surveys.[20] Using a participatory approach, the community determined that its local residents were six to ten times more likely to suffer from thyroid disease and that their risk increased relative to particular landscape and wind patterns pertaining to where people lived around Hanford. Other scientists who had testified in various court cases against the downwinders' health claims had only looked at the *average* incidence for certain cancers across the entire area.

Exposure of Yakama people in particular to Hanford contaminants began sometime in the fall of 1943 with the advocacy of the Wanapum (River People), a family band that still lives near Priest Rapids. They were initially viewed as an insignificant presence facing off with the ambitions of the Manhattan Engineering District. They weren't even noticed until Hanford reservation boundaries were thoughtlessly placed directly over areas where they fished. Historically, the Wanapum refused to join other Yakama bands in signing the Treaty of 1855, whom they derisively called "treaty Indians";[21] yet they decided to assert their rights of access to areas Hanford's engineers wanted closed.

To this day, the Wanapum still hold the spiritual belief that "they should not own land."[22] Their elders understood that attempts to keep them from fishing in such places would constitute a violation of the treaty they'd been placed under despite their unwillingness to sign. This also meant, unfortunately, that they had no deed to their fishing camps nearby Hanford with which to press their rights. Yet their humble status contained a silver lining in helping protect them from the engineers' efforts to evict them, as it became legally complex to rid a people from land they'd inhabited since time immemorial, even if they refused to "own" it in the European sense.

A brief period of conflict and negotiation culminated in the Wanapum and engineers' agreement that fishermen and their fish would be trucked back to Priest Rapids from the customary fishing grounds at White Bluffs, which lay within Hanford Reservation boundaries.[23] Hanford engineer Lieutenant Colonel Franklin Matthias grudgingly admitted to being impressed by the lead tribal interpreter—none other than William Charley, the storyteller of Coyote's Swing (see chapter 1)—whom he described as "a man of fair education although his appearance would not indicate as much."[24] At the time, this agreement was seen as a win against ongoing state and local efforts to erode Yakama treaty-guaranteed fishing rights,[25] but the victors could not have suspected that Hanford's mere presence would poison the sacred salmon and a river that had sustained them and their children for thousands of years.

To this day, the White Bluffs and Ringold sloughs and the Ringold 2 wasteway, all of which enter the South Columbia Basin Irrigation District and the Columbia River, still contain measurable low-level exposure to uranium-235 and uranium-238 (one-third the maximum recommended exposure for drinking water by the Environmental Protection Agency).[26] The U.S. Department of Energy officially disputes health effects of such low-level radiation exposure, stating that "scientists do not fully agree on how to translate the available epidemiological data on health effects from high radiological doses into the numerical probability (risk) of detrimental effects from low radiological doses."[27] The agency's quirky statement seems to mean that because the numerical means of expressing a danger have not been agreed upon, the danger shouldn't be thought of as existing. I recall speaking briefly with an IHS cancer researcher in 2001 who might disagree: he was officially charged with convincing River People not to consume potentially irradiated salmon bones.

Many Yakama families have long been aware of radioactivity impinging upon their health, land, and way of life. Revered Columbia River elder and Yakama leader Russell Jim said in 2002, "In our front yard down here [is] the oldest and largest nuclear facility that has ... bombarded this area with radioisotopes for 60 years. And we do not know what has happened to the gene pool of the Yakama Nation."[28] At the particular moment in time Mr. Jim made his remarks, I was still working at Yakama Indian Health Service Clinic with former colleague Dr. Rex Quaempts (Yakama), who lamented a lack of medical resources for the "5,000 women to whom his clinic should have given pap smears, only 1,100 [of whom] received the screening."[29]

Twenty years later, cleanup was still underway across this area NBC News called "the most toxic place in America."[30] Russell Jim reportedly suffered from throat cancer he attributed to Hanford's proximity[31] before he died in 2018. As to Dr. Quaempts's 2002 concerns, a decade later inadequate funding and lack of medical resources were still contributing to "disproportionate late stage rates of some screen-detectable cancers" among Native people in the Pacific Northwest.[32] Meanwhile, medical record linkage studies "conducted by tribal organizations and grantees suggest that cancer incidence is higher than national data suggest" for Native people across the United States.[33]

Yakama Nation is not alone in experiencing downwinder dangers. The Confederated Tribes of the Colville Reservation and the Spokane, Kalispel, Kootenai, and Coeur d'Alene tribes have also all been downwind of Hanford throughout its uranium production years.[34] Moreover, the Nez Perce, Confederated Tribes of the Umatilla, and Confederated Tribes and Bands of the Warm Springs all fish along Nch'i-wána, consuming Hanford-exposed migrating salmon that have "received higher doses of river borne releases which resulted from both accidental releases and normal operations that used Columbia River water to cool weapon-production reactor cores."[35]

Chronic exposure to low-level radiation isn't confined to just Hanford-adjacent communities, either. Uranium mining and processing contaminates groundwater for the Spokane in Eastern Washington, the Eastern Shoshone and Northern Arapaho of the Wind River Reservation, and the Navajo Nation, while over 1,000 unreclaimed open-pit uranium mines still dot the landscapes of South Dakota, Wyoming, Montana, and North Dakota, including in the southern Black Hills National Forest as well as in Custer National Forest near Lakota-Sioux lands.[36] According to one study, "the Environmental Protection Agency (EPA) has identified 15,000 abandoned uranium mine locations in 14 western states with about 75% of those on federal and tribal lands."[37]

Seventy years into Hanford's legacy, it seems fair to pose a question regarding ongoing genocide: Is unmitigated radioactive and chemical contamination on or near Native lands a result of deliberate action or inaction? If a jury were to consider such matters in relation to an individual perpetrator, the judge would likely instruct them regarding the difference between involuntary manslaughter, where there's no intention to kill, and second-degree murder, where an extreme and reckless disregard for life exists.

DEATH BY IHS

It is the United States Congress that continually underfunds the Indian Health Service. Serving 2.1 million people on an annual appropriation of $4.8 billion translates to $2,286 per Native patient—compared to $6,973 spent annually on individual inmates in federal penitentiaries.[38] This lack of health care provision *does not* represent a failure of a federal entitlement system like welfare. It is instead the mandated responsibility of Congress to provide quality health care to enrolled Native people in accordance with Article VI of the U.S. Constitution, which states that treaties constitute the "supreme law of the land."

However, simply delivering more funding for a treaty-stipulated right would appear to be an inadequate solution to the massive dysfunctional internal culture at IHS. In 2010, then chairman of the U.S. Senate Committee on Indian Affairs, Byron Dorgan, a Democrat, released a scathing investigative report of IHS's Aberdeen Area, consisting of twenty IHS and tribally managed service units serving 120,000 patients in North Dakota, South Dakota, Nebraska, and Iowa and employing nearly 2,000 people under an annual budget of $293 million. This investigation, Senator Dorgan wrote, was completed under a climate in which "numerous employees ... expressed fears of reprimand, retribution, and concerns about communicating with congressional staff due to emails and actions taken by the Director of IHS and local supervisory employees."[39]

These same IHS supervisors were characterized by the Laborers' International Union of North America as managers who were "either poorly trained, unqualified, or both" and who "typically either do not understand, or fail to respect, federal labor law."[40] Numerous instances of "managing" problem employees by shuffling them around were revealed through transfers, reassignments, and paid leave. Twelve employees under investigation for anything from inappropriate touching of patients to destruction of medical records to diversion of drugs received paid time off ranging from one and nine months, several on more than one occasion.[41]

Health care providers working at four different facilities in Aberdeen Area, including two hospitals, were found with "lapsed provider licenses, certifications, registrations, and privileges."[42] Six nurses were found working for IHS *after* receiving formal reprimands from or being suspended by state boards of nursing.[43] Dorgan's report noted that the Centers for Medicare and Medicaid Services had recently asserted that "Rosebud Hospital posed an immediate and serious threat to the health and safety of patients."[44]

The issues evident in the Aberdeen Area suggest that going to the Indian Health Service for an illness or injury might be a scary proposition. While little data exist on the direct effects of IHS dysfunction on patient health and well-being, we can get some clues regarding its hazards by examining IHS's own guidance to providers regarding "risk management" and tort claims—the types of lawsuits mounted against federal agencies.

Between 1987 and 2004, the number of tort claims alleging malpractice at the Indian Health Service more than doubled from about forty to about ninety-two per year.[45] Prorating from IHS's yearly growth estimate[46] of 1.7 percent in its service population, we might reasonably expect an increase to an average of fifty-six tort claims annually—provided we assume that IHS has failed to reduce its malpractice risks since 1987. Even using such a liberal assumption, the current number of tort claims the agency averages annually appears to increase about 60 percent over a twenty-seven-year period.

What are the allegations within these malpractice claims? They include missed or delayed diagnoses (35 percent); negligent medical management (18 percent), such as prescribing the wrong therapy or treatment, or improper or negligent surgery or anesthesia (19 percent); and other issues, such as poor perinatal care, drug treatment, and dental care.[47]

Thirty-nine percent of tort claims indicated permanent physical injury in the form of loss of function, brain damage, chronic pain, etc., while another 30 percent alleged wrongful death.[48] If about 30 percent of the legal claims filed against IHS are wrongful-death allegations, this would suggest twenty-seven Native people perish each year under circumstances felt sufficiently egregious by their loved ones to pursue legal action. How many more might die under suspicious circumstances without rising to this level of legal response? In its most recent (2018) edition, "an Agency-wide focus on patient safety and occurrence reporting"[49] was offered as an explanation for why "discussion of specific patient safety issues" was no longer part of this manual. The new edition is now at the same link as its 2006 predecessor but with *none* of the tort occurrence data. The 2006 edition no longer appears to be available to the public.

In 2016, the new chairman of the Senate Committee on Indian Affairs, John Barrasso, a Republican from Wyoming, reported again on Aberdeen, now the Great Plains Area, which services 122,000 Native people. In releasing his own report, *Reexamining the Substandard Quality of Indian Health Care in the Great Plains*,[50] Senator Barrasso noted that, "over five years later, the very problems identified in the Dorgan Report have not been resolved."[51] He described the Indian Affairs Committee staff members witnessing "firsthand the culture of cronyism and corruption that permeates the system."[52] Invited to testify at the Barrasso hearings, former Senator Dorgan remarked:

> There are some really great people, some people who care, people who sign up and commit their lives to the Indian Health Service and deliver good health care. Then I see something else.
>
> I see the weaving of friendships and favors, relatives, incompetence, corruption and yes, even criminal behavior. It has all too often and continues to be, in my judgment, overlooked, excused and denied. That cannot continue.
>
> No organization in America of which I am aware can work properly in those circumstances ...
>
> This is not some ordinary issue ... This is about people who die; this is about living and dying.[53]

It seems that the life-threatening dysfunction of the Indian Health Service is one of the few things Democrats and Republicans can agree upon. I don't know of any investigation similar to Dorgan's or Barrasso's occurring within IHS's Portland Area, within which lies Yakama Indian Health Service Clinic, where I worked from 2000 to 2004. I can only note that I have also encountered many good people at IHS—while having grounds to suspect numerous instances of corruption and malfeasance with life-and-death implications for Native people.

With regard to the UN/OSAPG points regarding deliberate genocide, what are the implications of chronically failing to fund and competently manage treaty-guaranteed health care services to such a degree that they represent an ongoing threat to the life and health of Native Americans? Under tort claims, no specific leadership, managers, or providers of services in a federal agency are held individually culpable for their actions. Instead, Congress sets up a pool of funding to settle claims across all federal agencies. What, then, drives accountability in IHS health care in relation to matters of life and death?

DEATH BY DIABETES

Native people experience the greatest incidence of poverty of all U.S. ethnic groups; nearly 27 percent of the enrolled population live at or below the federal poverty line.[54] At Yakama Nation, this statistic is greatly exceeded within the three major reservation towns: Toppenish, where 43 percent live below the poverty line; Wapato, where the rate is 46 percent; and White Swan, where it is 57 percent.[55] Moreover, an average of 16 percent of residents across these three reservation communities live at 50 percent or more below the federal poverty line.[56]

After starting work at Yakama Nation, I soon learned to ask whether a young person with whom I was about to meet had eaten recently. This was an especially important question on Mondays, because weekends didn't offer the relief of the National School Lunch Program, a resource continually targeted for cuts by the Trump administration[57] and recently restored by the Biden administration.[58]

I recall one young man answering that he'd indeed eaten over the weekend: "Yeah," he told me, "I had a bag of chips and a Mountain Dew." That was it: a shot of sugar and starch was all the food he'd had since his free school breakfast and lunch the prior Friday. Not surprisingly, "children who experience food insecurity . . . are more likely to experience chronic illnesses, acute illness, psychosocial problems, and psychiatric distress."[59] Are reactions to poverty and food deprivation best characterized as *mental disorders*?

Poverty and food insecurity work synergistically to exacerbate diabetes risk because the latter increases the risk of obesity, a diabetes precursor.[60] Between 2001 and 2004, Native people in the United States had the highest levels of food insecurity of all ethnic groups: 28 percent worried about having reliable access to affordable food compared to 16 percent of white people.[61]

Currently, 20 percent of Yakama people—one in five—suffer from type 2 diabetes.[62] Over many years, the traditional, healthy Yakama diet of foods like salmon, elk, venison, wild potatoes, chokecherries, bitter root, huckleberries, and other plants has been displaced, having been disrupted by colonization. Although group events and feasts may include such foods, many people "often rely on food-commodity and nutrition assistance programs and frequently purchase food from fast-food outlets and small grocery or convenience stores, which typically have a limited availability of high-quality produce and low-fat foods."[63]

Explanations for eating less nutritionally while experiencing food insecurity are multifactorial and range from lack of access to fresh fruits and vegetables to "thrifty genes" activated by food scarcity. Nutritional researcher Michelle Chino and her team note that among Native people "the goal for nutritionally stressed families [is to get] as many calories as possible from limited resources" and "[it] is hard to match the high calories per dollar from foods such as potato chips to the calories per dollar for green vegetables."[64]

Corporate food marketing and distribution exacerbates the diabetes threat. Yakama ethnic studies scholar Michelle Jacob has pointed out the ubiquity of Pepsi signs around Yakama Nation,[65] particularly in places where youth congregate, including at Yakama Nation Tribal School, where I've consulted over the years. She may not have noticed, however, a prevalent availability of sugary sodas inside schools at special events and at convenience stores nearby—poisons that one dark-humored Native educator identified to me as "Indian milk."

Yakama Nation Tribal School sign, sponsored by Pepsi. Diabetic socialization? Photo by author.

With regard to the UN/OSAPG points, if the continual pushing of a diabetes-inducing sugary health threat toward Native at-risk youth is not deliberate, is it negligent? What power does a Native community have in controlling lethal dietary threats directed at its people? Alongside readily identifiable environmental factors like the "food deserts" proliferating in many reservation settings, the historic disruption of more healthy traditional food availability, and the substitution of the USDA's so-called commodity foods for families living in poverty and want, diabetes remains, according to IHS, a heightened "genetic risk" for Native people. This seems a chronic mischaracterization of the facts.

BIGOTRY, HATE, SEGREGATION, AND EXCLUSION

In the 2017 NPR/Robert Wood Johnson Foundation's "Discrimination in America" survey undertaken by Harvard University's T.H. Chan School of Public Health, 35 percent of the 342 Native participants reported experiencing ethnic or racial slurs and 38 percent reported experiencing violence against themselves or a family member simply for being Native.[66] Among those living in "majority Native areas" like Yakama Nation, 55 percent reported they'd been personally discriminated against by local police, and 54 percent said they'd been discriminated against in applying for jobs and receiving equal pay.[67]

The percentages of Natives experiencing various forms of discrimination were not as high in the NPR study as those of African Americans but higher than those of Latinos. In my opinion, averaged overall findings obscured the heightened susceptibility to discrimination in the "majority Native areas" like reservations. Thirty-one percent of Native respondents described living in these areas versus 68 percent of Native respondents who said they were not living in such settings. This numerical balance appears to represent the overall U.S. census of people *identifying* as Native rather than those who are actually *enrolled*, more likely to live in majority Native areas, and to be entitled to IHS services. Native participants were recruited to the NPR survey not only under the criteria of identifying themselves as "only Native" racially but also if they identified as being of another race as well, provided they said they identified *most* with "being Native."[68]

In contrast, Native people identifying themselves as being of more than one race were excluded from the comparative ethnic analyses of the Stress in America survey administered by the American Psychological Association in 2016. In this sample of 199 Native respondents identifying as "Native only," participants reported experiencing more everyday discrimination than *any* other ethnic group in the United States. They reported more acts of discourtesy and disrespect, poorer service, and being treated as though they were less intelligent than any ethnicity in U.S. society.[69]

Both national surveys reflect real experiences in everyday Native lives. I recall speaking with several young women who'd transferred from public school to Yakama Nation Tribal School. I was curious to know why they'd requested to shift midway through the school year when they'd miss graduating with their class cohort. I learned that they'd all been in a public school classroom with the same *páshtin* teacher when he'd allegedly said, "I'm a racist, and I don't make any excuses. If you don't like it, you can complain to the school administration and see if they do anything about it." They'd complained to administrators, and nothing was indeed done—just as the teacher predicted—and this was why they had decided to transfer.

On another occasion, Sue and I attended a basketball game to support Yakama Nation Tribal School as they faced off with nearby Sunnyside Christian School, a predominantly *páshtin* school. We were astonished to hear parents from the Sunnyside team shouting racial epithets like "Hey, Savage!" or "You dropped the ball, Chief!" at Yakama students we were there to support. Nothing was done by the referees, and we were told that this was business as usual.

These anecdotes match experiences of Native youth nationwide. In 2010, Minnesotan Native students reported experiencing racial slurs from school personnel as well as exceedingly low numbers of teachers and workers caring about them.[70] Despite being only 2 percent of the Minnesota school population, they represented 7 percent of out-of-school suspensions, expulsions, and exclusions.[71] In 2013, Native athletes in Alabama watched as banners were unfurled by McAdory High School cheerleaders reading: "Hey Indians, get ready to leave in a Trail of Tears." School officials later apologized.[72]

Because such racist slurs and insensitivities arise out of abject ignorance, inclusion of Native history within American history curricula might seem a worthy partial antidote for all U.S. students and particularly crucial for encouraging students from beleaguered Native communities. Yet, in 2010, Arizona HB 2281 outlawed public school textbooks "designed primarily for pupils of a particular ethnic group" or that "advocate ethnic solidarity instead of the treatment of pupils as individuals."[73] Such exclusionary tactics are not far removed from UN/OSAPG criteria regarding "domination of media" in the analysis of deliberate genocide. They are served by the marketing clout of the conservative Texas Board of Education, members of which actively lobby publishers to create high school textbooks that "evidence a general lack of attention to Native American peoples and culture and occasionally include biased or misleading information."[74]

Native students report feeling more unsafe going to school than students from other ethnic backgrounds, and they also were most likely to be threatened with a weapon or involved in a fight while on school property.[75]

They are more likely to carry a weapon, typically to defend themselves.[76] Facing off against racial hate and discrimination, political groups and legislation devaluing their history and heritage, and unengaging textbooks undermining their motivation, Native youth have the highest high school dropout and lowest college graduation rates of any U.S. ethnic group. From 2005 to 2015, Native students were the only ethnic group to not experience improvement in reading or math.[77]

Additionally, these students are consistently overrepresented in special education programs nationally at 1.5 times the rate of other ethnic groups for "specific learning disabilities," and 2.9 times for services related to "developmental delays."[78] This overrepresentation statistic has sparked important debates regarding the quality of disproportionality research, particularly whether "the problem is not so much teachers' racial bias as the deeper structures of society based on socioeconomic inequality and unequal access."[79] I contend that the socialization of teachers and their resultant views on equal access, both subtle and overt, should count *as much as* "deeper structures." Teachers may not be at fault for a societal system with a demonstrable oppressive history, but they are certainly influenced by it. When researchers like Anastousiou and Kauffman argue the "medical model of disability" is not "necessarily followed"[80] in special education practice, I can't reconcile their presumption with what I've observed in the relationship between IHS clinics' ADHD diagnoses and public schools serving Native youth.

To what extent does Native youth experience constitute deliberate "widespread and targeted discriminatory practices" congruent with human rights violations in the UN/OSAPG points? If acts of racism and bias by workers in federal and state agencies, schools, and businesses are tolerated, swept under the rug, and/or minimized through ineffective, homogenized "diversity trainings," then these actors are tacitly permitted to continue to create hopelessness and limited futures for Native youth.

PSYCHIATRIC AND EDUCATIONAL STIGMA

Native people labeled as "mentally disordered" by the IHS—that is, with such diagnoses as major depressive disorder, bipolar disorder, posttraumatic stress disorder (PTSD), and/or attention deficit hyperactivity disorder (ADHD)— face negative social and economic stigmas that exacerbate their predicaments within U.S. society. Research suggests, for example, that most Americans feel more uncomfortable interacting with someone labeled "mentally ill" than with a person with severe facial disfigurement.[81]

The idea of public stigma includes discrimination occurring against people so labeled in obtaining a good job and fair housing.[82] Being considered among the "mentally ill" also evokes restrictive and authoritative attitudes in others, even (or especially) from mental health providers themselves.[83] Labeled people can be suspected of inhumaneness and dangerousness premised upon stereotyped media images[84] and are at higher risk of internalizing negative responses they experience from others around them. "Self-stigma" refers to the internalization of stereotyping and discrimination by others combined with self-attack and shame. Self-stigma can lead to a reduced sense of personal effectiveness, confidence, self-esteem, and self-worth.[85]

A special case is found in the overrepresentation of Native youth in public special education programs. In a large study of 11,000 adolescents using the Education Longitudinal Survey of 2002, both parents and teachers revealed lower expectations of students labeled with mental disorders tied to learning issues, and these biases contributed directly to poorer educational outcomes for these teens.[86]

DEATH BY VIOLENCE

Based upon my own analysis of reports issued by the Yakima County Coroner's Office, a Native person residing in the county between 2014 and 2016 was 4.2 times more likely to be murdered than a *páshtin*.[87] Elsewhere, enrolled Native people across the United States are exposed to violence at a rate averaging 2.5 times greater than other ethnic groups.[88] Thirty-four percent of enrolled Native women in the United States can expect to be raped in their lifetimes,[89] and 67 percent of these attacks will occur at the hands of a non-Native perpetrator.[90] Sexual enslavement and forced prostitution of Native women by EuroAmerican men is not just a historical travesty but a *contemporary reality*.[91,92]

According to the National Indigenous Women's Resource Center, more Native women go missing each year than those of any other U.S. ethnic group.[93] Between 1979 and 1992, homicide was the third leading cause of death for Native women,[94] and they are currently 1.7 times more likely to have experienced some form of violence in the past year than white women.[95]

Sexual violence is also experienced by 28 percent of Native men at some point in their lives,[96] while 34 percent, or one in three of these men, report experiencing some form of physical violence in the past year.[97] Native men suffer traumatic brain injury (TBI) from violence in their own communities at a higher rate and resulting in greater physical damage than any other ethnic group in the United States.[98]

Sexual and physical violence originated in Native families as a direct result of the destruction of cultural traditions, European colonization and rape, and the forced institutionalization of Native children in federally and mission-operated boarding schools from 1879 to 1970. This means that generations of Native children grew up away from their primary caregivers and in institutional environments, many of which were highly abusive.

Sixty-seven percent of the Native youth I met with from 2000 to 2010 reported both experiencing and witnessing physical violence.[99] Their reports to me were congruent with *general population* studies of reservation-based Native youth, not just those who have been identified as coming from families viewed as particularly troubled. In one such study, 77 percent of reservation-based Native youth reported at least one adverse childhood experience (ACE) of physical abuse, emotional abuse, sexual abuse, emotional neglect, physical neglect, and witnessing violence against their mother, and 40 percent of these youth had two or more such experiences.[100] Again, 33 percent of Native youth with whom I met reported being sexually violated, and 17 percent disclosed suffering from *both* physical and sexual violence.

Such numbers are startling enough, but 60 percent of Native youth I met with were also dealing with traumatic grief relating to the loss of an important loved one.[101] Ichishkíin Sínwit, the original language of Yakama people, contains words such as *cutla*, *tila*, and *pusha*, forms of address that are the same for people who are differentiated as grandparents and grand-children in Euro culture. Such Yakama words signify the extremely close bond of intergenerational relationships, and lowered life expectancy among Yakama elders adds to the overwhelm of children who've already suffered assault and must live with both violation and loss simultaneously. There have been many occasions when I've marveled at a student making it into school, given what I knew about what they were going through.

The vulnerability of Native people to organized violence was made more visible to all Americans through media coverage of the 2016 protests against the $3 billion Dakota Access Pipeline (DAPL) when the activism of Standing Rock, Cheyenne, and Yankton Sioux tribal communities sought to protect their people from yet more water contamination. On November 21, 2016, for instance, three hundred DAPL protesters were injured, including twenty-six seriously, having suffered cardiac arrest, bone fractures, eye injuries, hypothermia, and near loss of an arm when North Dakota law officers turned on water cannons, shot rubber bullets, and lobbed tear gas and concussion grenades at a portion of the crowd in below-freezing temperatures.[102]

Arrested DAPL protesters were strip-searched, kept naked for long durations in holding cells, hand-marked with numbers, and imprisoned in dog kennel–type cages.[103] The November DAPL assault constituted the apex of numerous other excessive force incidents, including one in which six people, including a six-year-old child, were assaulted and bitten by attack dogs under the direction of private security guards.[104]

I became curious about the brutality of police strategies at the DAPL protests. Patricia Donegal (formerly Campbell), author of *Torture and Its Psychological Effects in Northern Ireland*,[105] noted to me their similarities to British military abuses during Na Trioblóidí (the Troubles): "I followed the Dakota Pipeline struggle closely and I saw striking parallels . . . As I watched the brutalities meted out to the people it opened up many memories of my own trauma and vicarious trauma."[106] She described survivors of Na Trioblóidí who'd been beaten, stripped naked, hooded, abused, and isolated in solitary confinement using tactics adapted from sensory deprivation research findings in experimental psychology.

The highly visible, excessive force used by law enforcement against DAPL protesters hints at a more chronic problem. Since 1999, Native people have traded places year to year with African Americans in being most often killed by law enforcement officers.[107] In 2016, Natives held the highest per capita death rate by police of all ethnicities. Twenty-four Native people were shot to death that year either during police pursuit or apprehension; two of them were unarmed, and in two more cases, it was unknown whether they had a weapon or not.[108] In six of the other cases, the suspect possessed a knife, hammer, or pair of scissors.[109] From 2015 to 2016, a Native person in the United States was 2.7 times more likely to be killed by police than a white person,[110] while the actual number dying as a result of police response is thought by journalists tracking the issue to be greatly underestimated.[111] Near where I live with my family at the Suquamish Nation in western

Washington State, I attended Poulsbo City Council meetings and protests in 2019 following the police murder of Stonechild Chiefstick (Chippewa Cree), a father of six, which led to a successful $2 million lawsuit settlement with his family in 2022 after allegations of negligence, racist policing, and excessive force.[112]

The range and breadth of violence exacts a severe emotional toll upon many survivors: 67 percent of Native women[113] and 26 percent of Native men live each day with chronic traumatic preoccupations and intense safety concerns.[114] In fact, a less explored factor behind low representation in postsecondary education is the nearly 40 percent of Native women who report missing work or school due to violence exposure.[115]

How might the chronic ubiquity and extent of violence coming from outside tribal communities relate to the UN/OSAPG points? When the so-called dominant society allows its representative law enforcement to oppress, torture, and perpetrate murder, there is no longer an authority to call for help and protection from violence. Instead, the law of the street prevails, and the innocent are victimized as malevolent forces from outside their communities exploit vulnerability and hopelessness. Furthermore, the EuroAmerican justice culture of punishment favors the rich, exacerbates violence, and fails Native families by usurping community control and sovereignty in dealing with violent outsiders.

SIX

IHS Attempts to Prevent Native Suicide

DEATH BY SELF-INFLICTED VIOLENCE

It is something of an open secret that Native youth have the highest suicide rate of any ethnic group in the United States.[1,2] According to the Centers for Disease Control (CDC), suicide is the second leading cause of death for Native people aged fifteen to twenty-four years.[3] The first leading cause of death is "unintentional injury," and some researchers suggest that many self-poisonings classified in this way are in reality "undetected suicides."[4] In a 2020 study with over 10,000 participants during the COVID-19 pandemic, researchers found Native American subjects reporting the highest rate of suicidal behaviors on a standard questionnaire (Suicide Behaviors Questionnaire-Revised, or SBQ-R). Native individuals also reported the highest levels of food insecurity, which proved a highly significant factor in the suicidality findings.[5]

Native young women commit suicide at nearly four times the rate of their white female counterparts, and Native young men at twice the rate of white young men.[6] Such alarming statistics hide a much wider phenomenon. According to the CDC, for young adults, "There are approximately 100–200 attempts for every completed suicide."[7] By the second decade of life, violence through unintentional injury, homicide, and suicide accounts for 75 percent of deaths among American Indians and Alaska Natives.[8]

In 2000, during my first year at Yakama Indian Health Service, Blackfoot school counselor and friend Verna Smith (Pitá-aki) pulled from the back of a file drawer a survey by the Bureau of Indian Affairs recently undertaken with the local middle school students I was to meet.[9] She wanted to gently alert me that one in five of the students I'd be visiting had *attempted* suicide during the year prior to my arrival. Such numbers were little different from what I'd previously encountered while working in an inpatient adolescent psychiatric unit. Even more shocking is the discovery that such self-reports are not an anomaly in Native America. In 2015, this same school-based Youth Risk Behavior Surveillance System (YRBSS) reflected that 15 percent—and possibly as many as 24 percent—of Native middle and high school students across the United States attempted suicide in the past twelve months.[10] In 2019, this YRBSS question was altered somewhat, yielding findings that nearly 35 percent of Native high school students had seriously considered committing suicide.[11] In Yakima County between 2014 and 2016, an enrolled Yakama tribal member was 3.8 times more likely to commit suicide than a white person.[12]

To what degree is a society that tolerates widespread abuse, neglect, and lack of options for Native youth culpable for the hopelessness and despair leading to their suicides? How might that culpability relate to the UN/OSAPG points pertaining to deliberate genocide? If the severe so-called psychosocial stressors of "growing up Indian" continue to relentlessly encourage youth to take their own lives, then they are, in reality, a form of chronic oppression and constitute massive systemic violence perpetrated by EuroAmerican society.

IHS'S FAILED DRUG APPROACH

Officially oblivious to Native reactions to *oppression*, Indian Health Service practice guidelines emphasize that its primary care providers prescribe psychiatric drugs as the first approach to treating moderate to severe *depression* "whether or not" psychotherapy is available.[13]

Most doctors, like most people, assume suicidal behavior is *caused* by depression—an understandable conclusion, because many people who survive a suicide attempt meet psychiatric labeling criteria for severe major depressive or other disorders set by the American Psychiatric Association in 2003.[14] These guidelines state:

> The strong association between clinical depression and suicide and the availability of reasonably effective and quite safe antidepressants support their use, in adequate doses and for an adequate duration,

as part of a comprehensive program of care for potentially suicidal patients, including long-term use in patients with recurrent forms of depressive or severe anxiety disorders.[15]

We'll review the presumed effectiveness of antidepressant drugs in a moment. If we look at basic assumptions in this statement, should we assume that the "strong association" between feeling depressed and making a suicide attempt can be considered *causal*? Many people who report feeling severely depressed don't attempt suicide. Research conducted in the United Kingdom suggests that the implication of a causal link between depression and suicide "privileges depression over many other potential contributors to suicide, both proximal (e.g. alcohol intoxication, acute interpersonal conflict, access to lethal methods) and distal (e.g. poverty, unemployment)."[16]

Researchers reviewing completed suicides by Native people in Alaska and New Mexico found on average that 74 percent occurred while an individual was intoxicated.[17] Up to 64 percent of people attempting suicide in the general population in the United States are intoxicated by alcohol at the time.[18] The incidence of alcohol abuse, then, is another factor strongly correlated with fluctuations in population suicide rates, while alcohol intoxication carries the additional well-known risks of poor impulse control and obscured judgment.[19] Additionally, alcohol itself is a mood-altering drug capable of inducing temporary depressive mood states. Add to a mix of alcohol, impulsiveness, and impaired judgment other common elements among suicide attempters such as recent relationship loss and hopelessness,[20] and the inconsistent psychiatric concept of "depression"[21] becomes less salient than IHS practice guidelines may suppose.

Another way of thinking about heightened suicide risk in Indian Country is to look at it as a complex interplay of oppressive stressors magnified further by alcohol and other forms of intoxication. In this regard, a passionate plea for a shift in paradigm was issued by mental health researchers and providers in New Mexico writing in the *American Journal of Community Psychology* in 2010 when they asserted that *oppression*, not *depression*, plays a primary role in Native youth suicide:

> In summary, we found that American Indian/Alaska Native youth face multiple stressors and traumas, including: poverty, current institutional racism, micro-aggressions, and traumatic life events.

Furthermore, the current structures and emphases of behavioral health systems of care do not adequately address these challenges or integrate effective indigenous health practices.[22]

These writers described "high levels of violence and trauma exposure and traumatic loss" that link psychological distress and substance use among American Indian adolescents to "past and current oppression, racism, and discrimination," "disregard for effective indigenous practices in service provision, policy, and funding," and "the lack of inclusion of AI/AN participants in behavioral health intervention research" for so-called evidence-based practices (EBPs) in Indian Country as among numerous factors challenging the current behavioral health approach to Native suicide being emphasized by IHS.[23]

IHS behavioral health policies and providers which continue to stress prescribing psychiatric drugs as both a primary and desirable intervention for suicide and depression are controversial. For example, in 2010 the *British Journal of Psychiatry* sponsored an important debate effectively challenging the usefulness of antidepressant drugs for reducing suicide.[24] Claims of a rise or decline in the suicide rate in relation to the availability of such drugs have never been established. For instance, researchers looked at these drugs at the height of their popularity in four Nordic countries by surveying over 61,000 suicides and failed to find a link between antidepressant sales and declining suicide rates between 1996 and 1998. They were forced to conclude that "cohort effects or other cultural influences ... could theoretically have a bigger impact on suicide rates than any drug or psychotherapeutic/ psychosocial treatment" and lamented that "we are unable to convincingly comprehend suicide phenomena."[25]

It's also unclear whether active ingredients of antidepressant drugs actually lessen the subjective experience of depressed mood: 82 percent of the "clinical response" measured in the six most popular among these drugs pertains to the power of belief—that is, the *placebo effect*.[26] "Nocebo" effects—negative side effects in groups of research participants receiving antidepressant placebo—have also been detected, confirming the considerable power of patient expectations placed upon these drugs.[27] In fact, a case was documented in which an individual attempted suicide by taking twenty-nine antidepressant placebo pills, developed clinical hypotension, sweating, and an elevated heart rate requiring intravenous intervention, and then became completely restored within fifteen minutes of being informed he'd been enrolled in the placebo condition of the drug trial.[28]

Patient expectations can be enhanced through social indoctrination to scientific falsehoods. Alleged chemical imbalances I've heard described by IHS and other providers to Native patients regarding depression are one example of false science that serves the marketing desires of pharmaceutical manufacturers. "The chemical imbalance story, which is being told about all psychotropic drugs, even for benzodiazepines ('nerve' or sleeping pills), is a big lie. . . . [T]he idea that depressed patients lack serotonin has been convincingly rejected,"[29] according to Peter Gøtzsche, physician and professor of clinical research design and analysis at the University of Copenhagen and former cofounder of the Cochrane Collaboration. In her comprehensive book *The Myth of the Chemical Cure*,[30] British researcher and practicing psychiatrist Joanna Moncrieff writes:

> If people believe that it is brain chemicals that have made them depressed and that they only improved because a drug helped to rectify a chemical defect or imbalance, then they are likely to fear the recurrence of depression with every difficult period in their lives. In addition, they are not likely to recognize the things they did to help themselves out of depression, because they attribute their recovery to a drug. If in contrast they had managed to get through the period without taking a drug that they thought sorted out their biochemistry, they would have had an experience of self-efficacy that could build their confidence and help them face future problems with greater strength.[31]

By trying to prevent suicide by reducing Native "depression," the Indian Health Service overlooks or disregards a significant *lack* of evidence for its "first response" practice of prescribing antidepressant drugs. Ninety-two percent of FDA studies reporting *negative* findings regarding the ineffectiveness of these drugs were never published in relevant psychiatric or medical literature.[32] Writing in 2010 in *The Emperor's New Drugs*,[33] Harvard psychologist Irving Kirsch summarized multiple meta-analyses of FDA original clinical trials (obtained under the Freedom of Information Act) and concluded there is *no significant or meaningful clinical difference* between antidepressant drugs and sugar pills for reducing what the Indian Health Service calls "major depressive disorder." Researcher Michael P. Hengartner at the Zurich University of Applied Sciences concurred in 2017, noting:

> The pooled efficacy of antidepressants is weak and below the threshold of a minimally clinically important change once publication and reporting biases are considered. Moreover, the small mean difference in symptom reductions relative to placebo is possibly attributable to observer effects in unblinded assessors and patient expectancies. . . . Due to several flaws such as publication and reporting bias ... the efficacy of antidepressants is systematically overestimated, and harm is systematically underestimated.[34]

In early 2022, a research team lead by Erick H. Turner at Oregon Health & Science University found that half of studies indicating findings of ineffectiveness regarding so-called new antidepressants, such as Pristiq, Viibryd, Fetzima, and Trintellix, were not accepted for publication by professional journals or were mischaracterized as positive.[35] A 2008 study by these same researchers of "older antidepressants," like Prozac, Paxil, Lexapro, Zoloft, and eight other major brands, had already revealed even stronger "evidence for both study publication bias and outcome reporting bias."[36]

Others, such as investigative journalist Robert Whitaker (*Anatomy of an Epidemic*[37] and, with Lisa Cosgrove, *Psychiatry Under the Influence*[38]) and psychiatrist Dan Carlat (*Unhinged: The Trouble with Psychiatry*)[39] have effectively demonstrated how the pharmaceutical industry funds key opinion leaders for promoting its false science. Psychiatrists, meanwhile, are trapped in an ethical quandary threatening their professional survival. According to Whitaker and Cosgrove:

> In the United States, psychiatry is in competition for patients with psychologists, social workers, counselors, and other therapists who provide psychological services for people with psychiatric issues. If psychiatric drugs are not seen as helpful, the field cannot hope to thrive in this competition. . . .
>
> A medical specialty can only abandon a therapy when it has a replacement in the offing, as otherwise it might as well sign its own "going out of business" certificate.[40]

Having moved well away from sociological and psychological issues it once studied, the psychiatric guild ensnared itself with the drug industry in the 1990s to such a degree that it is more accurate to see its current providers as "psychopharmacologists." The motives of the Indian Health Service in allying the agency with psychiatry's psychopharmacological movement, however, seem less clear. I undertook an analysis of IHS and Medicaid public information that suggested between $50 million and $200 million in annual revenue comes to Indian Health Service and tribally run clinics from prescribing psychiatric drugs.[41] Additionally, chronic underfunding, lack of support for community-based alternatives, poor training in nonmedical crisis intervention and peer support, and rigid adherence to the "biomedical model" seem to solidify a sense at IHS that the psychiatric drug solution is the only viable response to suicide. In this, IHS's mimicry of the mainstream U.S. medical community is terribly misplaced.

Between 1999 and 2014—a time when these drugs peaked in popularity—the rate of completed suicides across the U.S. increased by 16 percent for all ages and ethnicities.[42] This increase was most pronounced among white women aged forty-five to sixty-four years (rising 80 percent) and white men in the same age range (up 59 percent). The primary culprit was the rising tide of prescription opiate addiction—a horrific problem in which the U.S. medical community was also duped by pharmaceutical manufacturers.[43] Yet, all along, IHS continued to emphasize an ineffective and, as we'll learn momentarily, dangerous drug solution while remaining seemingly unable to escape its own myopia. Tragically, the Native rate for completed suicides increased an average 63 percent during this same period.[44]

Astoundingly, IHS's drug approach may actually exacerbate suicidal behavior. A 2013 report on IHS suicide surveillance data between 2003 and 2012 issued in partnership with the Great Lakes Inter-Tribal Epidemiology Center (GLITEC) revealed that the Native youth suicide rate has continued to climb while that of other U.S. youth has leveled off.[45] Concurrently, a 2009 meta-analysis of 372 double-blind, randomized, placebo-controlled drug trials for all classes of antidepressants, including selective serotonin reuptake inhibitors (SSRIs), serotonin-noradrenaline reuptake inhibitors (SNRIs), other "modern" antidepressants (bupropion, mirtazapine, etc.), and older tricyclic antidepressants concluded that young people under the age of twenty-five years are at a 1.6 times higher risk for increased suicidal behavior while consuming these drugs, including for completed suicides, attempts, suicide preparation, and suicidal thoughts.[46] In 2019 a reassessment of original FDA trials checking the safety of newer breeds of antidepressant drugs (SSRI, SNRI) asserted the risk as even higher: "The rate of (attempted) suicide was about 2.5 times higher in antidepressant arms relative to placebo."[47] In 2020, researchers continued to debate the risk statistic, settling at 1.7, while concluding "an increased rate of suicide attempts, and possibly also suicides, among those treated with AD [antidepressant drugs] a reliable finding."[48]

There are contrasting opinions, but it is difficult to assess them, given potential conflicts of interest, entanglement with drug company funding, and the publishing biases I've mentioned. Pharmaceutical companies don't generally provide grants to researchers intending to undermine the marketability of their products, although this would constitute good public policy, because refuting *null hypotheses* that these drugs are *not* safe and *not* effective would be fundamental to an appropriate scientific methodology.

Thus, when I look at a recent study like "Medications and Suicide: High Dimensional Empirical Bayes Screening (iDEAS)," which audaciously offers a table suggesting that antidepressant drugs are "associated with postexposure decreases in suicidal events,"[49] I have to consider the study's authors' ties to an inherently corrupt pharmaceutical industry. As Suffolk University Law School professor Marc A. Rodwin remarks, "the root of the problem lies in the institutional corruption stemming from improper dependencies."[50] The primary researcher in the iDEAS study, Robert Gibbons, is a biostatistician who in 2007[51] used pharmaceutical funding and highly misleading data analysis[52,53] to challenge black box regulatory warnings about increased suicidal behavior among children and adolescents consuming SSRI antidepressant drugs. He also served on the FDA panel overseeing these warnings and voted against them, and he's been an expert witness for both Wyeth Pharmaceuticals and Pfizer. Similarly, fellow author J. John Mann has received funding from GlaxoSmithKline and served as an adviser to Eli Lilly and Lundbeck. Coauthors Kwan Hur and Jiebiao Wang are both biostatisticians rather than mental health researchers. And according to her bio, coauthor Jill Lavigne "develops and delivers campus and online course content in pharmacoeconomics, outcomes research, population health and leadership through quality improvement."[54] at St. John Fisher University while conducting suicide prevention research at the U.S. Department of Veterans Affairs (VA). Not surprisingly, "pharmacotherapy" for suicide prevention is still strongly emphasized at the VA[55] while veterans continue to take their own lives on average seventeen times every day[56] and at a rate 1.5 times greater than that of the U.S. civilian population.[57]

The most reliable evidence on the issues I've raised has been found outside of research funded by pharmaceutical corporate interests. This research moves beyond lack of efficacy for antidepressant drugs to suggest an unaddressed crisis in which the IHS treatment approach magnifies rather than decreases suicidal behavior. A high but unknown number of Native youth labeled with mental disorders by IHS providers have been prescribed these drugs, while the GLITEC suicide surveillance report notes that 54 percent of suicide attempts and 52 percent of completed suicides in Indian Country between 2003 and 2012 occurred within this same demographic of people twenty-four years or younger.[58] I was making such contentions when I first learned of this research twenty years ago and got into trouble for doing so. In 2018, Austrian medical researchers Martin Plöderl and Michael Hengartner reviewed youth suicide prevention research and flatly asserted: "We want to caution against the indiscriminate use of antidepressant drugs, which may worsen the problem they are supposed to treat."[59] I am sad and fearful about this broken, paralyzed system compounding the problem and exacerbating loss of life.

Likely due to poor provider compliance, the stigma about suicide, and other factors, IHS tracking of Native suicides is impeded by missing and incomplete information, making it difficult to detect the degree of substance involvement in 47 percent of completed suicides and 24 percent of attempts the agency has tracked.[60] However, another critically important finding within the GLITEC study is that one in three Native drug overdoses involved *the ingestion of psychiatric drugs themselves*. The majority of these drugs were prescribed by IHS providers and included amphetamines and stimulants, tricyclic and other antidepressants, sedatives, benzodiazepines, and barbiturates. Furthermore, GLITEC's suicide surveillance report doesn't specify what "other prescription medications" make up an additional 16 percent of medication overdoses, although they likely originated at IHS.[61] Drug overdose was responsible for 9.5 percent of completed suicides in Indian Country from 2003 to 2012.[62] Sadly, in 93 percent of Native suicide attempts, no follow-up resources or services were recorded as having been provided by IHS.[63]

Yes, I admit to having deliberately referred to antidepressants as "anti-oppressants." Is there any evidence that prescribing these drugs might represent an attempt to pacify reactions to oppressive conditions contributing to Native suicide? GLITEC's suicide surveillance report suggests that, in about 38 percent of Native suicide attempts and completions, *relationship loss*—death of a loved ones, including by suicide, or the ending of a relationship—was a primary contributing factor.[64] In nearly 16 percent of suicide attempts and 12 percent of completions, *legal, occupational, educational, and financial problems* were contributing factors.[65] Exposure to *violence and abuse* contributed to 13 percent of attempts and nearly 6 percent of completions.[66] Almost 27 percent of Native people attempting suicide and nearly 20 percent of those completing suicide were entangled in *substance abuse* and *addiction*.[67] Studies of Robert Agnew's "strain theory" among American Indian youth only bolster the relevance of psychosocial factors: caretaker rejection and verbal abuse, negative school attitudes, and perceived discrimination were significantly correlated with anger, depression, and suicidal behavior.[68]

The substance abuse/suicide factor is itself obscured through false and prejudicial linkages to a pseudoscience of "alcohol genetics," i.e., the "firewater" myth.[69] Substance abuse problems in Indian Country are in no way genetic, and old research pertaining to enzyme deficiencies in the metabolizing of alcohol has been thoroughly debunked.[70] Alcohol abuse in Indian Country is far more accurately linked to powerlessness, hopelessness, and family and peer transmission of self-medication as a tension-reduction response to chronic adversity.[71] Indeed, the firewater myth itself has actually been linked to reduced self-efficacy and rejection of harm reduction approaches among Native alcohol abusers.[72] I suspect one feels only more powerless to deal with a problem when indoctrinated by a false science that faults one's own "defective genes" instead of affirming and validating the oppressive realities within one's life.

Equating depression with suicide and psychiatric drugs with suicide prevention—ideas derived from IHS's medical model ideology—is an ineffective, dangerous approach that obscures the context and reality of oppression in the lives of Native Americans. Meanwhile, Native youth with a strong sense of cultural identity and family involvement have been found to be less at risk for suicide,[73] while youth experiencing family and cultural disconnectedness are at greater risk.[74] Such findings should constitute "evidence" too, yet of a very different sort. It was an obvious impetus within the community's desire to create Níix Ttáwaxt at Yakama Nation.

During her doctoral dissertation qualitative research in 2011, my former student, Seattle-area psychologist Kelsey Kennedy, interviewed numerous Yakama youth, community leaders, and elders in talking circles. Through her participatory design, community members revealed how much they *already* knew about factors behind local youth suicide—how "many of the homes on the reservation experience a severe lack of resources," "at times no clean water or food," and "many of the youth are hungry and are exposed to a lack of safety." Traumatic historical events were recounted alongside the transmission of violence in families: "We learned very early on through boarding school what abuse was, so it carried on from one generation to the next, you know." Participants noted that "the loss of language, our way of life and a sense of who we are has led current generations to feeling a sense that they do not really know how or where they fit in," and this has contributed to "an emptiness of understanding of the rituals and way of life."[75]

Not a single participant in Dr. Kennedy's study mentioned a shortage of psychiatric drugs or a need for better identification of major depressive disorder as factors in preventing Yakama youth suicide. Regarding the UN/OSAPG points, when should a mental health system ideology and reticent adherence to the Western biomedical model be considered complicit in Native self-violence and suicide? I believe it already is.

REACTIVITY TO OPPRESSION AS MENTAL DISORDER

Historically viewed as enemies and noncitizens, Native people across the United States have remained mostly unrepresented among elected public officials and economic leaders while living lives demonstrably shortened by environmental poisoning, cancer, diabetes, and suicide—difficult lives filled with more poverty, hunger, violence, bigotry, and lack of opportunity than any other ethnic group in the country. Given their beleaguered social and political status, how should we understand the U.S. mental health system's reframing of the troubling or troubled Native as "mentally disordered"?

Native hopelessness, substance abuse, nonconformity, rage, defiance, despair, demotivation, and the like are better conceptualized as reactions to unrelenting threat—that is, through day-to-day experience with domination, oppression, injustice, inequity, and colonization. This isn't a new idea: Frantz

Fanon wrote eloquently in 1961 about a similar political-psychological inter-section among colonized Algerians:

> It seems to us that in the cases here chosen the events giving rise to the disorder are chiefly the bloodthirsty and pitiless atmosphere, the generalization of inhuman practices, and the firm impression that people have of being caught up in a veritable Apocalypse.[76]

But do the adversities that Native people face constitute deliberate and genocidal acts according to the UN/OSAPG standards? In many ways, Native people are still treated like enemies. And within the current "behavioral health paradigm" IHS providers are unwittingly compelled to serve an indoctrination program teaching *Native people as disordered* rather than about society violating and abusing them. Until they feel fully able to challenge the very system in which they work, IHS mental health providers will continue to be forced into "openly [assisting] oppressive systems to continue to perpetuate supremacy."[77]

Having known, befriended, and worked with behavioral health providers from Native backgrounds, I feel I can attest to the power of IHS's indoctrinating influence in its current system. Nonconformity is not typically tolerated, and creativity is seldom supported or sustained. Culture-centered approaches may be accepted—provided they do not oppose or interfere with the dominance of the biopsychiatric model. Career survival is premised, then, on "going along to get along."

Here we see the great push of Coyote's Swing. I do not find the Yakama hero, Spilyáy, Coyote, trapped somewhere over the ocean in Germany as in William Charley's story but within the grip of imported Eurocentric biomedical ideology (with some roots in German philosophy). These notions represent what the UN/OSAPG describes as "exclusionary ideology and the construction of identities in terms of 'us' and 'them'"[78] and "unequal distribution of resources and power, and systems of domination ... that act symbolically or instrumentally to reinforce that domination."[79]

For over 150 years, the United States mental health system has sanitized and recast a murderous and intolerant society as the normative point of adaptation and assimilation for Native people it characterizes as "mentally disordered." To understand how this system's ideologies reassert its domination and how it might be opposed or co-opted toward its own betterment, we need to deconstruct its historical underpinnings.

SEVEN

Border Skirmish

DROWNING IN IHS CLINIC CULTURE

Our five-day road trip from Detroit to the Yakima Valley in 2000 was punctuated with countless sightings of white- and red-tail hawks, which my wife and I kept noting over walkie-talkies between our two cars. I had only two days with my family after we arrived before starting work with Yakama Indian Health Service Clinic. Settling into our new home in west Yakima, a secondary Washington city of about 70,000 people north of Yakama Nation, we marveled at the brown undulating hills of sage surrounding us and breaking up the landscape in ways unseen in flat Michigan. We busily sorted out boxes alongside the whereabouts of schools, gas stations, grocery stores, and churches while also managing to bless our new home.

During the Dream Catchers project in Michigan in the 1990s, I'd been taught to smudge, an ancient Plains Indian spiritual practice of burning sage and other aromatics that Western health research has only recently caught up to for its anti-bacterial, cleansing, and other ethnopharmacological benefits.[1,2] "We said prayers as a family in our new house & then burnt sage in every room," I recorded in my journal. I felt good to be embarking on a new adventure as we began to settle in.

This brief enchantment was irretrievably broken within my first few days on the job at Yakama Indian Health Service Clinic. I still possess notes describing my anxieties at the time as I hastily scribbled into a pocket-size memo book: "no furniture, no welcome, no briefing, no orientation, no lunch," "uncertain who I report to," "immediate philosophical disputes—

85

↑ medical model, ↓ therapy," "I was direct—don't buy into the concept of 'mental health,'" "honeymoon now over, if it ever began," and "a social worker … particularly hostile … sniping and sarcasm."

An irregular diarist, I took such notes because I rightly anticipated trouble. I'd been forewarned by one of the hiring managers that my new colleagues were hostile to the creation of the new "psychologist position." He expressed hopes they'd come around and I'd eventually supervise the "Mental Health Department." This possibility was attractive economic bait for pulling up our roots in Michigan and accepting the position, but it wasn't the deciding factor. Sue and I had placed our trust in the many mysterious and synchronous events happening to both of us during a time of great grief, some of which I've already mentioned. In any case, a promotion would never come to pass, and I attribute this to the conflicts that unfolded. I was hired as a "General Service-12," and a "GS-12" civil servant I remained for the next four years. It's the GS-13s who make the real money.

I believe the threat of my promotion potential seemed very real to my new colleagues, at least at first. I represented a potential boss they'd never sought, and they were furious. I hoped for alliances rather than friction, but I was naive about the negative pre-positioning of my role. The clinic's administration had let slip locally that in deference to prior tribal allegations about these same providers, the new psychologist would be expected to help shape them up. I knew nothing about the advance press, so I was shocked by the cold shoulder I received. I was more than not welcomed on my first day: I actually overheard people arranging lunch to discuss what to do about me and my arrival. I ate lunch alone at my desk, feeling somewhat dejected.

This freeze reached its iciest point a few weeks later with the first (and only) formal work complaint against me I've ever had, the fallout from psychotherapy work I'd undertaken with a sixteen-year-old Native teen I'll call Tessa.[3]

Only a few sessions in, Tessa had asked me point-blank if she *had* to take the psychiatric drugs she'd been prescribed. She was an older minor, and I felt uncertain how to answer. I wondered whether I wanted to go along with the idea of any Native youth having to ingest drugs against their will. In the state of Washington, teens over age thirteen can consent to mental health services without parent involvement, and I wondered: Did this include Tessa having a say in taking drugs she was prescribed?

At the time Tessa and I began meeting, about 50 percent of the Yakama Nation community (from various tribal backgrounds) were under the age of eighteen. Tessa happened to live in foster care with her aunt and was going through challenges similar to those of kids I'd known in the past and with whom I'd had some experience. I'll remind readers that foster care youth by definition are children who've experienced abuse and/or neglect—so-called adverse childhood experiences (ACEs)—of such severity that their situation has come to the attention of state or tribal social services workers. It is those workers who determine if youth must be removed from their families of origin to be cared for by relatives or foster care parents. This is a terribly hard job and a significant intrusion of the state into families' and children's lives, but—given the current state of societal morality—few alternatives exist.

Native children are placed in foster care at a rate 2.7 times greater than white children.[4] In Washington State, where Yakama Nation is located, the placement rate for Native youth in 2014 was 4.3 times higher than that of *páshtin* children.[5] There is a massive shortage of Native foster parent homes, and many children are placed in non-Native homes despite the protection of the Indian Child Welfare Act (ICWA) of 1978—the single most important legislation intervening in the ongoing history of removal of Native children from their families over the last 150 years.

In 2018, however, a Texas federal judge ruled that ICWA was unconstitutional and violated the rights of non-Native parents seeking to adopt Native children.[6] This case was mounted via broader legal strategies by right-wing, evangelical, and anti–tribal sovereignty groups to dismantle Native American self-determination by misconstruing the maintenance of community connections for children protected by ICWA into a deceptive language about the "civil rights" of aspiring adoptive parents. Fortunately, the judge's ruling was overturned on appeal in 2019.[7] In April 2021, however, "a sharply divided U.S. 5th Circuit Court of Appeals" struck down key parts of ICWA "giving Native American families preference in the adoption of Native American children" in a ruling that may find its way to the U.S. Supreme Court.[8] Clearly, ICWA is under constant attack.

Many good people make sacrifices to become foster parents and to try to help troubled youth grow up healthy and loved. Despite the biases people sometimes hold, the overall incidence of abuse of children in foster care appears lower than in the general population.[9] That's a mixed blessing, because the epidemic incidence of child abuse in the general U.S. population is nothing to write home about, and abuse does occur in the foster care system as well. When this happens, it layers trauma on top of trauma.

Like some youth, Tessa was exposed to extensive abuse both before and after her placement. She was savvy, street smart, and cynical about systems failing her. Having only just met me, she said, "This place sucks, the people here suck, and you suck." I took her attitude in stride, and I think accepting her prickliness had something to do with her opening up more.

It wasn't too long into our therapeutic alliance before she disclosed the horrific abuse leading to her foster placement: getting beaten by her intoxicated mom nearly daily with a heavy belt and fists. She and her siblings were removed from her biological mother's care when she was eight years old. She felt her younger sisters, from whom she'd been separated, blamed her for breaking up their family. By the time she was nine years old, Tessa's mother had died in a car wreck as a result of her "drinking and drugging." Her father had died in the same manner before she was born.

After her placement at twelve years old, she was sexually molested regularly by her foster mother's boyfriend. She eyed me suspiciously while briefly alluding to these assaults and then asked me what, exactly, I'd be writing down. Being able to confide without feeling "recorded" was critical to creating any trust with Tessa and youth like her. I often had to manage the curiosity of state workers, however, who knew the law regarding foster youth made my therapy work an open book for them. Many respected the boundary, but at times this could be a difficult dance.

This man's sexual assaults, Tessa said, were the main reason she'd chosen to become gang-involved. She sensed the state system could not protect her, and "Lower [Yakima] Valley" Indians were her nearest resource. Confronted one afternoon by a carload of these new homies, her foster mom's boyfriend moved out. He broke up with her foster mom and blamed Tessa. Her foster mom then appealed to state authorities to have her removed.

By the time we sat down together, Tessa had "blown out" of twenty-seven placements and developed notoriety as moody, defiant, and potentially combative. Her caseworker warned me she was a "fighter," and this amused me because Tessa was quite small. I found her fierceness understandable, and her "delinquencies" sometimes brilliant, sometimes dumb, but easy to predict given her distrust of adults. I was not surprised when she admitted she'd never volunteered details about this abuse to my other colleagues at the clinic. She didn't trust them, either, and had become accustomed to being minimized and disregarded. She was typically incredulous and suspicious, and I expressed gratitude that she'd been more open with me but wondered why.

"I don't know," Tessa said. "I just decided to. I didn't think you'd do anything to hurt me."

The only successful placements Tessa experienced were a temporary stay with her ailing grandfather John and, most recently, with her biological mother's half sister, Louise. John took Tessa into his home without conditions, and Tessa believed he truly loved her. Unlike nonrelatives, relatives in Washington State are not compensated for taking in a foster care youth, and that is a barrier that should change.

After John died, Tessa became very distraught while being shifted through numerous temporary placements and having to go to different schools. She acknowledged she began to "act up," and in response she was labeled psychiatrically and compelled to start taking drugs.

Today, as a member of the scientific and medical advisory committee for the National Center for Youth Law (NCYL), I am more aware of the vulnerability of foster youth being drugged against their will.[10] In 2016, NCYL helped achieve legislation in California limiting this kind of forced drugging and holding psychiatrists and psychiatric nurses more accountable for their prescribing behavior.[11] More recently, NCYL joined a lawsuit mounted by the nonprofit Children's Rights lodged against Missouri's Children's Division for similar practices.[12] Meanwhile, public revelations about migrant youth separated from their detained parents and placed in Shiloh Treatment Center near Houston, Texas, "a zombie army of children forcibly injected with medications that make them dizzy, listless, obese and even incapacitated,"[13] has provided a more publicized glimpse of this kind of ongoing chemical assault. Such violation of children's rights and futures continues and is widespread.

Louise worked several part-time jobs and cared for other foster children. She took Tessa into her care under the condition she follow "adult rules," which, given her own hectic life, was often influenced by state caseworkers and my IHS coworkers. Louise wasn't an uncaring foster parent, but she was often overwhelmed and sought support from these outside parties in order to keep her head above water.

Tessa found me unwilling to assume a role other adults had taken—in particular, acting like a quasi-parent and trying to control her. Ironically, she wanted to appear compliant with all concerned in our mental health department and the clinic because she desperately wanted more independence. This is why she'd *asked* me if she had to keep taking drugs instead of coming up with some means of subterfuge. She was seeking advice; she understood other adults held much sway over her, and she wanted to be viewed as "reformed" so she could somehow be released from their form of "care," i.e., forced drugging.

To complicate matters, her social worker passed along to my coworkers that Tessa's alternative school principal had requested they do a better job of "treating" her for "ADHD" by reassessing, and hopefully, increasing her dosage of methylphenidate, or he wouldn't allow her to continue attending certain classes in which she was viewed as disruptive. This kind of influence over the drugs youth take or don't take in order to obtain a public education has since been made illegal. Public school officials have been barred since 2004 by the Individual with Disabilities Education Act (IDEA, section 300.174) from insisting a student be drugged in order to attend school. However, there are many subtle ways of circumventing the law and pressuring students and caretakers toward such ends anyway.

It was the stimulant drug for her ADHD that Tessa particularly disliked because it made her feel "always jumpy." She'd already complained that it interfered with her sleep, but instead of having her dose reduced she'd been given another drug to help her fall to sleep that made her feel groggy in the morning. She readily acknowledged that she often felt edgy or bored or angry in school and at home, but "making a kid take drugs whose mother died from them" didn't make any sense to her.

In the beginning, I taught Tessa about breathing, meditation, and relaxation, and encouraged her to talk about her painful memories. I also echoed her own sense that gang life wasn't a good direction to go. At some point further on, I asked her what she knew about her cultural traditions and she bristled, "I don't know shit and don't want to. I hate being Indian. I wish I wasn't Indian." Tessa intuited "being Indian" as a primary explanation for how her life had gone so far. It would be many months before she discovered any curiosity about her cultural identity.

THE COMPLAINT

Tessa confessed she'd sometimes "cheek" pills she was given while showing an empty mouth to Louise and then spit them out. I was concerned about this behavior and decided to work with her directly on it because I felt if I disclosed what she'd been doing to others in the clinic, they would very likely try to hospitalize her in an inpatient psychiatric unit, where she'd be drugged further. Such a scenario would end any trust Tessa had tentatively formed with me and might be the last time she'd ever tell any adult about her secret noncompliance tactics.

I warned her about a chemically induced "depressive crash" from taking SSRIs and other antidepressants intermittently or withdrawing from them too fast, a problem known back then that has only recently begun to attract any degree of media attention.[14] These drugs continue nonetheless to be described as "nonaddictive" despite significant negative side effects of stopping their use prematurely.[15]

During this same session, Tessa upped her game, disclosing she'd sold some of her stimulant medication to her youth gang friends. I cautioned her about the precarious position she was putting herself in, and she responded that if she wasn't being forced to take drugs, she'd be less likely to take such risks. Besides, it gave her a little money.

Things were heating up, and I emphasized that I had no authority over her prescriptions while cautioning that if she got herself in enough serious trouble, we might not be able to work together anymore. Did she want me to "inform" on her? I told her I didn't want to do so. I suggested she instead talk about her strong feelings about the drugs with her aunt Louise, her legal guardian. She asked if I would help her.

Tessa and I had a joint session in which Louise mentioned she hadn't wanted her on drugs in the first place but IHS providers insisted. I recommended that she help Tessa advocate, so she could ease off drugs she didn't want to take. I realize now how ludicrous this advice was, as even today there are very few medical providers with adequate knowledge of appropriate protocols for psychiatric drug titration, including the psychiatrists who prescribe the drugs.[16] Over the years, I've seen many clients wean themselves too quickly off psychiatric drugs by following a given provider's advice.[17] They then begin experiencing mood problems as a side effect of drug withdrawal itself. A vicious cycle ensues in which the withdrawal is mistaken by the client and/or provider as confirming the alleged underlying psychiatric disorder is still at play, and the client is put back on the same or a different drug.

The written complaint against me came almost immediately after Tessa and Louise had their meeting with several coworkers. One of them alleged that I'd interfered with a "psychiatric treatment plan" and accused me of being an "obstructivist, paternalistic racist" for advising Tessa and her aunt about "medication." It felt strange to work so cooperatively with this Native youth and her guardian and to be called "racist" by a provider. To this day, I suspect I was seen as "obstructivist" for having a differing point of view and "paternalistic" because I was older than the coworker and happened to be a father. I was shocked by the vitriol.

Given the formality and bitterness of the complaint, I didn't seek direct dialogue (and the provider never spoke to me personally before writing the complaint to our supervisor). Instead, I visited the medical supervisor of the mental health department. I first explained that Tessa's aunt supported the change Tessa wanted to make. I described my first approach to her moods and defiance as consisting of supporting her ability to make proactive choices and exercise self-control, focusing upon her own strength and resilience in surviving the bitter experiences she'd lived through, and challenging her chronic sense of powerlessness. I now consider those goals unrealistic given the system with which we both became enmeshed.

This IHS supervisor's response was that I must apologize to the complainant and back off on what I'd said to Tessa and Louise. My "psycho-social approach" was considered to be of minimal value given Tessa's lengthy history of "acting out." I was to understand that her aunt was overwhelmed and didn't know enough to make informed choices on her niece's behalf. Tessa needed "stabilization with medication," i.e., drugs, and that was the end of it. Having no background in psychology or psychiatry, my own doctorate in psychology had insufficient credibility with my boss over the biomedical practices of my complainant, who was, I should understand, my fellow "team member."

But what I thought was a debate about ideologies and practices was not. The real issue between the complainant and me had more to do with power and esprit de corps. Afterward, I was encouraged to understand by several friendlier IHS colleagues that any officer in a uniformed branch of the U.S. Public Health Service *implicitly* (rather than formally) outranked a civil service psychologist like myself in all respects regarding decisions about IHS patient "care."

Whatever management ambitions I had until that moment vaporized. I suddenly realized that for me to be promoted meant nothing; I'd have no legitimate credibility or authority. This was humbling and painful but, strangely, good for me in setting me on a better path toward serving the Yakama Nation community. Looking back, the truth behind this medical power and dominance seems more obvious: IHS, a militarized federal health agency, holds the ultimate authority over the health care of Native people. Because of the waves I'd already made in raising Tessa's issue, my new job was now imperiled. I was a brand-new, junior-ranked civil service employee. I'd moved my family across the country only weeks before, was still within my first ninety days of probation, and could be terminated without cause.

Clenching my teeth, I decided I'd better do as I'd been told. The supervisor offered to shepherd my attempt at reconciliation, which proved very humiliating. My memo book notes from right afterward are staccato: "hostile meeting, letter of complaint, attempt to rebuild a bridge—I apologized and took full resp although I felt very offended; no reciprocal apology."

My fake apology resulted in being invited to weekly "team" meetings with mental health coworkers for the first time. I tried to believe some sort of peacemaking was underway, but I more accurately intuited an effort to please the supervisor. For several weeks I endured being completely ignored and listening to psychobabble. In every meeting, psychiatric drugs were presumed to be the crucial intervention for local Native people experiencing emotional turmoil and seeking help from the Indian Health Service. I eventually stopped attending.

INSIDE FIGHT

Tessa's quest not to be compelled to ingest questionable substances was marginalized and eventually disregarded entirely. My unwilling conformity mirrored her coercion. We'd become mired together beneath a form of domination much older than either of us. The craziness she felt within her emotional life echoed within the system dysfunction all around us. She'd introduced me to what I didn't yet understand about IHS "behavioral health" subculture, and I ended up retreating from a skirmish along its borders. I was forced to recognize that she and many other Native youth I'd meet would be forced to take drugs to sedate their reactions to oppressive systems and institutions that failed them.

I had a lot to draw on from my own teenage years. I identified with the circumstances of the many youth I saw, and this catalyzed my questioning, just as their defiance inspired me. I felt angry and no longer minded that my own in-house activism occasionally left me similarly maligned as an "acting-out adolescent."

My brief campaign began by using Yakama IHS Clinic's own database to pull together an internal memo asserting to medical supervisors a 75 percent probability that any Native youth brought in for "behavior problems" would be labeled with ADHD and provided with a prescription for stimulant drugs at their first contact. I also claimed that other youth clients familiar with illicit drug sales on the reservation informed me that IHS stimulant drugs sold on the street for up to $5 per "hit." I identified several potentially entrepreneurial families wherein each member had been diagnosed with ADHD and "medicated" by providers at Yakama IHS Clinic.

My efforts provoked only more hostility and acrimony, but I was unwilling to be cowed. I composed a second memo, a position statement from the "Psychology Department" (existent in my mind only with me as sole employee) in which I refused to go along with any ADHD label affixed to any Native youth by my coworkers or anyone else working at the clinic. As I said then, no evidence exists *whatsoever* that the EuroAmerican-centered, pseudoscientific concept of ADHD is any more applicable to Native youth.[18]

Whatever façade I had maintained as a potential "team member" crumbled. A year into working at IHS, I was a tenured federal employee and had become more difficult to terminate. For several more months I continued to write a series of internal memos to people in charge about emerging research on increased suicide risk related to SSRI antidepressant drugs as well as the chronic in-house lack of medical oversight in the prescribing of controlled substances, i.e., stimulants.

Nothing I said ever gained any traction, and I am still of the opinion that young Native people lost their lives due to negligence I witnessed and to which I tried to draw attention. Instead of any real change or objective internal investigation, ineffective and incompetent attempts at rebuttal to my memos were the norm. Eventually, I was specifically told to "cease and desist" looking into all such matters. Feeling I was about to lose my job, I opted to release my in-house ADHD "position statement" outside the building to tribal program directors. The rationale lay within my own IHS job description, which stated the new psychologist "consults with the local community." Obviously, I did not agree with my supervisor's desire that I obtain their consent prior to engaging in this form of consultation.

In response, I was placed on a PIP—a performance improvement plan—which I initially suspected would be the means by which I'd finally be fired. Strangely, a position posting for a neuropsychologist, suspiciously customized to fit with my own background, suddenly appeared at the Chemawa Indian School in Salem, Oregon. The mental health liaison at the Portland Regional IHS—the same person whom I'd alerted about overprescribing and mismanagement of psychiatric drugs, including potential links to local youth suicide—called and invited me to apply.

Under the PIP, I had all my notes and dealings reviewed late in the day each Friday—I presume to upset my weekend—while being coaxed toward this new position in Salem. Exhausted, I finally drove down with my family to check it out. The following Monday the position was "canceled." Was this a demonstration of power or dysfunction? I never found out.

Feeling on the skids toward unemployment, a friendlier clinic administrator confided that letters of support were being received from the Yakama community expressing gratitude for my services. Release of my internal ADHD memo outside the building had helped "politically," he admitted, even going so far as to pat me on the back. Tribal program leaders were aware of my predicament, and their letters made it more difficult for my critics inside the clinic to simply push me out.

"It's not easy being the only psychologist here," I wrote in massive understatement to my extended family and friends back in Michigan, not wanting them to know just how bad things were. "A Native domestic violence worker hesitatingly told me that I was viewed as a 'radical' by some tribal elements. She said, 'Don't worry, I am too' ... if that's the label I get, so be it. It does have its hazards, and I must exercise care in my decisions."

FINDING PEACE IN PATHWAYS CIRCLES

I don't know which saying applies more: "Time heals all wounds" or "Let sleeping dogs lie." My experience during my tumultuous first two years at Yakama Indian Health Service Clinic was somewhere between. Somehow the chaos and negative energy surrounding the complaint against me became linked to the various memos I'd been writing. I think the inference was that I was retaliating, but this was never true. I was advocating against what I saw as wrongdoing and malfeasance.

But I eventually stopped trying to rehabilitate the Indian Health Service. The still looming reduction in force and a major budgetary crisis gradually displaced the drama I'd created within the mental health department. A kind of truce ensued as I began to stick more to just seeing clients inside my office or going out into the "field." I interacted only with our Native receptionist, with whom I developed a friendship. I also continued to consult with clinic physicians from time to time, and the majority seemed to bear me no ill will.

From there, I was generally left alone and isolated at Yakama IHS Clinic. I soon became more involved with Yakama Nation Tribal School and Mount Adams School District in White Swan in a very rural area about twenty-five miles west of Toppenish. With the collaboration of school counselors, we began regular, weekly talking circles with troubled youth called "Pathways." Building off an article called "The Dream Catcher Meditation: A Therapeutic Technique for Use with American Indian Adolescents"[19] by Rockey Robbins, PhD, counseling psychology professor at University of Oklahoma, we purchased materials for each student to craft a dream catcher, the Ojibwe protective "spiderweb" weavings that are a popular pan-Indian tradition.

At the outset of designing this approach, my Blackfoot collaborator at Yakama Nation Tribal School, Verna Smith (Pitá-aki: Eagle Woman), suggested we stray somewhat from Dr. Robbins's suggestions. We decided instead to designate each of the four quadrants of the dream catcher like those of a medicine circle—that is, each representing a part of oneself: Heart, Mind, Body, and Spirit. My job was to create "incomplete sentences" for each quadrant to help our youth explore these parts of themselves and help us get to know them. "Incomplete sentences" are just that—a qualitative way of helping students express their struggles by having them complete sentences like "My three wishes are . . ." or "When I look in the mirror, I see . . ."

Collating students' completed sentences allowed us to report back what difficulties and challenges were going on in our "Pathways Circle" without naming names. Of course, we were very careful not to disclose unique responses in order to keep students from being identified. The reader can notice in the list below, which comes from one of our Pathways Circles, how seemingly "everyday" teen difficulties were interspersed with violence exposure:

> *Having divorced parents*
> *Being forced to wear hand-me-downs and totally stupid clothes*
> *Being the family scapegoat*
> *Being told to "sit up straight"*
> *Having your parents tell you what you will be when you grow up*
> *Realizing you're not the favorite child*

Being punished for telling the truth
Having an insufferable brother or sister
Being "snitched" on
Being grounded
Having your allowance cut off
Listening to parents fight
Being slapped by parent
Being hit by parent
Being spanked by parent
Being beaten by parent
Being tortured
Being sexually molested
Being kicked out of house
Being called bad
Being called lazy
Being called selfish
Making your mom cry
Being forced to apologize
Being told, "You should be ashamed of yourself"
Having your first realization that death is permanent
Being caught shoplifting[20]

Reporting such experiences about the struggles among the youth present in our circle helped them to open up with one another. It's true that Pathways Circles became important for these youth as another reason for staying in school. They wanted to come "to Circle" and they engaged with us as helpers, but even more importantly they engaged with one another. The bravery and support we witnessed between them reinforced our commitment to helping with intense emotional turmoil that would otherwise have been labeled as "flooding," "destabilizing," or "decompensating" by the mental health system. Pathways youth taught us all not to be afraid of strong feelings, and although we had moments of powerful anger and anguish, we never lost any of our youth to suicide and never saw or heard of any violence occurring between Pathways Circles members.

This positivity in Pathways likely arose by treating our circle as sacred space. We convened each session with a smudge of sage and sweetgrass smoke fanned over each participant with an eagle feather. We also said prayers and asked youth if they had any prayers of their own to offer. They often did. These spiritual practices set the tone for acceptance, respect, and self-disclosure.

Working on one's dream catcher helped provide structure, but, beyond this, Pathways was driven by youth participants, which corresponded to the best parts of Western non-directive group psychotherapy. There were rules, of course, which primarily consisted of being respectful, being discreet ("What's said here stays here"), and not breaking the circle by leaving early unless one felt too overwhelmed to stay (in which case one of us would accompany the student into the hallway).

We seldom had to ask anyone to leave, but it occurred a few times. The affected student would be tended to later on and always invited back. Who spoke and when in a Pathways Circle was up to the youth, and some students stepped into helper roles, encouraging others to speak. As facilitators, we did all we could to model close listening to every speaker, so that it felt more inappropriate to have any side conversations. If a side conversation did begin, one of the facilitators would gaze politely at the offending students while the other's attention remained riveted on the speaker, sometimes suggesting they pause for a moment and wait to see if the side conversation continued. This was often enough to resolve such situations. If this didn't work, we might openly suggest to the students to show the respect they hoped to receive when they spoke by being attentive to the speaker. It may feel surprising to some providers that such gentleness worked, but it did, and I think it had to do with the sacred ambience of the circle.

We also tried to help quieter and more withdrawn youth express themselves. Verna and I saw our entire role in Pathways Circles as encouraging self-expression, maintaining a sense of safety, and listening attentively. These efforts paid off as stronger bonds of connection developed between so many of the youth participants, who ranged from top students to gang members.

Another year passed, Verna accepted a position as a counselor in the Mount Adams School District, and we began convening Pathways Circles together in White Swan. Our "new" counselor at Yakama Nation Tribal School was the "old" counselor at Mount Adams, my *kála*, Levina Wilkins (Kussamwhy), a fluent speaker of Ichishkíin Sinwit (the Yakama language) and an Educator of the Year for the Washington State Indian Education Association. Kála brought with her Twelve Virtues of Níix Ttáwaxt (Good Growth; see chapter twenty). We integrated these virtues into Pathways Circles at both Yakama Nation Tribal School and White Swan, and they began to inspire the vision for a Níix Ttáwaxt program. I immediately noticed how the Twelve Virtues allowed participating youth to center themselves around expectations that had become obscured over generations and helped them toward a positive cultural identity.

In 2004, Tessa's enrollment at tribal school came as a surprise to me, as she lived some distance away. I saw her one morning in the hallway and she waved to me shyly. Several weeks later she spoke to Káła about joining Pathways Circle, where she became a leader to the other students. When Káła taught her about the Twelve Virtues of Níix Ttáwaxt, she immediately became excited. "*Yáych'unakl!*" she shouted with a big smile when she understood how to speak this word from her own original language. "Not Afraid of Any Type of Challenge; Courage ... ," she read aloud from the handout we'd supplied. "That's *me!*" She no longer hated being Indian, and she was on her way to learning about herself and her heritage.

CLINIC AS DYSFUNCTIONAL EPICENTER

Having multiple Pathways Circles to assist in facilitating helped me not only to survive Yakama IHS Clinic's dysfunction but, more importantly, to learn to love my work again. I also often visited Yakama Nation Tribal Jail and met with young clients housed inside. Before the new jail was built, this old jail was one of the bleakest places I could imagine. There were no windows, and the cells had dirty cement block walls, were each illuminated by a single dingy hanging light bulb, and had bars painted with flecked yellow paint. Many young people were put inside for nothing more than acting defiantly or running away from home. On one occasion I met with a young adult so impaired by chronic substance abuse, they couldn't form a full sentence. They'd ended up there because a state of Washington social worker could find no other way to put a roof over their head and keep them fed.

Concurrently, I undertook a home building project and woke up with my field of vision reduced to the lower left. I was proud for having diagnosed this myself as a field cut suggesting an injury, and it was soon confirmed by the IHS optometrist, who encouraged me to become much more concerned because I had a detached retina. That evening my wife and I had to leave our children with virtual strangers—a brother and sister from down the street— in order to rush to Spokane for emergency surgery to repair the damaged retina before I went blind in my left eye.

A bit weary the next day and lying on our couch with a patch over my eye, I received a phone call from the Portland IHS mental health liaison. Since I wasn't at work, this was very unusual, and I truly believed they were calling out of concern for my health. But they'd gotten wind that I might be thinking about "filing a complaint against the professional licensure" of one of my colleagues. It was true: I'd learned of a life-threatening incident in which this individual had, in my opinion, engaged in malpractice and negligence regarding the psychiatric drug imipramine, and I'd mentioned to someone I considered a close colleague that maybe I should file a complaint. But I didn't want to fight with the internal dysfunction anymore; I just wanted to keep making progress away from it. I told the liaison I had no idea what they were talking about, to which they responded, "Well, I'm just letting you know that if you follow through and file a complaint against one of your colleagues, your career at the Indian Health Service will be history." Lying back down, I decided this conversation felt like mob enforcement. All that was missing was the threat about breaking my legs. They didn't even wish me "Get well soon."

On May 23, 2002, the *Statesman Journal* of Spokane and many local papers around the Yakima Valley carried a story about another incident involving imipramine at Kirkwood Elementary School in Toppenish in which four fifth-grade students overdosed. They'd each been hospitalized in stable condition and were eventually released. I knew more about this crisis than was in the media. I'd been informed by an IHS supervisor that the psychiatric drug these children had overdosed on originated from the pharmacy at our clinic. The papers didn't mention that a prescription bottle full of the same powerful antidepressant drug, imipramine, had been delivered into the hands of a minor, a Native young person. Instead of delivering it to their relative, the child had taken it out to the playground and told other kids about a new way to "get high." Nothing was mentioned in the news stories about IHS as the source of this drug, but by then I'd thrown in the towel on further "risking my career" by speaking out publicly about IHS mismanagement. I did vow that one day I'd say more.

During my days in the clinic, few other care providers interacted with me except for the family nurses who'd been supportive of my in-house activism and shared many of my grievances. Their friendship and counsel as more seasoned IHS veterans validated for me that the clinic was just as dysfunctional as I suspected. We were among those who wanted to do something, but it was next to impossible to initiate proactive change. We knew speaking out meant "shooting the messenger."

One of these nurses eventually took on the role of messenger anyway. I still have a copy of a letter regarding general clinical conditions she sent directly to Tommy Thompson, then secretary of the U.S. Department of Health and Human Services, excerpts of which provide a snapshot of the clinic's climate back then, independent of my own impressions:

There are numerous, worsening situations in this clinic that are being ignored at local and regional levels.... The urgency and seriousness is heightened because this clinic serves a high risk population of more than 20,000 Native Americans.... It is doubtful that this clinic would currently meet standards set by the Accreditation Association for Ambulatory Health Care, Inc. (AAAHC), our accrediting body.... For the past several months, our staff has been informed that we were in a dramatic budget deficit ... During the past several months, we have been advised to restrict spending ... [W]e have been told to consider transferring or consider leaving IHS permanently ... [S]ome staff received RIF (reduction in force) notices ... We are now working in an unbearable situation ... We currently have three medical providers less than we had one (1) year ago. At that time, we already had an insufficient provider to patient ratio.... In contrast to one year ago, there are 45% fewer appointments available, representing a loss of more than 600 appointments per month.... The average patient wait for an appointment is four to eight weeks ... Nursing staff has been cut, and positions not allowed to be filled.... Our custodial staff has been cut to the point where exam rooms are minimally cleaned; this is a serious infection control concern, as well as disconcerting and distasteful to patients and staff.... Some disposable supplies, e.g. ear speculums, are cleaned and reused instead of being discarded and replaced with new items.... Pharmacy stock has been cut so dramatically that some essential medications ... are no longer stocked, and patients must buy those prescriptions out of pocket.... Some patients go without certain medications due to financial constraints.... The Yakama population have had seven (7) successful suicide attempts in the last four (4) months; six of the seven deaths were young people ages ten (10) to twenty-five (25) years ... Our Mental Health Department was reviewed six months ago by the IHS Portland Mental Health

> *Consultant ... and found to be out of compliance were IHS Mental*
> *Health standards in a majority of domains examined.... To date,*
> *however, the Yakama IHS Mental Health Department has made no*
> *apparent corrections or revisions ... Our new psychologist, Dr. David*
> *Walker, has made numerous requests for equipment, resources, training,*
> *and other expenditures, none of which have been acted upon.*[21]

The only outcome to this letter was the farewell I said to the messenger. A reserve military officer, she was compelled to transfer immediately to a locale so far from friends and family that she had to quit IHS entirely. At least she'd lived out the Yakama virtues of *yáych'unakl* ("courage") and *k'wyáamtimt* ("honesty, truthfulness").

THE SELF-QUIZ

While still in the Pathways Circle, Tessa continued working with me individually. Although we now met more often at school, she'd sometimes come to the clinic and wait for our sessions in a tiny area beneath a large red sign that read: MENTAL HEALTH DEPARTMENT. Many of my clients refused to sit anywhere near this sign and would ask me to find them elsewhere. Tessa didn't seem to mind: she'd already been well socialized into being a "mental patient."

Either pharmaceutical sales representatives or my colleagues would sometimes leave drug marketing materials in this area. IHS buys all its medicines centrally via various contracts and partnerships with the Department of Veterans Affairs and other public health agencies. Perhaps someone got the bright idea that they could stimulate more consumption of psychiatric drugs and more credibility for themselves through "direct-to-consumer" advertising. I suspect this to be so because when I taped up a 2003 article from the *New York Times* regarding new research questioning the safety of antidepressant drugs,[22] I received a raging memo from a mental health coworker (copied to my supervisor) demanding that I take it down immediately. My IHS supervisor concurred. I was not permitted to provide any counterpoint for Native patients to the pharmaceutical propaganda campaign underway in-house.

It was under these agency conditions that Tessa brought in a little form she'd "found" with an illustration of an agitated little bubble, rather than the happy and sad little bubbles more widely seen in TV advertising. The form read" "Take this Posttraumatic Stress Disorder Self-Quiz." I have saved the copy she brought me and have it before me now:

Identify the trauma in your past that is most disturbing to you now:

_____

In the past week, have you experienced any of the following symptoms? . . .
1. Have you been jumpy or easily startled?
2. Have you been physically upset by reminders of the event you listed above? . . .
3. Have you been unable to have sad or loving feelings, or have you generally felt numb?
4. Have you been irritable or had outbursts of anger?

. . . PTSD is a medical condition that affects your body, the way you think, and how you feel and act. . . . It's important to remember that PTSD is a real medical condition, like arthritis or asthma. . . .

The cause of PTSD is not entirely understood. Researchers and doctors have learned that people suffering from PTSD may have a chemical imbalance in the brain so the nerve cells cannot communicate properly. . . .

Many people with PTSD can benefit from treatment, which may include medicine, psychotherapy ("talk therapy"), or a combination of both. . . .

PTSD is a treatable medical condition.
Recovery is possible.[23]

Many mental health providers and lay people might feel Tessa *must* "fit," "have," or "be" the psychiatric diagnosis of "PTSD." Why wouldn't they? Tessa certainly felt so. "Complex PTSD" must be her tribe, her appropriate identity in the mental health world. Even my own views about the arbitrariness and negative stigmatization of this particular "functional psychiatric diagnosis," i.e., label, were still evolving back then. After all, people experience PTSD physically in the form of psychomotor agitation, poor sleep, and "triggering" of "hyperarousal" and "hypervigilance." Tessa, too, had been through terrible violence and loss, slept poorly, reacted very strongly, and felt anxious and sad often. Her "symptoms" seemed incontrovertible. I had also felt the physicality of "PTSD symptoms" within my own painful life experiences. Yet I already was beginning to feel suspicious about most psychiatric labels being a kind of "medicalized" or "psychopathologized" language for extremes of human suffering that have been part of normative human experience for thousands of generations.[24]

I pointed out to Tessa the fine print of the quiz's author: Pfizer Corporation—an organization calling itself "one of the premier biopharmaceutical companies."[25] I explained its primary purpose was to sell psychiatric drugs.

Tessa said she had most if not all of the "symptoms" and she hoped I could remove ADHD from her IHS medical chart and replace it with PTSD so at least she wouldn't have to take stimulant drugs anymore.

I explained I could *add* PTSD to her chart but I couldn't *remove* labels because I'd be seen as interfering with my estranged coworkers. This immutability of her "psychiatric poly-labeling" frustrated her, and she became quite irritated with me. I tried to help her understand the American Psychiatric Association's *Diagnostic and Statistical Manual of Mental Disorders*—from which such labels originate—is in its truest light a scientifically meaningless political document.[26] She didn't understand what I meant. I said that if I added PTSD to her chart, it might only make a stronger case for her to be forced onto more psychiatric drugs, deepening her disempowerment.

"But I am PTSD, right?" she persisted after my long-windedness. This seemed to be the most critically important question for her.

EIGHT

"Being PTSD"

WHAT DOES "BEING PTSD" MEAN?

It's beyond question that Tessa was physically and sexually violated, had lost her mother, father, and grandfather, and was exposed to multiple unsafe home environments that left her chronically feeling fearful, distraught, angry, worthless, and unlovable. She'd been maligned as a troubled, defiant Native young woman, and a poor, inattentive student. She blamed herself for the disruption of her family, suffered intense guilt and shame, and had trouble forming trusting, close relationships. She "acted out" in situations reminiscent of the extreme stress she'd experienced, especially any efforts to control or dominate her. To top all this off, she was also still a loyal gang member sprinting away from terrifying confrontations with bullet rounds whizzing by her ears.

Her life was fraught with predicaments that many reservation-based Native American youth face—poverty, racism, disempowerment, violence, and educational inequity—as well as those with which other U.S. foster care youth struggle.[1] Tessa drew me toward what I consider to be important ethical questions: Should her (very) heightened reactivity be considered a "mental disorder," a "political dilemma," or both? Would I take a role in encouraging her to believe her inner turmoil came from some unproven, pseudoscientific flaw, pathogen, or imbalance she carried? To what degree did I, as her helper, have a role in validating her reactions to *unjust* and *inhumane* circumstances?

Tessa's insistence about "being PTSD" struck me as ceremonial. Yet this ceremony originated from a culture oppressing her own. Disconnected from her family of origin, shoved into a mostly dysfunctional *páshtin* IHS and state subculture of providers and social workers serving as quasi-parents, Tessa sought my assistance in restoring her sense of self and giving her more control over her own life. If I'd go along with her "being PTSD," the label affixed to her would at least validate the violence she'd experienced. It would mean very bad things had happened *to* her, mitigating the stigma she felt about bad things having been done *by* her.

By asking me to relabel her, she was also doing what others insisted she begin doing: following directions. The Pfizer self-quiz clearly stated: "If you have identified a trauma in your past, if the symptoms are interfering with your daily life and relationships, and if any of these questions make you think 'this sounds like me,' discuss your answers with a doctor. Only a doctor or qualified healthcare provider can make a diagnosis of PTSD." I am a doctor, and she wanted me to do my job—that is, tell her she "was PTSD." Why shouldn't I?

POSTTRAUMATIC TRUTHS AND UNTRUTHS

I finally decided to bring Tessa into my dilemma by simply telling her the *truth*: what she was reading on Pfizer's self-quiz form was a *lie* or more specifically, a series of *falsehoods*. Tessa perked up immediately because she knew about lies and she could understand a con job—a hustle—too. I explained to her that PTSD is *not* and never has been a "real medical condition, like arthritis or asthma," as the quiz stated. Without being too technical, I helped her understand that there are no biomarkers or X-rays for identifying PTSD as there are for arthritis or spirometry for diagnosing asthma. Pfizer's analogy was a con back then—and there still is no solid evidence to support the company's contention on the self-quiz. The only way to "be PTSD" beyond having elevated scores on the Pfizer self-quiz is to answer more questions eerily similar to the same questions.

Researching the self-quiz more, I note now that its four questions were lifted from the Davidson Trauma Scale (DTS), considered a decent PTSD "diagnostic tool." When applied correctly to actual war combat veterans in a considerably longer format, research indicates the Davidson will be *inaccurate* in distinguishing PTSD from many other psychiatric labels 39 percent of the time.[2] This mid-level kind of accuracy is considered pretty good given the massive degree of overlap between *DSM* psychiatric labels—one of many factors that undermines their validity.[3]

From the DTS research, a brief diagnostic screening test called SPAN (startle, physiological arousal, anger, and numbness) was developed that demonstrated 81 percent accuracy in diagnosing PTSD when compared to diagnoses arrived at via three styles of structured clinical interview (SCID, SIP, and CAP),[4] which, in turn, measure statistically at up to 90 percent.[5] That is, if we do the math, the SPAN is 73 percent accurate overall in screening for PTSD in studies of the general population. Again, this is pretty good in comparison to the limited accuracy of numerous other psychiatric labels when they're studied. However, neither the SPAN study nor any pertaining to diagnostic interviews for PTSD include Native Americans within their samples or discuss how the unique experiences of these communities might apply to the PTSD psychiatric category. This is why we must ask what it means when SPAN, an incredibly abbreviated DTS of just four items, is then aimed toward a Native youth living under oppressive, marginalized conditions, sitting in the waiting area at the Yakama Indian Health Clinic. I believe the question reveals a psychopharmaceutical-industrial complex with no moral or ethical responsibility to explain itself, so caveat emptor: "consumer beware."

The pharmaceutical industry deploys Washington, DC's most powerful lobby, is relatively immune to public policies regarding its messaging, and has enjoyed nearly free license to bring its deceptions to the marginalized lives of Native young people and anyone else. Its marketing plan has worked well by conflating sales pitch with medical lingo in what Princeton philosopher Harry G. Frankfurt calls "a greater enemy of truth than lies are":[6] the academic philosophical domain called *bullshit.*[7]

OPPRESSIVE STRESS RECONSTRUED AS "DISEASE"

The quest to demonstrate an inborn "constitutional" (i.e., biological) inferiority pertaining to traumatic stress represents countless dollars spent upon a chimera. Findings to date reveal only that the "human stress response" can be observed for certain features at the brain level in *most DSM* labels, rather than being differentiated for PTSD alone. That is, people who receive a *DSM* label are often experiencing stress, which is simply common sense, and we can locate differences in their brains related to this stress, which is totally unsurprising.

In their white paper released in 2015 for the International Society for Ethical Psychology and Psychiatry (ISEPP), psychologists Noel Hunter and William Schultz point out the inherent limitations of "neuro-biologizing" PTSD and other *DSM* labels using brain scan technology such as CT, MRI, fMRI, and PET:

> The most consistent finding across all diagnostic categories is abnormalities in the hypothalamic-pituitary-adrenal (HPA) axis, which is an area of the brain that is specifically associated with trauma and stress. . . . Although many tend to take for granted that posttraumatic stress disorder (PTSD) is the only syndrome directly caused by traumatic events, we cannot say that trauma has any more direct causal link with PTSD than it does with other phenomena such as hyperactivity, psychosis, or depression. To conflate distressing experiences and the body's natural reaction to such experiences with biological disease is not only a giant leap in logic, but could also result in minimization and denial of the traumatic and stressful experiences that initially led to the emotional distress.[8]

Many have hoped to somehow link the human stress response with a *chemical imbalance causing* PTSD, but there has never been such a thing except within a *medical metaphor* created by biologically driven psychiatrists, psychologists, and other researchers. The only chemical imbalances existing with PTSD are those caused by the powerful psychiatric drugs alleged to "treat" this "disorder."

Additionally, biopsychiatric ideas coming from brain-scanning technology are often overblown in the media, and the brain biology thereby claimed for PTSD can't be effectively differentiated from the way humans respond in general to intensely difficult or extreme circumstances. Of course, most brain-scanning technology draws its basis from a theory of "neuro-vascular coupling," wherein changes in blood flow are thought to relate to the firing of clusters of neurons. Many lay people don't realize that areas not detected through this kind of scanning can represent important neural activity as well, much like a pattern of switches being on, neutral, or off to program the movements of a robotic arm. There are also theories of "neurovascular decoupling"—for example, that one area of the brain may have more blood flow, suggesting neural firing, while another area may have little or no blood flow change, but nonetheless, have a role in neural activity. Furthermore, neural activity is detected in other ways, such as electrically (EEG). These considerations have led several neuroscience researchers to conclude in 2014 that "the results from fMRI and other hemodynamic imaging methodologies for studying neural processes must be interpreted with caution."[9]

Then, in 2022, a critically important finding was published in the prominent scientific journal *Nature* from a large analysis of three data sets involving around 50,000 people, with forty-five researcher/authors reviewing "brain-wide association studies (BWAS)" using magnetic resonance imaging (MRI or fMRI) technology. The many studies this team reviewed were trying to detect "inter-individual differences in brain structure or function and complex cognitive or mental health phenotypes"—that is, the relation of specific localized brain areas to complex thinking and psychiatric labels like depression, PTSD, bipolar disorder, and ADHD. The huge collaborative determined that "BWAS associations were smaller than previously thought, resulting in statistically underpowered studies, inflated effect sizes and replication failures at typical sample sizes."[10] In other words, the very small sample sizes of the studies they reviewed and that have often been used in mental health training and presentations to promote popular conclusions about associations between brain areas and psychiatric labels are far too small to derive valid scientific findings; in fact, the studies averaged only twenty-five study participants. When such studies are discussed publicly in any conclusive way, which is still happening *all the time*, the presenters are engaging in false science by Western standards.

EPIGENETICS OF TRAUMA

I shudder to think of the ramifications of behavioral epigenetic research in its suggestions of an "intergenerational transmission of trauma."[11] Findings from this line of research are spreading rapidly through media and Native mental health quarters, and they appear overstated. The specific dangers are premature conclusions that parents traumatized by oppressive events in their lives are passing along through their genes a greater susceptibility to traumatic reactions in their children. In a 2019 review of such studies, Pamela Scorza and colleagues note:

There is considerable interest in the possibility that phenotypic traits, disease susceptibility, and even behaviors that are acquired through environmental interactions in one generation can be transmitted through epigenetic processes to future generations, however empirical evidence remains inconclusive and particularly scarce in human populations.[12]

Given the lack of accountability within U.S. society for its assaults on Native people, it must appear attractive to social justice activists to build a case that the oppressive events Native communities have suffered, past and present, made and continue to make a damaging imprint upon their children. But it seems quite dangerous to embrace such assertions prematurely because, well, the findings don't support them, and such assertions link back to a pseudoscientific legacy that continues to characterize the bodies and brains of Native people as defective, inferior, or limited. Consider, for example, that "most studies investigating epigenetic intergenerational transmission are based on animal models, leaving it unclear whether intergenerational epigenetic inheritance exists in humans" and "[d]ifferences in the epigenome between humans and mice do not permit direct inference to humans" while "animal studies cannot replicate complex social and community structure."[13]

As an example of this overenthusiasm, I recently attended a training alongside many Native community leaders in which the presenter claimed Native children who'd gone through "adverse childhood events," or ACEs, were prone to "DNA methylation" within their brains that predisposed them to PTSD symptoms. Again, Scorza et al. note that

the biological significance of DNA methylation can be difficult to interpret, as changes are often small and widespread throughout the genome and affect a variety of genes. Evidence also suggests that DNA methylation is driven by stable genetics and intrauterine exposure rather than intergenerational epigenetic inheritance.[14]

Enthusiasts for a human epigenetics of intergenerational trauma often point to a single study by epigenetics researcher Rachel Yehuda and colleagues at Mount Sinai School of Medicine using an exceedingly small sample of twenty-two members of the families of Jewish Shoah survivors. Scorza et al. admit that this study found "holocaust [*sic*] exposure had an effect on Cytosine methylation within the gene encoding for FK506 binding protein 5, an important regulator of glucocorticoid receptor sensitivity."[15] The idea is that this sensitivity will predispose offspring to secrete excess cortisol in response to stress. Yet Scorza et al. contend that such findings must be contrasted within the inability of this same research "to differentiate between epigenetic inheritance and social transmission, although the study did control for offspring trauma exposure and psychopathology."[16]

In 2018, Dr. Yehuda herself bemoaned the media and mental health hype, clarifying that "the attribution of any specific epigenetic mechanisms in human studies of offspring of trauma survivors is premature at this time"[17] and "to date, it has not been possible to validate models of potential non-genomic (epigenetic) heritability, except, possibly in animal models."[18] There is little doubt that babies are affected by stress in both their pre- and postnatal environments in their temperament, levels of activity and reactivity; we have known this to be the case for a very long time in developmental psychology. Yet a multiplicity of cultural and environmental factors, the phenomenon of reciprocal socialization between child and parent, and conceptual debates about what exactly is meant by "intergenerational trauma" present thorny difficulties regarding conclusions drawn from genetics and epigenetics.[19] Certainly, Scorza et al. realize this in their careful statement that "adversity in early childhood produces long-term alterations in endocrine and immune-inflammatory physiology, including greater hypothalamic-pituitary-adrenal axis reactivity and a greater pro-inflammatory state."[20] Again, this is a wordy description of the human stress response and seems true for everyone.

From conception, then, we know the learning by children of ongoing environmental threats is underway. Therefore, the "cultural transmission of traumatic experience," including its biological manifestations and implications for general community health, remains a critically important area of study. But this does not mean that sociocultural mechanisms for trauma transmission should be wantonly reduced to the current PTSD language used within biological psychiatry and epigenetics, and epigenetics researchers know it. As Amy Lehrner and Rachel Yehuda recently advocated, "The fact that children of traumatized parents may show differences in their stress response systems does not necessitate an interpretation that they are damaged."[21]

Given its own history, I suspect PTSD will remain what it has always been: a culturally nested category of metaphorical "disease" created by Western psychiatry. Can an epigenetics underlie the intergenerational transmission of a metaphor?

THE *DSM-5* KERFUFFLE

In 2011 an open letter protesting the *DSM-5* system of psychiatric labeling gathered signatures from "15,000 individuals and more than 50 mental health groups and organizations."[22] This open letter was inspired by the British Psychological Society's publicly stated skepticism regarding *DSM-5*'s lack of validity and its "concerns about any unsubstantiated shift in emphasis towards biological factors."[23]

This major credibility challenge rocked British psychiatry. Then, in October 2012, influential psychiatrist Thomas R. Insel, former director of the National Institute for Mental Health (NIMH) in the United States, wrote a blog on the institute's website in which he confessed:

> Terms like "depression" or "schizophrenia" or "autism" have achieved a reality that far outstrips their scientific value. Each refers to a cluster of symptoms, similar to "fever" or "headache." But beyond symptoms that cluster together, there should be no presumption that these are singular disorders, each with a single cause and a common treatment.[24]

By April 2013, Insel was declaring that a "weakness" in the newest *DSM*, the *DSM-5*,[25] as with prior versions, lies in "its lack of validity."[26] That would seem a pretty fundamental weakness for any classification system, especially one applied to millions of people worldwide.

Dr. Insel simultaneously proclaimed his own rededication to expanding the quest for detecting psychiatric disorders at a brain level, albeit by moving in an entirely different direction from using DSM labels. Launching his start-up, Mindstrong, in 2017, he admitted:

> I spent 13 years at NIMH really pushing on the neuroscience and genetics of mental disorders, and when I look back on that I realize that while I think I succeeded at getting lots of really cool papers published by cool scientists at fairly large costs—I think $20 billion—I don't think we moved the needle in reducing suicide, reducing hospitalizations, improving recovery for the tens of millions of people who have mental illness.[27]

Just a few days after Insel's lambasting of the newest *DSM*, psychiatrist David Kupfer, chairman of the *DSM-5* task force, shot back, "We've been telling patients for several decades that we are waiting for biomarkers. We're still waiting.... Efforts like the National Institute of Mental Health's Research Domain Criteria ... are vital ... But they cannot serve us in the here and now, and they cannot supplant DSM-5."[28] From former NIMH director Insel's perspective, the empty pursuit of biomarkers for psychiatric diagnostic labels had become too frustrating after seventy years of trying,[29] whereas for *DSM-5* psychiatric label maker Kupfer, having the newest bible disregarded by a former leader of psychiatry's most visible—and lucrative— federally funded research institute must have felt crushing.

The "new" direction both Dr. Insel and NIMH are following chases decidedly *old* ideas in the "biomedical model" of mental health, first theorized by Emil Kraepelin, a well-known German psychiatrist who wrote extensively in the early twentieth century. Herein lies NIMH's common ground with *DSM* creators. In *DSM-IV* and under the leadership of another *DSM-5* critic, psychiatrist Alan Frances, the master label makers declared their "non-theoretical" approach to be nonetheless "neo-Kraepelinian."[30] They were tipping their hats to earlier architects of *DSM-III*, an "'invisible college' of biologically-oriented psychiatrists,"[31] who'd broken with the older, Freudian labels of the *DSM-II*.

When my mother and father entered psychoanalysis, they were called "neurotic." I know this to be true because they sat me down at age sixteen, told me so, and declared I would eventually become neurotic too! But the shift from Freud to this biological language was one of economic necessity and arrived, not surprisingly, after insurance companies began questioning reimbursement for the lengthy psychoanalyses that were a primary source of income for psychiatry.

Indeed, it seems that even Kraepelin himself might not fit well with the many "neo-Kraepelinians" in the mental health system who so frequently embrace with near-religious fervor their correlational research findings from trendy neural technologies as proof of causal mechanisms at the brain level for the mental disorders they themselves design. Any under-graduate introductory psychology student must learn the age-old caveat that "correlation does not imply causation," but these researchers seem very reluctant to consider the brain as a unique organ "behaving" in response to its lived context and environment. They'd prefer to "reduce" such matters to brain tissue. And they do this despite the fact that Kraepelin himself "never doubted the somatic origins of madness" but "did insist that [the fields of] pathological anatomy and physiology were themselves incapable of grasping the complexity of the psyche."[32]

Dr. Kraepelin was himself an enthusiastic racist. Working under Ernst Rüdin, a prominent Nazi "race hygiene" psychiatrist, Emil Kraepelin was a fellow "ardent proponent of eugenics and 'degeneration theory'" serving German race-cleansing policies that contributed to the Jewish Shoah.[33] Why would psychiatry want to sanitize and repackage him? Regrettably, it appears many researchers are oblivious to the culture and history by which their own scholarly minds have been shaped over the last century.

As the official representative of the U.S. mental health system in Indian Country, IHS's policy and technical language also clearly favors the biological over the psychological and social—i.e., psychosocial—by promoting "an *etiological medical*[34] model [that] conceives mental illness as consisting of a disorder of the brain or a disturbance in the central nervous system which should be amenable to pharmacological or physical treatment."[35]

Tessa's complex case was framed by Western medical culture and its allied corporations, which demanded that I fulfill her need to "be PTSD." Métis Canadian social worker Natalie Clark worries this trauma "industry" will only further obscure the oppressive roots of troubled Native lives:

> The dominant discourses of "trauma" continue to define violence within normative neo-colonial constructions, thereby functioning to obstruct and erase the naming of certain kinds of violence such as experiences of racism, [and] structural violence enacted through state policy ...
>
> Left uninterrogated and unchallenged, this dominant discourse of trauma not only erases the harm done to Indigenous children and youth through policy but can also function to silence the local and Indigenous ways of knowing and of addressing the wellness of our children and youth. The definitions of trauma and the meanings we make of it are historically constructed and defined, and are shaped by the intersection of structural factors, including our access to power and our experiences of oppression. Further, these constructions of trauma shape what we consider as violence, what kinds of violence are erased, and the kinds of supports and access to services that flow from this.[36]

The psychopharmaceutical arm of the trauma industry already had its backfield play in motion by the time Tessa first called my attention to Pfizer's self-quiz. The quiz itself reflected a marketing plan to bypass mental health providers entirely and get drugs distributed directly through primary care practitioners via the emerging practice of "primary care behavioral health." The strategy worked exceptionally well, and its misinformation has widened to make more room for other paths toward the medicalization of emotional suffering and the sale of "chemical cures."

EURO-CULTURAL ROOTS OF PTSD

I would never deny that exposure to violence can contribute to lifelong suffering. But by what societal changes has posttraumatic stress disorder evolved to be so readily considered a "medical condition"? We have to trace its pedigree alongside psychiatry's long-term role in U.S. military culture. PTSD links historically to terminology like "shell shock," "combat fatigue," "traumatic neurosis," and even "soldier's heart"—terms reaching as far back as the American Civil War.

The prefix "post-" in "PTSD" refers to individual reactions after the fact, although many people experience high stress in facets of their lives chronically. "Post-" implies that an overwhelming experience of fear or anguish has ended, and this is not always the case.

"Stress" in "PTSD" is based upon the famous research conducted in the 1950s by Hans Selye,[37] the endocrinologist who borrowed the structural engineering term for his demonstrations of how animal physical health can be negatively affected by overwhelming social, psychological, and environmental demands.

"Trauma" in "PTSD" has a more complex backdrop, originating from the Greek "to wound or hurt." Initially, trauma was used only as it still is in emergency medicine: as a way to describe physical tissue damage. In 1892, however, an obscure Viennese neurologist named Sigmund Freud became fascinated with the ability of his Victorian patients—mostly women, many with a history of sexual assault—to displace their emotional suffering into their bodies and deny its existence altogether. "Trauma" as a psychological and emotional idea has its roots in Freudian psychoanalysis.

Pathogenic memories of assault, Freud mused, "failed to find adequate discharge in thinking, affect and motor reaction,"[38] and this "failure" gives rise to "symptoms" by which the sufferer experiences alterations in awareness and behavior. In Freud's ideas, we see the first merger of trauma as physical, material injury with "trauma" as a metaphorical, subjective sense of psychological and emotional overwhelm or wound.

Although Freud was unfairly skeptical of his patients' disclosures, ignorantly concluding their sexual assaults to be more likely fantasized,[39] the personal, inward subjectivity with which he described "psychic trauma" survives to this day. Many of Freud's original thoughts about the relationship between memory and trauma have also survived. PTSD is still often conceived within the Western mental health world to manifest residual, troubling, learned responses pertaining to unprocessed, unintegrated memories,[40] a mostly *unconscious experience* akin to Freud's views, and entailing avoidance, emotional upheaval, preoccupation, flashbacks, heightened reactivity, etc.

Without denying the persuasiveness of these concepts, it is important to recognize how these Freudian ideas influenced American psychiatrists and augmented their professional power prior to World War I. Ardent Freudian enthusiasts in the United States both reframed and obscured his theories and Latinized his concepts, even making it a law in New York State that only a medical doctor could practice psychoanalytic methods.[41] Freud was deeply concerned and asserted: "Doctors have no historical claim to the sole possession of analysis. On the contrary, until recently they have met it with everything possible that could damage it, from the shallowest ridicule to the gravest calumny."[42] Although he surely wanted to popularize his "psychoanalytic method," Freud, a physician himself, fiercely resisted the medicalization of his ideas:

> For we do not consider it at all desirable for psychoanalysis to be swallowed up by medicine and to find its last resting place in a textbook of psychiatry under the heading "Methods of Treatment," alongside procedures such as hypnotic suggestion, autosuggestion, and persuasion, which, born from our ignorance, have to thank the laziness and cowardice of mankind for their short-lived effects.[43]

As it does nowadays by pointing to an invalid pseudoscience of brain deficiencies that even Emil Kraepelin would not accept, American psychiatry in the early twentieth century co-opted Freud's teachings in order to profiteer off a method he hoped would be freely accessible to and liberating for everyone. Decades passed with American psychiatrists positioned as the sole experts on "psychological trauma" and maintaining their lucrative position as expert practitioners of psychoanalysis. As I finished graduate school in 1992, a lawsuit had just been settled finally allowing psychologists into psychoanalytic training institutes alongside medical doctors.[44] It has always been interesting to me how close in time this loosening boundary corresponded to psychiatry's full embrace of drugs as solutions to human suffering and their lucrative sponsorship by drug companies.

From its earliest days, the U.S. psychiatric guild proposed that people susceptible to being diagnosed with its new concept of "trauma as metaphor" must carry inborn weaknesses or defects. This stigma continues to survive in the concept of PTSD as "disability." In 1910, American Freudians like Smith Ely Jelliffe and William A. White were more specific about the demographics of people they felt were susceptible to such problems:

> **Psychopathic constitution**[45] ... More pronounced defects of character are seen in the *criminal* classes, many of whom lack the ordinary moral inhibitions and are properly classed as *moral imbeciles.*
> ... Many "shell shock" neuroses develop in this group.
> ... It includes a considerable number of the juvenile delinquents, of the recidivist type of criminal, of the paupers and prostitutes, of the ne'er-do-wells, the black sheep of the family, and at the higher levels of erratic, half-genius, half-crazy persons with brilliant spots here and there, but without continuity, whose efficiency is materially impaired and who live often a more or less wandering existence....[46]

We can still bear witness to the many people stigmatized by psychiatry as somehow being morally defective, weak, wacky, even criminal or rebellious. The roots of those labeled "traumatized" in Native communities and elsewhere are the same now as back in those early days: they come from impoverished backgrounds, from among the victimized, marginalized, oppressed, or nonconforming in U.S. society. In this way, the "traumatized" continue to be a reliable patient market population for American psychiatry, one that carries "PTSD" as its banner.

WAR EXPOSURE AND INDIAN COUNTRY

This medical metaphor of psychological trauma had a resurgence nearly a half century after World War I during the Vietnam era. Vietnam veterans returned home from a brutal, undeclared, and hated war. Native Vietnam veterans were twice as likely to see combat than white soldiers,[47] up to three times more likely to experience deprivation, and nearly two times more likely to witness atrocities.[48] These soldiers were "more likely than any other ethnic group to serve in the Marines (the branch of service with most combat duty) and in the northernmost sector of Vietnam (I-corps, the area under greatest enemy attack)."[49] They also received more combat service medals per soldier than any other ethnic group.

Today, Native Americans continue to serve in the U.S. military at a higher rate than any other ethnicity.[50] Consider this contribution carefully alongside the U.S. military's decision to identify terrorist mass murderer Osama Bin Laden as "Geronimo" in their search-and-destroy operation during Operation Neptune Spear in 2011.[51] Apache leader Geronimo has always been a great hero to Native people of the United States and a symbol of Native American resistance. After years of evading capture, he was held as a prisoner of war by the U.S. military until his death in 1909. For the U.S. military to identify Osama Bin Laden as Geronimo recapitulates EuroAmerica's "Indian as enemy" motif.

American society's involvement in warfare both before and after Vietnam has been continuous since prior to the Revolutionary War, and Native warriors have suffered on all sides.[52] There are countless historical instances of recruitment of Native American men and women to serve in territorial conflicts between EuroAmericans, French, British, Spanish, and others, with horrific results.[53]

Simultaneous to Native service, there have been the numerous U.S. military actions against their own people, i.e., the so-called Indian Wars. On the side of those who write the history, these wars are considered to have officially ended in 1898.[54] But the 1923 "Posey War" of the Paiutes is sometimes characterized as the "last Indian uprising,"[55] while the seventy-three-day occupation of Wounded Knee in 1973 by members of the American Indian Movement, resulting in two Native men killed and fifteen others wounded, involved the deployment of the South Dakota National Guard.[56] Not every media follower realizes that unloaded missile launchers were added to the mix of military vehicles as North Dakota National Guardsmen and police faced off with unarmed Dakota Pipeline protesters in 2017.[57] Distinguishing Indian Wars from police actions against Native people remains a question of perspective.

Despite common assumptions, what we call PTSD did not evolve out of psychiatric research on the stress of war[58] but through the medical guild's effort to find a singular terminology with which to characterize the after-effects of exposure to diverse forms of societal violence. There was a time not long ago when what we now call PTSD was divided into "post-Vietnam syndrome," "rape trauma," and "battered child syndrome," which at least offered greater specificity in associating personal upheaval with a specific cause. But rape trauma syndrome was brought into public consciousness by the feminist movement[59] and then roundly critiqued by this same movement for its pathologizing and medicalizing of survivors.[60] Battered child syndrome, while still in use by certain pediatricians serving our broken child protection system,[61] is now frequently replaced by the PTSD label with regard to abused children, thereby setting them up for identification by the psychopharmacological trauma industry.

Post-Vietnam syndrome morphed into PTSD through the activism of Vietnam Veterans Against the War, an organization that sponsored "rap groups" for veterans. These veterans felt the tremendous burden of "moral inversion"[62] and the "absurd evil"[63] of what they and many others considered an unnecessary war. Many felt enormously conflicted, ashamed, and plagued with involuntary flashbacks of horrific experiences as they tried to reenter an ungrateful and unwelcoming society. Post-Vietnam syndrome's moral and historical context has now been sanitized and rendered invisible by the PTSD label. Writing in 1973, just prior to the U.S. withdrawal from Vietnam, antiwar psychiatrist-activist Robert Jay Lifton noted:

> Some veterans, ambivalent about having the term "post-Vietnam syndrome" applied to themselves, suggest that it is more genuinely applicable to America at large. The psychological truth of that claim lies in the combination of cease-fire that is not quite peace, and the powerful war-linked residuum in the American people of confusion, guilt, rage, and betrayal. We have become a nation of troubled survivors of a war not yet over and still just distantly perceived.[64]

Attending many rap sessions, Lifton empathized with veterans' ambivalence about being labeled for their troubles individually, declaring:

> Large numbers of them feel themselves to be "hurting" and in need of psychological help, but avoid contact with the Veterans Administration—because they associate it with the war-military-government establishment, with the forces responsible for a hated ordeal,

or because of their suspicion (whether on the basis of hearsay or personal experience) that VA doctors are likely to interpret their rage at everything connected with the war as no more than their own individual "problem."[65]

The reinterpretation these veterans feared is exactly what occurred. Veterans Affairs psychiatrists built PTSD as a new categorical diagnostic label for the *DSM*, and, in order to qualify for help, veterans were expected to submit to being characterized as "disordered," a term akin to the "inferior constitutions" of shell-shocked veterans of World War I, who, like the delinquents, paupers, and other black sheep sharing their shame, were also subsumed beneath the medicalizing of psychological trauma.

The new label of "PTSD" effectively separated the psychological turmoil of Vietnam combat veterans away from what had *happened to* them: the experience of volunteering for or being drafted into a brutal war they'd ultimately be maligned for joining. PTSD reframed postwar reactions of enlisted man and draftee alike into an individual "service related disability," leaving American society and its leaders unaccountable for the human outcome of defective foreign policy by relocating it *inside* the survivors. This medicalized revisionism of PTSD continues to maintain a smoke screen over the choices made by American society in its unrelenting calls to war and its abuse, blaming, and segregating of its suffering citizen-soldiers. To me, it is a gaslighting diagnosis.

Soon it became economically and politically advantageous to apply "PTSD" to other violent social and political phenomena. Such efforts have typically represented a partnership between the medical guild, perceived as benevolent, and multiple corporate and political interests.

The unscientific ambiguity of psychiatric labels was repeatedly exposed by the pioneering efforts of psychologist, colleague, and friend Paula J. Caplan, initially through her firsthand account as a member of the *DSM-IIIR* task force in her book *They Say You're Crazy*.[66] Since then, many others have helped bring the mental health system's arbitrariness into the light of day.[67] Before her tragic death in 2021, Dr. Caplan offered a non-pathologizing, lay approach to helping veterans through her book *When Johnny and Jane Come Marching Home*. Therein, she describes the destructive illogic of posttraumatic stress as "disorder":

Like most studies of human behavior and emotional pain, those about PTSD are plagued by a wealth of problems in the ways they are conceived, designed, carried out, and interpreted. Some begin with "people who have been diagnosed with PTSD," and surprisingly often, no one checks to see if all of these people even meet the (unscientifically derived) PTSD criteria. When you interpret the results of such studies, it is hard to know where to begin, since you cannot be sure of much about whom you have studied, and you almost never know anything about their individual and social strengths and resources, which certainly affect treatment outcome. Similar problems apply to studies involving virtually any category of mental illness.[68]

PTSD is now a common means for establishing individual disability. The sociological "risk factors" that hide lived context and create "symptoms" have greatly widened: growing up poor or living in a crime-ridden, disadvantaged neighborhood,[69] driving a car on U.S. highways[70] (with the highest per capita death rate in the industrialized world), living in New Orleans's Lower Ninth Ward when the U.S. Army's Corps of Engineers misinterprets its own data in favor of saving money on hurricane disaster prevention,[71] or losing a loved one at the World Trade Center after successive U.S. administrations from both parties deploy misguided policies strengthening terrorism worldwide and hazarding retaliation.[72]

"PTSD" is now a form of lay vernacular, a mode of self-depiction, sometimes as a dark joke, other times more seriously. Mental health providers sympathetic to the pain of personal suffering are quick to cooperate with clients seeking to be so labeled. Given its popularity as a new identity, it is truly bizarre to witness the efforts of psychiatry and allied fields to reduce the PTSD phenomenon from its cultural and sociohistorical roots into a false biology. But the U.S. mental health system and its academics have for so long served mainstream corporate interests that the evolution and ubiquity of PTSD really only represents a case in point. When applied to the "special case" of Native Americans, I believe PTSD further obscures their lived context of ongoing oppression and genocide.

PART III

Building
Coyote's Swing

NINE

Collective Suffering

FORT SIMCOE

After I came to work at Yakama Nation, I wanted to learn as much as I could about the history of *páshtin* colonization in the area. It became an unusual source of relief to me to become more oriented to this history in relation to the stress I was experiencing trying to fit in at the clinic. As an outsider, I felt honored when I heard stories from my *kála*, Winátchapam elder Levina Wilkins (Kussamwhy), and numerous other elder friends.

I would also visit the library at Yakama Nation Museum and Cultural Center, especially its back room of rare books and tribal documents. I also bought books by local historians and visited places, particularly Fort Simcoe, a "Washington Historical State Park." This place is located in the heart of Yakama Nation land and features a restored governor's mansion, officers' quarters, old mountain howitzers, a stockade, and other outbuildings.

During my many visits, I would seldom see anyone else, although on one occasion a Civil War reenactment was being staged. I would walk around and often relocate the thick chain that was still set into the ground in the shell of a stockade. A small sign adjacent to it read simply: JAIL. It was just four walls of timbers with no roof. I couldn't think of any other use for this chain to be in the middle of the structure other than for people. I'd sometimes pull on it, imagining what it would be like to be shackled. Then I'd sit down on the broken edge of the jail wall and smoke a cigarette—an occasional stress behavior I blamed on IHS—and consider what happened to the Original People of this land.

The jail at Fort Simcoe in 1950. Only the chain and foundation remain. *Click Relander Collection, Yakima Valley Libraries.*

A BRIEF HISTORY

Although oral tradition records "an epidemic of smallpox"[1] around 1800, Sergeant John Ordway, traveling with Lewis and Clark and Sacagawea, describes a joyous meeting with the families who'd one day be called "Yakama" in 1806: "The head chief told our officers that they Should be lonesome when we left them and they wished to hear once of our meddicine Songs and try to learn it and wished us to learn one of theirs and it would make them glad."[2]

In 1814, European fur traders observed a crowd of as many as 3,000 men and many more women and children with an estimated 9,000 horses as they gathered and prepared roots.[3] They seemed to be living in abundance and harmony, "horse racing, foot racing, gambling, singing, dancing, and [holding] councils."[4]

After the Oregon boundary dispute was settled in 1846, Washington Territory was created out of claims ceded by the British North American colonial government to the United States. Only one year later, Christian missionaries Dr. Marcus Whitman, his wife, Narcissa, and eleven others were massacred by Cayuse warriors. Dr. Whitman helped many white immigrants and according to a contemporary, "looked upon them [Indians] as an inferior race & doomed at no distant day to give place to a settlement of enterprising Americans."[5]

As among the Yakama, traditional *twáti* (healers) of the Cayuse were considered all-powerful in relation to matters of birth and death, and for this reason failure to help patients could be a very risky business for the health of healers themselves. When Dr. Whitman began treating the Cayuse during a measles epidemic, many died, and this did not help his reputation among the survivors. Then mixed-blood wagon train passenger Joe Lewis intimated to the Cayuse that the doctor might be poisoning their children with the drugs he gave them. Lewis reportedly called these drugs "poison," and this added to Cayuse fears generated by the effects of "heavy drugs" Whitman had injected into watermelons several had stolen.[6] I've wondered if Cayuse suspicion and fear was further worsened by the sedative effects of the patent medicines Dr. Whitman likely used on them as well. These concoctions were often laced with alcohol, morphine, opium, cocaine, and other narcotics.[7] Cayuse brutality during the Whitman massacre notwithstanding, numerous incidents of Native poisoning by white people exist in the historical record.[8] According to Shasta oral history, for instance, during the summer of 1850 in California, whites deliberately poisoned one hundred Wintu people they'd invited to a "friendship feast."[9,10]

As a result of the Whitman massacre, 350 federal troopers were sent into the Blue Mountains.[11] Captured Cayuse massacre leader Tiloukaikt, "a heartbroken and conscience-stricken man"[12] who'd lost five children of his own to disease and war, pleaded with the Whitmans' adopted daughter, Catherine, to arrange to have him stabbed or shot to death rather than hung, which he believed would rob him of an afterlife. He was hung anyway on June 3, 1850.

In 1854 a Palus leader, Kamiakin, who'd been gathering intelligence on incoming *páshtin* while trading with them, joined Walla Walla elder Peo Peo Mox Mox (Yellow Bird) and Nez Perce leader Apash Wyakaikt (Looking Glass) in calling together a large council in the Grand Ronde Valley.[13] These men were alarmed by the pace of colonists coming into areas in which they hunted, fished, gathered, and camped, and felt they must be stopped. Kamiakin described numerous massacres of Native communities that had already occurred west of the Cascades. Many present heard stories from Delaware Jim, who'd settled among the Nez Perce, and told of the Trail of Tears and the forced removals of Original People to the east.[14] Despite Kamiakin's and the others' efforts, there wasn't sufficient resolve to form a confederacy.

In 1854, acting U.S. commissioner of Indian affairs Charles E. Mix directed Washington territorial governor Isaac Stevens to "effect the combination of all the bands into six or eight tribes, or to arrange half a dozen treaties, or less, so that every one of the tribes shall be party to them."[15] By 1855, a gilded EuroAmerican motive that had contributed to eastern tribal calamities was arriving at the doorstep of Native people in the Pacific Northwest: gold had been discovered in the Colville River.

Eighteen fifty-five was also the year that Stevens, accompanied by a troop of soldiers and Indian agents, convened the Walla Walla Council, hoping to carry out Charles Mix's instructions. He claimed his treaty meant the "Great Father" would care for his "Indian children" on land guaranteed to remain theirs "as long as the great sun rises in the East and sets in the West."[16] But the stories brought by Kamiakin, Delaware Jim, and others made "the transparency of the speeches ... so obvious" to the Indian leaders present "that it [was] a wonder the commissioners could not realize the ease with which the Indians saw through what they were saying."[17]

Yakama leader Owhi's disgust comes through in the English translation of his words: "What shall I do? Shall I give the land which is a part of my body and leave myself poor and destitute? Shall I say I will give you my land? I cannot say so."[18] Nez Perce elder Hal-Hal-Tlos-Sot (Lawyer) pointed to the Delaware translator (Jim?) and remarked to Stevens: "The red man traveled away farther, and from that time they kept traveling away further, as the white people came up with them. And this man's people ... are from that people. They have come on from the Great Lake where the sun rises, until they are now near us, at the setting sun."[19] Peo Peo Mox Mox simply remarked, "You have spoken in a manner partly tending to evil. Speak plain to us."[20]

Owhi and Kamiakin ultimately chose to provide their ink marks to the Treaty of 1855, but the significance of this gesture may have been unfamiliar to them, and "neither meant to ... approve the document, according to some of the old Yakimas who witnessed the signing."[21] In certain instances during his treaty campaign, Stevens actually "appointed the tribal chiefs who were to sign for their people."[22] In the oral history, Kamiakin refused to sign until

Stevens threatened that the river would run red with his people's blood if he remained resistant—and as he signed, he reportedly bit his lip until it bled.[23] Controversy continues to this day at Yakama Nation as to the right or freedom of choice these leaders actually had in making their marks.

EuroAmerican betrayals of the bands of people who would be designated "Yakama" began almost immediately. Twelve days after the treaty was signed, well before its ratification by Congress, and with Stevens's approval, the entire area was announced as open for *páshtin* colonization. The intrusion of whites continued unabated with the unrepentant announcing by Stevens that the land no longer belonged to the Original People who'd been occupying it for many thousands of years. Many tribal historians tell of rape and murder shortly thereafter against Native women out gathering food.[24] Furious over one such alleged event, Qualchan, son of Owhi, organized several warriors and killed a party of six *páshtin* miners.[25]

Indian agent Andrew Bolon tasked himself with investigating the killings of these miners, although he'd been warned by friendlier Yakama to stay away.[26] Warrior Mosheel and several others met him at a camp, where Mosheel possibly mistook him for Captain Nathan Olney, who'd recently captured and hung a number of Bannock warriors. Whispering, "This is the man who hanged my uncles and cousins at Wallula,"[27] Mosheel and his relative Stah-kin assassinated Bolon.

More intrusions and assaults and counterassaults followed,[28] and the legacy of the Whitman massacre, Bolon's killing, and other tensions fueled a blood rage among colonizers. In the taverns of The Dalles, Nathan Olney and his vengeful militiamen fanned the sparks for the "Yakama Indian Wars," which lasted from 1855 to 1858. Preparations for community defense had already been underway by Yakama families for years. Now driven from their food stores, Indian women and children entered the hard plateau winters and suffered greatly, sometimes starving to death as they hid. Yakama flight into the hills and ridges, away from *páshtin* gunfire, also took them away from the ancient nurturance of *Nch'i-wána*, the Columbia River. Their terror drove them to such a degree of haste that trade goods, beaded heirlooms, and religious symbols are still found by scavengers today. If captured, the warriors protecting them were purposely and publicly hung so as to symbolically leave their souls orphaned, as had been done to Tiloukaikt. Watching from the ridges and hills, these Original People witnessed such things happen to their many loved ones.

Peo Peo Mox Mox, now an elder seeker of peace for the Walla Walla, tried to parlay under a white flag but was tricked by Nathan Olney and his men into being captured along with several of his warriors. After they were invited to talk, Olney's escort, Lieutenant Colonel James K. Kelly, ordered them immediately tied.

"No tie men! Tie dogs and horses!"[29] Peo Peo Mox Mox yelled in defiance.

Olney's men claimed knives then were drawn from their captives' leggings,[30] but oral accounts state that Peo Peo Mox Mox and his warriors' deaths were outright murder. As Native women and children watched, the *páshtin* soldiers stuffed the bodies of their spiritual leader and his protectors into the widened hole of a sweat lodge as an intentional desecration.

According to Washington historian John C. Jackson, Dr. Shaw, Nathan Olney's regimental surgeon, "exhumed the body [of Peo Peo Mox Mox] and took off the ears."[31] Militia volunteer James Sinclair was more vivid about this dissection: "His skull was divided equally for buttons, his ears preserved in a bottle of spirits, and large strips of his skin were cut off along his back to be made into razor strops."[32] The leader's preserved ears were placed on display for anyone walking by to view at Smith's Apothecary in Portland, Oregon. "Apothecary" is an antiquated term for a pharmacist, which in those days was generally a physician. Peo Peo Mox Mox's dissection may represent the earliest instance of medical research performed on Native people in the Pacific Northwest.

Despite superior technology, it took three years for the U.S. military to defeat the Yakama warriors, a testament to a strategic resistance built out of maximizing the efficiency of dwindling numbers, familiarity with the terrain, accuracy with a bow and arrow, and several ancient muskets garnered through trade. The mountain howitzers proudly displayed at Fort Simcoe Historical State Park brought this resistance to a close; they were a devastating invention the warriors could not effectively oppose.

With defeat, the Treaty of 1855 was forced upon the ancestors of the people I've come to know. Given this history, it's no wonder I've never seen any Yakama friends at Fort Simcoe. The pillory where their grandfathers and grandmothers were bullwhipped is not on display. There is no plaque on or near the trees from which their warriors were hung. Soon the land "given" to the Yakama would become checkered with allotments created by the Dawes Act of 1887, the federal legislative scheme that stole another 50 million acres of land from beneath Native feet.

This is when the missionaries and teachers began to arrive. There's little left to identify even where the Fort Simcoe boarding school once stood. The children of the defeated were sent there to be trained in domestic tasks and cobbling shoes, trades for which they were considered best suited due to their racial "limitations." In his study *Away from Their Barbarous Influences: The Yakama Boarding School at Fort Simcoe*,[33] Yakama historian and former colleague James Smith describes the circumstances of these children. In 1889, Indian Service inspectors reported two Yakama children died from being whipped by Superintendent Samuel Motzer, while an unnamed ten-year-old boy was "taken to bed" and under medical treatment due to a beating. Smith describes Fort Simcoe boarding school as dirty, shoddy, short of teachers, and populated with incompetent, lazy staff members. "While Indian agents came and went with transfers and subsequent changes in administrations, life for Yakama students at the boarding school remained a constant cycle, punctuated by various episodes of neglect, regimentation, and occasional brutality," he concluded.[34]

SOUL WOUND AT CELILO FALLS

Under the authority of the Treaty of 1855 and other treaties, Indian people throughout the Columbia Plateau and River Basin were assigned to "tribes" designated by federal officials. When Lieutenant William Henry

Fort Simcoe Boarding School, 1900.

Boyle visited Indians along the Columbia and demanded that they move
to the Yakama agency, they refused to recognize his role or their treaty-
based relationship in a document they never signed. Historian Andrew
H. Fisher notes that "between 1860 and 1885, federal officials constantly
complained that many of the people assigned to the Umatilla, Warm
Springs, and Yakama agencies remained at large on the public domain."[35]
Resentment over not being represented in Isaac Stevens's treaty negotiations
but nonetheless deprived of one's ancient land rights became a resistance
movement as the "River Indian" cultural identity emerged from Sahaptin or
Upper Chinookan communities stretching along Nch'i-wána.

These Native people were considered renegades by federal officials. They
interfered with census taking and continually undermined allegedly benevolent EuroAmerican intentions. More accurately, they refused to abandon
their access to rich resources so that ambitious *páshtin* colonizers could take
them over. They complained openly of harassment to Captain Frank Kidder
Upham in 1884:

> [Pascappa], cheif [*sic*] of a small band living near Alder Creek,
> and Ko-tai-a-kon [Kotiakan] were particularly anxious that their
> grievances should be known; which were in effect, that while they,
> as a matter of principle, would not go to the reservation, and had
> never received any benefits or annuities therefrom, the agent at the
> Yakima reservation continued to send the Indian police after them,
> and particularly their children, insisting that they should be taught
> at the reservation schools, and [learn] of the religion of the agency,
> and that their hair should be cut.[36]

When Captain Thomas McGregor investigated rumors of River People
prepping for war, he found their source point among *páshtin* farmers trying
to appropriate Indian land. He asserted that "it [was] the wish of all the rest
of the whites living in the vicinity of the Columbia River Indians that they
be *let alone.*"[37]

The Treaty of 1855, a document governing River People that never had
their actual agreement, reads:

> The exclusive right of taking fish in all the streams, where running
> through or bordering said reservation, is further secured to said
> confederated tribes and bands of Indians, as [is] also the right of

taking fish at all usual and accustomed places, in common with the citizens of the Territory, and of erecting temporary buildings for curing them: together with the privileges of hunting, gathering roots and berries, and pasturing their horses and cattle upon open and unclaimed land.[38]

While this language seems unequivocal, River People have had to continually defend their fishing rights using a treaty they've viewed with great ambivalence. River Indian complaints about intrusion onto their established fishing "stands" were being sent to Yakama agent James Wilbur as early as 1881:

The Indians have always regarded these fishing stands as their own property, as much as the house or barn of any citizen; they never contemplated giving the whites the privilege of possessing them, but I believe when they signed the treaty supposed they were only giving the whites the privilege of taking fish at the fishery, from other stands.[39]

Of course, they hadn't actually "signed" the treaty to which Wilbur refers. By the late nineteenth century, *páshtin*-owned fish canning companies were dynamiting channels for "fishwheels," paddle wheel–like contraptions hoisting huge amounts of fish right out of the river.[40] The dipnetting River People could not compete with the machines placed in fishing spots without regard for their rights, their own catches declined substantially, and they took action to protect their treaty rights in court for the first time.[41]

In the years before 1920, River People took several cases before federal courts related to fishing rights along Nch'i-wána.[42] The overall outcomes were that treaty rights prevailed, yet decisions tended to describe Indian entitlements as pertaining to "tribal rights." The implication was that such rights could be applied upon *tribal* land only. This left the "usual and accustomed place" of the river itself completely off the map. States took advantage of the loophole by composing regulations governing so-called off-reservation fishing. These new regulations singled out tribal fishing methods and made them illegal.

Surrounded by commercial fishing opportunists, Yakama River People were now competing for their own ancestral inheritance. Deprived of their traditional methods, they were unable to catch enough fish to feed themselves and sell to make ends meet. Then Oregon outlawed fishing wheels on behalf of salmon conservation in 1926, and Seufert Brothers Company, a large commercial fishery, began recruiting River People for their new cableway system, hoisting fishermen out to rocky areas and islets from where they could more easily increase their catch and sell it back to the company. This meager effort at economic sharing backfired when poverty-stricken Indians from other reservations as far away as Alaska joined in the new labor boom. Seufert made no distinction between local Natives and others. Quarrels and conflicts ensued and the Celilo Fishing Committee was created in 1936 to aid in local arbitration and advocacy, but for years the committee's influence was limited by internal fighting. Regulations passed by the committee conflicted with traditional Yakama "unwritten law," and divisions in the community became exacerbated.

The subsistence and economic system of River People fractured; things must have seemed as though they could get no worse. Then came the dams: the Bonneville (1938), the Grand Coulee (1942), The Dalles (1957), and finally the John Day (1971). From that point until the present, attacks upon fishing rights along the Columbia have remained so vehement, vindictive, and chronic that whole volumes must be dedicated to fully describe them. Roberta Ulrich has documented the repeated failures of the Bonneville Power Administration and the Army Corps of Engineers to rebuild the River People's fishing sites—so-called in lieu sites to take the place of the old fishing spots they went to court to preserve.[43] I've known elders who wouldn't cross bridges over the flooded Nch'i-wána because they didn't wish to feel beneath their feet the graves of their ancestors, now flooded out by the dams.

And each time I drive by windsurfers plying the Nch'i-wána, one of the most popular sites in the world for this sport, I think of how a recreational area they enjoy was financed at the expense of River People and their ancestors. Sometimes I stop at Celilo to buy a few pounds of frozen salmon out of the freezer in the community longhouse, my $15 or $20 going into the slender pockets of the Original Guardians of this river. The sordid events at Nch'i-wána became yet another spiritual and economic wound when the last traditional fishing sites at Celilo Falls were flooded in the late 1950s with the opening of The Dalles Dam. Having honored me with this story, my *kála*, Levina Wilkins, concluded, "That was when our people truly went crazy. It was like all the rules changed or there were no more rules."[44]

COLLECTIVE SUFFERING | *135*

OPPRESSIVE SUFFERING REVISED

With their own language among the casualties, Native scholars, thought leaders, and elders have "borrowed" English words and phrases for describing the unique suffering community members have experienced generationally through historical and contemporary *páshtin* violence at Yakama Nation. They include "historical trauma," "intergenerational trauma," "soul wound," "cultural destruction," "colonization," "genocide," "forced assimilation," "loss of language," "boarding school," "termination," as well as more general terms such as "racism," "poverty," "life expectancy," and "educational barriers." These words are sometimes debated for their meaning, but they form a language for contemporary Native "mental health" discussions, research, conferences, and other events.[45]

I naively thought I'd encounter this borrowed language in written policies and procedures of the mental health system in which I was supposed to work. But I did not. The Indian Health Service's mandated mental health manual mentions "psychiatrist" and "psychiatric" twenty-three times; and "therapy" eighteen times; "pharmacotherapy," "medication," "drugs," and "prescription" sixteen times. It uses the word "treatment" a whopping eighty-nine times.[46] But the IHS mental health manual uses the word "violence" only once, and there's no mention at all of "genocide," "cultural destruction," "colonization," or "historical trauma"—or even "racism," "poverty," "life expectancy," or "educational barriers."

Put off by this ideological slight and on the heels of my encounter with Pfizer's PTSD self-quiz, I began writing "post-colonial stress"[47] for several months in the "diagnostic impression" area of IHS Patient Encounter forms for clients while still working at Yakama Indian Health Clinic. I was eventually told by the mental health liaison officer at the Portland-area IHS regional office to stop using this descriptor or face disciplinary action. Post-colonial stress, it turned out, is not a palatable concept to the U.S. Indian Health Service nor billable through Medicaid.

This is not particularly surprising. In its philosophies, the mental health system in the United States is almost entirely focused upon "individual Western selves" and thereby reflects a central EuroAmerican value system. This system may, on rare occasions, discuss more communitarian concepts but actually does very little to respond to collectively shared, rippling, residual, traumatic reactions to the *vertical*[48] and *horizontal*[49] violence of ongoing war, oppression, and social calamity. And yet one need not look far within American society at large to encounter this kind of reaction to violence in many forms. It just seems to be disregarded in the realities of Indian Country.

Consider the attacks on the World Trade Center and the Pentagon in New York City on September 11, 2001. Six months afterward, about 6 percent of Americans living *outside* the New York City area fit psychiatric labeling criteria for "PTSD" as a result of media exposure alone.[50] A simple maneuver on a calculator tabulates 17 million Americans reacting in a prolonged and visceral manner to the violence they were witnessing virtually. This is not to mention what people living in New York City were experiencing. In a separate six-month post-9/11 study of more than one hundred relief workers working in New York City who had *not* been on the scene of the attacks, nearly 5 percent reported acute anxiety and depression lasting for months just from listening to stories of survivors.[51] Such transmission of collectively experienced trauma is not an isolated phenomenon: social workers counseling victims of the 2011 Japan earthquake and Fukushima meltdown also reported higher levels of "secondary traumatic stress" despite *not* having been on the scene;[52] Israeli university students hearing televised reports of terrorism felt significantly elevated levels of "vicarious trauma."[53]

The U.S. mental health system, however, decontextualizes reactions to violent events by marginalized communities in reframing them as problems of the individual. In King County, Washington, a better housing allowance is obtained for incoming refugees escaping war and political persecution if they demonstrate that the traumatic effects of torture or deprivation they've endured make them "severely mentally ill." Conversion of a horrendous collective refugee experience to an individualistic language of psychiatric disorder qualifies one for a better place to live. In Native America, then, I see very little difference: the "individual Indian" must also be decontextualized, labeled, and even characterized as "disabled" by "mental illness" to qualify for desired help and services.

Seemingly pertinent ideas of *stress process* and *stress proliferation*[54] offered by Leonard Pearlin remain untested and virtually unknown to mental health system researchers. Perhaps these sorts of ideas, which emphasize psychosocial dynamics rather than phony biological explanations, are not where the priorities of corporate and guild interests supporting mental health research lie. In 2013, Dr. Pearlin noted:

When we look at the etiology of mental health, we are able to see a convincing example of how personal problems may often have their beginnings in social problems. This message needs to be underscored and repeated, for when the political climate of society shifts to the right, a contrary message tends to arise, namely, that social problems start as personal problems. We can assert that what has been learned and what will be learned in the future will continue to go directly against the grain of such a claim. Personal problems can be and often are reflections of structures and contexts in which people lead their lives.[55]

I watched in admiration as a sociological perspective found traction in Indian Country for a time when Les Whitbeck and colleagues surveyed American Indian parents using a "Historical Loss Scale" and "Historical Loss Symptoms Scale" in 2004. This was an effort to disentangle "proximal" versus "distal" (i.e., historical from current) factors in participants' reports of grief, depression, and anxiety.[56] These researchers wondered:

> Are we dealing with actual historical issues or more proximate grief and trauma from the daily lives of often economically disadvantaged people who live with constant overt and institutionalized discrimination, severe health issues, and high mortality rates?[57]

Study participants came from two reservation communities in the upper Midwest of the United States and two Canadian reserves in Ontario. Over 50 percent of parents in the Whitbeck study reported thinking about the loss of their language and spiritual traditions at least weekly, while roughly 35 percent did so daily or even several times a day. Over 33 percent also thought about the loss of their culture daily or several times each day. And more than 63 percent reported thinking about "losses from the effects of alcohol on our people"[58] at least weekly—with an impressive 45 percent reporting they thought about such losses every day, with nearly 16 percent doing so several times a day.

Whitbeck's team's findings also revealed that around 15 percent of parents often or always felt sad or depressed and roughly 14 percent felt shame in thinking about historical trauma and loss.[59] Twenty-one percent reported often feeling uncomfortable around white people and nearly 15 percent often distrusted the intentions of whites in relation to such thoughts.[60] Nearly 23 percent often felt angry when they had these thoughts, with 6 percent reporting they frequently felt enraged having such thoughts.

The Historical Trauma and Loss Scale used by Whitbeck and his colleagues was created out of focus groups with elders; that is, community members themselves helped to create the scale. The initial 2004 study was extended with similar results among Native youth in 2009.[61] Moreover, in 2013 the scale was demonstrated to be significantly correlated with EuroAmerican mental health measures of anxiety, depression, PTSD, and proneness to substance dependence.[62] I couldn't help but think these researchers were making genuine progress in articulating the oppressive realities of "generational carry."

A CHALLENGE TO HISTORICAL TRAUMA

Despite its populist roots, the relevance of such sociological findings is currently challenged by certain social scientists seeking to determine whether the term "historical trauma" itself merits academic acceptance. This "borrowed language" descriptor, which I've heard applied for nearly twenty years to describe the "spiritual wound to the heart of our people,"[63] is now being studied by social scientists for its "construct validity" using statistical methods.[64] I suspect the effort originates from those who don't believe in the term or its utility. Setting the stage for an attempted debunking in 2014 were Laurence Kirmayer, Joseph Gone, and Joshua Moses, who argued in an opinion piece in *Transcultural Psychiatry* that

> establishing definite causal linkages across generations in the case of historical trauma is exceedingly difficult, perhaps even impossible. Studies are necessarily retrospective and constrained by limited data and recall bias. The fact that individuals attribute their problems to past events does not prove a causal link.[65]

I'm surprised that a psychiatrist, an academic clinical psychologist, and an anthropologist would assert that attribution in a family or community of current suffering to past events should *not* be considered at least to some degree "causal evidence." *Story*—i.e., "his-story" or "her-story" or "their-story"— has always served as a modus operandi in each of these professions. It seems academic *gaslighting* to imply that the childhood kidnapping of a Native grandmother to boarding school, where she was raised by an institution and sexually assaulted and/or beaten for speaking her own language, wouldn't have the potential to create lifelong grief, rage, substance issues, emotional distance, or other difficulties that could interfere with forming bonds and promoting positive development with her children or, indeed, their bonds with and development of their own children.

Whenever we see someone shaking, crying, and hyperventilating, we cannot open their head to know why: they must somehow *tell us a story* of their pain. All so-called diagnostic inquiry within mental health practice is premised upon this approach. "Field study" in anthropology is also dependent upon asking "cultural informants" why people do what they do, including why they suffer as they suffer. Social science research *writ large* is plagued by such complexities, making a criticism of historical trauma for not having a "definite causal linkage" seem specious.[66]

What is also strange is the seeming disregard for existent Western social science empirical evidence for the generational features of what Native people are calling "historical trauma." There are already solid studies of adult-to-child transmission of attachment problems,[67] intergenerational domestic violence risk,[68] family transmission of child maltreatment[69] and substance abuse,[70] and, indeed, generational features of traumatic reactions to oppression.[71]

There are also wider sociological phenomena to consider: the boarding school era itself left only 175 of 300 spoken tribal languages surviving.[72] Legal threats to the protection of the Indian Child Welfare Act (ICWA) continue to hazard a return to Native child adoption away from relatives and home communities. Even Temporary Assistance for Needy Families (TANF), which ended the entitlement features of Aid to Families with Dependent Children (AFDC), pushes upon Native families to either face sanctioning or leave their reservations to find jobs elsewhere, a pressure akin to forced assimilation and termination.[73]

Kirmayer, Gone, and Moses[74] also elaborate on their worries about "historical trauma" becoming a potentially damaging form of *self-stigma*:

> The more popular the historical trauma concept becomes the more likely individuals are to think about their problems in this way and to produce narratives and attributions that confirm the model.[75]

These stigma and threats to identity they fear—for which they provide no evidence—seem very similar to the negative stigma of psychiatric diagnoses already widely applied in Indian Country for which there *is* evidence.[76] The question arises, then, as to whether Native people prefer being labeled by a dubious Western mental health system or sticking with terminology favored by their elders.

I believe empirically oriented researchers in Indian Country could make themselves more useful by testing shaky Western bioreductionist "constructs" that continually subvert a deeper understanding of the Native community, family, and person facing off with chronically oppressive forces, while "colonizing the mind" with misinformation that negatively affect Native identity. But I've found that even commenting upon the problems and dangers of this biopsychiatric ideology can sometimes leave one maligned by smart scholars who have had less opportunity for firsthand observation. I suppose this is an occupational hazard for any anti-authoritarian trying to work within a liberation psychology framework in Indian Country.[77]

SHIFTING CONSCIOUSNESS

Eduardo and Bonnie Duran and others call the shared, generational trauma of Native people a "soul wound."[78] Reading their work just before I began working at Yakama Nation was inspiring, but as a stranger in a strange land, I needed to learn more. In 2001, about eight months after I started working at the clinic, and with my funding request firmly denied, I traveled on my own dime to the first annual Healing Our Wounded Spirits conference held at Grand Ronde, Oregon. There I met a new friend, Dr. Joseph Stone[79] (Blackfoot), who took time to mentor me as we built fire together for a sweat lodge ceremony. This lodge included several male conference speakers: Joe, Eduardo Duran (Apache/Tewa) himself, Tom Ball (Klamath/Modoc), as well as local Native healers and counselors and several Lakota sun dancers. Our evening sweat was extraordinarily hot and purging physically, emotionally, and spiritually. This powerful memory is a touchstone for me, one in which I felt honored to vow alongside others to do all we could to help the people we served. I also recall with gratitude the support I felt in reclaiming my family's Missouri Cherokee heritage.

At the conference the following morning, I briefly met Maria Yellow Horse Brave Heart (Hunkpapa/Oglala Lakota) and listened as she introduced her ideas about historical trauma for the first time to many attendees.[80] I witnessed firsthand the empowering effects of her terminology on Native people present that morning: it was like a light bulb being turned on. Several months later I realized with surprise that Maria had integrated into her own thinking certain psychoanalytic writings from Jewish Holocaust survivor and trauma psychiatrist Henry Krystal.[81] I'd met with him and heard him speak on numerous occasions about generational trauma long before I came to Yakama Nation at our Thursday graduate case conferences in the mid-1980s at the University of Detroit. In 2015, I had the great pleasure of alerting a very elderly Dr. Krystal just prior to his death to his influence in Native circles, a fact of which he was not aware.

Any outsider seeking to ally with Native people must consider the Durans' timeline of traumatic eras affecting Native communities. These eras include First Contact, Economic Competition, Invasion and War, Reservation and Relocation, Boarding School, and the Termination periods.[82] *Coyote's Swing* suggests Mental Health Revisionism as an addition to this timeline.

An ordering of collectively shared traumatic events along linear, Western time helps familiarize learners with what "has happened" to Native people "in the past." Yet it seems important to remind my reader again of the string of the Yakama time ball and its knots and relevance to this very moment. Blackfoot scholar Wendy Running Crane notes:

> In Euro-American tradition time heals wounds, erases memories, and brings distance between who exists today and who existed in the past and in the future for the Euro-American thinker. Like the waters of a stream passing by, the Euro-American believes the past is gone forever and will not be back. For the Blackfoot thinker, ancestors and descendants are but two days away from the now; their energy can be accessed. Knowledge is never lost because it can be sought out again.[83]

While training at University of Detroit in the mid-1980s, I was immersed within a unique psychodynamic, phenomenalistic understanding[84] that shares common ground with both the Yakama and Blackfoot perspectives. We learned that the past is not *truly historical* per se but a phenomenon of one's current psychology. From within this viewpoint, the "historical" in "historical trauma" is best considered to be *within the present*.

We can imagine how this would be so in the effects of domination and perpetration on both Native and white consciousness relevant to the present moment. Through the Blackfoot way described, we discern "historical trauma" as quite near, occurring with immediacy in the stories of yesterday's ancestors, today's heroes, and tomorrow's visionaries. The critical importance of such stories is aptly demonstrated by Native people themselves: in their ceremonies, conversations, and understanding of their complex relationships with the so-called dominant society. William Charley was trying to tell just such a "living story" when he depicted Coyote's Swing for his friend Lucullus McWhorter.

On the other hand, the categorizing and historicizing of individual or shared trauma as a "distal" and environmental "factor"—as can be seen, for instance, in anything the U.S. mental health system touches from "intake" protocols to the subjection of "historical trauma" to Western empirical analysis—makes invisible the immediacy, accessibility, and relevance of a calamitous collective history shared by both Native and non-Native.

I've coined the term "generational carry" to help capture the moment-to-moment reenactment or replay of oppression. I believe such reenactments occur often and impinge upon both Native and non-Native people—upon their physical bodies, upon their emotional and spiritual well-being, upon their relationships with the world, but most particularly upon their immediate consciousness.

Generational carry informs my sense of moral duty to familiarize myself with the cultural-historical narratives affecting my own consciousness and interpretation of the world. In trying to be a good helper, I am continually asking myself whether I'm resisting or serving the metaphorical force of Coyote's Swing. In Native ways I've been taught, mind, heart, body, and spirit are inextricably linked to here-and-now experience in relating with the living world and beyond. In this way, I am brought to question and challenge the contradictions brought about and promoted through the U.S. mental health system as "abstractions of postconquest consciousness" that are foreign and constantly being imposed upon the lives of Native people.

ON PORCH AND RIVERBANK

Having smoked a borrowed Pall Mall on the front porch of a dilapidated house with a Yakama fisherman who could not fish or feed his family due to politics along Nch'i-wána, I did not wish to construe his emotional state as "major depressive disorder." No, he was suffering from oppression. I did not wish to apply "panic disorder" to a Native young woman mired in intense worry about high-stakes tests at her school that might make or break her only opportunity to go to college. She was understandably panicky about racist barriers she faces as a member of a marginalized class of people. I don't want to label a Native child with "ADHD" who'd rather touch and hold what he's being taught about in the apprentice-style learning of traditional eldership—together, *in solidarity*, and yet *in his own way*. I'd prefer to view him as sustaining a kind of consciousness that remains precious for all of us.

Stopping along the picturesque Lewis and Clark Highway along the Columbia Gorge, I see the pictographs on rock formations and hear the echoes of Yakama warriors yelling defiantly across Nch'i-wána how they will *never surrender* their homeland. I hear these echoes again when a Native young man at tribal school steadfastly refuses to speak with me. The tears of generations greet me when a Piikáni woman weeps during a ceremony and apologizes to her Creator for "speaking in a borrowed language." In all these ways, I find *historical trauma* among the people living it.

TEN

Exploring the Soul Wound

A TRAIL OF TEARS

About four hundred years before my first day at Yakama Indian Health Service Clinic, a brief and mostly peaceful period of trade along the eastern seaboard of North America was beginning to erode. Their numbers growing, invading Europeans contemplated what actions they could take to displace Original People whom they perceived to be in their way. Military technology, including more armed personnel as the colonial population increased, became their spearhead strategy, yet even then deployment of its power was not without controversy. For many early colonists, war could only be mounted against Native people after being sanctioned by God's Will as interpreted exclusively by a Christian elect. In fact, Puritan leaders used the term "war" on purpose to sway mixed opinion about its morality among ambivalent white colonists. War was justified violence; massacre was not.

In 1637, about five years after struggling onto the Atlantic shore after leaving Europe, British infantry ensign Richard Walker, my generational grandfather, participated alongside hundreds of other English Puritan militiamen in a massacre of the Pequot people that had to first be reframed as "war." Sparked by killings of an unsavory sea captain and a trader of questionable repute, this so-called punitive action was stoked by leaders in a manner not so different from certain U.S. military misadventures of today. The largest Pequot village was set ablaze and up to 1,000 people fled into European rifle fire. I'm saddened to say my own ancestor's rounds were likely among them. The murdered were mostly women and children.[1]

My awareness of Captain Walker's actions in itself reveals the privilege of my literate ancestors who recorded their participation in Native genocide. Yet such travesties had a fallout of their own and troubled the moral reasoning of white people even back then. Christian leaders soon emerged hoping to save the souls of the Native people that other Europeans were trying to destroy. Their first question—and it must have felt urgent—was whether a Native person actually possessed a soul to save.

Several years after the Pequot massacre, missionary John Eliot explained to two male Christian converts from the Nikmuk that Jesus Christ understood their prayers, telling them that "if hee [He] made Indian men, then hee knows all Indian prayers also."[2] Eliot's belief that Christian missionaries should learn to speak Wampanoag fluently was premised upon a basic assumption of Native humanity and coupled with a dedication to teaching Native people to read. Through such reasoning, education became a key offering of missionaries seeking to appeal to eastern North American tribal communities.

Eliot's Wampanoag interpretation of the Bible, *Mamusse Wunneetupanatamwe Up-Biblum God*, preceded by three years his 1666 book, *The Indian Grammar Begun*, and firmly established the principle that Christian conversion of Native people depended on first recognizing their capacity to learn the word of the Lord and then apply it to their lives. Once educated biblically, God would decide the fate of their souls. John Eliot and Christian missionaries like him were the first to apply Christian humanism to Native people in a movement that would last for hundreds of years.

I suspect their efforts to save souls form the historical basis for today's U.S. mental health system in Indian Country.

WHOSE SOUL NEEDS SAVING?

One of my first duties to the souls of Native clients I saw at Yakama IHS clinic consisted in having enough tissue on hand. Before a client arrived, I'd often tug tear-soaked tissues left by the prior client from between the cushions of a comfortable chair I'd repurposed from the clinic kitchen. *Why did my loved one commit suicide? How can I ever be close to anyone? Who will ever love me? Why am I shamed for mentioning abuse? How will I feed my children? What do I do with this anger? If I was abused, will I be an abuser? How will I ever stay sober? Being this poor, how can I make it? Where do I go if I feel unwelcome everywhere? How do I put away my grief in losing everyone I've ever loved? Can I ever sleep again?* "Tomorrow, I will drive a client to her sister's grave," I wrote in my journal, "I may offer a tissue to wipe the tears away ... she wasn't there to protect her."

I'd already been a psychotherapist for many years but never exposed to such sorrow among so many. The psychiatric drugs my colleagues insisted upon seemed to dishonor this pain, but when people wanted the pills despite my warnings about their side effects, I had to acknowledge an attraction to numbness familiar to me from my own past. Losses stacked upon losses inside my tiny office, violation upon violation in tearful disclosures, sometimes all situated within the same person.

I needed some means to keep my own balance, and it came about by accident the first time I walked into the vestibule of the Tribal Youth Center (TYC). (I've obscured the actual facility name and identities of these workers in order to protect their privacy as some of them continue their good work in the small, close-knit Yakama Nation community.) My visits became a near daily habit. A counselor I'll call Truman would greet me with a big smile. He was funny and happy in constant juxtaposition to the teens in his charge. Humor is very important in Native America, and I never saw him waver from gentle teasing, cajoling, and corny jokes. If I'd been a teen in trouble, I'd have easily confided in him. His good cheer was an important medicine to everyone he encountered.

Once inside TYC, I'd often sit down with Tory, who'd pull together a smudge of sage or sweetgrass, alternately talking or listening. He had long braids and was active in the "Red Road" recovery movement.[3] He teased not only the youth but me, too, with subtle innuendoes I wouldn't initially understand. My delayed reactions brought him great delight.

At first, I didn't understand that people at TYC were trying to help me. The elders there—Eva, Val, and Tania—would often talk to me, and they'd teach me without me realizing it. They became golden for me, and remembering our interactions is still a great relief. They provided me with a kind of "orientation" that the IHS never offered to their cultural community.

My own opinions as a psychologist and person proved helpful to them, I'm certain, but I came to understand the empathy, kindness, and wisdom that emanated from them was a means of showing me how I might best get to know the youth with whom we'd be working. They took me under their wing, and I am forever grateful for the great medicine of their friendship.

I once asked Eva if my role as a psychotherapist held any meaning within her cultural ways.

"Sure," she replied with a wink. "You are a kind of *twáti*,[4] Doc Walk, who helps people bring out their tears."

Given the depth of grief I'd been witnessing, I wondered if doing so could be considered truly helpful.

"*Nye*," she answered. "What's taught in the outside society, you might even think crying is no good, but that's not our way. If you don't bring out your tears, you can get very sick." Then she laughed and counseled me further: "But you need to grow your hair long, Doctor, because the Creator, Tamanawash, can't see you to help you. Also, you ought to go to the *xwyách*[5] and draw out the poison you've been hearing. Otherwise, it's going to make you sick too."

It was Tory who took me to my first sweat lodge, showing me how to bless the fire heating the smooth river stones red-hot and the proper way to enter the sacred lodge. He eventually taught me the role of a leader, the pourer of cold water, in starting prayers and other forms of honoring for the twelve or fifteen naked men who'd entered the pitch-dark lodge very early on a weekend morning. I was taken many times through the four rounds, each followed by a break, the timing of which was up to the leader: Welcome, Honoring or Prayer, Suffering, Closing. Eventually, I was invited to other sweat lodges offered by different families and communities, and I found great differences in how such things were done. All of them made clear that no one ever charges money for participation in a sweat lodge. It is very wrong to do so.

I had to stay away from the lodge for some years due to my own health issues, but lately I've been able to return. The Suffering round is the most important for me and fills me with reluctance. It is often the longest and hottest. Sitting in the dark beneath a dome of woven saplings covered with blankets, I turn inward as cold water is poured directly onto red-hot stones inside the center pit around which we all sit. The heat of gushing steam may sometimes feel suffocating and nearly intolerable. I invariably start to think about dying. Along with others present, I hear myself moan inwardly as the leader pours repeatedly and the very hot steam rises even higher. I'm brought into direct contact with my body's limitations, the fleeting nature of my life, and its fragility. I pray for help and guidance within this temporary sphere of existence. Then the leader speaks, perhaps setting the stage in what he says or discloses about the darkness of our spiritual pain. Each one present then speaks as we move around the circle, and to the extent we wish to do so we share our vulnerabilities and pain. There is drumming, singing, crying out, tears, laughter, and amplifying of one another's prayers.

Where else have I ever experienced such intimate care for my suffering? From those early days of Tory's hottest lodges, I still hear him begin by saying, "This is the path back to our Mother. . . ." I look now at the devastation being wreaked upon our planet and think of these words as among the most important of my life. What good will ever come of a species who abuses its Mother? I was much awakened to my responsibilities to the earth in the sweat lodge.

The first time I completed all four rounds, I lay on my back beneath the stars, watching the moon move across the sky, completely relaxed and restored. I do not know of any comparable Western practice because the sweat lodge is not therapy; it is a sacred ceremony. In the sweat lodge, I find no Post-Enlightenment alienation between my physical and spiritual self. I feel part of the earth, and my own well-being cannot be distinguished from the health of the planet I'm borne upon. I discern all my relations scattered in Seven Directions (east, west, north, south, up, down, and within) across the universe.

At some point Tory asked me to lead the lodge. I was completely taken aback. With a confidence I felt I hadn't earned, he wanted me to help in creating *healing* space for men I'd been sitting with in the dark for weeks. He needed a break, but the lodge had to continue. Would I help? If I said yes, it meant that I must not fail to build fire very early for several Saturdays, many hours before others arrived and be ready when all were present to lead all four rounds with them. This was a commitment in the Native way, and I was humbled.

The English word "healing" derives from the Greek *heil* or *hal*, a term that is at the root of the Western concept of "health," but which moves beyond freedom from injury or disease toward the *sacred* or *hal*-y, i.e., "holy." The sweat lodge was a "healing" practice in this sense, although the roots of the English word are obscured by today's mechanized approach to the body.

To be a "leader" for the lodge was not a privilege. I was not "entitled" or "awarded." I was simply being asked to serve. Unlike other participants present, I would be someone to pour water and set the tone for each round. The core virtue from the Twelve Virtues of Níix Ttáwaxt, which we used in the Pathways Circles: *Piná wait ku kw'atáni,* was taught to me by *kála* Levina Wilkins, and translates roughly to "He or she gives it all away" (i.e., "to be grateful just to help others"). This is Yakama esteeming of true leadership—that is, the virtue of being grateful for the ability to help others.[6]

By being included and taught in the *xwyách,* the sweat lodge, I was helped onto a path back to my own soul. I shed many tears in the dark and also laughed a great deal. I don't look at the world in the same way as before. I now seek to treat all my relatives and Mother Earth with *tma'áakni,* respect. I'm still working on *Piná iwaat ku kw'atáni* . . . and will likely do so for the rest of my days.

MORE SOUL HEALING

In the midst of much learning in early 2001, I was invited to a Yakama Indian Shaker healing gathering far out on the reservation. As the third-largest reservation in the United States, Yakama Nation covers nearly 2,200 square miles, and one can drive for hours before leaving its boundaries. I arrived at this very rural family home early, the first on scene. Despite the cultural rudeness of my Euro timeliness, I was politely directed toward a seat among a circle of chairs still being set up around the living room.

In my ignorance, I mentioned how glad I was to be included and permitted to observe the ceremony. I was immediately informed there was no way I'd be permitted to just be a witness: all present, including me, would be expected to "minister" to several people seated in single chairs placed in the middle of the living room's circle. I began to feel anxious because this was unexpected, and I felt uncertain and completely out of my element.

As each person arrived, he or she would walk around the seated circle very lightly touching the fingers of one hand to the palms of others present and then touching their own hearts before they sat down. This powerful gesture moved me. All mirrors and pictures were soon turned toward the walls. Many more people began to arrive, and the room was darkened and candles lit.

The ceremony commenced and took over three hours. It was emotionally and physically exhausting, and there were times I wondered whether I'd make it. My Euro clock kept intruding until compulsiveness itself died. As the ceremony progressed, someone reached for my hand and I was pulled into dance, song, prayer, the ringing of handbells, and the laying on of hands by Shaker ministers and all of the rest of us to heal the afflicted. We "brushed off" the burdened shoulders of those in anguish, in tremendous need, and then we clapped their pain, grief, and worry up into the heavens. The bells and singing continued the entire time; it became very warm, and tears and sweat intermingled in near darkness.

"Nothing to do with the old Pennsylvania Shaker faith," I wrote to a friend back in Michigan shortly afterward. My intellectuality makes me wince now as I struggled to describe what "seems a combination of Native beliefs and practices with Roman Catholicism." I mentioned how the devout religious faith of the Indian Shakers was founded in the 1890s through the visions of John Slocum and his wife.[7] I forcibly described what I determined as the "psychology" in the event, writing that "many here believe when we are psychologically disturbed, our soul begins to wander from our body," and a "person with an absent spirit can be taken over—by the alcohol spirit, for example. Shakers have the gift of restoring the soul to the body and of purging negative spirits."

I was caught in the same liminal space some of my Native friends call "between two worlds," yet I was entering from the opposite direction: from EuroAmerican to Indian. I was experiencing strange insights, and they chipped away at me, exposing the solitary sadness of the individualistic culture within which I'd been raised:

One begins to cry. A Shaker holds her in his arms. In a trance, he cries as well. She has witnessed aloud being a victim of sexual abuse and rape. The Shaker weeps with her, loudly groaning. He lifts his hands to the air—sending negativity and pain away.

I myself begin to get choked up. My Western eyes try to focus on what is happening in intellectual terms, but I don't like doing that. I want to be with this event in an honest and emotional way. There are times when Jung, Campbell, all those types of rationalizations only serve to distance us from what these people seem to know to their very core. I imagine what it might be like to be in one of those chairs—to have that amount of touch and care focused on me. To know that all present are aware to at least some degree of the deepest facets of my troubles and hardships. They know me and have known me all my life; some grew up with my parents, some grew up with my parents' parents.

The relatedness and connectedness seem generally unimaginable to a white person. We have lost this kind of thing long ago. But in trying to be totally present with what is happening, I recognize a deep longing within that has been invisible. It is about being raised among my own people, EuroAmericans, and how much we long for and envy the riches present here. White alienation from the self and one another, our social inhibitions, the compensations we go to in order to offset what we lack in relation to each other. I not only sense all this—I feel a tremendous spiritual tragedy. A calamity of unappreciated and unknown breadth. Like a capacity we once had but surrendered in favor of all the craziness, neuroticism, materialism, and selfish egocentrism that pervades. I don't mean to ennoble or romanticize what is here—there are a bunch of different people just as challenged as anyone to survive, truly more so, but they have preserved a practice so powerful and potentially healing. I am absolutely convinced that to sit in one of those chairs would be incredibly healing for anyone. And I feel the presence of God—all around, within each Shaker, an amazing energy of Love and Care. It is hard to describe that feeling ...

After the Shaker ceremony, a long table was set up and various foods brought in. I noticed several people present whom I'd seen individually in psychotherapy. This made me self-conscious because I felt uncertain of the boundaries involved. Given my training, I knew I couldn't acknowledge knowing them at all without their informed consent. Yet to fail to acknowledge them seemed a very impolite thing to do from a Yakama perspective.

"Hey, cuz!" one announced. "You ought to talk to Doc here with all you and Lolinda been dealing with!"

The other party stared down the table at me, obviously incredulous. My face turned cherry red.

"No kidding, he's helping!" said my fan. "I go see him every week."

All faces then turned toward me, but I must have looked aghast. An elder chuckled and then asked me to offer a prayer—I think to help me out of my social predicament. But this only deepened my awkwardness further: I'd never in my life been asked to offer an impromptu prayer to a roomful of people. I remember gripping both my knees tightly underneath the table as I improvised, but I have no recollection at all of what I said.

We finally began eating, but more questions ensued. What does a therapist do? Who are my family? Where did I grow up? Is my family religious? Do I believe in a Creator? Do I hunt? Fish? What do I think about alcohol?

At some point I knew I must somehow share more about myself or I'd leave feeling I'd failed in some important way. I had a self-conscious sense that my education and socialization as a psychologist, combined with the individualist loneliness of my culture of origin, made me appear emotionally distant in ways I abhorred. I was being invited to be a part of something I'd never encountered and to accept a form of public accountability I'd never had. Continuing from the note I wrote home to my friend:

> I talked more deeply about my own spiritual beliefs. I expressed my commitment to the work I was doing but also shared my own lack of confidence, imperfections, the great suffering I saw, and the need for their prayers and help and guidance from Creator. People listened and just moved on to more "testifying" over dinner. On Monday, my attendance at the Shaker meeting had clearly made it into the "moccasin telegraph"... Many, many people already knew of my presence and what I had said....

THE *KÁATNAM* AND WÁASHAT

Over the years, I've been invited to naming ceremonies, funerals, and other events at the numerous *káatnam* (longhouse) at Yakama Nation, places of the Wáashat (dance gathering) with their powerful architecture of massive cedar spans. Therein, the Seven Drum tradition continues to thrive, and as the singer's voice lifts (in a way that sounds mournful to me), men and women rise from their benches to stand on the plank floors opposite one another, separated by gender and the packed earthen span between each side upon which many will dance. Their movements, songs, and prayers are knots strung on this community's time ball by the Ghost Dances, Prophet Dances, and many visions of their ancestors who received this faith of resilience and survival. Wáashat ceremonies celebrate and refresh the prophecies heralding the rising of the dead, salvation, and a renewal of the Yakama world.[8]

Wáashat connects participants to their sacred land through the very ground beneath their feet. Everything done in the *káatnam* is a kind of prayer—from the preparation of food in the kitchen, where sadness and anger are not permitted, to the specific body turn and hand gesture prior to entry into the main hall. Here, Ichishkíin Sinwit is often spoken, the old songs are preserved and sung, traditional clothing is usually worn, and the "Indian way" is intensively taught to the youth. As an informant told anthropologist Helen Schuster in 1974:

> *Wáashat* is just pure faith. Just prayers. We only believe in something high up ... like heaven, but we have no word. That's the old Indian religion we've always had.[9]

Wáashat drumming and singing intermingles with Indian Shaker practices at events across the reservation. When the drums or bells sound, I am taught to stand up respectfully and swing my arm gently at the elbow, fist lightly closed, in a movement once recorded by Lewis and Clark in their journals.

I recall a powerful ceremony for a young teenage girl receiving the Indian name of her ancestor. This event culminated in a giveaway where every person present received something substantial from her and her family. I still have the blanket I received. The crescendo of the giveaway came when she removed her gorgeous regalia, ornate with handmade beadwork by her grandmother, to reveal her street clothes underneath. She then presented this masterwork to her cousin, enacting the leadership gesture of *pinaá íwaat ku kw'aláni* (self-denial and gratitude; humility)[10] and exhibiting the positive values with which she was raised.

Shortly after I began working at Yakama Nation, my oldest son and I decided to attend a "First Foods Feast" to represent our family, the rest of whom were unable to go. This traditional spring ceremony, Waykáanash Ká'uyt, celebrates the return of *núsux*, the salmon, and is open to the public. However, we accidentally drove to the wrong *káatnam*—that is, one in a different locale from the one to which we'd been invited. The Native friends we were to meet were not at this *káatnam*. We both felt confused and shy as we walked up to the entrance, and I couldn't see anyone I recognized. But suddenly people emerged from inside to greet us, as though we were long-lost friends who'd been to this place many times before. An elder Yakama man escorted us inside, taught us the proper way to enter, sat down with us, and then explained in English the significance of every song and movement for the next several hours. The profound welcome of this community left a life-changing impression on both of us, and that's not to mention the food, which was incredible.

It's taken me years to articulate the boundary line my family and I have often been invited across by the people of Yakama Nation. I consider its meaning carefully as I report my experiences. They do not mean that I can behave as though I've been "raised to" ways I was invited to learn about. On the other hand, I am permitted to honor and participate in them. Yet the honor of these teachings comes with a personal dilemma. Culturally, I can never fully return to who I once was, nor can I remain permanently within the world that I've been invited to enter. Like many Native friends, I now walk in two worlds, but, as I've said, I entered from a different direction.

I've sometimes said to my clients, "You can't step in the river in the same place twice." Through their generosity, I became a friend to many and a relative to several Yakama families ... but I must always be the brother or uncle from somewhere else. I've taken the Indian ways shared with me forever to heart and work to apply them to my life. I am deeply grateful. I will always feel welcome in this community, and I know of no other place on earth where I've ever felt this way.

POSITIVISM, THE QUANTIFICATION IMPERATIVE, AND THE QUALITATIVE

There are other outsiders who've journeyed further along than me into this community. I was once present in a Yakama sweat lodge where a *páshtin* man professing no Native heritage had been a brother for many years. I listened to him sing all the traditional songs during our sweat in fluent Yakama language. I never learned any to the degree he did, but I was glad to be taught at all.

Like me, psychiatrist E. Mansell Pattison, likely the first contemporary mental health consultant to tribes in the Pacific Northwest, was very affected by what he was allowed to witness and partake of in the mid-1960s, so much so that he wrote passionately about the limitations of Western approaches to emotional and psychological healing. For instance, he said in 1972:

> The Indigenous healer is of importance as a comparative model of psychotherapeutic methods ... And the Indigenous healer is important as healing resource within Western society itself. For although scientific psychotherapy is the paradigm among the intellectual elite of the West, there are many groups of people within Western society who do not ascribe to the scientific world view, and who do not seek or accept help from the professional psychotherapist.[11]

Dr. Pattison worked as a psychiatrist at a time prior to today's false technocracy of alleged brain disorders and drugs, well before the rise of "biological reductionism" in Indian Country brought along its psycho-pharmaceutical-industrial complex. Describing his support of a Yakama ceremony for an adolescent girl he termed an "exorcism," Pattison wrote:

> The alternative which I followed was to take the traditional Indian belief system *for real*. To accept the interpretation of cause and effect within that system for real also. And to support an intervention within that system that would indeed be *real*. [italics in original]
>
> My point is that I was not playing a game . . . as if my system of psychoanalytic interpretation was the real system, while their interpretation was a fake system. No, the traditional Indian belief system and the psychoanalytic belief system are two different ways of looking at and acting upon this life situation.[12]

Pattison was ahead of his time in questioning who "owns the reality" of healing in Native America. I also take Indigenous healing *for real*, and to do so increases my acceptance with community members while placing me at the fringe of my own profession—where I've sometimes sensed I'm viewed as having embraced "shamanism" or moved well out of my element, neither of which feels true or fair.

I am instead encountering and respecting forms of healing knowledge more ancient than European medicine by thousands of years. My particular view derives from powerful personal experiences I've had in relation to that knowledge as well as recognition that the allegedly material "realities" of "evidence-based practices" of the Western mental health movement are, in truth, cultural *metaphors*. The allegedly scientific within the U.S. mental health system in particular cannot claim to superiority over Indigenous healing practices—and, indeed, may be its inferior.

James Nelson and Brent Slife[13] use the term "positivistic naturalism" to describe Western psychology's generally negative treatment of the healing claims of spiritual practices and ceremony. Positivists favor a logical and systematic study of causal relationships in establishing what can be considered legitimate in Western mental health "healing." Thus, applied psychology and psychiatry—relatively new fields of human endeavor and philosophy intimately tied to Western individualism, industrialization, and domination—secularize the sacred, the spiritual, the soul, away from their philosophic purview. These professions position their positivism instead as a substitute for spiritual wisdom by proposing that measuring and categorizing human behavior and then assigning "meaning," "medicating," or "motivating" practices to helping the distraught or the disturbing.

Positivist naturalism has major implications toward obscuring specific life situations with which Native people struggle as well as their own spiritual understandings and solutions. Non-Native mental health providers meeting with Native clients every day hazard remaining entirely oblivious to an indoctrination process within the various psychotherapies they offer and recommend.

For instance, in their "quest for natural laws or law-like causal regularities in the universe"[14] that fit with a view of the human as mechanized, positivistic naturalists may be ready to sacrifice the sacred human being of the sweat lodge or the displaced soul of the Indian Shaker home meeting for the sake of the rationalist "cognitive-behaviorist." Such mental health providers are trained to serve the dominant culture's desire for certainty about why we do what we do or why we suffer.

The U.S. mental health system writ large continually misapplies psychological "universalism" through its research and application in Indian Country of screening tests or "self-quizzes" and its culturally nested concepts, i.e., laws and causes, for "depression" or "PTSD." Even more destructively, this nonsacred and non-Native philosophy uses its "positivity" to try to convince Native people themselves of supposed "disorders" and associated quasi-explanations of chemical imbalances and/or brain defects.

This outsider impetus toward Native America represents a *quantification imperative* by which EuroAmerican cultural values become *operationalized*.[15] Western social science specifies Native human beings as "subjects" and tries to isolate their variability from other facets of their life and in particular their locally lived context with their own unique language, history, and cultural and spiritual practices. Via this imperative, a Yakama person becomes interchangeable with any other Native person globally. Maori, Cree, Tulalip, or Yąnomamö are thereby remade into "depressed Natives" or "Indigenous substance abusers" from decontextualized realities. Various methods and statistical maneuvers are repeatedly applied by elite trained professionals charged with measuring "publicly observable phenomena"[16] that "maximize repeatability and reliability (law-like regularities), sometimes even at the expense of validity"[17] in a massive global numerical study of "Indigeneity."

What could possibly be missed? Psychologist Jack Martin at Simon Fraser University offers some clues:

> Psychological phenomena are meaningful, relational, non-extensive, interactive, socioculturally and historically constituted phenomena with moral and political significance. All of these attributes of psychological phenomena are non-quantitative. None of this is to deny that aspects/dimensions of such phenomena can be constructed along quantitative lines ... However, when this is done, the result typically is a "watering-down" of the phenomena of interest ... with the predictable consequence of studying not quite what one claims to be studying.[18]

Unfortunately, the same positivism imbuing many mental health studies of Native people shares its roots with other doctrines that amputated the hands of those refusing to embrace its Christian Lord. I have my friend and colleague Steven Newcomb (Shawnee Lenape) to thank for alerting me to this "domination code," or implicit language of power, traceable to papal (i.e., Christian) decree. If we turn Western cognitivism back to look at itself, we find this "code" embedded in the unconscious proclamations of many outsiders working in Indian Country, such as within my former mental health coworker's assertion that IHS "has always and will always use the medical model." Similar absolutist metaphors form the "image-schemas" that populate "the deep cognitive structure of the conceptual system of federal Indian law."[19] Steve elaborates:

> Ironically, although the meanings that are understood as constituting the "constraints" of federal Indian law are the result of imaginative processes that take place in the brain, even those of us who are Indigenous have been educated and conditioned to think and talk about these constraints of federal Indian law as if they were something *external* that rule *over* us [italics in original]. However, because the ideas that constitute federal Indian law and policy are a product of the EuroAmerican imagination, this means that the constraints of federal Indian law and policy originated in and are the result of the EuroAmerican imagination and social conventions. We as Indian people become coparticipants in this process.[20]

What Steve discerns as a code of domination within the U.S. legal system is equally salient within the "biological reductionism" of the U.S. mental health system in Native America.

THE HUMAN SPIRIT AS BIOLOGY

Reductionism is a generally laudable philosophy of physical science seeking to explain complex phenomena by isolating and specifying relationships between simpler elements. The misapplication of this philosophy within the U.S. mental health system was strengthened by the formal proclamation of the "Decade of the Brain" by President George H. W. Bush in July of 1990. By this act, the ground was laid for a resurgence of research into detecting alleged defects, impairments, and genetic deficiencies in the brains of the troubled and/or troubling in U.S. society.

In 2015 this futile pursuit led critical psychology writers Dolores Albarracin, Alain Ducousso-Lacaze, David Cohen, François Gonon, Pascal-Henri Keller, and Michel Minard to assert:

Since the 19th century, the failure of scientists to discover biological markers of mental disorders or illnesses has been accompanied by the misleading claim that real and necessary progress is being made. The distortion of research findings ... is commonplace in the field of mental health.[21]

The domination code within biological psychiatry and pharmaceutical marketing currently negates the restoration and rejuvenation of Native healing approaches. Instead, a foreign social, political, and cultural force imposes a language of "evidence-based best practices" within Native mental health serving psychiatric guild interests. W. Joseph Wyatt, psychology professor at Marshall University, and Donna Midkiff, director of therapeutic services at River Park Hospital in Huntington, Virginia, noted in 2007:

The American Psychiatric Association is engaged in self-serving advocacy of biological causation, and ... does so in the absence of conclusive scientific evidence. The psychiatric guild is evidently urging blind faith in the theory of biological causation, but is unable to produce the research evidence that would confirm it.[22]

The U.S. Indian Health Service (IHS) is the major purveyor of this guild's biopsychiatric ideology in Native America, and Native people often have no other resources to learn about alternative views pertaining to what the agency currently calls "behavioral health." There have been recent encouraging signs of in-house questioning, however. Consider, for example, strategy "III.B.2." of the Indian Health Service's *American Indian/Alaska Native National Behavioral Health Strategic Plan, 2011–2015*:

> Recognize the heavy influence of biomedical models in IHS as well as the need for more integrated care by creating a track within the various IHS health conferences and meetings that addresses behavioral health and integrated care.[23]

Sadly, this glimmer of organizational self-reflection is followed immediately by strategy III.B.3: "Assist the Indian Health System to make needed prescribed psychotropic medications available to persons served...."[24]

The history of this domination code in Native "mental hygiene" is directly traceable to male physicians of European descent inhabiting positions of authority and power over Indian health care for more than 120 years. They themselves are misled by their own history. In truth, even the iconic professional ancestor of today's Western bio-dominated view, Emil Kraepelin, decried the "naïve materialism"[25] of brain anatomists of his own time, while psychiatric historians Eric Engstrom and Matthias Weber conclude: "As paradoxical as it may sound in a Neo-Kraepelinian age, Kraepelin would have agreed with those who later sought to 'denosologize' his legacy."[26] Even the Kraepelin worshippers must reconcile with his encounters with the Indigenous people of Indonesia, where he noted that "the essential characteristics of a people are displayed in their religion and mores, in their spiritual and artistic achievements, in their political and historical development."[27]

BECOMING CONSTRUCTIVE

When I began graduate training at University of Detroit Mercy in 1986, I was fortunate to encounter teachers challenging the rising tide of biopsychiatry and the privileging of human quantification over qualitative understanding. By the time I arrived at Yakama IHS Clinic, I'd already been "traumatized" within my own personal life, and I carried within me the realities of what it feels like to suffer intensely, to become withdrawn, and to feel crazy. I'd also been through an internship and postdoctoral training in both short- and long-term psychiatric units. On many occasions I'd witnessed highly reactive people escalated by the reactivity of their "providers," who sometimes chased them down, compelled them into four-point restraints, and then "provided" them with haloperidol for refusing to conform or for frightening them by becoming a "danger to self or others."

I've held down people myself, which I hated having to do, including children trying to plunge knives into their chests or adolescents trying to drop large rocks on my head. I've been immersed in other people's sweat while trying to keep them from beating one another up, and felt the air of chairs whizzing over my head as fists were being shaken in my face. I've administered "neuropsychological screenings" to inpatients suffering permanent brain injury from electroconvulsive "treatments," co-led and trained interns in group psychotherapy with people labeled "actively psychotic," and worked extensively with individuals who heard voices, had visions, held frightening belief systems, or all three at once. This includes a Native young woman who informed me she saw her friend who'd committed suicide standing next to me and checking me out.

"What does he make of me?" I asked her.

"Maybe he'll trust you," she answered softly. "Maybe not...."

Long before I arrived at Yakama Nation, I realized that what gets called the "self" is constructed mostly out of what we're born into and experience, just as our "culture" refers to a great, living, dynamic story in which we come to play a part. Mi'kmaq-Acadian Charlotte Loppie describes an intersection between constructivism and Indigenous belief:

Western constructivist and Indigenous paradigms generally agree that reality is a product of multiple human constructions, woven from the fibers of individual and collective context, perception, and action. Each construction evolves over time and exists for as long as it is useful or until a new construction takes its place as a more reliable or relevant representation of reality. Reality is transformative and transactional. More simply put, each interaction represents a new negotiation, which creates the context, text, and subtext of human understanding, which is thus experienced within existential and embodied domains.[28]

A University of Detroit mentor, Patrick Kavanaugh, wrote from a psychoanalytic perspective along similar lines:

> The subject of contemporary times is understood as an *historical subject* spoken by language, history, and the specific discourses of the culture: He or she is constituted by interrelations and interconnection and is understood as being *something more* than the sum of his or her identifiable "parts." People and the external world are understood as shaped, if not constructed and constituted, by language, texts, codes, and images. [italics in original][29]

I believe my training and philosophic beliefs predisposed me to be at odds with the Yakama IHS medical model of bioreductionism and biopsychiatry. It is also why I felt drawn toward the cultural teachings of various Native friends. Although not entirely clear to me at the time, I came into Indian Country as a constructivist and liberation psychologist.

I was in no way the first to the party. Eduardo Duran and Bonnie Guillory, together with graduate student Michael Villaneuva, had already asserted over a decade earlier—in January 1990 (seven months prior to Bush's "Decade of the Brain")—that "the very tools that are available to research psychologists are contaminated with the ideology of White supremacy" and "policies of service delivery have been an integral part of a system that is searching for any means of social control in order to continue the social, political, economic, and spiritual exploitation of Third and Fourth World peoples."[30]

While their seminal paper was still "in press," I was "acting out" my own anti-authoritarianism as a graduate student by blowing internship interviews through my refusal to videotape clients. But Spanish Jesuit psychologist Ignacio Martín-Baró went much, much further, only to be gunned down by U.S.-trained Contra soldiers, sacrificing his life, and birthing the liberation psychology movement itself from his adopted home of El Salvador.

Martín-Baró's belief that "a psychology of liberation requires a prior liberation of psychology"[31] was only beginning to have an influence on others at that moment. By this, he meant providers and researchers in applied Western psychology should deeply consider their own history, take responsibility for their legacy in serving political and social domination and oppression, and then deliberately reconstruct their practices and methods. "Social forces," like psychology, he wrote, "are historical realities, and it is precisely this historicity that tends to be ignored in the dominant psycho-social analyses."[32]

Of these two principles, *historicity* and *concientización*, the latter was borrowed from Paulo Freire, whose *Pedagogy of the Oppressed* I first read during my solo lunches in my dimly lit office at Yakama IHS Clinic while often in big trouble for my views. *Concientización*, as I understand it, refers to the emerging awareness of being enmeshed in a historical predicament alongside a growing sense of agency and capability for intervening in it. I remember the palpable sense of this truth I had as I was first reading about such ideas inside the clinic. This state of awareness comes, according to Freire—who wrote from within a radically new view of education—through a given educator's capacity to "re-present" the universe, i.e., reality, back to a community in a manner that reveals its oppressive situation.[33] I've felt a sense of responsibility to try to serve this idea for many years now.

Concientización is both the teaching and learning of a capacity to "perceive social, political, and economic contradictions, and to take action against the oppressive elements of reality."[34] For Martín-Baró, *concientización* represented the awakening of a critical consciousness, and he saw this as particularly important for psychologists themselves if ever they were to effectively serve liberation. I must note that psychologists do not "provide" liberation but through their self-reflection and service to people *are themselves assisted toward it*. My own experience at Yakama Nation has felt very much allied with this idea.

I have so far asserted that the U.S. mental health system in Native America homogenizes, masks, and pacifies community reactivity to chronic social and political maltreatment and oppression by labeling, stigmatizing, and drugging individual Native suffering, falsely asserting that a "mentally disordered" Native suffers from a defective or imbalanced brain, and intervening ineffectively and even dangerously in the tragedy of Native suicide.

I've contended that models informing this mental health system are heavily skewed toward mainstream corporate interests and wider EuroAmerican political phenomena and values rather than relating to the unique situation, history, or ways of knowing protected by generations of Native people. This state of affairs is easily demonstrated by the whole-cloth importation of ideas about "trauma" that ignore genocide, cultural destruction, and the lack of control that Native people continue to experience in the course of their own healing journeys.

I've suggested that even community-grown or sanctioned concepts like "historical trauma" are at risk of being co-opted and rebranded. I'm still awaiting Pfizer's self-quiz form for postcolonial stress. I've also tried to illustrate the profound spiritual and philosophical disconnects between what I understand of the Yakama view of healing and Western positivism, biological reductionism, and the etiological medical model within Indian Health Service policies and practices.

Closely allied with *concientización*, Martín-Baró asserted the need to recover "historical memory," or *historicity*.[35] Thus far, I've only hinted at a pedigree of U.S. mental health practices in Native America; for example, in referring to Freud's early ideas of "psychic trauma" or Puritan John Eliot's acknowledgment of the Native soul and its redemption, and the implications of positivism and the quantification imperative in research in Indian Country.

In now offering more about the history of the U.S. mental health system's complicity in Native oppression, it's my hope that Native people and those whom they count as allies will draw their hearts and minds together to address the paradoxes between what seems to be past but is present and what seems to be new but is actually quite old.

ELEVEN

"The Continuance of Their Race"

GENERATIONAL ITERATIONS

There was a fifteen-year-old Native young man I knew quite well; I'll call him James.[1] He was fortunate to have a wonderful, loving grandmother, his *kála*, Eloise, who'd survived a great deal of tragedy in her life. Her son, James's father, had been sent to boarding school out of state in the mid-1980s for "behavior problems." As a result of criminal connections, he'd gradually become a main resource for local cannabis (well before its legalization in Washington State). James's father was still in prison as an accessory to murder when I met Eloise. He'd been a driver at age sixteen when his comrades took aim at rival gang members. By then he'd also fathered James.

Eloise's daughter-in-law and granddaughter (also *kála*) were involved in methamphetamine, the most abused drug among Native women in Washington State at that moment. They'd first gotten involved in this cottage industry as a way of supplementing their income in the HUD project neighborhood where they lived before becoming addicted themselves.

The meth problem was worse at Yakama Nation than it is now, partially due to law enforcement jurisdictional issues on the reservation and the ease of smuggling from Mexico into the rural backcountry. Less attention is paid to reservation lands by federal, state, and county authorities, and drug cartels know it. Also, rigorous enforcement by Canadian authorities on illegal pseudoephedrine importing from China to British Columbia had mostly shut down Yakima Valley meth labs, and the bulk of meth now came from Michoacán, Mexico.

Among other effects, methamphetamine makes one feel very powerful and strong. Used by pilots on both the Allied and Axis sides of World War II, it was abandoned for lesser amphetamine alternatives when people started to show hyperaggression and erratic behavior as side effects. But its appeal resurged in the 1980s via biker gangs, who hired chemists to synthesize it and then stored their stashes in the crankcases of their motorcycles—hence its old nickname, "crank."

I've spent much time with people who've successfully backed away from meth addiction. (It's a fiction that one can't do so, although the road is very difficult.) They've told me about their gradual migration from abuse to addiction via the sense that meth helped them work several jobs, made them very organized, or greatly improved their sex life. One domestic violence survivor told me she became a meth addict by using it as a means to stay wide-awake for days at a time while grasping a loaded pistol and protecting herself and her baby from the man who'd vowed to kill them both.

The meth phenomenon quickly stimulated existent small youth gangs in both Upper and Lower Yakima Valley to affiliate in various ways with incoming representatives of rival Sureños or Norteños gangs. Florencia-13 (or F13), among many others, became a subject of local graffiti all over Yakama Nation land.

As I began working there, I quickly came to know Native young people who'd been shot at. Some ended up wounded or murdered. I developed a cheat sheet to help me keep track of fluctuating youth gang names, tags, and affiliations. The climate of gang violence I knew well back then has continued, unfortunately, and reached a crescendo in the murder of five people in White Swan in 2019, which brought national media attention.[2]

James was involved with F13 and imperiled as the "last one standing" in his family. Eloise was all he had, and she hoped to save him from the imprisonment or addiction all around him. She had her own story to tell me of being kidnapped by local ranch hands working part-time for boarding school officials. Yet her family name was associated with eminent Native leaders of legendary wisdom. Eloise did all she could to teach James about their family story. But, surrounded by chaos and at such a vulnerable age, he sometimes found it difficult to pay attention.

Eloise called me at the suggestion of another elder, and we got to know one another over coffee. She brought me a small baggie stuffed with huckleberries she'd handpicked from a secret spot she once went to with her husband up on Pahto[3] before he walked on. She wept as she talked about missing him and her hopes for James. The honor of her gift was profoundly traditional: I was being formally approached as an accepted helper and healer. She explained what a great artist James was, expressing her heartfelt desire to help him stay in school. Her poor health limited her ability to talk him into abandoning the path he was on. She told me, "He's too far gone for me to reach; maybe you can." Her appeal to me felt enormous, and I worried about disappointing her.

James still visited Eloise regularly and went to school, and this was where I first met him. He'd long since been channeled into special education, the catch-all environment for any child considered ill-suited for one-size-fits-all public education. The special education teacher thought I was going to update his "learning evaluation." She introduced me to James as follows: "This is Dr. Walker. He's going to test you to figure out your impairments and deficits." If someone had told me a teacher would say this to a student, I would have been incredulous. But I have my own profession's history to blame for her academic socialization.

James agreed to speak with me only because Eloise wanted him to do so. First, I apologized for the confusion and tried to distance myself from the teacher's introduction. He responded by telling me a brief story about a white counselor he knew in middle school who'd told him, "Indian kids shouldn't aim too high." He described this same person as pointing to a Native janitor in the school and saying, "But don't end up like your uncle there."

James's story hung in the air between us like a question: Was this what I meant by expressing open disapproval about the way his teacher had introduced me to him? He was telling me about the breadth of his own experience in being maligned and excluded. His willingness to do so was a positive signal, and we started off in counseling together doing quite well.

About a month after our first meeting, Eloise had a massive stroke and died. I went to her memorial and stood outside listening to Indian Shaker songs being sung and bells being rung. The funeral home was packed, and as the service ended, I saw James exit with a crowd of relatives, including his mom and sister. They all appeared devastated. The presence of the community certainly helped, but I knew James faced more anguish after Eloise was buried.

After this, whenever James showed up for classes, the principal, teachers, and I would try to encourage him to stay in school. I believe he was willing to continue meeting with me only because he saw me as an extension of Eloise's last wishes. Soon, James began missing school so frequently that he faced expulsion. His truancy seemed an expression of grief: if Eloise was gone, so was he. He'd lost hope; the world that told him not to aim too high must be right.

The few sessions that followed Eloise's efforts to intervene in James's gang involvement led him to believe he'd stressed her into having her stroke. He told me he appreciated talking with me, but I wasn't enough to keep him in school. I had to accept this: Eloise was James's only real "psychotherapist" (from the Greek, *psyche*, goddess of breath and soul, and *therapeia*, healing). I couldn't coordinate my schedule to get to the various places he slept anyway, and I wouldn't have felt safe doing so. But Eloise wouldn't have hesitated.

One day, a nurse at a small hospital called me to say James had gotten into a terrible fight. He'd specifically asked if I'd come visit him. As it turned out, I was the only one called. I got there about two hours later and found him in his hospital bed with both arms covered in thick white bandages. His face and forehead had nicks and abrasions. An IV drip with painkillers made him a bit loopy. In a slurred monotonic voice, he explained that he had received seventy or so stitches in various places on his arms. Beneath his numbness, superficial apathy, and toughness, James let me to know he'd been beaten to within an inch of his life. He was still only fifteen years old.

Nurses flitted in and out to tend to his lacerations. One nurse was quite kind, and I recall gazing at James's quiet eyes as she so gently moved his arms to work with his dressings. I wanted her to clean him up better, or sit with him and watch TV for a few minutes, because I knew I'd have to leave. I wanted her to know he'd just lost Eloise, who would have sat all night praying for him. I felt like an uncle who wasn't doing and couldn't do enough.

James brushed off my attempts to locate his mother or sister. "I wouldn't want them around right now," he chuckled at his bandages, wires, and monitors.

His eyes glazed while he tried to smile, and I felt how sad he was. I asked where he would go after he was discharged. He said, "I never sleep in the same place twice," making necessity seem more like choice. Then he seemed to realize something in my question and looked at me intensely. "I'll run if you or anybody else tries to put me anywhere."

I stayed by his bedside for another half an hour or so, watching *SpongeBob* with him. A couple of times I mentioned being sorry about his injuries. This was my very indirect way of saying, "I'm sorry your *káta* isn't here." I felt that to say anything like that out loud would have been too much.

I finally made it to the doorway, and I think we both realized that when I left he'd be utterly alone. I said goodbye anyway, and James nodded at me but looked straight ahead. I stopped by the nurses' station and asked if any of them had time to sit with him. The kindly nurse said she'd try, but shift change was coming. I got into my car, took out my keys, and wept.

The doctors kept him for a while to watch for infection. The state already knew about James through them, of course, and I don't believe anyone else ever visited him other than me and a beleaguered social worker. This worker found a group home for him in Spokane, well away from his gangster friends. James resisted the idea wholeheartedly, but she laid out what would happen if he didn't comply, and he finally gave in.

After that, I would hear about James periodically at a weekly Local Indian Child Welfare Advisory Committee (LICWAC) meeting. Eventually, he made good on his vow to run. I never saw or heard from him again. I still have a photo he gave me a few weeks before Eloise died. His fanciest gangster cap is inverted on his head and multiple chains hang around his neck. He's holding his hand up by his face making a gang sign, staring back, completely lost. The thread of generations comes through him. The last knot Eloise could tie on her time ball was threaded in faux gold around his neck.

Several years went by, and I heard from another client that James sold meth and had bought a fancy motorcycle. I'm sure he'd never owned anything of such value in his entire life. A few more months passed before I learned he'd gone "over the high side" out on Canyon Road between Ellensburg and Yakima. I was too late to go to his funeral.

I carry other stories like that of James in my heart. No special professional armor can ever shield me from the premature demise of children like him caught in inescapable situations. One summer day, several of my graduate students watched in shock as their professor wept on the shoulders of a tearful grandfather during a Treaty Days gathering at Yakama Nation. I could only explain that my impromptu meltdown was a part of their professional orientation to Native America.

MORTON'S SKULLS AND GENERATIONAL CARRY

When I think about the special education teacher introducing me as a detective of "impairments and deficits" or a middle school counselor telling James "Indian kids shouldn't aim high" or pointing to an uncle's work as a claim to shame, I feel a duty to understand how these ideologies have survived so that we might surface, expose, and unteach them. I suspect they date all the way back to initial contact between Europeans and Native peoples of North America. My focus here, however, is necessarily placed upon their lines of descent through the U.S. mental health system.

On a summer day in Philadelphia in 1830, a young professor of anatomy, Dr. Samuel George Morton, felt stymied. A recently graduated physician from the University of Pennsylvania, he was preparing an introductory lecture he'd entitled "The Different Forms of the Skull as Exhibited in the Five Races of Men," but he was short on actual examples to show his students.

"Forcibly impressed with this great deficiency in a most important branch of science," Morton wrote, "I at once resolved to make a collection for myself."[4]

Today, we might call Morton "racist," but he was not necessarily an evil person. In our current time, the word "racist" carries undeniably violent and oppressive significance. We benefit by tracing today's violence to older academic beliefs rooted in white supremacy. Morton and others like him simply believed in the scientific validity of "race" as a form of human classification. This constitutes the heart of a racist view, of course, but not enough of us think of it as a basic assumption leading to violence and disaster, even today. There are still many academic "racists" of this sort around.

More particularly, Morton believed in the intellectual superiority of the "Caucasian ... [as] characterised by a naturally fair skin, susceptible of every tint"[5] over all other races he described. Through his writings, Samuel Morton fortified the place of "races" in American academic science while simultaneously helping to deepen the concept of a supreme white race entitled to use its presumed intelligence to rule over all others.

By the mid-nineteenth century, Morton's ideas were "reified"—that is, so well accepted that "race" was now imbued with a "thingness," solidified and beyond conceptual debate. At the same moment, similar scientists in the United States and Britain were beginning to promote *polygenism*, which proposed a hereditary view of separate races and racial characteristics.

Even way back then, Morton's ideas were not without controversy. He was challenging anatomists like Johann Friedrich Blumenbach (1752–1840) and James Cowles Prichard (1786–1848) who, while also embracing white supremacism, considered the presumed intellectual and moral superiority of European people to arise not from an inherent, inborn capacity but instead from "influences of history and environment on one original stock, and . . . these influences could be reversed if the conditions of 'less favored' races were changed."[6]

To be born inferior but capable of some potential—we can bear witness to these ideas in the middle school counselor: Don't aim too high but also reach your potential. They are the same "seeds of redemption" for souls of peoples presumed barbarous and/or savage by European Christian missionary clergy. They are also a historically philosophic core of the U.S. mental health system in Indian Country.

Writing about Native people of North America in 1839 for his first book, *Crania Americana*, Morton argued for a racial hierarchy, a "primitive distribution of mankind into races" favoring the "Caucasian" with "the highest intellectual endowments."[7] He was relying upon the cultural values with which his lived context was imbued. He was also pointing to what he considered to be solid evidence regarding Native people:

> I have in my collection four Cherokee heads for which I am indebted to the kindness of Dr. J. Martin of the United States Army. On comparing with the one belonging to the Phrenological Society, I find them all small, the largest not equalling the average of European skulls, and the mean of the series giving but seventy-nine cubic inches of internal capacity, while the mean of facial angle is seventy-six degrees.[8]

It would be instructive to learn where these Native heads were obtained, especially by an Army surgeon. However, we must turn instead toward the pseudoscience of Morton's "craniometry," where we can see the positivistic *quantification imperative* being applied to Native people possibly for the first time—long before measures of their depressive moods via the PHQ-9 or their traumatic experiences using the PTSD self-quiz (both Pfizer creations).

During his lifetime of frailty and disease—ending ten years before the publication of Darwin's *On the Origin of Species*—Morton established himself as "the father of biological American anthropology."[9] Pausing in his cataloguing of the more than eight hundred skulls of North American Native people he'd collected, obsessively detailed, and sketched, he reflected an unexpected sympathy belying his "racist" prose that suggests a rather complex character:

> A system of encroachment and oppression has been practised upon them since the first landing of the Europeans on the shores of America: their lands have been seized upon with the most frivolous

of pretences, and they have had no redress at the hand of the white man: wars have been fomented among them to procure their mutual destruction; and when they have been weakened by the conflict, the common enemy has stepped in and seized their possessions. They have been taken in their villages, or inveigled on ship-board, to be sold into slavery; and in fact every art that cupidity could devise has been put into practice to deprive them of liberty and life. Is it surprising that a people thus oppressed should retaliate against their oppressors? Or shall we stigmatise them as treacherous when they have received so much treachery at our hands?[10]

What to make of Dr. Morton? How can his context as an academic "racist" be understood alongside his psychosocial sympathies? In the history of Western social science, Samuel George Morton became iconic in characterizing the Native American as a "mental being," and his *Crania Americana* constituted a seminal *observer effect* for an emerging Native mental hygiene movement that brought about the stigmatizing and oppression he apparently abhorred.

By "observer effect," I'm borrowing from professor and cyberneticist Stuart A. Umpleby's assertion that scientists, including social scientists, can greatly affect society through the ideologies they embrace. Or, as Umpleby has it: "We are aware that theories affect society.... [T]hat is why we create social science theories."[11]

No matter how sympathetic he may have felt toward Native people, Morton's theories were germane to a generational ideology of white supremacy. This idea of observer effects is not new—but what might we learn from it with respect to *historicity*? Mark Amadeus Notturno of the Interactivity Foundation (and a friend of Sir Karl Popper) suggests that

different observers may have different characteristics, including different sensory capacities, beliefs, and biases; that their different characteristics may affect the nature and quality of their observations; and that theories may have impacts upon the systems they describe when we apply them to alter those systems."[12]

Many Native epistemologies recognize the interdependent web of existence and the idea that one's personal actions and biases may radically and chaotically alter entire life systems. Researching implicit metatheories within the applied social science that informs the mental health system, especially in relation to their embedded ideas of white supremacy, would seem an important direction to consider before applying these ideas directly to Native communities.

It seems reasonable to say that a well-positioned social observer, Samuel George Morton, once told a story about a "Native race" and his belief in the intellectual superiority of "Caucasians." This story was soon picked up by many EuroAmericans of his time and taught to their children as well as to Native children. Today it represents a prime example of how a trumped-up belief can be recast as "fact" and create untold misery. I've chosen my wording of this last sentence deliberately.

Of course, Samuel George Morton's research was famously impugned in 1981 in Stephen Jay Gould's *The Mismeasure of Man* as "subjectivity directed toward prior prejudice."[13] In other words, Gould considered Morton unconsciously biased. One might hope Gould's analysis laid Morton's premises to rest, but as recently as 2016 a debate emerged within Western academia in which Gould himself was accused of biasing his critiques of Morton's early skull measurements. Others rose to Gould's defense, asserting the claim of "prima facia evidence of unconscious bias in *Crania Americana* remains intact."[14] And still we see popular contemporary political scientists like Charles Murray defend the false belief that "race" is "more than a social construct," and "class structure is importantly based on differences in abilities that have a substantial genetic component."[15]

It is both amazing and frightening to consider such debates continue 170 years after Samuel George Morton. I wonder how far his "observer effect" will extend into the future. His particular version of human "races" remains so intrinsic to academic medicine, anthropology (initially ethnology), psychology, education, and sociology that these fields can't seem to extract themselves. Countless journal articles still divide by race, analyze by race, and rejuvenate another theory that evolved from his ideas: that of "race difference."

GALTON'S EUGENICISTS AND NATIVE STERILIZATION

If whites were superior, as Morton and others had proclaimed, scientific white men of an emerging industrial age felt they should be able to prove it. Lewis Henry Morgan extended Morton's system of cranial volume measurement for his book *Ancient Societies; or, Researches in the Lines of*

Human Progress from Savagery Through Barbarism to Civilization.[16] Morgan proposed cranium measurement as a means to scientifically substantiate the alleged limited intelligence of Native people. He was highly influential among numerous founding cultural evolutionists within the new field of *ethnology*, which would eventually be renamed *anthropology*.

Like mid-nineteenth century French ethnologist Joseph-Arthur, comte de Gobineau,[17] cultural evolutionists asserted a "parallelism between biological evolution and cultural evolution."[18] Famous cultural evolutionists include Herbert Spencer, Sir James George Frazer, Sir Edward Burnett Tylor, and Hutton Webster. These early anthropology theorists believed cultures foreign to their own should be evaluated against the European ideal of "civilization." Assuming Native Americans had little capacity for extending the concept of an agricultural community, for instance, Morgan claimed they represented "the zero of human society," with "no help of elevation."[19,20] Under his and others' influence, an era of frequent pilfering of Indian graves began.

Building upon cultural evolutionism, Sir Francis Galton established himself as an intellectual elder and seminal observer for future generations of applied psychologists, founding an international movement for which he coined the term "eugenics" in 1883. He described his new pseudoscience as a means to "improve the human stock" by giving "more suitable races or strains of blood a better chance of prevailing speedily over the less suitable."[21] Competing with his cousin, Charles Darwin, who certainly approved of his ideas,[22] Galton asserted his social version of natural selection by which northern Europeans and EuroAmerican "stock" should somehow eventually come to reign over everyone else.

Galton and his many followers stimulated a global agenda for identifying those races least suitable for continued existence.[23] Not surprisingly, Native people of North America became a favorite target. Galton never made any direct observations of American Indians, having never met any. Yet, from his cozy armchair early in his career, he proclaimed them to be "naturally cold, melancholic, patient, and taciturn" with "youths [who] treat their parents with neglect, and often with such harshness and insolence as to horrify Europeans who have witnessed their conduct."[24] He contended "[their] mothers have been seen to commit infanticide without the slightest discomposure," suggesting this was the means by which "numerous savage tribes have died out in consequence."[25] They "nourish a sullen reserve, and show little sympathy for each other, even when in great distress."[26]

Later on in his career, Galton relented, at least partially, accepting that "[t]he Red Man has everywhere great patience, great reticence, great dignity," but nonetheless possessed "the minimum of affectionate and social qualities compatible with the continuance of his race."[27] The phrase has hints of ethnocidal intent to us now, and this seems accurate; hesitation about "the gradual extinction of an inferior race" was to Galton an "unreasonable" sentiment resting upon "some confusion between the race and the individual, as if the destruction of a race was equivalent to the destruction of a large number of men."[28]

Such rhetoric was not unusual, and as a founding father of Western psychology Galton's ideas were widely read and accepted. In 1889 he was invited to address a conference on physiological psychology in Paris with other major psychology figures like William James and Jean-Martin Charcot.[29] Carl Jung credited Galton as a resource for the free associative method that contributed to psychoanalysis[30] and liberally applied racial evolutionist ideas. Jung wrote in 1930:

> Racial infection is a most serious mental and moral problem where the primitive outnumbers the white man. America has this problem only in a relative degree, because the whites far outnumber the coloured. Apparently, he can assimilate the primitive influence with little risk to himself.[31]

James, in contrast, sparred with academics applying Darwinian theory to social phenomena and viewed "talk of the contemporary sociological school about averages and general laws and predetermined tendencies, with its obligatory undervaluing of individual differences, as the most pernicious and immoral of fatalisms."[32] The historic adjacency of these iconic psychology figures to Sir Francis Galton signals the degree to which his ideas were nonetheless considered relevant, scientific, and authoritative.

Eugenics took off with near-religious fervor,[33] causing a Galton contemporary, sociologist Caleb W. Saleeby, to remark "in all quarters of the globe, north and south of the Equator, there are bodies of persons who are interested in this matter."[34] Prominent followers within American psychology became members of the advisory committee to the recently founded American Eugenics Society, including Edward Lee Thorndike, James McKeen Cattell, Carl Brigham, Lewis Terman, Robert Yerkes, G. Stanley Hall, Charles Hubbard Judd, Robert Sessions Woodworth, and

Henry Herbert Goddard.[35] In all, six presidents of the American Psychological Association remained closely engaged with the American eugenics movement through the mid-1920s.[36]

Henry Herbert Goddard and his protégés were likely the first to apply eugenics concepts to intellectual assessment through the U.S. Public Health Service, out of which the Indian Health Service would one day emerge. These psychologists were early gatekeepers at the country's borders. Immigrants who failed their screenings at Ellis Island received a chalk-marked "X" high up on the front of their right shoulders, which meant they were considered "mentally defective," and were not allowed to enter the United States.

Goddard was a pioneer of psychological testing who greatly increased the prestige of academic positivists in intelligence measurement by translating French psychologist Alfred Binet's IQ tests into English and then adding the term "moron" to that of "idiot" in demarcating degrees of poor performance. For his own part, he strongly believed that "no feeble-minded person should ever be allowed to marry or to become a parent."[37]

U.S. Public Health Service psychologists administer IQ testing to immigrant woman, 1917.

Goddard's translation of Binet's intelligence tests was readapted by his eugenicist colleague, psychologist Lewis Terman, into what Terman awkwardly entitled the "Stanford Revision and Extension of the Binet-Simon Intelligence Scale." This test evolved into the Stanford-Binet Intelligence Scales, which are still in use in both research and learning disability determination today.[38]

The Stanford has an even darker past, however, for helping determine whether an individual should lose the right to reproduce. For example, California, one of twenty-four states to enact sterilization laws for people determined to be feebleminded, used the Stanford-Binet "as the primary psychometric measure of mental deficiency" and "led the nation with 6,787 court-ordered sterilizations" by 1930.[39] Having administered similar tests, I've often wondered what it must have been like for applied psychologists to have the role of helping decide if someone would be allowed to have children or not. Did they ever object to this application of their profession on moral grounds?

Alongside developing the Stanford-Binet, Lewis Terman suspected "mental deficiency" to be very common among "Spanish-Indian and Mexican families" and, like Goddard, asserted "if we would preserve our state for a class of people worthy to possess it, we must prevent, as far as possible, the propagation of mental degenerates."[40] Both men were supporting the mission of *negative eugenics*, which aims to reduce births among those considered inferior via sterilization or propaganda and contrasts with *positive eugenics*, which entails promoting increased reproduction among those of EuroAmerican lineage, particularly so-called Nordic or Teutonic "racial strains."

Terman also echoed an ideology that had already infiltrated the educational philosophies of American Indian boarding schools:

> The fact that one meets this type [feebleminded individuals] with such frequency among Indians, Mexicans, and negroes suggests quite forcibly that the whole question of racial differences in mental traits will have to be taken up anew and by experimental methods....
>
> Children of this group should be segregated in special classes and be given instruction which is concrete and practical. They cannot master abstractions, but they can often be made efficient workers, able to look out for themselves. There is no possibility of convincing society that they should not be allowed to reproduce, although from a eugenic point of view they constitute a grave problem because of the unusually prolific breeding.[41]

Lewis Terman was elected president of the American Psychological Association in 1923 and joined Henry Goddard on the advisory committee of the American Eugenics Society in 1925. By the time psychologist Nathaniel D. Mttron Hirsch published *A Study of Natio-Racial Differences*[42] in 1926, several other psychologists had already launched research on Native youth in boarding schools. Given his emerging belief in the "constitutional psycho-biological deviation" of "juvenile delinquency,"[43] Hirsch hoped to generalize the "blood quantum" concept of Native tribal membership more widely outside of Indian Country.

With a nod back to craniometrists like Morton, Hirsch mentioned "the Cephalic Index [head circumference] under the circumstances, could not be taken"[44] but stated authoritatively in his table "A Comparison of the Intelligence of the nine Types *without* regard to National groups" that individuals with dark hair and black or brown eyes had the lowest average IQ.[45] In this way, he impugned Native youth on two fronts: by comparing them with undesirable foreigners and by depicting their own negative "anthropometric characteristics."

FEEBLEMINDED AND STERILIZED

The most famous eugenics survivor was Carrie Buck, who was Tutelo, a tribe initially inhabiting areas of what would become Virginia and North Carolina that fled north in the eighteenth century and were adopted by the Haudenosaunee, also known as the Six Nations of the Iroquois Confederacy.[46]

TABLE 30
A Comparison of the Intelligence of the nine Types
without regard to National groups

Type of Coloration	Nos.	I. Q. Av.
1. Light Hair and Blue Eyes	232	98.6
2. Light Hair and Gray or Hazel Eyes	157	98.1
3. Light Hair and Dark Eyes (Brown or Black)	26	92.9
4. Medium Colored Hair and Blue Eyes (Brown or Chestnut)	413	97.0
5. Medium Colored Hair and Gray or Hazel Eyes	456	96.7
6. Medium Colored Hair and Dark Eyes	381	94.0
7. Black Hair and Blue Eyes	165	94.6
8. Black Hair and Gray or Hazel Eyes	218	94.4
9. Black Hair and Dark Eyes (Brown or Black)	858	90.6

Table of IQ by hair and eye color from Nathaniel Hirsch, *A Study of Natio-Racial Mental Differences*, 1926.

Carrie, whose mother, Emma, had been detained at the Virginia State Colony for Epileptics and Feebleminded, in Lynchburg, grew up in foster care raised by a white family.[47] She was eighteen years old, poor, and uneducated when, after being raped by her boyfriend, a nephew of her foster parents,[48] she became pregnant and, soon thereafter, a test case for forced sterilization in Virginia. Testimony was given as to her "mental defectiveness evidenced by failure of mental development, having chronological age of 18 years, with a mental age of 9 years, according to Stanford Revision of Binet-Simon Test"[49] when she lost her U.S. Supreme Court challenge to Virginia's Racial Integrity Act of 1924 and was sterilized against her will.[50]

Prior to World War II, eugenicists in U.S. society created public policies leading to the forced sterilization of more than 60,000 individuals. The tragic stories of Native survivors of this era were still being told among Abenaki tribal members[51] and Canadian Aboriginal communities[52] when I began working at the Indian Health Service in 2000.

Inspired by American and British eugenics thought leaders, U.S. public sterilization legislation evoked great interest among German Nazis, including psychiatrist Ernst Rudin, who became chair of the committee on race psychiatry of the International Federation of Eugenics Organizations (IFEO) in 1932 and eventually president of the IFEO itself.[53] Rudin was director of the department of genealogy and demography at the Kaiser Wilhelm Institute of Anthropology, Human Heredity, and Eugenics in Munich, supported in part by the Rockefeller Foundation on behalf of its mission to locate "the genetic and neurological basis of traits such as criminal propensity and mental disease."[54]

If this ideological goal sounds eerily similar to the Neo-Kraepelinians of the *DSM* and today's biopsychiatrists, the generational carry is not coincidental. The Kaiser Wilhelm Institute of Anthropology, Human Heredity, and Eugenics was founded as the Institute for Psychiatry in 1918 by Emil Kraepelin, an "ardent proponent of eugenics and 'degeneration theory.'"[55] The name was changed in 1924[56] when Rudin took over as institute director and linked German biological psychiatry to its wealthy oligarchy of eugenics sympathizers in the United States.[57]

One of those helping locate the alleged racial-genetic mental disease of deviance was psychiatric sadist Josef Mengele, who shipped body parts of murdered Jews, including pairs of eyes, from Auschwitz back to his mentor, Otmar Freiherr von Verschuer, at Kaiser for study during World War II.[58] Records of the institute were lost or hidden after the war, and although several key staff members were prosecuted by Soviet and East German authorities, many more escaped safely to the West, and became "denazified."

With the horrific revelations of the Jewish Holocaust, eugenics fell into public disfavor after World War II, and enthusiasts began couching their ideologies within softer language. Nonetheless, use of the term "eugenics" survived the war and continued to be used in public health training into the late 1950s. Intelligence tests used for demonstrating racial superiority were now respun as tools for the "disadvantaged."

Psychiatrist Paul Lemkau exhibits these types of revisions in his postwar (1949) textbook, *Mental Hygiene in Public Health*.[59] Lemkau rationalizes segregation and lowered expectations for "mentally deficient" children who typically would have been impugned as inferior along racial lines prior to the war:

> It is accepted that mentally deficient children need special attention in the educational process, and special classes are set up for them. . . . [B]ut the general trend is to lessen the amount of academic work the child is called upon to do and increase the manual part of learning, further increasing this trend as the child becomes older until he is learning the rudiments of some trade or skill in which he can work after the school years.[60]

Little difference can be seen between Lemkau stating these children should be "learning some trade or skill" and Lewis Terman's call that they be "given instruction which is concrete and practical."[61] Lemkau also believed individuals deemed feebleminded contributed to illegitimate births, poverty, and disease, and modern public health should take more responsibility for intervening. He continued to rework eugenics-based ideas into a genetic determinism consistent with today's biomedical mental health philosophies at the Indian Health Service:

> A good deal of the constitutional core on which the personality structure is built is genetically determined. Mental hygiene must then concern itself with the improvement, so far as possible, of this genetically determined core.[62]

In this kind of language, we find the nucleus of today's special education classroom. Although "mainstreaming" to regular classrooms has since been mandated in many places, the stigmatizing features of special education "determinations" still negatively affect many children's futures.

This is particularly true regarding diagnosis of Native children across Indian Country with ADHD. The evolution of this psychiatric diagnostic label is linked historically to the "feeblemindedness" label affixed to children in Indian boarding schools. In my opinion, ADHD is its contemporary equivalent. Rates of ADHD diagnoses for Native children have consistently tracked as the highest of any ethnic category, climbing steadily since 1997, and only recently have rates for children from other backgrounds caught up.[63] ADHD diagnosis among all U.S. children living in poverty increased by 50 percent between 1998 and 2009 under policies of "early intervention" promoted by the CDC, IHS, and other agencies. Each ADHD-labeled child qualifies for special education services, a circumstance that may bring extra funding sources to poorer, less resourced schools but also creates an incentive to diagnose.

I attribute the proliferation of ADHD diagnoses in Indian Country to the "domination code" of the biomedical model at the Indian Health Service. Pseudoscientific claims abound at this federal agency, such as that of psychiatrist Elise Leonard, a deputy director of behavioral health for IHS Phoenix, who cited a variety of biopsychiatric research findings to her in-house colleagues in an April 2013 webinar while asserting ADHD is "about 80 percent genetically determined."[64] And yet *no gene, brain lesion, or chemical imbalance for ADHD has ever been established or replicated in research*, much of which is easily critiqued and debunked.[65] A false biopsychiatric ideology reflected by Dr. Leonard and many other physicians continues to prevail in the U.S. mental health system in Indian Country, a phenomenon of remnant eugenics philosophies, political oppression, and corporate marketing masking itself as science.

The Indigenous Peoples Council on Biocolonialism[66] has commented upon the implications of genetics pseudoscience for subjugating Native American epistemology:

> By focusing on reactions to changes in genetic materials in organisms (including humans), genetics takes a very mechanistic view of the world. Life forms are viewed as mere machines, in that the research tries to change one part of the "subject" organism in order to get different "output" ... This view is in conflict with a view that recognizes the interrelatedness and interdependence of all living things. Tampering with one aspect of creation necessarily has effects on all other aspects.[67]

There continue to be academic opinion leaders who minimize or sanitize the role of applied psychology and psychiatry in eugenics.[68] And in both under-graduate and graduate psychology training, students are often accountable for understanding Sir Francis Galton and his followers' contributions to statistics and psychometrics but are seldom taught to recognize their oppressive and marginalizing purposes. In particular, graduate clinical and counseling psychology training demands students master statistical principles of the bell-shaped or normal curve (Gaussian distribution)—isolated by Galton's biographer and admirer Karl Pearson—but don't contemplate its original purpose in supporting the hereditary entitlement of the British aristocracy.[69] After all, it was the bell curve's "objectified entitlement" that found funding from wealthy, elite white Americans backing eugenics and its many goals,[70] including compelling the forced assimilation of Native American children.

EUGENICS' GENERATIONAL CARRY AND EMMA

Emma[71] visited with me for several months regarding an unrelenting grief, an "ambiguous" loss[72]—that is, one without ceremony or community recognition but unbearable in its force.[73] Her two children had reached adulthood, but each died tragically, one from disease, another in a car wreck. Emma was overwhelmed with constant regret, but these losses were only the part of the picture. If only she'd been able to have more children, she told me . . . but that opportunity had been taken from her long ago by physicians at the Indian Health Service. Emma had been coerced into having a total hysterectomy during the 1970s when she was in her early thirties, a fate occurring not at the height of the eugenics era but two generations later.

Writing for *American Indian Quarterly* in 2000, law professor Jane Lawrence noted that "various studies revealed that the Indian Health Service sterilized between 25 and 50 percent of Native American women between 1970 and 1976."[74] Although sterilization can be considered a necessary medical procedure for a woman's health, coercion became part of the picture for many Native women visiting IHS during this period. In an examination of just four out of twelve IHS hospitals, a Government Accountability Office (GAO) study found that patient consent to steril-ization was not "informed"; in other words, Native women were not made aware that they would *not* lose treaty-guaranteed federal or welfare benefits if they declined the procedure.

These women reported that physicians approached them with a "recommended" sterilization procedure when they were entering labor, while medicated, without an interpreter for those who spoke only their Native language, and often in tandem with state social workers who would threaten them with loss of their children if they did not comply.[75] Additionally, the Native women interviewed by GAO researchers indicated that physicians failed to inform them that sterilization was irreversible or that other, less invasive options were available.[76] Such manipulative and coercive practices continued despite a court order by federal judge Gerhard Gessel that women must be fully advised of their reproductive rights prior to undergoing sterilization.[77]

What motivated these doctors? Relying upon contemporaneous research conducted by the Health Research Group and Dr. Bernard Russell, Lawrence offers several compelling ideas:

> The majority of physicians were white, Euro-American males who believed that they were helping society by limiting the number of births in low-income, minority families. They assumed that they were enabling the government to cut funding for Medicaid and welfare programs while lessening their own personal tax burden to support the programs. Physicians also increased their own personal income by performing hysterectomies and tubal ligations instead of prescribing alternative methods of birth control. Some of them did not believe that American Indian and other minority women had the intelligence to use other methods of birth control effectively and that there were already too many minority individuals causing problems in the nation, including the Black Panthers and the American Indian Movement. Others wanted to gain experience to specialize in obstetrics and gynecology and used minority women as the means to get that experience at government expense. Medical personnel also believed they were helping these women because limiting the number of children they could have would help minority families to become more financially secure in their own right while also lessening the welfare burden.[78]

The effects of these physician biases were disastrous. In the 1970 U.S. census, the average Native woman in the United States had 3.79 children; by 1980 that average had fallen to 1.99. No other explanation can hold a candle to IHS coercive sterilization in explaining this dramatic decline:[79] this was a direct extension of pre–World War II negative eugenics being practiced in more recent times, more evidence of *generational carry*. The drop varied among tribal communities; by the end of the decade, Apache women, for instance, had half as many children as in 1980.[80] Although the Native population in the United States has since rebounded, there are still many whose lives were irrevocably altered by underground eugenics at the Indian Health Service.

My client, Emma, was a survivor. What she experienced was part of a system-wide phenomenon, but the ethics of what happened has still never been truly contemplated—at least, not publicly—by the Indian Health Service. In his careful analysis of Native sterilizations of the 1970s, medical ethicist and physician Gregory W. Rutecki concludes:

> The cultural evidence supports, at least for I.H.S. physicians exempt from greed, a push towards sterilizations and abortions within Native American communities consistent with the predominant medico-cultural zeitgeist—responsive to eugenic aims. That particular tendency again betrayed a critical fact alluded to before: eugenic philosophy and practice persisted in the U.S.A. despite the Nuremberg Trials.[81]

For decades after World War II, Native women were stereotyped as hypersexual and had limited access to birth control. Native girls apprehended after running away from boarding schools in the late 1950s were presumed to have been promiscuous and faced highly traumatic, "routine" examinations upon their return. Psychiatrist Robert Leon observed in 1960:

> There are a number of frankly psychotic children ... There are quite a number of severely neurotic children.... After a girl had run away from the boarding school and been brought back, she was almost immediately taken to the health service for a pelvic examination.[82]

Pre-World War II eugenics efforts to limit the births of Native children also continued into the 1960s through the attempted indoctrination of Native female patients throughout the IHS system who were shown pictures of parents with many children and few horses, then pictures of parents with few children and many horses in efforts to persuade them toward becoming sterilized.[83] There was little effort made to counter this propaganda.

Are there any signs of generational carry for eugenics sterilization ideology today? If so, I suspect they might be found in carefully worded dialogues about "free" provision to teenage Native women at Indian Health Service clinics of birth control patches such as Ortho Evra—which the Food & Drug Administration (FDA) has warned can cause fatal blood clots[84]—or perhaps injectables such as Depo-Provera—with side effects of modified menstrual bleeding, reduced bone density, increased risk of cervical cancer, and heightened risk of sexually transmitted diseases. Injectables are twice as likely to be offered to American Indian women than to EuroAmerican women via what at least one researcher calls the "sterilization racism" of health care providers.[85]

Another means of detecting the generational carry for eugenics in Indian Country is by more unconscious means—that is, by simply reviewing the very common side effects of the antidepressant drugs that are prescribed so liberally through the Indian Health Service. Many of these side effects affect procreation, specifically, through reduced libido and sexual dysfunction in up to 73 percent of patients taking them,[86] which can turn into "persistent" sexual disabilities after discontinuation.[87] A persistent, i.e., permanent, sexual disability after discontinuation of a drug would seem to me to represent a sterilizing agent. Further risks include reduced male fertility[88] and decreased birth weight and gestational length.[89]

By the time we met, Emma was an elder. Working with her, I wondered if there was some aging physician somewhere who would characterize his efforts a success because she'd spent time on welfare while raising her kids and had to rely on food stamps. Deprived of the option of having more children to allow her the joy of grandchildren, perhaps he'd still consider Emma a living expression of his political views. She lived alone, often mourning children she'd been lucky enough to have with her for a time, and longing in vain for more—an impossibility because of what he'd done.

TWELVE

Generational Carry: Boxing to Boarding School

AN INVITATION TO FIGHT

Alvin,[1] a short, muscular youth, strolls around our classroom, refusing to join our Pathways Circle—the program my Blackfoot co-facilitator Verna and I have inserted as a "health elective" at Yakama Nation Tribal School in an effort to create a positive climate of peer support for certain students living in challenging circumstances. Alvin's disruptiveness is causing other youth to shut down, and several are clearly annoyed. Although Verna is the stronger presence in the room, he seems to have identified me as "white man in charge." I can't quite figure out what to do.

His behavior reminds me of stories about rebellious youth during the American Indian boarding school era—the fires set at Flandreau and Haskell Indian schools in 1918–19 and the lighting fixtures that were broken, the threats to abduct and "string up" the principal.[2] Curtis Thorpe Carr, a Creek elder, told American Indian studies professor K. Tsianina Lomawaima in 1994, "We used to *deliberately* do things just to show that we could do it and get away with it ... I happened to be one that ... couldn't stand somebody telling me what to do every minute of the day or night."[3] Boarding school students reportedly "dawdled at their tasks, stole food to supplement a diet of mush, smoked cigarettes, and played pranks."[4] Native boarding school scholar Brenda J. Child wrote that "rebellion was a permanent feature of boarding school life, and runaways and stories of resistance figure

187

prominently in the letters and reports from Haskell and Flandreau during the years they operated."[5]

Alvin doesn't realize I support his skepticism about authority, including any attributed to me. I recognize in his disposition to challenge me a positive facet of generational carry, an important anti-authoritarian tendency in Original Nations to which my colleague Bruce Levine has alluded.[6] I'm from a subculture where respect is earned, not presumed or granted by rank.

Unfortunately, Alvin's challenging disposition has created a legacy for him. He has already been labeled with oppositional defiant disorder (ODD) and conduct disorder by mental health providers contracted at two public schools from which he's been expelled. The stigma of these labels causes him much frustration, as his defiance gets attributed to his "mental problems." Given what labels have done for him, he has ample reasons to anticipate somebody like me as a threat.

Alvin struts toward the teacher's desk and tampers with Verna's eagle feather, a sacred object. She is irritated, out of ideas, and tired of insisting, "Alvin, please sit!" She's about to ask him to leave. We both also know our circle represents his last chance.

On an impulse, I decide to improvise and stand up, walk across the room, stop a few feet in front of him, and ask him how he makes a fist.

Alvin ceases pacing and squints at me. "You serious?"

In my younger years, I tell him, I earned a black belt in taekwondo, Korean karate. I admit to being a bit out of shape, but I also assert that I instructed for a time. To a lesser extent, I'm mirroring his bravado and letting him know I'm not scared of him. Mostly, this is true. I shrug and simply clarify that I'm curious about how he goes about making a fist. Verna is looking at me incredulously and clearly a bit nervous.

"Like this," he says, moving forward, and clenching his fist in my face.

"Really," I respond, trying not to flinch. "Well, I hope you don't hurt yourself."

"Wha?" He smiles contemptuously. Verna may think I've gone crazy.

The tension rises a notch, and I turn sideways to him, assuming a nonverbal stance I learned from crisis intervention training somewhere. Other youth in our circle look fascinated. Are we going to fight? There is a remote possibility of having to defend myself, but I'm confident I can block any initial assault Alvin might try. We're about four feet apart.

I nonchalantly make a fist of my own, raising it slowly, and hold it forward to explain what I've been taught about the best way to avoid damaging one's hands in a self-defense situation. I keep emphasizing "self-defense" as I speak. I'm trying to respond to whatever worries he might have about being dominated by me while placing us as on equal footing physically and trying to remember that he is likely the one feeling intimidated here.

"I don't start fights. I finish them."

"I figured," I respond. We stand in our balancing act, holding fists a few more seconds. I know whatever "authority" I will have must emerge from respect, not through coercion or force, even though he's very accustomed to that version.

"Well, I sure wouldn't want to fight you, Alvin," I say, raising my eyebrows. "You look pretty strong. Besides, you're probably too fast for an old fart like me."

The other students giggle, Verna laughs, and Alvin looks around. Tension breaks.

"I just thought I'd give you some advice on how not to hurt your hand," I conclude as I sit back down. Alvin is left standing in the center of our circle, glancing sidelong at several students, some of whom still smile faintly at him.

"Come on . . . sit," one girl whispers. A brief pause, and then he mutters, "Cool," and accepts the seat next to her.

A few weeks later, Alvin sits weeping about his mother's death while this same girl and his younger brother—another new addition—hug him. Of course, this was back in the days when touching was still allowed in school. Alvin had lowered his guard in response to the medicine of Pathways. Verna, who brought so much through her spiritual traditions, was initially skeptical of my desire to keep our approach as nondirective as possible. But the inner resources of youth that others had given up on came forward and allowed them to help one another, and she soon saw how that could happen.

Alvin eventually asked me to show him some karate. Was I being truthful on his first day? From fact to promise, it's my responsibility to be true, so I strained a groin muscle doing a spinning hook kick. He seemed impressed that an old man could actually kick.

One day Alvin showed me his "rap sheet" printout of behavioral infractions from his last school before he'd come to us. There were quite a few parallels in its language to the prison system. This document came from a public school, not a jail. I asked him what it meant to be cited for "loitering" or "violation of probation contract."

"Most of that stuff, like 'violated class rules' or 'probation contract,' has to do with me not wanting to wear an orange vest."

"Orange vest?"

"Yeah. You have to wear an orange vest if you need to use the bathroom or go anywhere in the building. I told them I wouldn't do it. Not ever. They'd make me put it on, but then I'd take it off."

"But I don't understand: Why do you have to wear an orange vest?"

"It's like a hall pass. They can just look at you and know you're allowed to walk around."

"Ah, I see. But you wouldn't wear it. How come?"

"Because I know what they're up to."

"What do you mean?" I asked.

"My older brother is in prison. He has to wear orange. I'm not wearing orange at any school I go to. Period. I'm not going to be treated like I'm going to prison."

Most of Alvin's "infractions" had to do with the battle lines drawn around this orange vest policy. Behind Alvin's fighting demeanor, he'd thought more carefully than others in charge would have ever suspected about what he defied and why. He wanted to be recognized and respected and was quite willing to reciprocate when he knew he could trust someone. This was especially so regarding peers because he felt ashamed and stigmatized by troubles in his family. He wasn't going to allow school officials to reinforce a publicly negative view of him.

Verna got Alvin involved in a boxing program, and this made a positive difference in his life. Last I heard, he was competing as an amateur.

BOXING AND RACE PSYCHOLOGY

How could there possibly be "generational carry" into Alvin and me comparing fists that day? Boxing is a European invention introduced in Indian Country through the curriculum of American Indian boarding schools via the required *Course of Study for the Indian Schools of the United States: Industrial and Literary* issued in 1901:

It is necessary to look into the physical condition of pupils and give them the training that will counteract the influences of unfortunate heredity and strengthen the physique, in order that they may be able to bear the strain that competition in business and earning a living will impose.[7]

Boxing became wildly popular in boarding schools in the 1920s and 1930s. School boxing clubs were generally top-notch and team members won Golden Gloves amateur championships. "School administrators, coaches, and businesses in the vicinity of boarding schools enjoyed boxing, and thrived on the revenue and local publicity gained through fights,"[8] while white people drove for hours from nearby cities to attend American Indian bouts. Boxing's popularity "reflected a very real atmosphere of physical violence and intimidation that existed among boys at boarding schools"[9] but also offered a release from gender segregation and mundane domestic training for girls and young women,

SKP	SKIPPED CLASS
RDC	RUDE/DISCOURTEOUS
LOI	LOITERING
VCR	VIOLATED CLASS RULES
RDC	RUDE/DISCOURTEOUS
UET	UNEXCUSED TARDY
MML	MISSED MATH LAB
RDC	RUDE/DISCOURTEOUS
LCM	LACK OF CLASS MATERL
RDC	RUDE/DISCOURTEOUS
RDC	RUDE/DISCOURTEOUS
RDC	RUDE/DISCOURTEOUS
UET	UNEXCUSED TARDY
VCR	VIOLATED CLASS RULES
MWD	MISSED WK DETENTION
VPC	VIOLAT.PROBATION CON
RDC	RUDE/DISCOURTEOUS
RDC	RUDE/DISCOURTEOUS
VCR	VIOLATED CLASS RULES
VCR	VIOLATED CLASS RULES

Excerpt from a Native youth's "behavioral rap sheet" from Toppenish School District. Transcribed from author's photo.

who were also recruited to fight. Public enthusiasm for seeing Native youth fight with one another and other "races" became so unwieldy that the Bureau of Indian Affairs outlawed boxing at its schools in 1948.

While exploitive of students, who were often required to participate, boxing could also be cathartic and a rare means of proving oneself. One participant recalled channeling his feelings about physical abuse he'd suffered from a white "advisor" into winning bouts: "I used to think about the time when I grew up. I said, I'm going to be a fighter. I'm going to tangle with that Mr. Stein . . ."[10] A local champion later noted how boxing helped him feel better about being Indian:

Well, I'll tell you, you got the pride. . . . If there's any race that's speaking different languages, outside of you, well you got the pride to demonstrate that you going to be in there fighting . . . Because you're an Indian, well you going to show what an Indian can do.[11]

EuroAmerica controlled all aspects of curricula in American Indian boarding schools, and boxing reflected a long-standing Euro cultural obsession. In New Orleans in 1892, when "Gentleman Jim" Corbett knocked out heavyweight champ John Sullivan, who had held the title for over a decade, the news traveled far beyond the crowd of 10,000 to a flashing white beacon light on New York's Pulitzer Building. With Corbett's pugilistic strategies triumphing over Sullivan's brawn, scientists wanted to know about human physical capabilities, including several early psychologists.[12]

In 1895, philosopher Richard Meade Bache, a great-great-grandson of Benjamin Franklin, asserted that a skilled Black American boxer could beat a white boxer because so-called primitive races such as Africans and Indians possessed stronger "automatic reflexes":

> Men, in proportion to their intellectuality, should tend less and less to quickness of response in the automatic sphere ... In a word, the automatic superiority of the less intellectual man being greater as such than that of the other, and his intelligence quite equal to the purpose of pugilism, he would win in a pugilistic contest.[13]

Bache mounted the first published academic psychology study of American Indians when he compared eleven Native individuals of unknown tribal affiliation with twelve "Caucasians" and eleven "Africans." Experiments were designed at his request by Lightner Witmer[14] at the University of Pennsylvania. A pioneer of psychological measurement who may have originated the term "clinical psychology," Witmer walked the same halls where craniometrist Samuel Morton had researched Army-donated Indian skulls seventy-five years earlier.

Witmer used a "magneto-electrical apparatus"[15]—a device we don't learn much about—in order to shock participants, presumably timing how fast they removed their hand from the shock. His findings supported Bache's stereotyped views of "primitives"—that is, that both American Indians and African Americans showed faster reaction times than "Caucasians." Morton's race categories were intrinsic to the Bache-Witmer research design.

As far as I can tell, this work was the starting point for researching Native race difference theory in the realm of applied psychology. Witmer was a student of eugenics psychologist James McKeen Cattell. Cattell became president of the fledgling American Psychological Association in

1895 and set the stage for psychology's role in supporting eugenics: "For many, the leading interest in organic evolution is in its application to social evolution."[16] Cattell believed people measured as having inferior intelligence should be sterilized and reportedly offered $1000 each to his children if they chose the child of a professor as a mate.[17]

THE FORK IN THE ROAD

Another student who earned his doctorate under James McKeen Cattell was Robert Sessions Woodworth,[18] who became a popular mentor to many psychologists at Columbia University for years to come. Among Woodworth's many students were two of particular import in the history of the U.S. mental health system in Native America.

Otto Klineberg was the first psychologist to visit Yakama Nation, and he did so as a graduate student who would fundamentally challenge race difference theory. It was an astonishing discovery for me to learn that Klineberg's 1927 study at Yakama Nation was likely his earliest move in this direction. A bold thinker, he faced withering criticism for opposing established white supremacist ideology by suggesting there was no such thing as "racial inferiority."

Klineberg recruited "120 full-blood or almost full-blood children living on the Yakima Indian reservation" in central Washington State "and 110 white children living in the town of Toppenish, in the heart of the reservation, and known as the Reservation City,"[19] ranging in age from seven to sixteen years to compare on several tests of performance speed and accuracy, some of which were forerunners to IQ subtests utilized today. He noted that although the Native children were slower in speed, they were *more accurate* in their answers than the *páshtin* children. He concluded:

> Those who look for economic interpretations of social and psychological data will have little trouble in this case. Speed seems to have a place in a competitive society, but there is little economic competition among the Yakimas. Not more than 15 per cent or 20 per cent of the able-bodied men earn their living by farming and herding. The others live on the rent which white people pay for the use of their land. Fishing and berry-picking supply them with the greater part of the food which they require.[20]

In this way, Klineberg brought a brand-new "cultural thesis" forward that antagonized race psychologists of his time. His experience with the Yakama evidently set his own career path in a unique and rich direction. Only twenty-seven years old, he returned to Columbia University and pioneered the field of multicultural psychology, authoring *Race Differences* (1935), *Negro Intelligence and Selective Migration* (1935), and *Race and Psychology* (1951), among many other works. He wrote forcefully in 1935:

> The human race is one, biologically speaking. There are no subvarieties whose genes are mutually incompatible, or whose crossing will necessarily lead to degeneration....
>
> Racial antagonisms must be understood in their historical and social setting; they have no basis in biology. The assumption that they are the inevitable result of group differences merely serves to hide their true causes.[21]

Otto Klineberg received a Guggenheim Fellowship, went to China, and studied emotional expression among the Chinese for a year. His brilliant achievements reached a crescendo in 1954 when he testified on behalf of the historic Supreme Court decision *Brown v. Board of Education*, which led to national school desegregation. He once remarked upon the significance of his early days among the Yakama:

> This was an unexpected discovery ... [I]t was the substantial variation in speed which struck me as the real difference in their behavior.... [S]ince so many intelligence tests and performance tests are based upon speed, in part, this seemed to me to be a fundamentally important factor.[22]

Klineberg never visited the Yakima Valley again as far as I know. Instead, he took the path of lecturing, writing, and advocating back at Columbia University. For me, a strange synchronicity draws me toward this legendary psychologist. Like him, I studied emotional communication among mainland Chinese—for my doctoral thesis. I finished my final dissertation draft during the first week of March of 1992, the same week he passed away. Nearly single-handedly, Otto Klineberg created the academic perspective of cultural psychology that I immersed myself in for three years, earning me the degree that permitted me to come to Yakama Nation in 2000, the very place where he'd first been inspired. This is the nature of the

Yakama time ball, and I'm amazed to locate the knots of such a legendary psychologist on the same string holding my own in this community's collective memory.

During the 1940s, another Columbia student, physical anthropologist Thomas R. Garth Jr., began hiking throughout the Pacific Northwest, stealing bones from Native graves[23] in the ways of the cultural evolutionists. In 2003, I found myself in the incredible position of sitting inside a sweat lodge with an elderly Yakama leader celebrating the return and burial of some of these stolen bones. His solemn songs welcomed an end to the tragic *páshtin* penchant for absconding with the sacred remains of Native loved ones. I thought about the checkered life of the bone thief's father. He was a prominent early "Indian psychologist" who took a much different road from the one pioneered by Otto Klineberg. His name was Thomas Russell Garth, and he, too, attended Columbia University and studied under Robert Sessions Woodworth.

THE NATIVE ACCORDING TO GARTH

New students at mission- and federally operated American Indian boarding schools arrived in an environment by which, according to a 1941 doctoral researcher, "they could be taught to give up their old habits, ideals, and religion and become a settled, self-supporting people with the ideals, language, and religion of their white neighbors."[24] These children served, quite literally, as a captive population for early applied psychologists. Neither they nor their parents could object or even consent to psychological test research, which was simply built into their day, presumably through the permission of a superintendent. Their "intelligence" was tested long before the ethical constraints of contemporary research were formulated. There were no institutional review boards to approve research designs or other factors to interfere, nor were any parties held responsible regarding potential negative effects of this research on the personal status checks familiar to us today that we call "self-esteem," "self-worth", and "self-concept."

Psychological and educational testing occurring in Indian boarding schools was introduced in the mental hygiene context of "race betterment." Given their presumed inferiority, Native children forced into these schools would have their sacred hair shorn and be redressed in burlap smocks (often made by themselves) or dungarees. They faced punishment, often severe, for speaking their own language and were compelled to learn "industry" and "a Christian way of life."[25] When not voluntarily surrendered to this ordeal by families facing extreme poverty and deprivation, the commissioner of Indian affairs managed funding set aside by Congress for "child snatching" by police, the chasing and capturing of these children "like so many wild rabbits."[26] I try to remember how the bad dreams and night terrors some kids experience came true for these children.

The residential school facilities into which they were brought often had poor ventilation and sanitation and were rife with health and fire dangers. Their nutritional needs were frequently neglected, and they died regularly of various preventable diseases. Alongside the brutality and sexual and physical abuse for which these schools became notorious, children endured strict, military-like daily regimens in rigid classroom environments governed by Bible instruction and the rod, training in farming, stock raising or manual labor for older boys and domestic arts such as sewing, cooking, and cleaning for older girls.[27] Most students beyond third grade became a source of labor to the operation of the boarding school itself.

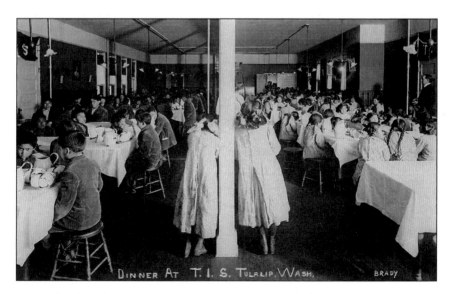

Frederick Brady photograph depicting dinner at Tulalip Indian School, 1912. Note the somber mood and hands off tables. On the right side of the room, might that be a white pastor leading prayer? *Museum of History and Industry, Seattle.*

According to media studies professor Stephen Petrina at University of British Columbia, race betterment advocates mounted concerted efforts to survey sections of the U.S. population, hoping to detect "defectives," because

mental deficiency had been causally linked, by interventionists, to crime, delinquency, deviance, legal entanglement, poverty and vice. If selected at school age or earlier, children could be contained or treated and, simultaneously, the individual and social effects of mental deficiency or feeble mindedness could be prevented.[28,29]

Thomas Russell Garth, whom I try to think of less as a villain and more as a potential colleague were he living today, was a particularly passionate white psychologist trying to establish his career via research within these American Indian boarding schools. As an academic, lackluster achievements left him an outsider to the glamour of Ivy League schools, but he found a niche and

Fort Simcoe Boarding School girls stand in front of a block house in burlap smocks likely of their own making. According to my Yakama *káɫa* Levina Wilkins, children resistant to instruction were locked inside a similar structure, and some chose to speak their language anyway so as to express their defiance. Photo by Jerome Peltier. *Northwest Museum of Arts and Culture/Eastern Washington State Historical Society, Spokane, WA; item L97-29.98.*

dedicated a life shortened by asthma to the research he undertook. It appears that the more he got to know Native Americans, the more he wanted to help them. He does not seem to have been a malicious or bad person, a key observation in understanding his admixture of benevolence and flawed ideology.

Garth was also not the first or only applied psychologist in Indian Country, but he was undoubtedly the most prolific.[30] It's likely his intelligence research fortified the established stilted curricula of boarding schools, and yet he came to regret his conclusions and took the brave step of publicly retracting them near the end of his life. His final study's implications, however, were no less devastating to Native children than his lifetime of research.

Garth was born in Paducah, Kentucky, in 1879 in humble circumstances and to a devout Christian family.[31] His doctorate under Robert Sessions Woodworth at Columbia University came a decade earlier than Otto Klineberg's, leaving him more directly socialized into the eugenics pedigree of the time. Woodworth was a careful mentor, more conservative than James McKeen Cattell, and with respect to racial measurement questioned "whether the tests are fair to the different races compared. We need to have our eyes open to the elements of unfairness, so as to make allowances for them."[32]

Thus, Thomas Garth was taught to be conscientious. He asserted that researchers in race psychology should have to take a test to prove they were not racially prejudiced. He demanded that claims by eugenicists about "race difference" must be subjected to rigorous scientific method:

> Racial psychology means nothing unless it uses the methods of and devices of scientific psychology that have been tried out and perfected with great care in the laboratory. . . .
>
> In making investigations in race psychology, therefore, the first thing we must do is to measure the mental processes to be studied; secondly, we must maintain standard conditions; next the subjects measured must be representative of the racial group studied; and finally, we must interpret our results in the light of all the facts.[33]

As a devout positivist, Garth didn't confine himself to only researching intelligence. Over the course of nearly two decades, he conducted studies—mostly with Indian children and mostly in the southwestern and southeastern United States—on personality, will, community of ideas, reaction time and mental fatigue, work persistence, handwriting, and color-blindness. He undertook many of these studies himself or in collaboration with graduate students, even including his son, bone thief Thomas R. Garth Jr. Many were collected for his 1931 book, *Race Psychology: A Study of Racial Mental Differences*, a research review.

Garth had both predecessors and contemporaries. E. C. Rowe had already applied Henry Herbert Goddard's revision of the Binet Scales to 268 Indian children in Michigan in 1914 and declared that only 5.8 percent of them had a mental age equal to their chronological age, while 79 percent of a sample of "547 white children" were measured as being at chronological age level.[34] Walter S. Hunter and Eloise Sommermier, whose work was cited by Nathaniel D. Mttron Hirsch in describing the "immigrant threat," applied the 1911 version of the Otis Intelligence Test, a group-administered, paper-and-pencil test, to 715 Indian children at Haskell Indian Institute in Lawrence, Kansas, and contended these children were also deficient in intelligence compared to 1,366 white children.[35]

In contrast, educational psychologists J. A. Fitzgerald and W. W. Ludeman remarked upon more positive findings, having used the group-administered National Intelligence Test with Indian children at St. Mary's Mission School in Springfield, South Dakota, and the Santee Normal Training School in Santee, Nebraska: "Your attention is called to the fact that not one child can be classed as feeble-minded."[36] By 1934, however, B. F. Haught weighed in with the majority view, describing several studies at federal boarding schools (likely among the Zuni and at Albuquerque and Santa Fe) showing "there are no periods of acceleration in the mental growth of the Southwestern Indian up to age sixteen. Retardation is constant from the ages of six to nine" and "[i]n mental age the Indian of the Southwest is from 1.0 to 4.7 years below whites."[37] The positivist methods and quantification imperative of these applied psychologists built the Native inferiority stereotype that became solidified in white people's minds and in what Native children were told to believe about themselves.

An outlier for this period is the 1928 research paper by Elmer Jamieson (Canadian Mohawk), the first known Native psychologist, mentored by Peter Sandiford at the Ontario College of Education, which would eventually become the University of Toronto.[38] In other places, this particular article has been misconstrued.[39] Sandiford himself certainly embraced the "imperial racism" of his time but seems to have permitted Jamieson's psychosocial arguments to stand. Certainly, the article depicts the blood quantum thesis that the higher intelligence test scores of "mixed blood" Haudenosaunee children from the Six Nations of the Iroquois in Ontario were due to greater degrees of "white blood." But I believe we hear Jamieson's voice coming through in the article's contention that

> language handicap, irregularity of attendance, inferior social status and lack of heterogeneity in the environment which goes along with inferior status, must be considered as three of the most important factors which have resulted in the inferior performances of the Indian children on the intelligence and the achievement tests.[40]

Intriguingly, while the Jamieson and Sandiford study is cited by Thomas Garth in a 1930 review article, he obscures its implications. Garth only points out "a large group of mixed bloods [had] an I.Q. of 97."[41] Psycho-social contentions about language, culture, socioeconomics, and education were entirely absent from Garth's 1931 book, *Race Psychology*, and this study was cited only in a table with a brief description that further distorted it as research regarding "mixed blood" Indians.

To be fair, Garth does touch upon the nonconformist views of Otto Klineberg, landing firmly on the fence between his own social Darwinism and a more open acknowledgment of cultural difference. He clearly struggled with a desire to avoid being racist:

> Any disposition on our part to withhold from these, or similar, races, because we deem them inferior, the right to a free and full development to which they are entitled must be taken as an indication of rationalization on account of race prejudice; and such an attitude is inexcusable in an intelligent populace.[42]

Despite his ambivalence, twenty of the twenty-five studies Garth reviewed for *Race Psychology* supported race difference theory, favoring the notion that American Indians were significantly less intelligent than EuroAmericans. None of the studies discussed by Garth supported equivalence or superiority of intelligence for American Indians. Just as he had done with Jamieson and Sandiford, Garth cited in his appendix the study by Fitzgerald and Ludeman, the researchers who'd lauded their failure to detect a single "feebleminded" Indian child. He refrained from commenting upon such findings, which would have countered the dominant mental health discourse.[43] In sum, Thomas Russell Garth became complicit with a mainstream white supremacist viewpoint, despite misgivings he signaled at various points.

The work of Garth and others inside American Indian boarding schools influenced policies within which Native children were presupposed to be best suited to a life of domestic servitude or manual labor. Although public sentiment at the time appeared solidly turned against racial intermarriage, Garth himself undertook five of the seven Indian IQ studies favorably comparing "mixed blood" children to "full bloods" and had done so as early as 1921. Additionally, he was prone toward making statements such as "mixed bloods excel full bloods by 11%" or mixed bloods were at "Rank I" compared to a variety of "full bloods" who came out at lower ranking IQ scores.[44]

In a show of personal integrity, Thomas Russell Garth eventually reversed course. Just prior to his untimely death from asthma in 1939, he sent public signals that his conclusions about American Indian

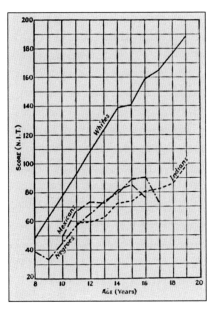

Garth's chart of highly biased "IQ" test scores comparing white students to Mexican, "Negroe," and American Indian students inside boarding schools using the National Intelligence Test (NIT), the civilian version of the Army Alpha-Beta tests. From Thomas Garth's *Race Psychology* (1931).

intelligence, premised upon decades of work, were fundamentally wrong.[45] By then, however, he and his students had already exerted a significant influence in the opposite direction. The stereotypes about inferior Indian children they'd helped create moved from boarding schools into the public school system.[46,47] Prominent and reputable individuals in applied psychology and psychiatry did not question or challenge the white supremacist presumptions Garth had fortified. Instead, they built their reputations on them.

By 1937, Thomas Russell Garth was a "specialist" with the Bureau of Indian Affairs. Contrite over erroneous conclusions, his last study pertained to taking Native children out of their families and into white homes. In this, he noted simply that Native foster children raised in white homes had IQs

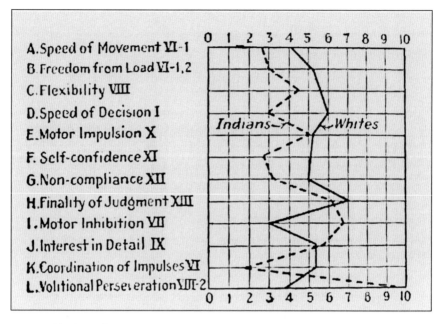

Garth's chart of the evaluations by three white judges of "Will and Temperament" factors among American Indian boarding school students compared to white students. From Thomas Garth's *Race Psychology* (1931).

11 points higher than those raised in "hogans."[48] Garth was saying he was wrong about inborn inferiority in these children; what mattered was to raise them in white homes.

After his death, and throughout the 1940s and 1950s, Indian women came under increasing attack as unfit mothers, and white adoption was seen as a means of rescuing their children from them. Indian motherhood became so maligned that, by the late 1940s, between one-quarter and one-half of all American Indian children were living in institutions, foster care, or adopting homes.[49] Native children showed promise "if only ..." they were not living with their own family and culture.

Additional means were brought to bear for the "white socialization" of Native children. By the 1930s, when Garth and others were publishing their highly biased findings widely, nearly half of all Indian people receiving formal education were attending boarding schools.[50] On the basis of their presumed limited intelligence and other deficiencies, these students were regularly shuffled into "outing programs," which placed them in residential homes and farms under the supervision of white families, presumably to address their "defects of character." This is how research by Garth and Mary A. Barnard regarding "will-temperament" became topical. They compared this characteristic among full-blooded Pueblo, Diné, Apache, and Sioux students from two federally run boarding schools and found white students "show a greater amount of self-confidence than do Indians" and "appear to have stronger personalities."[51] Elsewhere, Garth declared low ratings were also found among Native youth in judgment, intensity, reasonableness, and independence on a personality measure when rated by a white judge comparing "Indians of varying degrees of blood" to successful students at Chilocco Indian Agricultural School in Kay County, Oklahoma.[52]

Girls shipped to outing programs from the Flandreau Indian School in South Dakota to surrounding towns as domestic servants in 1932 received room and board and a meager weekly salary of $1 to $4 for cleaning, washing, ironing, serving meals, and often looking after small children.[53] These young women frequently challenged the setting in which they found themselves:

> Time after time they broke the rules of their contracts and continually tested the patience of their employers by staying out late, smoking, and refusing to be celibate.... Employers often described the Indian girls who worked for them as sullen and uncooperative and commented that they were puzzled by their employees' personalities.[54]

Many forlorn Indian girls and boys chose to quit or run back home from their experiences (and were often apprehended and returned). In 1928 the Meriam Report criticized outing programs as "mainly a plan for hiring out boys for odd jobs and girls for domestic service, seldom a plan for providing real vocational training."[55] Outing programs were involuntary servitude, which in some quarters might be called slavery.

The programs of race difference and outing fell out of favor, but their influence carried down into educational settings generationally. In 1968, for example, an astute but frustrated teacher recorded the ugly socialization experience at Birch Island Indian Day School in Ontario:

> From the first day these youngsters enter school, the screws are turned and twisted; racial disapproval, criticism of parental and community standards, odious comparisons that shame him and

strip him of his self-esteem, that point up his short-comings as a human being; ruthlessly applied pressures seemingly deliberately designed to break his spirit and make him conform to white society's expectations.[56]

In 1969, the U.S. Congress finally acknowledged the appalling situation of American Indian education in its 4,000-page report, *Indian Education: A National Tragedy—a National Challenge*. Spearheaded by and dedicated to recently assassinated U.S. senator Robert Kennedy, the report's new chairman, Senator Edward Kennedy, noted that "one-fourth of elementary and secondary educators and teachers—*by their own admission*—would prefer *not* to teach Indian children; and Indian children, more than any other minority group, believe themselves to be 'below average' in intelligence."[57]

The forceful words in this federal government report written over 50 years ago are surprising in their contemporary relevance:

> With attitudes toward Indians being shaped, often unconsciously, by educational materials filled with inaccurate stereotypes—as well as by teachers whose own education has contained those same stereotypes and historical misconceptions—it is easy to see how the "lazy, dirty, drunken" Indian becomes the symbol for all Indians. When the public looks at an Indian they cannot react rationally because they have never known the facts. They do not feel responsible for the Indian because they are convinced that the "savages" have brought their conditions upon themselves. They truly believe the Indian is inferior to them. The subcommittee found this climate of disrespect and discrimination common in off-reservation towns which educate many Indian students in their public schools. The Indian is despised, exploited, and discriminated against—but always held in check by the white power structure so that his situation will not change.[58]

The prejudice and bigotry to which this report alluded had been fortified for many years by the eugenics and mental hygiene movements in Indian Country. As a practicing psychologist, I bear witness to the survival of descendant psychological tests and measures by which this same prejudice continues through frequent misuse and misapplication by school psychologists; so-called cultural interpretive caveats that violate publisher guidelines (and elevate "standard error of measurement"); a casual disregard or ignoring of the lived context of students, their histories, and their family circumstances;

ongoing lack of representative normative data; and the many ethnocentric-
ities and cultural biases of the quantification imperative and assessment
processes themselves. Additionally, the technical research of intellectual tests
used in special education determinations across Native America has recently
revealed they are actually measures of literacy, an educational discrepancy
with strong links to discrimination and marginalization.[59]

SCHOOL AS JAIL, DEFIANCE AS IDENTITY

Several American Indian boarding schools remain in operation today, and
although their philosophies and practices have changed significantly—and
proactively—with the times, at least one had its own jail until recently. In
2006 the family of sixteen-year-old Cindy Gilbert Sohappy accepted a $1.8
million lawsuit settlement following her death from alcohol poisoning after
being abandoned by staff members in the Chemawa Indian School jail in
Salem, Oregon.[60] Describing her torturous journey from the Warm Springs
Reservation to retrieve her niece's body, Cindy's aunt Corinna Sohappy
recounted to the U.S. Senate Finance Committee in September 2004:

> Cindy was lying with her right hand extended upward. She had
> blood around her mouth and nose, and on her shirt.
>
> The staff could not explain to me why she was bleeding. I tried
> to move her arm to rest it across her chest, but she was already cold
> and her arm very stiff.
>
> Throughout her life, Cindy had rarely gotten herself into
> trouble. . . .
>
> My nephew, who also attended Chemawa at the time, had
> followed Cindy to the jail that evening to make sure that the staff
> gave her the supervision she needed. He had seen how intoxicated she
> was, and warned the jail staff that it was not safe to leave her alone.
>
> My nephew told me that while Cindy was being carried into
> the cell—since she was too drunk to walk on her own—the jail staff
> made jokes about her.
>
> Until that morning, I did not know that this dreadful jail even
> existed at Chemawa. . . .
>
> Other relatives of Chemawa students told me about the annual
> homecoming celebration at the school, when as many as 92 students
> have been locked into these 4 small cells at one time.[61]

Ms. Sohappy is describing the generational carry of domination and coercion that killed her niece just as it killed Native youth in boarding schools in the past. In sharing her grief, she shows us what once happened still does.

In their handbook *Reading and the Native American Learner*, released by the Washington Office of State Public Instruction in 2000, Joe St. Charles and Magda Costantino coined an alternative term, "oppositional identity," to describe the open or subtle resistance by which Native students clash with educators and helpers who fail to recognize their cultural identity, traditions, sense of daily reality, or family values.[62] Such terminology may help clarify the nature of Native youth defiance and resistance while offsetting the stigma of their various psychiatric labels, but it does not address the prejudices and stereotyping they continue to face.

Attributions and decisions by educators, contemporary mental

A 1887 engraving featuring the perceived virtues of the Chemawa Indian Boarding School in socializing Native children toward domestic vocations. Note the dominant stance of the white overseer as he removes his glasses and holds them loosely. *University of Washington Libraries, Special Collections, NA4018.*

health workers, and tribal juvenile court officials about limited intelligence, conduct problems, oppositionality, inattention, or other alleged character defects among Native youth rehash an ongoing historical assault. I believe an "anti-authoritarian counterculture" embedded in the hearts and spirits of Native youth since the inception of the boarding school era has been a key to their resilience and survival.

THIRTEEN

My Generational Carry

"REAL INDIANS"

When I was a little boy in 1962, I brought incessant questions to my grandma Donna whenever she'd visit, or we visited her: "Are we Indians? How can we be?" I couldn't reconcile my pink whiteness with TV images of bronze Tonto (Jay Silverheels, Canadian Mohawk), olive Cochise (Ricardo Montalban, Mexican), or chiseled Geronimo (Chuck Connors, EuroAmerican). She'd answer, "Well, you tan red, don't you? We're part Cherokee, and that's all I know."

I have a vivid early memory of visiting them in North Carolina. My parents, sisters, and I would often go with Grandma Donna and Grandpa Verwin Walker on an all-day excursion from Hendersonville to Oconaluftee Indian Village in the Eastern Cherokee Nation. On one of these occasions Dad made a wrong turn into a camp of indigent families situated in a meadow along a river. I remember seeing a cluster of rusty, broken trailers with their roofs covered in tarps, the dogs chasing our car and black-haired kids with worn clothing running up to our station wagon rear window as Dad was trying to turn around. My blue eyes met their brown eyes.

"Who are they?" I demanded, astonished.

"Those are *real* Indian people, Davy," Dad said.

A precocious child, I wondered, *Well, who, then, were all the people dressed up and making crafts at Oconaluftee Village?*

In my memory, as we pull back out onto the highway, I catch a glimpse of women hanging clothes on a line near a ringer washing machine sitting by a trailer. Numerous extension cords stretch up the side of a telephone pole.

"Why do they wash their clothes outside?" I ask.

"Because they're poor, Davy," Mom answers.

I understand that our family is *not* poor, but I am too young to understand what it means to *be* poor.

"That's just how they do those things," Grandma Donna says a little sharply, and she seems self-conscious about my questions.

About a year later, a genuine Cherokee Togs fringe jacket arrived in a big box shipped from Pryor, Oklahoma, in time for my seventh birthday. I was awed by its craftsmanship, and I knew in my own childlike way that this was more than just clothing. My parents were shocked by the expense, and I somehow understood Grandma and Grandpa Walker didn't have much money. But it would be many years later before I understood the Cherokee-ness Grandma Donna wanted to wrap me up in.

She was too debilitated by stroke to answer any more questions before she died. They persisted, and as a young adult I copied her letters to my dad regarding what his brother, Uncle Ed, would call "this Indian thing." In the mid-1980s I created a research project for my minor thesis in anthropology untangling the story of Grandma Donna's grandfather (and mine, fifth generation) in relation to Cherokee factionalism during the Civil War. This project took me inside genealogical libraries, where I pulled down dusty books that had never been opened before and traced leads.

By the time Grandma Donna died in 1990, I still hadn't filled in the blanks in the story she had told us—a story of Native grandmothers hidden within our family's past by fear and shame. I brought my search with me as I started working at Yakama Nation, but I didn't want anyone to know. I didn't want to be another "wannabe from the Wish'um tribe."

"*Ni kso ko wah*," my Blackfoot brother Long Standing Bear Chief said to me when I reluctantly recounted my search to him in 2000. "In this way, we say 'all my relatives,'[1] and of course you want to know. You want to know who you are!" He laughed at my self-conscious whiteness and pushed me to work harder to recover our lost Cherokee story. He often spoke to me about what "being Cherokee" should mean to me.

"You have to say, 'So what?' to what other people think. I myself have French and Scottish," he told me, looking down at his dark brown arm. "And I've wanted to know more about my white ancestors. There are no full bloods left. The blood quantum thing was a white man's creation anyway and has nothing to do with being Native. But I will tell you: you must stop saying you're 'part Cherokee.' Maybe you should listen to your grandma's reasons for putting the connection in that way to keep it quiet. You're either Cherokee or you're not."

"Well, it's your bloodline," my Yakama *káła*, Levina Wilkins, later counseled. "And just because you're mixed doesn't mean their story isn't important." She then told me about her red-haired, blue-eyed great-grandfather.

Long Standing Bear Chief, my *káła*, and numerous other friends motivated me to find ways to unmask an "invisibility" in my family. The currently fashionable genetic tests for whether one is "Native" or not do nothing to reveal such hidden stories, and that has always been the most important thing in my own way of searching. Besides, both the nonprofit Council for Responsible Genetics[2] and the American Indian and Alaska Native Genetics Resource Center at the National Congress of American Indians[3] conclude DNA tests professing to detect Native family heritage are simply invalid. Specific to Cherokee heritage, there are numerous convoluted EuroAmerican kinship ties related to intermarriage across hundreds of years, and the DNA testing issues are only exacerbated.[4]

I find this DNA testing trend ironic in the extreme. For centuries, white society professed great ambivalence about "racial" admixtures. Au courant DNA tests would have been a source of scandal and suppression one hundred years ago. Donald Trump and certain followers enjoyed mocking seemingly legitimate Cherokee family heritage in Elizabeth Warren's family,[5] but she would have been far better off avoiding the DNA test garbage. Of course, family stories are not enough for racial purists and some tribal genealogists but make no mistake: calling anyone claiming Native American descendancy a "Pocahontas" insults *all* Native people. The Canadian Constitution Act of 1982 recognizes Métis people as "aboriginal" and as having their own culture. No such recognition or identity exists in the United States, so insults and derisions become low-hanging fruit in the ferocious identity politics of today.

FROM THE TRAIL OF TEARS TO NATIVE MENTAL HYGIENE

My justification for depicting our Cherokee family story here is that it navigates the same "mixed-blood" boundary line that brought the U.S. mental health system to Indian Country. By telling it, I'm able to unravel my own time ball further in parallel to the earliest features of this system.

Grandma Donna wrote letters to my father and uncle about my sixth-generation paternal white grandfather[6] Alfred Hirton Barlow

The author with mentor and close friend, Long Standing Bear Chief (Blackfoot Pikaani, 1941-2010), shortly before his passing. Photo by Susan L. Walker. *Author's collection.*

marrying a Cherokee woman, Elizabeth Gibson, on June 23, 1834, near Murfreesboro, Tennessee. I was born 122 years later to the day. Alfred would be characterized in PC academic terms these days as an "Appalachian backcountryman." But he'd more likely be called "white trash" by broader society and in my family, a category that became a common fate for orphans fleeing court-ordered servitude, the "dangerous refuge of waste people, and the spawning ground of a degenerate breed of Americans."[7] Cherokee women were already marrying such "low-class" white adventurers and traders well before the First Cherokee War ended in 1761. These white men were often landless squatters whom it's hard to fault for realizing in these inter-cultural liaisons the tangible benefits of shared land stewardship. For the Cherokee, such arrangements were one more strategy for keeping the peace with intrusive whites.

I've tended to think of Grandmother Elizabeth Gibson as a former slave of mixed Cherokee and African heritage. All I've had to base this intuition upon is a vivid dream I recorded in my journal shortly after coming to work at Yakama Nation around the time Long Standing Bear Chief was encouraging me in my Cherokee search:

*I am with her in a forest, and I know who she is. . . . I can't quite look
at her; it's as though I'm unable to turn my head. In the distance, I hear
voices with British accents shouting instructions.*

"*They've gone this way!" yells one voice.*

I'm suddenly aware we're being pursued.

"*Run!" Elizabeth Gibson seems to say within my mind.*

*We sprint through brush together, into a grove of young saplings,
and I hear galloping hooves behind me getting louder. We stop suddenly,
stooping down, barely breathing, and I hear the snort of an approaching
horse. Elizabeth reaches out her hand and touches my shoulder, alerting
me to not trip over the root of a tree nearby my foot.*

*Without any words, she warns me to be extremely careful to avoid
making any noise of any kind, not even to breathe, or we'll both be killed.*

I startled awake and thought about this dream for days. My first meaningful, Western, psychodynamic understanding concluded it reflected my fears about legitimizing Grandma Donna's claims—that is, that I'd be participating in a kind of tokenism. I should not make too much noise about Elizabeth's presence at the "root" of my family "tree." I was ignorant then of the history of Native enslavement by white colonists or the fact that a vast majority of such slaves were "noncombatant women and children," and Elizabeth could have been among them.[8]

The author with *káła*, mentor, and close friend, Kussamwhy Levina Wilkins (Yakama/ Winátchapam) in 2020. Photo by author.

I decided to ask several Native friends at Yakama Nation what they thought. My interpretation was "one way," I was politely advised, and then I was counseled, several times sternly, to "pay attention" because my lost grandmother was teaching me. This metaphysical view felt less palatable back then than it does now, but I listened carefully and tried to remain open. After all,

The author's paternal grandmother, Donna Barlow Smouse Walker (Missouri Cherokee descendent), lounging outside her trailer while vacationing circa 1962. Photo by George Lee Walker. *Author's collection.*

I told myself, similar concepts exist in Western psychology, from Carl Jung's "collective unconscious" to experiments in generational memory.[9]

But thinking about Elizabeth "teaching" me only highlighted her obscurity. I yearned to know more about someone I couldn't possibly know except in dreamland. Years of genealogical effort brought little pertaining to who she and her husband, Alfred, actually were. The names of her parents remain uncertain,[10] while he claimed he'd been orphaned at an early age shortly after being brought from North Carolina to Tennessee along with his brother. They both must have had relatives, of course, but their remote locale left these people veiled as well. All that was objectively clear was that certain U.S. census takers encountered white and Cherokee people living adjacently and relying upon one another in the small community from which they originated. From there, Alfred and Elizabeth stepped out of the piney Appalachian shade and married one another in 1834.

A more distant relative on my mother's side with the remarkable name of Return Jonathan Meigs Sr. must have had a radical influence on their lives. Return began serving as the first United States agent to the Cherokee in 1801 and worked for twenty years to reestablish ties after the Second Cherokee War. He was esteemed by both sides of the Cherokee–white divide for his role as primary communicator regarding U.S. treaties and defender of Cherokee land rights and well-being before his superiors in Washington.

Unfortunately, Return also believed the best way to deal with chronic white intrusion was to have the Cherokee "volunteer" to move elsewhere. He was probably the first white leader to recommend they resettle on lands west of the Mississippi, and he actually succeeded in persuading a small number to leave for what is now Arkansas.[11] However, Return then reportedly "tried to coerce the tribe into total removal to the West,"[12] and these efforts didn't go nearly as well. His views integrated with earlier writings of Thomas Jefferson as a touchstone for policy makers in Washington. They became a nightmare for the Cherokee people.

In 1823 the Christian Doctrine of Discovery became solidified into U.S. law in *Johnson v. M'Intosh*. In this decision, Supreme Court justice John Marshall asserted white people had "a right to take possession [of land], not-withstanding the occupancy of the natives."[13] Marshall combined his importation of papal decrees alongside biblical doctrine to create a carte blanche for enacting the vision of Manifest Destiny celebrated by Andrew Jackson's Democrats.

This dream—in which Christian whites inherit the earth beneath the feet of Native people of the eastern United States—came true, and I suspect its seeds still ferment within the bigoted political landscape Native Americans face in the United States today. Andrew Jackson described the thrust of Democratic ambitions to Congress in 1830:

> Doubtless it will be painful to leave the graves of their fathers; but what do they more than our ancestors did or than our children are now doing? ... And is it supposed that the wandering savage has a stronger attachment to his home than the settled, civilized Christian?[14]

Many whites vehemently opposed Jackson's idea, especially those who had intermarried or had friendships or trade dealings with affected eastern Native communities. In his elder years, Grandfather Alfred Barlow hinted about this to a county historian, who noted: "Mr. Barlow was originally a Whig, and says he sticks to it yet."[15] While the Whigs were not always consistent,[16] between 1830 and 1842, Whig party members in Congress voted in favor of pro-Indian rights over 84 percent of the time,[17] and Indian "removal" was among the most potent movements they opposed. Frontier hero Davy Crockett, a U.S. congressman for Tennessee, ran on the Whig platform and called Jackson's efforts "wicked and unjust."[18] He believed he lost reelection for doing so.

In a six-hour speech spread out over three days and lambasting Andrew Jackson, Senator Theodore Frelinghuysen of New Jersey eloquently expressed the Whig moral indignation regarding Indian removal:

> However mere human policy, or the law of power, or the tyrant's plea of expediency, may have found it convenient at any or in all times to recede from the unchangeable principles of eternal justice, no argument can shake the political maxim—that where the Indian always *has been*, he enjoys an absolute right still *to be*, in the free exercise of his own modes of thought, government and conduct.[19]

Cherokee principal chief John Ross worked with white allies of Whig and other persuasions to fight Cherokee removal in the U.S. Supreme Court. Regrettably, *Johnson v. M'Intosh* held firm as Marshall's court refused to hear the Cherokee suit against the Indian Removal Act and then subsequently vacated the state of Georgia's conviction of a white man for illegally occupying Cherokee land.[20] The reality of a forced march imposed upon many eastern Native people away from their homelands took hold, and this became a trauma and tragedy with which Elizabeth and Alfred would become entwined.

THE DEMISE OF CHEROKEE FEMININE POWER IN FAVOR OF LUNACY

Until then, Cherokee women oversaw land held in common through their matrilineal clans, considering its nourishment, ecology, and needs in relation to the survival of future generations. As early as the 1760s, Cherokee leader Oconostota publicly asserted the matrilineal nature of land along Saluda Creek in what is now western South Carolina being gifted to the sons of intermarried Scottish traders Alexander Cameron and Richard Pearis:

> Our beloved Brother, Mr. Cameron, has got a son by a Cherokee woman. We are desirous that he may educate the boy like the white

people, and cause him to read and write, that he may resemble both white and red, and live among us when his father is dead. We have given him for this purpose a large piece of land.[21]

Historian Tom Hatley clarifies a subtle strategy behind such gifts:

Cherokee headmen ... attempted to create *métis* leading men on the margin of white and Cherokee societies through cessions of land that directly enhanced the economic standing of red/white families.... [T]hey hoped to create a buffer between the Cherokee towns and the growing backcountry farmer-hunter populations.[22]

I'm not too confident in Hatley's depiction of this "buffer" strategy as being male in origin. Elsewhere, he describes days of dispute at Sycamore Shoals treaty council in 1775 when the "Great Grant" of 20 million acres across Tennessee and a portion of Kentucky to Judge Richard Henderson and Nathaniel Hart was at stake. Both men happened to already be married to white women, and therefore Cherokee matrilineal kinship with them and their offspring could not be achieved.[23,24] When deliberations broke down, Cherokee women, who formed at least half of the thousand or more people in the tribal delegation, walked out.[25] They eventually returned and reluctantly agreed to the sale, but their walkout demonstrated Cherokee feminine power and must have astonished the white men who were present.

Matrilineal sway over land and resource dispensation was not just part of Cherokee culture. Similar tribal practices drew European men toward Native women from the earliest moments of intercultural contact. English immigrants discouraged by colonial hardships or primogeniture at Jamestown colony abandoned their posts so frequently to join surrounding Natives that anti-fraternization laws with severe punishments were instituted to stem the loss of labor.[26] After Bacon's Rebellion against British governor William Berkeley in 1676, white men "who had been ignored when huge land grants around Jamestown had been given away [went] west to find land, and there they encountered Indians"[27] with whom they began to create families. In America's later colonial period, Cherokee territories in Appalachia experienced an immigration of refugee Scottish Jacobites, reviled by the English for supporting the "Great Pretender" to the British throne, Bonnie Prince Charlie.[28] These Scots were poorly suited to their new environment—but they esteemed the potential similarities between Native mountain dwellers and their own censured Highland clans.[29] The "Scot-Cherokee" identity emerged in just this manner, while similar voluntary white assimilations included survivors of the failed Irish Rebellion of 1798.[30]

Frustrations regarding cultural "appropriation" today would be hard to categorize regarding these un-racialized "white Indians" of the past who adopted practices of the society to which they'd become wedded, learning its language, and even joining warriors in fighting against former brethren. In 1676, for instance, "renegado" English colonist Joshua Tift reportedly "married one of the Indian squaws, renounced his religion, nation, and natural parents, all at once fighting against them" alongside the Narragansett during King Philip's War.[31] Although asserting that he'd been compelled by the Narragansett as their captive, a Native woman who had been caught described Tift as encouraging the warriors in all they did. Tift became the only EuroAmerican colonist ever executed by being hung, drawn, and quartered for high treason against the king.[32]

These adopted whites and their métis offspring were an affront to biblical literalists of the day and were often deeply resented by other colonists. During period of British colonial unrest prior to the American Revolution, inter-married Scophilite families (named for one of their leaders) were viewed by local colonists as dangerous "banditti"[33] but soon reconceived as "disaffected Insurgents from the back parts of S. Carolina, N. Carolina & Georgia"[34] after over 1,000 of their men were recruited by British army major general Augustine Prévost against the Continental Army in 1778. These families became specifically targeted for massacre by armed "Regulators,"[35] who saw their ready acceptance of Cherokee values as both an obstacle and affront. While Regulators might tolerate European men marrying Native women, they were revolted by Cherokee female empowerment. Historian Tom Hatley notes:

> The image of a Cherokee society in which women were dominant, and in which all Cherokee were equal, threatened the fragile pater-nalism of the backcountrymen who aspired to the status of planter and slaveowner.[36]

As Europeans married among them, the Cherokee buffer strategy began weakening ancient tradition, and continual gifting of or bargain sale of lands to white men and their "mixed" progeny caused internal friction and disunity. When a highly lucrative land cession to white trader Nathaniel Gist led to closure of the ancient "Warrior's Path" to the Six Nations of the Iroquois,

Cherokee leader Dragging Canoe had had enough. He and his followers formed the Chickamauga, who called themselves Ani'-Yun'wiya, or "Real People," to distance themselves from Cherokees whom they considered too acquiescent to greedy European values and derisively called "Virginians."[37] In the English language translation, Dragging Canoe declares: "Should we not therefore run all risks, and incur all consequences, rather than to submit to further loss of our country? Such treaties may be all right for men who are too old to hunt or fight. As for me, I have my young warriors about me. We will hold our land."[38]

Thus, while Minutemen loaded volleys at Bunker Hill to hold what they claimed as "their" land, numerous intermarried Cherokee-white families siding with Dragging Canoe armed themselves to protect the land of these Original People. Thomas Hatley notes: "Chickamauga towns included many *métis* members as well as Cherokee from the tribal heartland.... [And] from the beginning the Kituwan dialect was mixed with the English of white Tories, traders, and black refugees."[39]

The Cherokee became devastated through their support for the British during the American Revolution and were compelled to make many more land concessions. So-called unclaimed land was left up for grabs, and since land ownership itself was foreign to many tribal people, white people simply took it. According to Vine Deloria Jr. and David E. Wilkins, "there was no question [that U.S. founding fathers] believed they owned the clear legal title to the lands they had wrestled away from Great Britain."[40] Long before Justice John Marshall's Supreme Court decision, any Native-occupied acreage Congress happened to deem "wilderness" might serve as a Revolutionary War veteran's paycheck. In this way, Colonel Hardy Murfree was provided a congressional land grant for wartime service,[41] and, as a man of means, he and his followers began pushing their claim through the fledgling United States' renewed version of European "right of title."

The Chickamauga harried and attacked these intruders around what would become Murfreesboro up until about 1794 and just prior to Tennessee statehood. By then, Dragging Canoe had been dead for two years, and members of his resistance movement were losing steam. They began returning to broader Cherokee society, and I suspect they felt quite vexed by the intermarried families and offspring now holding Cherokee leadership positions. The powerful ascendance of these families was an outcome of the very gifts of land the Chickamauga had resented.

PROGRESSIVES, TRADITIONALISTS, MATRILINEAL SUNDOWN, AND RISING LUNACY

Turmoil was also occurring in Cherokee gender politics, including opposition to an emerging European patriarchy. Certain mixed Scottish-Cherokee leading men arose to protect a matrilineal system, echoing their own Pictish roots.[42] In 1819, leader John Ross, Koo-wi-s-gu-wi (Mysterious Little White Bird), seven-eighths Scottish and a member of the Anitsiskwa, or Bird Clan, through his mother and grandmother, signed a new law protecting matrilineal property rights in Cherokee-white intermarriages. This law cautioned that "any white man who shall marry a Cherokee woman, the property of the woman so marry, shall not be subject to the disposal of her husband, contrary to her consent."[43] Such a legal protection must have seemed incredible to unfamiliar EuroAmerican men, but its force would not last long.

In 1826 the influence of Christianity on the mixed-blood elites brought an ostensibly more "civilized" way to Cherokee towns that had always had their own council houses.[44] Groups of "well-to-do, highly acculturated Cherokees"[45] called a constitutional convention to centralize a republican government linking these villages together. This idea was not palatable to many Cherokee people, and U.S. commissioner John Cocke, appointed to try to negotiate Cherokee removal, reported to the secretary of war that

> the mixed bloods are known to have been for some time at the head of affairs and passed laws so contrary to ancient customs that the native Indian is ready to revolt.[46]

The opposition meeting these mixed "progressives" were so-called traditionalists who formed a poorer majority. Many wished to expel the missionaries from their midst. Some even considered Christian hymns of damnation a form of conjuring with the potential for casting an evil spell.[47] Others mounted all-night dances replete with sorcery of their own adjacent to the Christian missions to express their resentment of the condemnation of their ancient ways.[48]

By centralizing national governance and creating the position of a principal chief, an older total consensus model of local governance where all voices were presumed equal became abrogated. But the most powerful change was the "political system [through] which the [Cherokee] Constitution of 1827 . . . excluded from government most traditionalists."[49] Local community responsibility, interdependence, and mutual healing now gave way to laws which "relieved individuals within the nation of responsibility for their own welfare."[50] On October 14, 1826, a decidedly Western ideology redefined visionary or spiritual affliction into its concept of "madness," i.e., a loss of personal agency and reasoning faculties. This view, descending from Christian doctrines of demonic possession and European notions of witchcraft (detailed within the *Malleus Maleficarum*),[51] became codified into Cherokee national laws:

> *Resolved by the National Committee and Council,* That a child under the age of twelve years, whose tender age renders it improbable that he or she should be impressed with a proper sense of moral obligation or of sufficient capacity, deliberately to have committed an offence, shall not be considered, or found guilty of any crime or misdemeanor; *nor a lunatic or a person insane without lucid intervals, shall be found guilty of any crime with which he or she may be charged;*[52] *Provided,* the act so charged as criminal shall have been committed in the condition of such lunacy or insanity.[53]

This appears the first European mental hygiene doctrine brought into Native America, and it had little in common with traditional Cherokee healing. It was a foreign creation. Interestingly, the law included a provision "that any person counselling, advising, or encouraging a child under the age of twelve years, or a lunatic, or an idiot to commit an offence, shall be prosecuted for such an offence when committed, as principal."[54] In this way, some remnant of older, interdependent values lingered.

THE "MIXED" IN ME

All of these developments were recent history around the Murfreesboro home of woodsman Alfred Barlow and Cherokee woman Elizabeth Gibson when they married. Shortly before Grandma Donna's first stroke in 1970, she transcribed a letter she'd received from her cousin Pauline describing one of their sons, my fifth-generation paternal grandfather Mathew James Barlow, as "Indian, [but] he was very blond and blue-eyed according to Mama."[55] In my research, I began to realize how the intermingling of cultures meant many mixed Cherokee could be described in this way. Yet there were also many white people repulsed by any "degree" of connection with their Cherokee relatives.

"Mama" was Laura Jane Barlow, Mathew Barlow's daughter and Donna's aunt. Laura, Pauline said, "despised Indians" and "knew nothing of Indians except the wild Plains Indians who raided and scalped and massacred and were objects of fear and hatred."[56] Grandma Donna didn't share Aunt Laura's antipathy and wrote in notes to Pauline's letter that she'd been told by her own mother, Mary, Laura's sister, that "my great-grandfather [Alfred] was a guard on the Trail of Tears," and "if this is true," then Elizabeth Gibson, Donna's great-grandmother, "was a FULL blood Cherokee."[57]

Donna's capital letters express her longing to magnify her Cherokee self through the same blood quantum metaphor by which U.S. and tribal officials sought to shrink it. She lamented that "if Aunt Laura and my mother had known that we were more Cherokee they would never have told it as they hated the Indians so and were ashamed of having Indian blood."[58] Their revulsion was juxtaposed by her own Cherokee pride.

In 1835, about six months into Alfred and Elizabeth's marriage, decades of stalwart Cherokee resistance to forced removal collapsed beneath the Treaty of New Echota, an illegitimate document endorsed by a faction of "progressives." They'd acquiesced to certain white leaders who had carried forth the aims of Return Jonathan Meigs Sr. and determined that going west was key to Cherokee survival. As a result of their actions, 16,000 Cherokee people were soon rounded up from their ancient lands, forced into stockades, and then onto *nu na hi du na tlo hi lu i*, "the trail where they cried," the Trail of Tears. Alfred and Elizabeth were taken along with them.

THE "DETERIORATING INFLUENCE" OF CIVILIZATION

From the standpoint of the fledgling U.S. mental hygiene movement, the *Medical Examiner* reported in 1845 that Dr. Charles Lillybridge encountered "more than twenty thousand Indians" during the Trail of Tears tragedy and "never saw or heard of a case of insanity among them."[59] As well, said the *Examiner*, a certain Dr. Butler, "a devoted Missionary and Physician among the Cherokees," was told by "an intelligent Chief, a man now 80 years old," that "he had never known a case of insanity among his people."[60] Writing in 1863, even an early icon of American psychiatry, Isaac Ray, founding member of the Association of Medical Superintendents of American Institutions for the Insane (which would eventually morph into the American Psychiatric Association), remained less persuaded regarding "Indian insanity": "If the savage is more exempt than the sage from mental infirmities, as he probably is, the fact is to be attributed to his greater exemption from all the deteriorating influences of civilization."[61]

But "deteriorating influences of civilization" continued to exert themselves upon these Original People, and in 1838, 4,000 Cherokee refugees found themselves pushed out of their detention camps at Fort Cass, now part of Charleston, South Carolina, onto the Trail of Tears' Northern Route, passing north of Murfreesboro along sections of what is now U.S. Highway 70 South from McMinnville[62] and within a few miles of Alfred and Elizabeth's home.[63] Starving and dying, these bedraggled souls were forced to follow the route north of town after being threatened with tolls and tariffs if they tried the shorter way through. A few made their way on horseback or in wagons, but many more came on foot, driving cattle and pigs and carrying wares or whatever they could hurriedly gather with bayonets at their backs.

Although it's always possible Alfred and Elizabeth joined this exodus voluntarily, it would not have been an appealing prospect. They had three toddlers to care for by then, and it seems more likely they, too, were pushed off their land by General Winfield Scott's 7,000 federal troops, who combed through the hills of Georgia, Alabama, North Carolina, and Tennessee[64] with orders to do their dirty removal work "by any means necessary."[65]

Two years after some 2,500 to 4,000 Cherokee perished on the Trail of Tears from hunger, exposure, and disease,[66] Alfred and Elizabeth resettled between Neosho and "Marysville,"[67,68] Missouri, only thirty miles west of the Northern Route's entry into Indian Territory.[69] The land Alfred and Elizabeth chose had been recently annexed by the new government of the Western Cherokee Nation and lay only a few miles from its borders. They resettled on a cultural buffer as intermarried Cherokee families had been doing for decades.

Grandma Donna's memory about being told as a child that Alfred was a guard on the Trail may have had more to do with his orphan (likely) brother, Larkin Barlow, who is listed as a guard with the North Carolina Regiment, Company I, Ashe County Volunteers, Cherokee Removal.[70] Alfred is not, although he may have taken on such a role informally.

"Guards" on the Trail of Tears were not the federal troops who abused and forced people from their homes. Unable to stop Indian Removal at the Supreme Court, Principal Chief John Ross and his allies succeeded in obtaining funding for guards to be hired by the Cherokee government. Witnessing the desperation of their escorts, many of these men hunted or fished to try to help.

Elizabeth ended up where she was not supposed to be. The Indian Removal Act of 1830 compelled all Cherokee to relocate *inside* Indian Territory, which would eventually become Oklahoma. Between 1845 and 1906, Missouri state law declared: "No person shall give to any Indian a permit to come or remain within this state; nor a permit, or other instrument of writing, with the intent to induce any Indian to come or remain within this state, except the proper agent, under the authority of the United States."[71] Staying in Missouri with her husband and children was clearly risky. We must add to this that Alfred was not entirely law-abiding, which must have left her feeling even more vulnerable. He and his son William were indicted for "selling goods and liquors without a license" in 1886.[72]

In this way, my sixth-generation Cherokee grandmother Elizabeth Gibson became a refugee from refugees. Hiding out with her family in Missouri meant she'd never be "recognized" as a citizen of the new Western Cherokee government. Alongside many other such women and their children, she became disenfranchised. Former Cherokee Nation of Oklahoma councilwoman Julia Coates describes these waylaid Cherokee:

> There are probably 1,000–1,500 people who simply could not be accounted for.... [I]t is likely that most of these people did not die, but simply dropped off the trail to stay with relatives or return to the eastern Cherokees, [and] by the action of choosing not to complete the journey, they had effectively relinquished their citizenship in the tribal government.[73]

The chilliness of Coates's words lies in the presumption that women like grandmother Elizabeth Gibson had any choice. It is more likely that most Cherokee in Missouri after the Trail of Tears did not have the means or wherewithal to return east and were women like Elizabeth and her children. Many adopted Christianity, and Alfred and Elizabeth "related their experimental acquaintance with religion"[74] in 1848 at New Salem Cumberland Presbyterian Church, a frontier evangelical ministry antithetical to the mainstream Presbyterianism of the day.[75] According to Trail of Tears historian Joan Gilbert, Cherokee remaining in Missouri "kept low profiles in fear that the government would somehow, sometime, descend and pack them off to reservations."[76] This, of course, had just happened, and any form of public visibility must have felt vulnerable, even terrifying.

As years passed, Missouri Cherokee ancestors kept their personal histories hidden, even from their own children.[77] This has helped me understand that the suppression and secrets in my own family are not necessarily only about shame but also about the oppressive forces these ancestors faced. Their very survival depended upon an ability to "pass for white, or black, or a vague mix of ancestry."[78] To me, this need for covertness made them no less Cherokee.

FLIGHT OF THE NEXT GENERATION

The American Civil War divided the Cherokee and many other tribal communities forcibly removed into Indian Territory. Initially, the general sentiment was to stay out of the white man's war, but powerful slaveholders resenting the federal government's role in Indian removal now began to promote Southern sympathies.[79] Meanwhile, a sizable number of Cherokee felt drawn to the Union stance by their moral and religious views and concerns about a rising tide of local violence.

By the time Elizabeth Gibson died in 1862, the entire region around her and her family in Pineville and Neosho, Missouri, was mired in anarchy and chaos. Cannon and small-arms fire echoed through their hills. Colonel John T. Coffee's Confederate marauders were active locally, and numerous skirmishes and battles occurred near Alfred and Elizabeth's home.[80] General Stand Watie's Cherokee forces and Union troops skirmished regularly in nearby groves and meadows. Regarding the civilian threat, Vernon County historians immediately to the north wrote in 1887 that local conditions were rife with terror: "Every raid meant a robbery and plundering—maybe a house-burning and a murder."[81]

In North America's most vicious war to date, people living in southwest Missouri and Indian Territory were suffering more than anyone anywhere. Elizabeth Gibson and her children had to hunker down very close to a mayhem long remembered by eyewitnesses and reported by researcher Amanda Cobb-Greetham:

> While the men were fighting, the women and children were raided
> by bands of Northern soldiers, Southern soldiers, Pins, and outlaws.
> According to [survivor] Elizabeth Watts, raiding parties would "go

all over the country, burning all the houses, barns, and cribs, and carrying all the beds and chairs away, and killing or driving away the cattle."[82]

Perhaps such circumstances explain why particulars of Elizabeth's death were never recorded, and Alfred remained evasive. "During the war his house and fences were all burnt," a county historian explains in relation to Alfred in his short biography in 1897, "but they caught from the forest fires. He says the Rebels treated him well and he never had an enemy in his life."[83]

Alfred was lying. The 1856 marriage between their son, Mathew James Barlow, and another Cherokee grandmother, Elizabeth Jane Albina Alexander, fractured the family over the issue of slavery. At their wedding, our family story recounts, this young couple refused to accept the "gift" of an African slave couple from Elizabeth Gibson's brother, Mat Gibson. Uncle Mat then reportedly swore he'd "tie the knot" for their lynching nooses for sullying his honor. The newlyweds, my great-great-grandmother and great-great-grandfather, galloped off on horseback from Pineville, crossing the border into Arkansas by night ride to escape execution.[84]

SLAVERY AS DIVIDING LINE

Black slaves were forcibly marched by their Cherokee masters on the Trail of Tears,[85] where they, too, suffered and died.[86] By then, adoption of African slavery was already eroding older Cherokee beliefs about human freedom, interdependence, and matrilineal obligation. Prior to European contact, Cherokee reportedly held no beliefs about race difference or superiority,[87] and their use of African slaves commenced through their new relationships with European colonizers.

Although a form of human bondage using war captives existed prior to European contact, historian Theda Perdue concludes that "Cherokee bondsmen bear so little resemblance to European slaves that the term 'slave' can perhaps only be used inaccurately."[88] "*Atsi nahsa'i*, or 'one who is owned,'"[89] were eligible for adoption by matrilineal clans and, when it was granted, were able to partake of similar rights. While clearly deprived of freedom and forced into servitude, these bondspeople were seldom mistreated, permitted to advocate for their needs, and often considered family members.

European colonization radically altered such practices by adding key ingredients of dehumanization and materialism to the trading of enslaved African people. In the early days of contact with white slave owners, many eastern Native people recognized African slaves as their relatives, i.e., fellow human beings, rather than property, and sympathized with their plight, sometimes helping them run away. Terrified of possible alliances between slaves and Natives, white owners began propagandizing stories to slaves aimed at creating distrust and fear of their rescuers while simultaneously recruiting and rewarding Native "slave catchers."[90] Of course, such indoctrination came about within the wider context of exposing Native people to many other foreign ideas, often rooted in Christianity: ruling over rather than cooperating with nature, striving to achieve a higher status than others, possession over sharing as a measure of prestige, and a patriarchal family structure derived from "the domination of these Europeans whose empires rested on plantation slavery."[91]

It was the brutal objectification of African slaves that spun the kind of controversy erupting around Uncle Mat Gibson's "gift" to Mathew and Elizabeth Jane. Their marital rebellion reflects a response to a deep Cherokee factional tension—but was this couple's behavior a taking of sides, a stand for justice, or both?

Christian abolitionists were on the run throughout the region, often routed by militia recruited by slave owners.[92] And yet Cherokee principal chief John Ross, a member of the Christian mixed-blood elite and a slaveholder himself, vacillated on Black slavery to such a degree that he initially supported Cherokee alliance with the South. By 1862 he'd repudiated this alliance with his fellow slaveholders but been arrested by Union troops and sent into exile with his Quaker wife, Mary, to Washington, DC.[93] In 1863, pro-Ross, marginalized "full-blood" Cherokees, followers of Baptist missionaries Evan and John Jones, gathered at the Cowskin Prairie Council,[94] a few miles west of Alfred and Elizabeth's Pineville home, to pledge their allegiance to the Union. I don't know whether or not my great-great-grandfather Mathew Barlow was there, but I believe his wedding story suggests he would have been sympathetic.

Evan and John Jones were influential spiritual leaders who viewed slavery as a sin, expelled slaveholders from their churches, and inspired formation of the antislavery Keetoowah Society as a rebuke to the Cherokee Southern planter leadership.[95] Many Keetoowah followers would eventually become

Union soldiers and signal their rejection of all they considered antithetical to being Cherokee by wearing crossed pins on or beneath their lapels, earning them the sobriquet "Pin Indians," or "Pins." As noble as their moral stance might seem, Pins became just as notorious for raids and offenses against tribal women and children throughout Indian Territory.[96]

As the Civil War commenced, lines of conflict over African slavery bisected my own ancestors: Lemuel Green Barlow, Mathew's brother and my great-great uncle, and James Ambrose Gibson, a likely cousin through Elizabeth Gibson, joined the Confederacy together and fought with Stand Watie's Confederate Cherokee forces. Matthew and Elizabeth Jane, however, held firm to the stance they'd taken and, like many abolitionists of the time, fled north from Arkansas to Kansas, where Mathew enlisted with the Ninth Kansas Cavalry (Union) as a blacksmith. He faced off against his own family members at the Battle of Pea Ridge, where more than 3,000 men were killed or wounded.

After the war ended, Uncle Mat Gibson's blood oath against my blue-eyed Cherokee grandfather Mathew may have been transacted. He died under mysterious and somewhat ludicrous circumstances—from "insanity" brought about by hemorrhoids, according to the attending physician. I believe generational grandfather Matthew James Barlow was poisoned.

Elizabeth Jane Alexander Barlow became a widow under dire circumstances. Destitute, she was compelled to leave Kansas and seek support from her anti-Indian daughter Laura back in Missouri. She was instead "encouraged to go to the Indian Agency and register so that she would receive benefits from the government."[97] She reportedly refused, explaining "she had been disowned by her people when she married into the white race."[98] Such an explanation seems an accurate if simple depiction of the common experience of disenfranchised Missouri Cherokee women of the time. Ultimately, Laura took Elizabeth Jane in and cared for her for the rest of her life. She left her mother's grave near Stillwater, Oklahoma, unmarked.

Other ancestors were less ambivalent about our Cherokee heritage: Uncle Lemuel Green Barlow and two of my great-great aunts, Sarah and Elizabeth A. Barlow (unrelated by blood to Elizabeth Jane), all married and settled in the Cherokee Nation after the Civil War.[99] Still others moved back and forth as the social climate evolved. James Ambrose Gibson became ordained with the traveling Indian Mission Conference. John Wesley Barlow,

The author's paternal great-great-aunt, Sarah Barlow (Missouri Cherokee descendent), daughter of Elizabeth Gibson and Alfred Hirton Barlow, who migrated with the Cherokee Trail of Tears. *Author's collection.*

The author's paternal great-grandmother, Mary Safronia Barlow (Missouri Cherokee descendent), 1930s. *Author's collection.*

my great-uncle, and my great-grandmother, Mary Barlow, are both described in various genealogical sources as "mixed-blood Cherokee." I've described myself similarly on occasion.

My grandma, Donna Barlow Smouse Walker, was born into poverty in 1901 in a log cabin near Hog Creek along Indian Meridian Road near Newalla, Indian Territory, at a time when a concerted effort was underway to create a state called "Sequoyah." By 1907 her white father's alcoholism spiraled out of control and he abandoned her, her mother, and her older half brothers. In 1973 she recollected into my Uncle Ed's tape recorder about living "all around, and like I told you, I went to eighteen grade schools, so that's why I don't know anything."[100] Her father, still an occasional figure, "wouldn't give my mother any cash, but he'd buy me anything I wanted—shoes, a new dress, or whatever. The trouble was he wouldn't come back in time before my toes were pokin' through my shoes."[101] She never finished high school, working instead as a telegraph operator for Western Union until 10:00 or 11:00 p.m. to help her mother, a home nurse, make ends meet.

Hers is a story about what happened to Cherokee people. Louis Owens, the astute Choctaw-Cherokee-Irish professor of English and Native American Studies at UCLA who tragically took his own life in 2002, wrote eloquently on the deliberate obscuring of mixed families:

> Silence a people's stories and you erase a culture. To have graphic evidence of this phenomenon, all we have to do is look at a map. Mapping is, of course, an intensely political enterprise, an essential step toward appropriation and possession. Maps write the conquerors' stories over the stories of the conquered.[102]

Grandma Donna felt so ashamed about her humble roots that she persistently resisted friendly overtures from my well-to-do and more educated maternal grandparents. She was also quite possessive of her two sons and never bonded well with my mother. Being Cherokee was a rare point of pride for her, and I feel her own hardscrabble life was a transcendent echo of that of our forebears on the Trail of Tears. I'm convinced the Cherokee Nation of Oklahoma will never officially "recognize" Missouri Cherokees like her or their descendants. In this way, our disenfranchisement remains another painful feature of Cherokee history.

I know she loved me in her own way, and I now understand the fringe jacket she gave me as the only way she could communicate a story she could not tell about our lost Cherokee grandmothers and the demise of their matrilineal power, to be whispered in hints and secrets, but never so completely hidden that her grandson couldn't follow the map.

FOURTEEN

Entering the Asylum

MENTAL HYGIENE AS THOUGHT REFORM

I've often wondered how Cherokee "progressives" must have thought because they represented such a profound change in consciousness evolving over a very short period. Conflicting ways of knowing social and material reality had collided for decades, and after the Civil War they demanded quick resolution to meet terrible changes immediately at hand. Since many Cherokee progressives were drawn to Christian humanism by white missionary education, their agenda of spiritual, material, and educational uplifting must have felt imperative, a rescue attempt of one's brethren, the families left indigent and ruined by oppression and forced removal.

As for the older, traditional Cherokee ways, perhaps Cherokee progressives concluded that the newly established cultural compass simply no longer pointed that way. Such a circumstance alone would induce chronically high levels of stress among the Cherokee majority. However, to such a revelation, we must add ongoing factionalism, chronic white intrusion and land exploitation, and internecine warfare across a relatively lawless Indian Territory in the post–Civil War Reconstruction era.

I've sometimes used the provocative phrase "thought reform" to depict the forced assimilation of Native people in the United States. I borrowed this modern-day phrase from the deliberate political coercion and attempted "brainwashing" of dissidents and nonconformists from 1955 to 1969 during the Hundred Flowers Campaign and Cultural Revolution in China.[1] A more recent version of the same approach is seen in China's forced imprisonment of at least one million Muslim Uyghurs in encampments in Xinjiang, where they are subjected to "ideological 'education transformation.'"[2] "Thought reform" was what we see in the history of American Indian boarding schools. It is the social enactment of the consciousness-altering *intention* of domination, and it is sobering to consider its purpose in China, as it has been in the United States, which is "not to gain compliance but to produce conversion."[3]

The first expression of the early U.S. mental hygiene movement in Indian Country was embedded within a similar "conversion" of the Cherokee tribal community to Christianity. Historically, we can link early Christian missionaries considering whether eastern Natives actually possessed souls to "progressive" Cherokee converts partnering to save them. These religious conversions expanded through cultural transactions with EuroAmerican men, especially via intermarriage. Among Cherokee, federal and religious authorities installed and then partnered with powerful Christianized elites in the "civilizing" of holdout savage souls relabeled as "traditionalists." I believe this process traces forward all the way to the creation of a priestly caste of secular professionals identifying and intervening in Native "mental disorders" and "mental illnesses," filtering out genocidal and oppressive correlates and reframing them as deficiencies and impairments of individualized Native selves.

Such conversion was never just religious but holistic. For fifty years Welsh preacher Evan Jones, cofounder of the Keetoowah Society with his son, John Jones, worked to convert his mostly traditional, "full-blood" Cherokee followers not just *toward* Christianity but *away* from their long-established rituals, dances, and especially reliance upon *adonisgi*, medicine healers. Jones clearly saw his mission in disrupting and replacing a worldview. According to biographer William G. McLoughlin, he insisted to his Cherokee protégés that

> instead of adapting themselves to the cyclical rhythms of nature, they must now accept a linear view of progress ... God meant man to subdue nature and utilize its resources to improve his condition. This meant adapting new values—individualistic self-reliance in place of communal cooperation—hard work, self-discipline, thrift, enterprise, and accumulation of private property for each man's family. Christianity would assist them in adopting and sustaining a

new ethic attuned to the market economy of the United States. To adhere to the old religion under their new circumstances would be to fly in the face of history and God's will.[4]

I don't believe Evan Jones's Cherokee followers surrendered their sense of personal agency or became victims of some kind of mass hypnosis. There are likely few singular reasons why these Cherokee accepted, promoted, and practiced European ways. Contemporary clichés such as "Like father, like son" or "We're married now, and I'm in charge" or "Stockholm syndrome" do not capture the breadth of this American thought reform movement.

African slavery certainly played a special role. As in many other places in Native America, the blood quantum metaphor developed into a social currency entirely reversed from its sense today. Being a slave owner; passing as white in appearance, manners, and demeanor; and being of higher economic standing while embracing Southern virtues like gentility and honor brought the "successfully civilized" Cherokee an aristocratic aura and presumed superiority. While there were "full-blood" Cherokees keeping African slaves, they were considerably fewer in number than—and much less likely to obtain the ease or status of—the intermarried, "mixed" planters.[5] In fact, traditionalist slaveholders were more often described by ex-slaves and observers as rejecting practices of European chattel slavery and treating them as kindred, being masters in "name only"[6] and possibly sustaining remnant ethics of *atsi nahsa'i* bondage.

The Keetoowah Society responded to the loss of status and place among this poorer, traditionalist class through the promise of Christian redemption. Ironically, the intermarried planters who practiced chattel slavery helped build the Cherokee reputation as a "civilized tribe." European mental hygiene ideas became more attractive as part of their adopted mores of conformity and deviance arising through their new social status. They modeled civilized behavior to the whites with whom they traded and related, and at the height of their dominance their African slaves approached 15 percent of the entire Western Cherokee population.[7,8] Of course, the slavery that the abolitionist Joneses railed against, and that the intermarried elite preachers lauded, was a key factor in dividing the Cherokee Nation.

It was two years into the American Civil War, which from its outset was more immediately about African slavery than it could ever be about states' rights for Cherokee people, that Indian agent W. G. Coffin described several thousand Cherokee people "entirely barefooted, and more than their number have not rags enough to hide their nakedness."[9] And after the war concluded, the people of Cherokee Nation became only more brutalized for taking the wrong side again, this time through their formal embrace of the Confederacy. Once again, they were forced to cede more land, this time 10 million acres, to the United States government.

LOCKING UP THE CRAZY INDIAN

Massive community upheaval and the disempowering of matrilineal clans—political and social consequences of domination and oppression—brought Cherokee progressives to first envision a new home for their "disadvantaged citizens."[10,11] Clan roles were collapsing and with them mutual obligation: EuroAmerican individualistic values were displacing an older sense of interdependent responsibility.

Some historians praise the compassion of the leaders who built the first mental hygiene facility in Native America, but they may not have fully considered the factionalizing and upheaval leading to its necessity. Historian Julie L. Reed admits that "when clan kin could not provide, they expected their broader family—the Cherokee Nation—to step in. The number of requests to the council for national pensions increased significantly after the war."[12] She celebrates the first asylum in Indian Country as "an institution that could serve multiple categories of residents ... [that,] given the number of pensioners, presented the possibility of an economic savings."[13] To me, such a conclusion does not adequately represent an ongoing power struggle between a victorious minority of progressive, intermarried elites and a marginalized majority of Cherokee traditionalists.

This Cherokee "social services" movement started in 1866, only three months after President Andrew Johnson declared the Civil War ended, and when the Cherokee National Council appointed a committee to look into improving care of children left orphaned by the war's violence and secondary famine and disease.[14] Initially located in the Cherokee Male Seminary, efforts at establishing more permanent housing stalled until 1877, when conflicts of interest were resolved regarding the purchase of deceased wealthy Cherokee planter Lewis Ross's estate. In its early days, the Cherokee Orphan Asylum became a point of pride with its well-appointed facilities, philosophical emphasis on family and nurturance, Cherokee staff and teachers in the majority, and curriculum efforts supporting Cherokee language and traditions of its mostly "full-blood" children.

The needs of the blind, enfeebled, disabled, and "insane" came next. The new facility, located five miles south of Tahlequah, Oklahoma, was christened the "Home for the Insane, Deaf, Dumb, and Blind of the Cherokee Nation" but was more commonly referred to as the "Cherokee Asylum." According to a masters thesis on Cherokee architecture written by Ellen Dement Hurd and accepted by the department of architecture at the University of Washington in 2019,

> The Insane Asylum building was a brick building in the Italianate mode. The four-story building had a rectangular plan and a hipped roof. The symmetrical façade had a projecting central pavilion with five bays of windows and a front gable. The central bay had a one-story porch with a flat roof, paired bracketed columns, and wooden railings carved with circular Chippendale-style designs.[15]

Any dispossessed, disabled, blind, distraught, non-conforming person, destitute and causing concern or trouble to the community, became eligible for admission to Cherokee Asylum, either voluntarily or involuntarily, through the testimony of two other citizens. As Julie Reed suggests, "embedded in the admissions policy was an acknowledgement of the inability of families to meet the basic needs of disabled Cherokee people."[16]

Earlier legislation enacted by progressives in 1826 and declaring "lunatics" and "idiots" not legally culpable for their actions was now methodized within "An Act in Relation to the Asylum for the Blind, Insane, and Others," passed in 1875:

> Every applicant for admission to the asylum, should by himself, guardian or friend, present to the steward an application in writing showing cause of admission, and that he was destitute of means of support, and had no relatives able, or willing to be burdened with his support, and the same was to be certified by two respectable citizens.[17]

This admission process was smoothed for "lunatics":

> In case the friends or relations of any lunatic shall neglect, or refuse, to place him in the asylum, and shall permit him to go at large, it shall be the duty the judge of the district court wherein such lunatic

may reside, or be found going at large, on the suggestion, in writing, of any citizen of the district, to order the sheriff to take charge of such person, and place him in the asylum, and the steward shall receive and provide for him until otherwise directed by the board.[18]

After involuntary admissions, determinations regarding the "sanity" of a lunatic became the purview of the asylum's board of trustees in consultation with its medical superintendent. This was the beginning of a formal legal process known as "Indian lunacy determination."

When Cherokee Asylum opened its doors in 1877, its board of trustees and medical superintendents were unified by their Christian humanism, despite having come from both sides of the Civil War. Charles Thompson (Utselata), principal Cherokee chief, was the board's de facto president.[19] During the war, he'd switched sides from the Confederacy to the Union and become a Keetoowah Society member.[20] A devout Baptist deacon who preached in his Native language on Sundays,[21] his métis mother reportedly spoke only Cherokee.[22] "S. Foreman," another trustee, was likely Reverend Stephen Foreman, a Princeton graduate who helped translate the New Testament into Cherokee.[23] His son, John A. Foreman, became the first steward of the asylum[24] and was once a major with the Third Indian Home Guards on the Union side.[25]

Trustee Dennis Wolf Bushyhead was the mixed Cherokee son of Reverend Jesse Bushyhead, who shepherded his flock along the Trail of Tears.[26] Like Foreman, Dennis was educated at Princeton, but he had traveled widely and recently returned home at the time Cherokee Asylum opened. He once worked as a clerk for Chief John Ross and would himself soon be elected as principal chief of the Western Cherokee Nation.[27] Trustee Wilson Sanders accepted his role as the asylum's first superintendent.[28] A Cherokee Nation attorney, he'd fought for the Confederacy in Company I of the Cherokee Mounted Rifles under General Stand Watie.[29]

The asylum's first doctor, i.e., medical superintendent, Edwin Poe Harris, was a white man who once served with the Missouri Militia, answering the clamorous call of Governor Claiborne Jackson, who'd sent secret secessionist communications to Jefferson Davis.[30] Looking back two decades after the war, Harris declared he'd "gotten mixed up in the politics of the [Cherokee] country and owing to his influence with the then ruling party he was intensely hated by the opposite party,"[31] evidently referring to his close friendship with Principal Chief Lewis Downing.

As a physician, Harris was not shy about proselytizing his political view "to show the Indians their only hope of existence lay in an abandonment of the title in common by which they [held] their lands"[32]—that is, matrilineal clan rights. His views contradicted those of Reverend Walter Adair Duncan, the Cherokee intellectual and supervisor of the Orphan Asylum, who told the *Cherokee Advocate* in 1894: "Land in severalty has filled the world with homeless men, women and children."[33]

Harris's "open and somewhat defiant mode"[34] to matrilineal common title was trumpeted via his partnership with Elias Cornelius Boudinot, son of the assassinated signer of the Treaty of New Echota, in their newspaper, *Indian Progress*.[35] Harris rankled many, and at one point, "the opposite party obtained control of the country and ... [he] was forced to leave to escape assassination."[36] His one-year tenure as Cherokee Asylum's medical superintendent appears to have been politically tumultuous as well.[37]

His replacement, Dr. Walter Thompson Adair, reportedly once served as surgeon for the Confederate First Cherokee Mounted Rifles.[38] He was the son of George Washington Adair, a signer of the Treaty of New Echota who had avoided assassination.[39] Both Harris and Adair had been assigned, in 1863 and 1865 respectively, to "Boggy Depot"—a central spot for citizens of the forcibly removed Choctaw Nation—and perhaps Harris recommended Adair as his replacement. It was Adair who would stay in the role of asylum medical superintendent for some time.

MENTAL HYGIENE IN CHEROKEE ASYLUM

The Cherokee National Insane Asylum was the first Indian "lunatic asylum." It was likely a difficult and depressing place for both inmates and staff members, and to gain a better sense of what it was like, I rely a little more than I'd like upon Carl Steen's overly rosy 1943 paper, "The Home for the Insane, Deaf, Dumb and Blind of the Cherokee Nation" (the original name of the Cherokee National Insane Asylum). Steen cites the annual steward's report (filed by Robert Wofford) as reflecting that, under Adair's supervision in 1882, "two substantial wooden cages"[40] were constructed and placed in the asylum "inside the northeast cell room, for the safe keeping of the more unruly and unmanageable inmates, at such times as it became necessary to restrain them from harm."[41]

These cages, in which inmates were confined for unknown durations, were likely the first documented use of psychiatric restraint in Native America. Their design is uncertain, and I'm unable to verify whether they bore any similarity to "Utica cribs," the notorious and highly claustrophobic devices consisting of "a bed with sides and a latched top that opened"[42] that were recommended as a more appropriate restraint than "strong rooms"[43] at the 1874 meeting of the Association of Medical Superintendents of American Institutions for the Insane, forerunner to the American Psychiatric Association.

Strong rooms and Utica cribs are the antecedents to the "quiet rooms" I've encountered in inpatient psychiatric facilities, places where I've seen out-of-control patients forcibly shackled into four-point restraints and injected with haloperidol and other substances. "Chemical restraint" has become more normative these days than locking people into confined spaces when they become threatening or disturbing, but quiet rooms remain common. The Cherokee Insane Asylum's need for contraptions to manage the "unruly and unmanageable" suggests a similar need for some chemical means by which to compel inmates inside of them. The psychiatric drugs used at the time included chloral hydrate, alkaloids (opiate derivatives), and—most popular for patient "management"—bromides. Bromides were highly toxic, accumulated in tissue with lasting effects, and induced lethargy, hallucinations, and delirium.[44]

About four years after these cages were built, Steen notes, Adair created a list that distinguished inmates he considered "competent" from those deemed "incompetent." His method for tabulating the distinction was "whether or not the patient was able to be trusted with any funds which might be placed within his care through any means."[45] Out of a census of twenty-one people, Adair determined nine female and five male inmates to be incompetent.[46]

In assessing the troubled or troubling Native's capacity to manage money, Adair's psychiatric competency evaluations became another first in Indian Country, presaging the competency commissions of the Burke Act thirty years later that would determine an Indian's capacity to make decisions regarding her or his own land allotment, including whether to farm or sell it.[47] Evaluation of Native competency continues into the present time, such as when, shortly after I arrived at Yakama Nation, I declined to be part of an examination undertaken by the Bureau of Indian Affairs of an elder who refused to allow a cell tower to be built on his land allotment.

By 1882, Steen describes an average yearly census at the Cherokee Insane Asylum of twenty-two people. Its doors had been open for only five years, and already twelve people had died within its confines—that is, an average of 10 percent of people entering the asylum each year. He quotes an unnamed, undated report, likely issued around 1883, as providing an implicit explanation of the high mortality rate:

> The Asylum is not intended as an infirmary for those who are poor and unable to pay a physician. Many are admitted under the head of descrepitude [sic] purely with a desire to obtain medical treatment. On these cases the law should per very expelicit [sic]. A young person cannot be decrepit. Inmates should be regular in habits, have regular exercise, and should not be allowed to straggle over the country ad libitum. They should be so managed as to forbid a free and unrestrained intercourse between the sexes.[48]

"Decrepitude" means very elderly individuals. Traditional family care of elders had become disrupted by matrilineal clan demise, war, and poverty, and the asylum was apparently being viewed as a last-ditch alternative. By "ad libitum," the report writer is using the older, longer form of "ad lib," meaning in this context that inmates should not be allowed to move about freely. Thus, freedom of movement and "intercourse" (Victorian code for sexual relations) was to be curtailed within the Cherokee Insane Asylum, though well before the emergence of the British and American eugenics movement.

According to Steen, Adair's salary was arbitrarily cut in 1887, but he fought back and won. However, he'd evidently had enough and decided to concentrate on his practice in downtown Tahlequah. A recently minted Cherokee physician, twenty-three-year-old Joseph M. Thompson, was selected over five other candidates in 1888 as the new medical superintendent for all public health needs at Cherokee Nation, including the asylum.[49] Sources predating Steen describe Thompson as a "courteous, refined gentleman" and "no participant in gambling, whisky drinking, or even the use of tobacco."[50] His father, Johnson Thompson, was a prominent local merchant and a former quartermaster of the Confederate First Cherokee Regiment whose own education had been "obtained in private schools maintained by the Georgia planters."[51] Thus, the family's pedigree was connected to slaveholding Cherokee planters who left voluntarily with the Treaty of New Echota signing party.[52]

When Dr. Thompson began his role, there were twenty-four patients in the asylum census,[53] and high mortality continued to plague the facility. In late 1890, Thompson sought funds for a nurse after the deaths of three inmates during the past year. By 1892, "six idiotic and six insane" were described in a census that had grown to its highest point at thirty-four. Blind, disabled, and infirm people likely made up the remaining inmates, but this is not clarified.

There are clues to specific inmate problems emerging for staff members within an unusual recommendation from a special report by the new steward, John R. Meigs, and issued to Colonel Johnson Harris, principal chief of the Cherokee Nation, in September 1893:

> Some early action should be taken to relieve the institution of the care and custody of unauthorized inmates. "P.S." a white U.S. citizen with no claims to Cherokee citizenship whatever—and "Jonas" the colored adopted Cherokee Freedman who is at the Asylum without "due course of law."[54]

The staff of the Cherokee Insane Asylum were likely considerably more compassionate than those to come. Yet a review of the lives of certain inmates[55] suggests the facility was also exploited as a means for being rid of the unwanted or maligned. Additionally, as Steen notes, "non-citizens of the Indian Territory, those who had been permitted to live in that country, and by no means trespassers, had trouble taking care of their unfortunate."[56] There were no similar facilities for the problematic white intruders onto Cherokee land who had arrived with anticipation and primarily through the ambitions of railroad companies lobbying to dissolve Cherokee and other Indian nations.[57] For these white people forming what would become the new state of Oklahoma, housing for those who did not fit among them would become the impetus for the Oklahoma State Hospital for the Insane.

By 1893, Cherokee Insane Asylum was operating at a deficit and becoming run-down. Steen reports that steward Meigs appealed to the trustees for better bedding and needed repairs to the furnace grates, broken windows, pumps, and pipes in the bathrooms and the watershed. In 1892, medical superintendent Joseph Thompson left, and for several years, Richard L. Fite contracted as medical superintendent at both male and female seminaries, the insane asylum, and the jail[58] before making room for Charles McClelland Ross, great-grandson of Principal Chief John Ross,[59] who was at least associated with if not supervising all of these institutions until his untimely death in 1908 after being electrocuted by a fence.[60] While Choctaw historian and professor Devon Mihesuah describes Ross as medical superintendent through the closure of Cherokee Insane Asylum,[61] Carl T. Steen's 1943 paper tracing asylum expenses includes Fite as the medical supervisor of that particular institution through 1908, its final year.[62]

By 1898, the board of trustees was abolished by order of U.S. president William McKinley, and the Cherokee Insane Asylum was placed under federal control. Historian Julie Reed iterates that with pressures toward "allotment and dissolution, the Cherokee Nation 'donated' the asylum facilities" for use by any insane persons.[63] Steen abstracts from the report of yet another new steward, Sam Manus, who seemed desperate to find anyone in authority to care for the building's leaking roof, unsafe stairways, and poor bedding for the remaining ten inmates.[64] Two more inmates died that year.

In 1903, the Cherokee Insane Asylum became uninsurable, and all inmates were moved into the national jail in Tahlequah, conflating psychiatric confinement with legal incarceration. They stayed there, and by 1904 things had improved somewhat. The census came up to eighteen inmates, yet the annual report's depiction of the oldest among them, "Jack Spaniard," at 108 years, stretches credulity and was likely a ruse,[65] while another inmate described as being eight years old seems both sad and terrifying.

Steen names Fite as the contracted medical superintendent overseeing Cherokee Asylum towards its demise. He was a local doctor with a practice in Tahlequah and helped the facility limp to its closure in 1908. Whether the remaining ten patients transferred to the Oklahoma State Hospital for the Insane actually represented its final census or had been "valiantly assisted through trial and misfortune due to mental ailments," as Steen contends, remains for others to verify. I cannot imagine things went quite so well.

The need for a brand-new facility to house Indian lunatics was now a pressing issue.

FIFTEEN

Locked Inside Hiawatha: Josephine's "Delusions"

INTRODUCTION

The Hiawatha Asylum for Insane Indians was an American gulag operated by the U.S. federal government, primarily housing Native people made forever invisible to their families and the world outside. Many would be considered political prisoners today and died in total obscurity, forgotten. For the next four chapters I will seek to unravel the asylum experiences of several Native inmates. Of course, they have long ago walked on, and legally the confidentiality of their federal medical records expired fifty years after their deaths. I'm unable to fully consider the desires of family descendants, but I have decided to presume they would want to know who these ancestors were and what they went through. For these reasons, I use their real names.

To remind my reader of a point made earlier regarding the definition of "mental disorders," today's American Psychiatric Association states that

socially deviant behavior (e.g., political, religious, or sexual) and conflicts that are primarily between the individual and society are not mental disorders unless the deviance or conflict results from a dysfunction in the individual.[1]

Let us bear this caveat in mind in learning what "conflicts" between these individuals and the dominant society brought them to such a horrific place. Simultaneously, we will learn of the mental hygiene practices of the time and seek to identify Hiawatha's echoes in the U.S. mental health system in Native America today.

Until recently, I could not locate any comment upon the Hiawatha Asylum from professional organizations associated with American psychiatry. In May 2019, the American Psychiatric Association annual meeting sponsored a session on its 175th anniversary "history track" that mentioned the history of the U.S. mental health system in Indian Country, including the Hiawatha Asylum, while completely neglecting to describe its direct complicity with its profoundly oppressive and violent practices.[2] That is a stupendous oversight.

RIDING BETWEEN THE CHEROKEE AND HIAWATHA ASYLUMS

Narcissa Josephine Rider, who went by Josephine, exemplifies just such "socially deviant behavior ... and conflicts," and yet she spent much of her life confined in the Cherokee Insane Asylum, the Hiawatha Asylum for Insane Indians, and the Oklahoma State Hospital for the Insane. She was the granddaughter and niece to men who signed the Treaty of New Echota and were then executed.[3] Her own father, a soldier in the internecine "Tom Starr War,"[4] was dead by her third birthday, and she buried her mother before she turned sixteen years old.[5] In 1870 she married a veteran named Jackson Foreman,[6] who'd served under Confederate general Stand Watie.[7] Before 1874, however, she'd conceived a daughter, Maude, by a second Cherokee husband named Richard Martin Walker.[8] By 1878, Walker had left her and Maude behind to marry another woman.

Not very long before all this, such challenges in the lives of Josephine and Maude would have been responded to by members of their clan, the Ani'Ga'tâga'wi, or Wild Potato Clan.[9] Matrilineal relatives would not have frowned upon Josephine's successive relationships or upon Maude as an "illegitimate" child, who would have been embraced as one of their own. Historian Rose Stremlau notes that "late-nineteenth-century Cherokee women retained enormous autonomy to engage in a range of sexual relationships"[10] and "sexual and marital relationships" in Cherokee society often "were characterized by fluidity rather than permanence or exclusivity."[11] Yet, for Josephine, the rapid erosion of clans meant an urgent need to find a new husband to support her and Maude. Josephine's very life was determined by political, religious, and gendered conflicts existing between the two worlds she was forced to inhabit with her daughter.

By 1882, she'd married Allen Gilbert and had another child, a son.[12] Allen was a white farmer who may have adopted Maude, and marriage with Josephine was likely mutually convenient. Gilbert had recently lost his Cherokee wife, Kiamitia West,[13] which meant he'd also lost his Cherokee citizenship, including the right to farm any Cherokee land held in common. A privilege enjoyed by intermarried white men to buy Cherokee citizenship for $500[14] had been repealed five years earlier in 1877. Having lost Kiamitia, Allen could retain control over land he'd already been farming only by marrying another Cherokee woman, and this seems a likely part of his relationship with Josephine.

At some point about five years into their marriage, Josephine was briefly placed in Cherokee Insane Asylum, and it is unclear why. When I say "placed," I mean she probably did not go voluntarily. She wasn't inside for long, but the implications would come to haunt her. Medical Superintendent Walter Thompson Adair remarked in his annual report of 1887 that she'd been discharged "on furlough."[15] She'd come into the asylum at the same moment as her younger cousin, Ruth Belle Rider, daughter of Charles Austin August "Gus" Rider, who served in the Cherokee legislature for multiple terms.[16] Whatever troubles brought them separately or together, Josephine eventually returned to live with Allen until he died in June 1898.

Only three weeks after Allen died, the Curtis Act passed Congress, forcing the Cherokee into abiding by the Dawes Act of 1887 and finally ending the tribe's battle to sustain common land title through matrilineal affiliation. The tribal government was abolished, and U.S. federal courts and Indian agents found themselves with vast new powers over legal and other dealings of Cherokee people. This power extended to the oversight of Cherokee Insane Asylum.

Under the Curtis Act, the secretary of the interior placed Inspector J. George Wright in charge of Union Agency, all schools in Oklahoma Territory, the Choctaw and Chickasaw Mining Trust, revenue inspectors for the Cherokee and Creek, and tribal commissions surveying and laying out town sites for populations of over two hundred.[17] And in 1904, Inspector Wright also accepted responsibility for all "insane persons" in Indian Territory as well as authorization of all oil and gas pipeline rights of way.[18] The linkage between these seemingly disparate responsibilities will not be lost on the astute reader.

INTO HIAWATHA

On a lingering "Indian summer" day in October 1905, an aging Josephine Rider first caught sight of high front gates arched with a sign reading "Hiawatha Asylum" in Canton, South Dakota.[19] She was by then very far from home, fifty-seven years old, short, and heavy. She'd nonetheless apparently been a handful for Captain John Calhoun West, brother of Kiamitia West, deceased wife of Allen Gilbert. A notorious figure among the Indian Police,[20] Captain West was charged with bringing her to the Hiawatha Asylum from the Union Agency at Muskogee, Oklahoma. He'd had to lock her in his jail for several weeks before compelling her along the 400-mile journey away from what had been her lifelong home in Bartlesville.[21] The evidence suggests Josephine didn't go without a fight.

The Hiawatha Asylum for Insane Indians was opened by U.S. federal authorities in Canton, SD, in 1899 as the Cherokee Asylum entered decline. Hiawatha would soon become an American gulag. *South Dakota State Historical Society, 2009-07-02-012.*

As they entered the gates, she probably noticed the seven-foot-high woven steel prison fence surrounding her,[22] a feature not found at the Cherokee Insane Asylum. She was soon escorted into Hiawatha's main

Handwritten note to Indian Agent George Wright on oil company stationery from Josephine Rider's son-in-law, William Ross II, requesting that she be committed to Hiawatha Asylum and forcibly conveyed there by Indian policeman John West. *National Archives and Records Administration, Fort Worth, TX, RG 75, ARC ID# 649158.*

building, where she'd have found its two floors and four wings mostly empty, lit by the cold austerity of newfangled bright electric lights.[23] No artwork of any kind was permitted, and, oddly, there were very few chairs. Inmates were expected to sit on their beds if they weren't lying on them or walking around aimlessly, provided they were permitted to walk around at all.

Despite having recited a government policy on several occasions to not accept any Native inmates at Hiawatha Asylum that had sufficient revenue for their support from their estates, Indian agent J. George Wright applied funds derived from Josephine's oil leasing royalties to cover all her travel expenses and West's transportation pay. In a sad irony, her connection to land that would have been hers by birthright now helped pay for her coercion and confinement. The oil royalties collected in her name were controlled entirely by William P. Ross II, her son-in-law and legal guardian, husband to Maude and father to her granddaughter and toddler grandson. Ross himself was a nephew to Chief William P. Ross, a founding trustee for the Cherokee Insane Asylum.

In early 1903, William P. Ross II had forced Josephine to be confined at the Cherokee Insane Asylum again for several months before allowing her to come live with him, his wife, and their children. About two years later he accused Josephine of swinging a chair at her granddaughter, and this was one of the reasons he gave for sending her to Hiawatha.

As guardian in control of her wealth, son-in-law Ross must have arranged for the three prominent white men in Bartlesville to attest that Josephine was without means. He'd begun his campaign to have her confined for the second time in her life by writing to Indian agent Wright in September 1905 about his own effort to transport her to Russell, Oklahoma, to live with her sister, Sue. He said he "could not manage" her over the trek of several hundred miles, and at Muskogee he'd appealed to Captain West, her cousin, to take charge and force her elsewhere.

Ross had obtained guardianship of Josephine in late 1902. His word on her misdeeds would have carried sufficient power to send her into Cherokee Insane Asylum and then to Hiawatha. Presciently, he'd already obtained a U.S. court order in August declaring her an Indian lunatic and, in the process, hired a Bartlesville physician to document that "she was very nervous, very restless, and . . . very angry at times and making threats."[24] This physician also stated that she was suffering from "hallucinations in regard to money and property." Anything Josephine would say about her financial situation, apparently, was now to be regarded in terms of insanity.

Just a few months prior to her confinement, in fact, Ross had bought two hundred acres of land south of Bartlesville and converted this land into an individual allotment in Josephine's name using new provisions from the Curtis Act. He had testified to the Cherokee Land Office clerk, "She owns a home in the land I am selecting."[25] Of course, as Josephine was under Ross's guardianship, she no longer had any real home to own anywhere. For all intents and purposes, this land now belonged to her son-in-law, and it proved highly lucrative.

The oil royalties Ross managed in Josephine's name were "bonds of the Kansas and Texas Oil Company." By June 1906, the *Petroleum Review* was reporting plans "to construct a pipeline from the company's property in Bartlesville,"[26] expanding on what the *Weekly Examiner* had extolled in 1903 as "the first well drilled in Cherokee Nation outside of Cudahy's" upon "the Ross allotment . . . the most important well that has been drilled in this section."[27]

Thus, when Hiawatha's gates swung open, and Captain West presented Dr. John Turner an "Order for Delivery of Insane Indian,"[28] Josephine was confronted with a fait accompli: "The United States Court . . . having issued an order adjudging Josephine Rider, a Cherokee citizen, to be insane and remanded her to your custody . . ." meant she'd been removed entirely from her prior life and made powerless. Turner signed the "Receipt for Delivery of Insane Indian": "I hereby acknowledge to have received from William P. Ross, Guardian . . . custody of the insane person noted."[29] In this way, Josephine's final defeat in a fierce family battle was sealed.

The intake paperwork from Hiawatha describing her as "very angry at times" and "making threats" is all that remains of her voice. She'd lost her home, land, clan, and family; she no longer held control over her own body or her future. Sitting on her bed, she was now briefed about her new life in this special American gulag.

Hiawatha would become for Josephine what seminal asylum researcher and sociologist Erving Goffman called a "total institution" governing every aspect of her life through "a series of abasements, degradations, humiliations, and profanations of self."[30] Asylum superintendent Oscar Gifford described the patients arriving at the new facility as "miserably wretched."[31] In the chain of command beneath Gifford were Assistant Superintendent Dr. Turner, a financial clerk, a matron, a seamstress, a laundress, a cook, a watchman, an engineer, two attendants, and two laborers. Everyone working there lived on-site.

Twenty-one Hiawatha inmates per floor were expected to share a single toilet and bath, but capacity would overflow to twice that number eventually. Josephine, however, arrived to only twenty or so fellow inmates in the entire facility. Turner described them as suffering "epileptic" and alcoholic dementias, "acute" or "chronic melancholia" (depression) or mania, or simply "congenital imbecility," i.e., "feeblemindedness."[32] He regimented each inmate's life to consist of proper sleep (bedtime at 8:00 p.m. nightly), vegetarian meals, outdoor activity (working on the asylum farm), and regular hot baths. Visits from family members were forbidden, as was Native dancing. Beading and basket-making were permitted, as were board games, cards, sewing, baseball, basketball, and horseshoes. But such activities didn't generate much interest among the imprisoned, and the able-bodied often sought work in the laundry, the kitchen, or on the farm to mitigate their endless boredom. Becoming a source of free labor also helped establish privileges and a possible means of escape. There were many such attempts at Hiawatha Asylum, but very few successes.[33] According to Hiawatha historian, Todd Leahy, "Patient care took priority . . ." in a list of forty rules governing employee conduct, but "kicking, striking, shaking, or choking patients as methods of control" were sanctioned, and "[a]ttendants were to insure the patients were non-violent and never profane."[34]

After Josephine's first year, Turner described her as "changed markedly" and "now quiet and quite reasonable."[35] His positivity may have made her optimistic, but she would never go home again. Turner's ongoing friction with Gifford over releasing inmates he considered "cured" kept Josephine inside Hiawatha for three more years. By 1909 he had quit, and Josephine's son-in-law, William P. Ross II, easily arranged for her transfer to the Oklahoma State Hospital for the Insane at Norman. I could find no further record of Josephine Rider afterward. It's likely she lived out the rest of her days there.

SIXTEEN

Locked in Hiawatha: Emily's Demise

QUEEN EMILY

Let's turn now to a Native woman who embraced the "deteriorating influences of civilization"[1] with a passion. Emily Waite may have been an enrolled Chickasaw woman, but she was far more interested in her Swedish heritage. Her older sister, Irene Kerr, an accomplished artist, detailed Emily's impetuous nature as a young adult: her refusal in 1882 to return to Oberlin College following her first year; her insistence that her property be "divided from the estate which mother held in common with her unmarried children"; her spending of her family's wealth, derived from the rich bottomlands they owned,[2] upon "a handsome wardrobe"; and her efforts to enter "a gay society life."[3]

After straying to California and working for a time as a maid, Irene said Emily returned to finish her degree at Oberlin and, in 1899, wrote to her family that she was leaving for Paris. Once situated, she began teaching French children and soon became fluent in French and German. Her letters home were "filled with abuse of the American people who she termed 'Foreigners'" and "emigrant usurpers," asserting "the Indians were the only true Americans and the nobility of America."[4]

Emily may have been reflecting a felt kinship with the romanticized *sauvage noblesse* often erroneously attributed to Rousseau. It's important to make the correction: this stereotype actually originated from racist anthropologists who'd successfully infiltrated the anti-racist Ethnological Society of London and recast the American Indian as an obsolete and dying race.[5] Whatever Emily's internalization of her "Indian-ness" represented to her, she was clearly more closely identified with her European heritage and proclaimed her intention to "live in Europe among the better class who preferred to remain at home where they belonged."[6]

Emily's family began to feel that she was becoming "unbalanced" through her declarations, but this was only the beginning of her escapades. After travels through Spain and Italy, she settled in Sweden, where her pursuit of her European roots became a total obsession. On October 8, 1897, the *Norman (OK) Transcript* carried a lengthy story entitled "American Girl Who Would Be Queen."[7] Emily, disguised under the pseudonym "Miss Louise White," had, according to the paper, gathered "an immense amount of documentary evidence"[8] that she was the rightful queen of Sweden.

According to the *Transcript*, Emily traced her family's ancestry to Gustavas IV Adolf, who'd been dethroned in 1809. Her claims found many Swedish followers, and Emily was described as "deeply interested in the various social, political and religious problems" of her new land, "familiar with Swedish literature," and "constantly studying the conditions of the Swedish peasant."[9] The fact that the sitting king of Sweden, Oscar II, could not claim the ascent she could from Gustavus IV made her suddenly very popular. There was doubt, however, as to her ability to actually press her claims because women had been prohibited from ruling for almost one hundred years. Emily was not deterred, however, and promised to provide "papers and documentation" she'd "collected and which she [said would] be put in evidence at the proper time ... [to] establish her relationship, it is claimed, to the old rulers of the country."[10]

Meanwhile, she'd taken up residence in lavish splendor in a posh hotel just down the street from King Oscar. An uncredited *Transcript* reporter declared her apartment to hold "interior decorations ... [that] compare favorably with any palaces on the continent."[11] Further, he gushed, if she "ever comes into possession of what she so confidently claims is her own, she will have beyond doubt the most beautiful and costly home in the world."[12]

I suspect Emily made a singular mistake in her meteoric ascendance to rival the king of Sweden, and this was her embrace of individualism and intent to "rely on her own resources"[13] rather than consider the impact of her behavior on her family. She came from people "well known both in society and in business in Indian Territory."[14] Her rebellion against them had lifted her from dropout rich girl to persuasive candidate for royalty in a period of only four years. Amazingly, she'd impressed her European followers "with a remarkable suit based upon a relationship of this nature which seems to establish the fact that she is the present and rightful Queen of Sweden"[15] as well as "the benefits good education and good breeding secure."[16] On the other hand, the *Shreveport (LA) Progress* opined that unless she "disguises herself as Joan of Arc and successfully downs the whole of Sweden before her sword there is not much likelihood of her ever getting near the throne."[17]

Despite living a high-society life and convincing many of her royal hue, Emily was now a significant public embarrassment for her family. By 1899 she'd sustained a massive fall from celebrity, been somehow compelled to return home, and was being held against her will in the Oklahoma State Hospital for the Insane, referred to at the time as "Oklahoma Sanitarium." How this occurred is unclear. Inside the sanitarium, she was reportedly prone to ripping her clothes apart when bothered by others, while if left alone she would give no trouble.[18] However, her family felt that her psychiatric treatment there was "without effect."[19]

In 1904, Irene wrote again to J. Blair Shoenfelt, Indian Agent for the Five Civilized Tribes as "Mrs. Perry N. Kerr," stating that "our sister is only partially demented, but not sufficiently sane to be safe in our families. We have kept her case as privately as possible and would request that you kindly do the same."[20] In his own affidavit, her husband and prominent local attorney Perry Kerr added that Emily "is so unpleasant" to her sisters, "they will hardly go in her presence."[21] Perry attested that Emily was apparently very angry and "[would] not speak to her sisters or brother, and they are all afraid of her."[22]

In 1905, the family's banker, S. J. Garvin, offered a notarized statement to Shoenfelt's office describing Emily as "without means, except an allotment as a Chickasaw Indian, which, however, is not subject to sale; and that she has no relatives or friends to give her proper care and support; that it would be best to the interest of all concerned to have her placed in an asylum by the Government."[23] By this time Emily was certainly no longer a candidate for queen of Sweden. Attorney J. T. Blanton followed suit, and her ties to family wealth were erased, making her eligible for forced incarceration in Hiawatha Asylum. In early August 1905, Emily was "conveyed" from the Muskogee

Indian Agency to Hiawatha by order of the "Indian Office" at a busy time when her transporter—a Hiawatha employee whose name is illegible to me—described "3 of us . . . on the road nearly all the time conveying patients to that asylum."[24]

FROM QUEEN TO LUNATIC

In providing the intake information for Hiawatha Asylum, Dr. David W. Griffin, resident physician of the Oklahoma Sanitarium for the Insane (later Oklahoma State Hospital) determined that Emily suffered from "delusions of grandeur," believing "she [was] the queen of some foreign country."[25] Unlike the Swedes, attorneys, and journalists she'd persuaded, Griffin did not believe her. On November 12, 1905, she was taken before a jury of twelve white men—Indians were not allowed to serve on juries—at the United States Court, Southern District, in Indian Territory and declared insane.

Preparations had already begun in 1904 through Irene Kerr to have her moved to the Hiawatha Asylum. It seems no wonder that Emily would be enraged. She'd succeeded in living as a queen for some time in everything but name; now she'd been reduced to poverty and powerlessness. In supplying intake paperwork for Hiawatha, Griffin described her as having "a strong will power," a belief that "she is Lady Bloomington and of royal blood," who "repudiates her relations here" and "desires to return to her home in the east."[26] But with "a number of delusions on various subjects,"[27] Emily was going nowhere, and Griffin recommended she have two guards for her transfer.

In 1906, Dr. John F. Turner, assistant superintendent and physician at the Hiawatha Asylum, undertook his rounds and noted that Emily looked "the same as a month ago" and that "she remains in her room most of the time, unmolested."[28] He did not record whether she'd destroyed any more of her clothing.

Emily Waite remained an inmate of the Hiawatha Asylum for Insane Indians for the next twenty-four years. She died there in 1929 at the age of fifty-nine and was buried in the asylum cemetery. Across the period of her long confinement, she witnessed the steady devolvement of the coercive and ill-conceived Hiawatha Asylum into absolute bedlam, a place one contemporary federal investigator described as "a living burial."[29]

ASYLUM FOR INSANE INDIANS,
Monthly Report Regarding Patient.

Canton, So. Dak. *Oct 1* 190 6

Report regarding *Emily Waite*

Physical condition *Good*

Weight *158*

Mental condition *Same as month ago.*

Remarks: *She remains in her room most of the time unmolested*

Very Respectfully, *John F. Turner*

Physician and Assistant Superintendent,
Indian Insane Asylum, Canton, S. D.

Hiawatha monthly "progress report" on Emily Waite written by psychiatrist and assistant superintendent John Turner: "She remains in her room most of the time, unmolested." *National Archives and Records Administration, Fort Worth, TX, RG 75, ARC ID# 649158.*

Unnamed female inmates who "often worked in the kitchen" (handwritten on back of photograph). Date unknown. *National Archives and Records Administration, Kansas City, MO, RG 75.*

SEVENTEEN

Locked Inside Hiawatha:
Two Eyewitnesses

HUMMER'S DRIVE

Much of the brutality that Emily Waite and many other Native inmates met at the Hiawatha Asylum for Insane Indians came about through the neglect and incompetence of its new director, Dr. Harry Hummer. A psychiatrist, Hummer took over in 1909 as Hiawatha Asylum superintendent after Oscar Gifford resigned following Dr. John F. Turner's complaints that his lack of oversight had led to a "full-term, bastard, imbecile" being conceived by an inmate. This baby boy was removed for an adoption that never materialized and died three months after being taken away from his mother.

Hummer had interned at St. Elizabeth's Hospital in Washington, D.C., where superintendent William Alanson White introduced such humane reforms as abandoning straitjackets and opening a beauty parlor. Such indulgences apparently did not impress young Dr. Hummer. He fought with his fellow staff members from the moment he arrived at Hiawatha, and Turner was quickly replaced by Dr. L. M. Hardin, a physician from Leech Lake Indian Boarding School, whose investigation by the Indian Office for unknown reasons had led to his transfer.

Hardin got along no better with Hummer and rallied staff members against his immaturity and arrogance, writing complaints to the Indian Office about his harsh treatment of inmates, including solitary confinement, food rationing, and the conscription of inmates as personal servants.[1] Hummer was repeatedly vindicated by outside investigators, however, even surviving accusations by his secretary in 1914 that he'd sought her out for sex while his wife was off evaluating two girls at the Santa Fe Indian School.[2]

Hummer retaliated against his adversaries by firing any who wouldn't resign. Hardin was gone after three months, and Hummer became both superintendent and sole physician for the next seventeen years. He seldom did any actual work with inmates, only rarely taking on an interview when it interested him.[3] Hummer fervently embraced the American eugenics movement and felt no Indian should be released from his asylum without first being sterilized. He didn't have facilities for such operations, and therefore very few inmates were released while he was in charge. In thirty-three years of operation, nine out of ten inmates discharged from

Harry Hummer, the notorious Hiawatha Asylum superintendent who developed the facility into an environment akin to what inspector called "a leper colony." Date unknown. *National Archives and Records Administration, Kansas City, MO, RG 75.*

Hiawatha left by dying. Eighty-three percent of the 120 inmates who died there lost their lives during Hummer's tenure, 52 as a result of his negligence during a 1924 tuberculosis outbreak.[4]

Yet, in 1916, Hummer's career was ascendant: he was expanding facilities to eighty-five beds and building new provisions for hydrotherapy and a solarium.[5] Hydrotherapy treatment, often considered punishment by anyone receiving it, included forced bathing for hours or even days in tubs circulating warm water or being swaddled with wet, freezing bedsheets. Attendants often only had to mention hydrotherapy to obtain compliance from inmates.

In 1927, Hummer sent a report indicating he had thirteen Native children and youth under age eighteen in the asylum.[6] Inmates lived behind locked doors, some bound in straitjackets. During a subsequent investigation, one paraplegic Native girl was discovered struggling on the bathroom floor

```
Crippled         Asylum for Insane Indians,
Children.           Canton, South Dakota,

                       April 22, 1927.


The Commissioner of Indian Affairs,

    Washington, D. C.

    Sir:

        Responding to Office circular dated April 13, 1927

    I have the honor to report that we have the following

    children here who appear to belong to the class to which

    you refer.

    Name.                Age.    Defect.    Grade.    Recommendation.
    Fairbanks, R.,        14.    Idiocy.    None.     Should remain.
    Frenier, Henry,       12.    Idiocy.    None.          do.
    Hayes, Robert,        16.    Imbecility. None.         do.
    Mankimetass, E. F.,   14.    Imbecility. None.         do.
    Richards, Alfred,     16.    Idiocy.    None.          do.
    Antone, Milsie,       15.    Dementia,p.None.     Is improving.
    Faribault, Baby,       ¾.    Imbecility. None.    Should remain.
    Moss, Amelia,         10.    Epileptic.  None.         do.
    Shawano, Annie,       17.    Epileptic.  None.         do.
    Yazza, Zonne,         18.    Epileptic.  None.         do.
    Roberts, Henry,       18.    Epileptic.  None.         do.
    Wolfe, Roy,           18.    Epileptic.  None.         do.
    Kalonuheskie, E.,     18.    Imbecility. None.         do.

    All of the above named children properly belong in an

    institution and are incapable of acquiring any degree of

    education.  Milsie Antone appears to be recovering from an

    episode of dementia praecox and will probably be discharged

    in the course of time.

                            Very respectfully,
                            H. R. Hummer  M. D.

    HRH*HRH                         Superintendent.
```

Harry Hummer tallies the number of Native children and youth being held in the Hiawatha Asylum for Insane Indians as of April 22, 1927, for the Commissioner of Indian Affairs. *National Archives and Records Administration, Kansas City, MO, RG 75, Box 2.*

where she'd been compelled to sleep half naked on a filthy mattress. Other inmates were found chained to iron pipes, the keys to their shackles "lost." One man had spent three out of the past six years locked in his room. Some people wore chains that had to be sawed through to remove. Others were found tied to beds, soiled in their own excrement.

For many years the asylum had been used as a convenient dumping ground for any Native person troubling an Indian agent or other vested parties by resisting government policies, authority in general, or the ambitions of powerful interests. Some, like Peter Thompson Good Boy, whose heroic story of in-house resistance I detailed in 2015 for *Indian Country Today*,[7] actively sought to obtain outside assistance, to no avail. I found this letter within one of the dusty boxes I opened at the National Archives and Records Administration facility in Fort Worth, Texas, but there was only a very rudimentary translation on separate piece of note paper. I was grateful when the staff at *Indian Country Today* arranged to have Peter's smuggled letter in phonetic Lakota, which never made it past the front doors, translated. Therein, he offers a rare eyewitness glimpse of how inmates fared in Hiawatha:

> My friends, at this time I would like to share something with you. Well, this hospital poses a concern. Therefore, I ask that it be taken care of at the Indian Office. Well, there are several men that work here, and they are employed through Lakota monies. Nothing is done correctly. Men were ill and died here. They endured severe ill treatment. That is why many have died here. Therefore, I choose to help. An individual (man) from a higher power to pursue such as [in] the Supreme Court we are entitled to. That is why men who work here do their work according to black hand. Men who are ill [and] get a little upset are killed immediately. So that is why the law was given to the Indian. If there was something filed against these men, they should be brought in front of a grand jury. These white men need to be found guilty now. That is why I am telling the truth. It was then I was coming back from the dining hall. He's got it in his mind we are going to die of starvation. I also would like to have an inspector come here. Whenever there is one coming here, we would like to visit with him. My relatives, we endure severe ill treatment. So that you can take this letter and get it written in English and give it to Cato Sells, Commissioner Indian Affairs, Washington, DC. He would be the person I suggest. My friends, I shake your hand. Peter T. Good Boy[8]

Peter's remark about "black hand" refers to extortion in the early days of organized crime.

Hiawatha's notoriety finally gained enough momentum to become scandalous even to white people. The *Helena (MT) Independent* ran a front-page story in October 1933 with the headline "Sane Reds Confined in Asylum."[9] Investigating for the Indian Office in 1932, Dr. John Holst compared Hiawatha to "a leper colony."[10] With public disclosure that many Native people at Hiawatha were actually sane, the facility was soon closed.

Peter Thompson Good Boy's letter of June 8, 1916, written in phonetic Lakota and seeking outside intervention for the brutal abuses going on at Hiawatha Asylum, never left the building. *National Archives and Records Administration, Fort Worth, TX, RG 75, Ind Pt files 1910–16.*

Those few deemed still insane were transferred to St. Elizabeth's Hospital, Hummer's alma mater. But William Alanson White had passed away years before then, and his more humane values had already been replaced by experimental "treatments" such as insulin injection, electroconvulsive shock, and prefrontal lobotomy.

HELEN GROTH'S ESCAPE

An unfortunate tendency of some researchers interested in Hiawatha Asylum for Insane Indians is to depict its philosophies, methods, and practices as anomalies. In fact, Indian lunacy determinations through state-operated insane commissions were a widespread method of managing and controlling Native nonconformity without allowing access to due process. How dark and nefarious these efforts could become was brought to light by another source of eyewitness testimony: Helen Groth's letter of complaint to the

"Investigation Committee of Affairs at Indian Asylum at Canton, So. Dak.,"
which was entered into the official record of the Hiawatha Asylum's investigation on September 29, 1933.

Helen fought tooth and nail to keep her health and mind stable while
forcibly hospitalized at another asylum, Yankton State Hospital, after she
attempted suicide as a result of Hummer's attempts to forcibly confine her at
Hiawatha. What she went through is best shared in her own words, and I've
transcribed her handwritten letter to the Hiawatha Investigatory Committee
in its entirety below:

926 W. 9th St.
Sioux Falls, S. Dak.

Investigation Committee of affairs at Indian Asylum at Canton,
So. Dak.

Gentlemen: As an individual who had personal experience
with the Supt. of the Hospital, Dr. Hummer, I take this means of
acquainting you with a few facts concerning his method of adding
to his income, which under law is stabilized, and should be sufficient
for his needs.

As a result of overwork and fatigue I fainted and then became
hysterical after strenuous reflex stimulation and prodding of persons
who had been called in to help out. The doctor in attendance was
know[n] to have been under the influence of morphine for at least
six months, asked me if I'd heard evil spirits, etc. the nights previous.
He called in the doctor on the insane commission who said he'd
have to take me to the hospital for a little treatment, that I was
dangerous and insane. They called the police station and forcefully
took me to the county jail (a place in which I'd never been before).
I found out afterward, and have a portion of the medicine, that
my husband had been drugged and was ordered to stay in bed for
several days. Cocain was used to keep him drugged and from clear
enuf thinking to come to my rescue. Remained in County Jail from
Dec 26th until Dec 28th—during which time I was not examined
or questioned by any member of the board. I was sane all of this
time but was not allowed to communicate with anyone except the
two other women who had been put there for unprintable reasons.
After being slapped in the face three different times by the jailer, I

was taken to the courtroom where I was promptly informed by the doctor on the board that I was insane. It was, as you might know, somewhat of a surprise to me. At the end of his questioning me he had no answers on his questionnaire blanks. Upon asking him to put all his cards on the table at once and tell me what the foolishness was all about, another board member decided to adjourn and see if it would not be better to wait and see if a mistake had not been made. I was placed back in the jail and my mother was summoned from Missouri and I was paroled into her custody.

At the public library in the So. Dak Revised Edition of 1919 I found out that not having been a resident of the State for 1 year I was not eligible even to be summoned before the board. I wrote out the law and placed it before the judge who grudgingly issued me a document declaring me free and capable of caring for myself.

Finally as I was going about my affairs in the customary manner the doctor after deciding he'd made a mistake that might prove damaging to the commission, managed to convince my husband that I was a danger to my family and had him take me to Canton to have Dr. Hummer (an expert Federal physiatrist) to examine my mind. After all that had transpired I was nearly paralyzed with fright and refused to go to the Asylum at Canton where Hummer was to examine me. Finally Hummer came into the court house at Canton where he questioned me for ½ hr. or so, insulted my mother who was with me, thumbing his nose at her and asking if she would rather go back to her home in Missouri or with me, where I was going for about six months of "hospitalization." His entire manner was one of burly brutality, insolence and co-operation with the doctor who had advised my unsuspecting husband to take me there. After the short session of questioning he charged my husband 12.50 for his work.

Blows rained upon me by the jailer who testified I was violent, the ordeal of trying to figure out just why I was being held in jail, trying to do my work at home and then realizing that Hummer meant to testify against me at a new session the board was calling to protect themselves, I became unnerved to the extent that rather than be committed to an insane asylum when I knew I was not insane, I committed my soul to God and took 1½ oz of iodine, with the full intention of dying rather than undergoing the stain of insanity upon myself and my family.

However, it was not be that way and a physician was called in time to pump my stomach. I was given a good strong shot of morphine to allay the pain and I presume also to allay my thinking powers. Dr. Hummer was called to the board meeting the next day and testified that I was a maniac and also had homicidal or suicidal tendencies. That "suicidal tendencies" was a break for him after the way things turned out. After they held me at Yankton and found out I was not insane, and I established my status quo upon release, I went and asked to see the document as it was filed in probate court hence my knowledge of the evidence. I do not know how much the county paid him for this trip or if the doctor on the county commission paid him, but I do know that the Dr. on the County comm. received $41.80 fees. It might be well to investigate Dr. Hummer's activities in connection with the County Insane Commissions in the surrounding territories. Also it might be interesting to investigate why several pure blood Indians who have money are being held at the So. Dak. State Hospital at Yankton. Perhaps they wish to do them up in such a hurry that the money will go to this crooked state of So. Dak! Governor Berry and the two emmisaries from the state could be more beneficial in investigating conditions at Yankton than at Canton.

I've lived one year in New York City and know that the east is a more healthful climate than So. Dak. There's more outbreaks of infectious and contagious diseases in this section than many others. Typhoid is particularly menacing on account of the alkali water. If conditions and methods are comparatively as had at Canton as they are at Yankton, they're unthinkable. I'd say, move them to Washington where intelligent people are interested in science and progress, and where specialists are interested in knowing when and when not a person is insane. Send home the ones that have been framed in and treat the others, as real eastern scientists and doctors have learned how to so do. Instead of beating, starving, force feeding, insulted, ridiculed and mentally and physically misused as in this state, treat them as unfortunate human beings with partial mentality and brain power that might be fully developed by consideration, kindness, restraint if necessary, endocrine treatment, and other methods known to mental specialists.

They die so fast at Yankton that they keep 15 to 20 holes dug all of the time to receive the bodies. Instead of treatment they give them luminal and shots of morphine to keep them quiet. They have no sanitary water drinking method in the receiving sick room, but have one glass at a faucet in the sick room toilet, out of which all patients are required to drink. Some are syphallitic, some chronic ghonorreah, some sleeping sickness, I presume, etc. Knowing a little about hygiene, I washed my hands thoroughly and drank of the luke warm terrible water flowing from my palm. Patients feverish and begging for a cold drink were given this slop while the attendants carried the ice to their quarters to be used for their own thirst.

I received no treatment whatsoever except what I could do for myself. Got the iodine that was eating the mucous membrane out of my intestines and stomach by first asking for milk and then being refused then demanding to be put on a milk diet, getting my blood in a better condition in a hurry to offset the probability of a toxic condition by eating one or two teaspoons of syrup with its glucose. This was in a container on the table each meal. I had to demand iodine, which was grudgingly given, for my irritated toes and feet which were abraised and swollen from being forced to push a broom around the floors to collect the dust. These <u>exercises</u> were forced upon <u>aged</u> patients for 2 hrs. immediately after dinner and 1½ hrs. after supper. The dish was chiefly starch and patients were so intimidated they were afraid even to ask for mineral oil. The accumulation of toxic poisons with the resultant injury to their systems can be readily understood. One girl 18 yrs. old wanted to get down to walk on the grass at Easter time and instead of being allowed to do so, either by herself or accompanied by one of the ignorant attendants there, she, in desperation, jumped from an unprotected 2nd floor balcony while the attendants possibly were either playing bridge or knitting rugs out of the silken garments belonging to patients.

Sometimes I wonder if some of the names mentioned in this letter should not be considered in the investigation now being carried on in connection with the possibility of a narcotics ring in Sioux Falls and the surrounding territory.

In all seriousness I would suggest, as a result of coming in personal contact with Insane Commissions in So. Dak, that it would be a really fine measure to move the 93 Indians to the Washington Hospitals. It would be a fine economical measure and I feel sure it would not hinder relatives in visiting their insane members as that is seldom done anyway.

Yours, for Roosevelt and his whole-hearted activities in connection with all NRA [National Recovery Administration] measures,

Very respectfully,
Mrs. Helen J. Groth[11]

EIGHTEEN

Locked in Hiawatha: The Soldier

FROM THE TRENCHES TO HIAWATHA

Among the Native veterans of World War I held inside Hiawatha Asylum for Insane Indians was Robert Winans. I'm indebted to Dr. Susan Burch, professor of American studies at Middlebury College and a fellow researcher on the people of Hiawatha, for helping me learn about him.[1] Robert was a citizen of the Mandan, Hidatsa, and Arikara Nations. He came from the same community as psychiatric survivor Pemina Yellow Bird, whose article "Wild Indians"[2] first alerted me to the existence of Hiawatha Asylum. He is buried at Indian Scout Post No. 1 at Fort Berthold Indian Reservation, which is cared for by the Old Scouts Society.[3]

Robert was interviewed by Hummer on December 11, 1930, over four years after being incarcerated in Hiawatha on April 7, 1926, according to Hummer's notes.[4] It's unclear why the neglectful Hummer suddenly became interested in him, but Robert's responses to Hummer, like Peter Thompson Good Boy's, suggest he wouldn't have shied away from challenging him.

During the war, Robert, like numerous Mandan men, probably volunteered as a scout under Colonel A. B. Welch, Field Artillery Section, Third Army.[5,6] This section fought during the Marne Defense, the Châlons-sur-Marne Offensive, and the Meuse-Argonne Offensive. These key battles of World War I involved American soldiers helping to turn the German tide toward armistice. There's little question that Robert experienced heavy combat while patrolling the fields and trenches where over 144,000

Americans died or were wounded in just four months. Robert's combat exposure involved witnessing the very worst of human atrocity. Medical science hadn't yet progressed to match the devastating new technologies of gas warfare, machine guns, barb wire, and mass bombardment that he and his fellow soldiers endured.

Unnamed male members of Hiawatha Asylum's baseball team. Are we looking at Peter Thompson Good Boy or Robert Winans? Date unknown. *National Archives and Records Administration, Kansas City, MO, RG 75.*

Hummer's handwritten interview notes suggest his utter ignorance of the significance of Robert's service. I also detect a subtle sarcasm coming through in Robert's responses as he speaks of his experiences. What follows are several exchanges I've selected:

(Why admitted?)[7] "I was sick and seeing visions."

(What caused?) "Believe I got the cold because of getting a horse out of a river." [mustard gas often permeated horse's manes][8]

(In Army?) "9 months ... Fort Riley, I was first in Fort Dodge ... First volunteered August 1, 1917 ..."

(Discharged?) "I had sore eyes [another reference to being gassed?]. January 9, 1919"

(What caused visions?) "I don't know where they came from ... [S]omebody reported that I drink whiskey, that I was a heavy drinker. Somebody made it up. [underlined by Hummer with a note next to it: "persecution"] I just drink 3 times. That's all I drink. Home brew. Boys bought it."

[Robert is reporting drinking whiskey after the war and during Prohibition when industrial alcohol was often used for home distilling. Government regulators mandated purposely contaminating this type of alcohol with "quinine, methyl alcohol and other toxic chemicals"[9] to foil bootleggers and consumers. Industrial alcohol and the added chemicals could induce powerful hallucinatory experiences as well as blindness.[10]]

(Use peyote?) (nods affirmatively)

"When sick, saw Devil about 5 miles away. He was black. He moved, hit the church about 5 miles away, didn't move. I just thought the Devil was after me ... This devil disappeared."

(How long since last saw Devil?) "I only saw him one day. I got scared. I thought he might kill me."[11]

Hummer also records that Robert Winan jumped out of a second-story window and hit himself in the head with an axe. Perhaps he did so while intoxicated, but I also feel skeptical of Hummer's reports, given Helen Groth's letter. I suspect that Hummer had no compunction about making up or lying about reasons inmates needed to be held in Hiawatha. Additionally, Hummer seems to have missed the relevance of Robert's regular use of peyote obtained through the mail by a Pawnee friend, to his spiritual visions. When asked by Hummer how long he'd used peyote, he told him, "About 4 years, I guess."[12]

In these brief exchanges, we also see Hummer's efforts to rework Robert's turmoil, spiritual experiences, and alcohol issues into "persecutory delusion." In this way, a U.S. combat veteran was maligned for his suffering so as to keep him imprisoned. From my perspective, Robert's visionary day "running from a threatening black Devil" was a compelling and poetic means of depicting the death of battle coming after him.

I initially couldn't find out much more about Robert in the National Archives materials and concluded he'd been one of the rare inmates who had succeeded in getting discharged by Hummer. Further scrutiny proved me wrong. In Dr. Burch's scans from the National Archives in Seattle—the Hummer interview materials were at NARA in Washington, DC—I discovered Robert's name on an undated "Occupational List" for inmates in Hiawatha Asylum.[13] Therein, Robert is described as follows: "Assists farmer. Trusted. Takes out the horses and drives alone to the fields, etc." In a letter to Dr. L. L. Culp, special physician in charge of Canton (Hiawatha) Asylum, dated December 16, 1933, written on behalf of lead investigator Dr. Samuel Silk after the investigation, exposure, and shutdown of Hiawatha and Hummer's dismissal, a list of seventeen patients is mentioned with instructions:

> ... that the following named patients be discharged from Canton and returned to their homes, as they do not show in his [Silk's] estimation sufficient mental derangement to justify holding them further in an institution of this kind.[14]

In other words, this letter contains a partial list of those inmates being held at the Hiawatha Asylum for Insane Indians considered "sane." Robert Winans was on this list and described as being thirty-seven years old. By then, this U.S. Army combat veteran had been imprisoned into forced labor for well over seven years. Perhaps some other researcher may be able to discern whether Robert took the Army Alpha and Beta tests after his enlistment to fight for a country that didn't count him a citizen. It remains possible that this early psychological testing compelled him into the front lines of the Great War, only to come home thereafter to the terrible fate of being locked into Hiawatha. The connection remains to be made. Whether or not this was what happened, we can only wonder to what degree exposure to the war or to Hiawatha led to Robert's early death in 1939 at forty-four or forty-five years old.

ANOTHER GENERATIONAL ECHO

As Operation Iraqi Freedom commenced under a storm of national debate in 2003, Native Americans remained the least represented ethnicity in post-secondary education in the United States. At that moment in time, I found brochures promoting free administration of the military psychology placement test called the ASVAB (or Armed Services Vocational Aptitude

Unnamed male inmates circa 1920s who appear to be dressed to work on the grounds. Are these American combat veterans of WWI? *National Archives and Records Administration, Kansas City, MO, RG 75.*

Battery), placed front and center on the Yakama Nation Tribal School reception counter, suggesting to low-income Native families and youth a great opportunity for educating and career building. We know now that only 15 percent of veterans successfully complete a college degree using G.I. Bill funds,[15] and for this and many other reasons the strategy of military recruitment in public schools remains a controversial idea.[16]

At least 70 American Indians and Alaska Natives lost their lives in Operation Iraqi Freedom or Operation Enduring Freedom and 513 were wounded.[17] Among those killed was Lori Piestewa, the first American servicewoman to die in combat. She was a single Hopi mother who reportedly joined the military not so much out of patriotism as because she felt it a morally sound way of escaping economic dependence on her parents and building a future for her children.[18]

"We're not rich enough to send her to college," her brother told *Rolling Stone* writer Osha Gray Davidson in 2004. "When you have obstacles in your way, you take what life offers."[19]

Lori made the ultimate sacrifice at the Battle of Nasiriyah, and her best friend and fellow soldier, Jessica Lynch—rescued from certain death in an Iraqi hospital—found herself pulled into a deceptive Pentagon public relations campaign. Jessica Lynch testified in 2007 before the U.S. House Government Oversight committee her frustrations with U.S. military officials' efforts to propagandize a false story about her as a heroic, white, "little girl Rambo from the hills,"[20] when, as she stated:

> My hero is my friend Lori who died in Iraq but set an example for a generation of Hopi and Native American women and little girls everywhere about the important contributions just one soldier can make in the fight for freedom.[21]

It is likely that Lori drove a truck on the day she was killed because the ASVAB said this was the kind of military role to which she'd be best suited. Yet "the Department of Defense has conceded that there is no direct validity evidence for the [ASVAB] student testing program"[22] and "minority females suffer a double jeopardy as they often score lower than both white females and males of their own racial or ethnic group"[23] on the test. Although I couldn't locate similar findings regarding the ASVAB, the older Armed Forces Qualification Test (AFQT), which is incorporated within the current ASVAB, demonstrates that the lower a recruit's scores, the more likely they will end up exposed to combat.[24]

The ASVAB is a descendant of the very first U.S. military recruit psychological screening tests used, the Army Alpha and Beta tests. These 1917 tests were published in the civilian-version, paper-and-pencil National Intelligence Test (NIT) often used by Thomas Russell Garth in American Indian boarding schools. The Army Alpha and Beta tests were similarly mined for early versions of the SAT (Scholastic Aptitude Test),[25] a test that remains "not only ineffective but also destructive for Indigenous students."[26]

When the United States entered World War I in 1917, thousands of Native American men just like Robert Winans stepped forward to volunteer. Among them was a small cohort of 124 Native volunteers who became research subjects for the Army Alpha and Beta tests. Little did they know that the highly biased test findings would count against them, just as the ASVAB worked against Lori Piestewa.

At the forty-seventh annual meeting of the American Neurological Association in June 1921, Colonel Pearce Bailey, "eminent" neurologist and member of the American Medico-Psychological Association—the former name of today's American Psychiatric Association—was invited to speak about Alpha and Beta research.[27] He'd been cross-functional partner within the Army's Division of Neuro-Psychiatry and integrated the tests into the division's overall examination of recruits.[28] Bailey described 62 percent of the Native volunteers in the Alpha and Beta study as "mentally deficient," i.e., "feebleminded,"[29] and told his audience:

> The American Indian, or Amerindian, as H. G. Wells calls him, is primitive like the negro, and exceeds even him in mental deficiency. He is not as much below the United States average in alcoholism or drugs as the negro ... In other conditions, namely, neurologic, psychoses, psychoneuroses, endocrine and constitutional psychopathic states, he is far below the United States average. His high mental deficiency percentage leaves little room for anything else.[30]

Of course, we know that Bailey was missing something in his own time. "Indian lunacy determinations" had already been underway for decades, and the Hiawatha Asylum for Insane Indians was only part of a larger picture of forced Native institutional incarceration. It was a critical insight for me to discern that a conceptual bridge had occurred around this time between the eugenics stereotype of the "dumb Indian" and its descendent, the "crazy Indian."

As these Native men headed off to the Great War, the *Statistical Manual for the Use of Institutions for the Insane*,[31] the earliest forerunner to today's *Diagnostic and Statistical Manual for Mental Disorders, Fifth Edition* (*DSM-5*),[32] was being published by the American Medico-Psychological Association. This early *DSM* recommended institutional censuses of "American Indians" (among other "races") held in insane asylums, and certainly the Hiawatha Asylum counted among them. What is truly sickening here is the convenient creation of new categories of psychiatric disorder that combine inferior intelligence with psychopathology, such as "mentally deficient with psychosis," "mentally deficient without psychosis," and "constitutional psychopathic inferiority without psychosis."[33] In this way, Native inmates already locked up for "feeblemindedness" were made eligible for new psychiatric labels more akin to what we see today. Similarly, concepts of inferior potential strung by history into today's ASVAB placed the life of a single Hopi mother in harm's way.

NINETEEN

Today's Indian Asylums

HARD TIME

The "Indian insane asylum" may be a thing of the past, but the full tilt of Coyote's Swing still pushes its way through Indian Country, having absorbed its intent. Native American men are currently imprisoned in the United States at four times the rate of white men.[1] In 2012, 48,000 inmates incarcerated in U.S. prisons or jails were American Indian, Alaska Native, Asian, Native Hawaiian, or Pacific Islander veterans.[2] Efforts to break apart this category of people currently described as "Other" by the Justice Department have been thus far unsuccessful.[3] According to the Department of Justice's Bureau of Justice Statistics: "Although AIAN [American Indian/Alaska Native] inmates made up less than 2% of the total U.S. jail population in 2014, the number of AIAN jail inmates increased nearly 90% from 1999 to 2014."[4]

Between 2010 and 2015, the rate of Native people incarcerated in federal prisons grew by 27 percent, and research in Minnesota and Arizona reveals they receive more severe and longer sentences than white people.[5] Patterns very familiar to African American youth are also suffered by Native American youth, who receive more severe sentences from juvenile justice systems[6] than white youth and are 30 percent more likely to see their cases adjudicated rather than to have charges dropped.[7]

Despite historically having no police system and favoring restorative and restitutive approaches to violation and deviance,[8] Native communities throughout North America have been influenced toward growing more lockup facilities for their young people. Addie C. Rolnick, a Critical Race Studies Law Fellow at the University of Nevada, notes that at least sixteen new juvenile facilities were built in Native America between 1998 and 2013, and many upgraded, despite the total number of juveniles incarcerated staying constant or declining during this time period. Tribal courts lock up youth as a primary response to drug, alcohol, and other nonviolent offenses.[9]

Imprisoned by their communities for nonviolent offenses, are these youth experiences similar to "Indian lunacy determinations"? Are they just today's casualties strung upon a time ball of destruction and domination going back centuries? This expanding system in Native America appears to reflect that of the dominant society, wherein 15 percent of inmates held in state prisons in 2016 were there with a drug offense as their most serious crime.[10] How might the mindset for locking up today's Native youth echo that involved in the institutional confinement of their ancestors in boarding schools and lunatic asylums?

Between 1999 and 2014, the daily census of American Indian and Alaska Native male jail inmates nearly doubled, rising from 5,500 to 10,400.[11] Over 40 percent of these inmates were between the ages of eighteen and twenty-nine years old, and 45 percent had been in jail for one to six months.[12] Like yesterday's asylums and boarding schools, today's U.S. jails and prisons are brutal and depressing places where emphasis is placed upon maintenance and compliance. Although exact numbers are hard to determine due to the collapsing of Native people alongside Asians and Pacific Islanders into the category of "Other" tallied by the Bureau of Justice Statistics, I feel confident in guesstimating that at least two hundred Native men and women took their own lives while under correctional "supervision and care" in state or local jails between 2000 and 2014.[13,14]

Simply by being Native, members of tribal communities already experience a heightened risk of violence exposure prior to incarceration. How might jail exacerbate an individual's sense of being chronically unsafe? Little seems to have changed since Human Rights Watch noted back in 2004:

U.S. prison inmates have been beaten with fists and batons, stomped on, kicked, shot, stunned with electronic devices, doused with chemical sprays, choked, and slammed face first onto concrete floors by the officers whose job it is to guard them. Inmates have ended up with broken jaws, smashed ribs, perforated eardrums, missing teeth, burn scars—not to mention psychological scars and emotional pain. Some have died.[15]

In Washington State prisons in 2013, 16 percent of "use of force" cases—during which guards applied anything from their fists to pepper spray to shock sticks—were mounted against inmates inside prison mental health units.[16]

Within this context of induced psychological distress, Human Rights Watch notes that 20 to 40 percent of inmates are labeled with psychiatric disorders.[17] There are few helpful services available to troubled or troubling prisoners, who end up in isolation significantly more often than other inmates, an experience that in itself enhances terror and agitation and can stimulate hallucinations in just about anyone.[18] The primary approach to "treatment" of these inmates carries life-threatening implications.

In prisons and jails, "mental health interventions are often limited to medication oriented to responding to immediate crises and not tailored to the individual prisoner's needs, strengths, and goals for recovery," Human Rights Watch noted in 2015.[19] After randomly selecting for analysis 699 post-release records of the deaths of former prisoners of the Washington Department of Corrections, physician-researcher Ingrid Binswanger and colleagues were compelled to admit:

> Receipt of psychiatric medications in prison during the 60 days prior to release was associated with all-cause and overdose death.... [F]actors that may have contributed to this association include poor continuity of medication treatment for mental health disorders after release, difficulty coping with the stress of the transition to the post-release environment among people with mental health disorders, or medication interactions which predispose to overdose.[20]

Binswanger and colleagues had less to say about the brain-disabling effects of psychiatric drugs themselves,[21] their many side effects,[22] or their potential relationship to predisposing inmates toward prescription medication abuse.[23] Given the horrid circumstances that inmates must endure, coupled with the fact that they are deprived of resources to help them better prepare for adapting to the world outside, reliance on psychiatric drugs alone cannot be implicated as having "caused" these inmates' deaths. However, these drugs do not seem to have helped their post-release adjustment.

GOING INSIDE

I recall visiting an inmate inside the Yakima County Jail.[24] Just as one might protect oneself against tuberculosis in the 1920s when entering Hummer's Hiawatha Asylum, I had to first be fitted with an anti-tuberculin mask beforehand. I will call the inmate "Joshua" because he reminded me of the song I wrote called "Joshua Maiden" and was similar in appearance to the elder Diné man I'd met so long ago in a Detroit nursing home.

By the time we met, Joshua had lived homeless for many years. He was destitute, prone to alcohol bingeing, and resided—or more accurately slept—in a place referred to locally as "the Jungle." There are numerous sites in the United States similarly named. Joshua told me he was a Vietnam veteran. He'd been arrested following a fight with another homeless man. He'd already had a history of run-ins with the Toppenish Police Department. Astonishingly, a city judge had even banned him from wandering around inside this reservation town. The fight occurred in the city of Yakima, and he was arrested by Yakima police.

Joshua had been diagnosed with tuberculosis while in jail and was receiving treatment. He was still considered infectious and didn't seem to be getting better. When I met him, Joshua was bottoming out, and he wanted a Native healer to come visit him. I received a call from Yakama Nation Police Department asking if I'd go, and I indicated I definitely shouldn't be thought of in such a way. Perhaps someone from the Indian Shaker Church or Wáashat longhouse could visit him, I suggested. But no one was available, which I didn't really understand.

The tribal police officer was aware I would sometimes offer a smudge of sage inside my office at Yakama Indian Health Service Clinic if clients requested, although the practice was not part of Yakama tradition. He then asked me point-blank if I would be willing to take a smudge over to the Yakima County Jail and pray for a few minutes with this elder. Nobody else was going to do it.

I'd never been inside Yakima's jail and was struck by the many security doors and gates and searches I had to pass. Eventually, I was taken to an outdoor exercise area on an upper floor of the jail building. Joshua was brought in wearing handcuffs, which were taken off. He was a small man with long braids, physically thin and frail. Like me, he had a mask over his face. We greeted one another in muffled tones, and I stooped down to block the chilly breeze coming in from an open overhead door. I lit a pile of white sage I'd prepared in my abalone shell.

The scent blossomed over both of us, and I felt a bit nervous as we both lifted our masks briefly. Here I was sharing my breath with a man very ill with a dangerous, highly infectious respiratory disease. This was many years prior to the COVID-19 pandemic when the risks of such a situation became so prominent in so many minds. But I knew it was dangerous then, and I consciously wanted to go ahead. I was scared, but I wanted to do it.

We blessed ourselves together with smoke and said brief prayers for Joshua's healing. He had tears in his eyes as he rose up and extended his hand toward me. Should I shake it? I was ashamed of my inner revulsion and decided I must, and I'd wash it before leaving. We did so in an Indian way with a very light touch.

After we shook hands, Joshua said in a frank and very quiet voice, "Thank you, sir. This is the nicest anybody's ever been to me."

He pulled his mask back down over his face, the guards put his handcuffs back on, and then they took him away. I never saw or heard about him again. As far as I know, he or someone very much like him is still locked up somewhere in Native America.

PART IV

Dismantling
Coyote's Swing

CHAPTER TWENTY

Hope and Reason

"PREVENTION"

Despite my efforts to avoid doing so, I carried numerous assumptions when I began my work over two decades ago at Yakama Nation. I thought I'd be involving myself in something new and innovative, but the U.S. mental health system in Native America, wound upon a time ball controlled by the Indian Health Service, holds oppressive knots strung back to the Cherokee Trail of Tears. I arrived at Yakama Nation naïve and idealistic, drawn toward helping to prevent the suicide and despair that I felt were by-products of social inequity, racism, bigotry, and marginalization, not reflections of broken brains or faulty genetics.

I began this book to assuage my grief over what I've seen firsthand and felt powerless to change. To my mind, the U.S. mental health system in Indian Country prevents very little, and I'm asserting this from direct experience. I've done what I can to describe a system rife with falsehoods and infected with historical and contemporary oppression, paternalism, and racism. The sadness of the story I've carried within me for so long has caused me to revisit my own approach to taking care of myself and others and also changed my relationship with the word "prevention."

Prevention is a central purpose of the "mark" I'm trying to make in the Blackfoot way I described earlier in this book. I want to prevent further erosion of traditional pathways to healing and growth that are still critically important to survival in Indian Country. I believe the Original Peoples of North America should have sovereign control in defining what "mental health" or "mental well-being" means for them as well as in designing and implementing ways that they feel are needed to increase these attributes within their own communities. Even if their decisions ultimately include the very practices I've criticized, that is not my business; I've already exercised the great privilege of making the case for change to the best of my ability. Again, I do have faith that Native communities will know how to use funds being set aside under treaty guarantees for such purposes more effectively than the federal government—the historic and contemporary perpetrator of oppression against them—and I see a welcome role for allies and scholars to help immeasurably even as they relinquish the control they currently maintain directly or through Public Law 93-638 ("638") (The Indian Self-Determination and Education Assistance Act) and its grant-making provisions (described in chapter 3).

Until that change is made, my preventive efforts remain focused toward continuing to get the word out and stopping expansion of this "one-size-fits-all" paradigm of "mentally disordered" Natives currently promoted through the U.S Indian Health Service, its tribal grantees, and grant-dependent academics. Culturally, epistemologically, and philosophically, the U.S. mental health system in Indian Country has never been Native American. As I've tried hard to demonstrate, this system evolved instead out of Christian humanism, Western individualism, the quantification imperative, naturalistic positivism, and eugenics. I call upon anyone with the heart and spirit to rectify this egregious situation and prevent further expansion of this system's legacy of coercion, imprisonment, forced sterilization, conscription for manual or domestic labor, promotion of Native inferiority, drugging, and revising of reactions to oppression through false discourses on deficiency, brain or genetic defects, and/or other flaws.

My own naivete aside, the great presumption of the U.S. mental health system is that it somehow improves Native lives. I say, "Prove it," because the tragic social problems of Native America, including traumatic abuse and violence, suicide and substance dependence, have continued unabated after 140 years of this Western "mental hygiene" paradigm. I've provided evidence that this system actually exacerbates the problems it has created. I find no historical or current evidence of *substantial* or *enduring positive effect* of its capacities for reducing violence, suicide, substance abuse, or disease or in improving education, wellness, nutrition, discrimination, or employment for Native people. I truly welcome being corrected.

Certainly, one can point to a plethora of research articles from academic and professional mental health journals about the shared desperation of a hypothetical homogenized "race" of Native Americans vaguely drawn from some community or several somewhere in a certain region. Conclusions from this methodology are never valid for any specific Native community anywhere. I also dispute the patronizing efforts to protect tribal confidentiality by obscuring cultural-historical context and geographical locale that help sustain this imaginary Native. Beneficiaries of such research designs are not *communities* but those who negotiate keeping hidden the lived context of survivors of oppressive trauma while leaving them to carry the undeserved shame and stigma of entirely human reactions to violence they've suffered.

Communities should control their own research as well as make their own decisions about whether to keep private the findings about themselves or to collaborate with other communities and researchers regarding the distribution of such information, perhaps to serve social and legal action and activism. How can lawsuits or other efforts to achieve justice and restitution ever be mounted if specific communities are persuaded to keep themselves anonymous in research articles about a contrived "race" of Native Americans? How will federal, state, local, and religious entities ever be held accountable?

The U.S. mental health system continues its "diagnosing" of Native mental disorders in individuals in service to what it calls "acculturation pressures"[1] and then "treats" them through three primary, nonexclusive means: *sedation, pacification*, and *thought reform*. As if ignoring the proverbial elephant in the room, this system colludes with broader U.S. society in its denial of oppression in Native America. Liberation psychologists Mary Watkins and Helene Shulman assert:

> Such an individualistic and elitist approach makes it increasingly difficult to understand that one's personal difficulties are often shared by others. Without this knowledge, attempts to gain insight into the causes of these difficulties are directed solely to one's own individual biography, itself seen out of social and historical context. This myopia precludes actions taken together to change the larger context that contributes to personal misery.[2]

Every youth client or family member I've ever met at Yakama Nation, or from many places all over Indian Country, has been uniquely tied to complex interdependent relationships and stories demanding to be understood. In

Indian Country there is, in fact, no positive "treatment outcome" for a single individual until their family and community are raised up too. It is within these widened parameters that there remain many opportunities for outside professional and paraprofessional allies to *accompany* and serve an ongoing need for cultural resurgence and the transcendence of generational pain.

MORE ON "RESEARCH"

Over the last two decades, the U.S. mental health system, generally working through IHS and/or the agency's tribally managed "638" programs, has popularized a "community participatory research approach" for studies conducted in Indian Country. Certainly, Western *quantitative* and *qualitative* research methods remain potentially highly useful to Native communities. But what gets called "community participation" is more often a "stick" of outside intrusiveness into Native affairs offered alongside the "carrot" of potentially increasing funding or services.

Provisions for how "community participation" will happen are always conditional. For example, the "Circles of Care" and "Gathering of Native Americans"/"Gathering of Alaska Natives" grants awarded by the Substance Abuse and Mental Health Services Administration (SAMHSA) include funding for programs promoting community and cultural engagement, which are desirable targets to many communities. When Circles of Care team researchers visited one school I've frequented, they carried with them prepared forms specifying questions for a preformatted "community participation" exercise. I was struck by the confines of this allegedly consultative process. There was no genuine council provided at all.

Use of this kind of "methodology" embeds outside interests and covertly sneaks a domination code of biopsychiatric language in Indian Country. For example, Circles of Care provides a "Mental Health Facts Sheet" for grantees informing Native community participants about links between "treatment" of "mental health disorders" and the "Native worldview" including "herbs, plants, nature" and "psychopharmacology."[3] Diametrically different worldviews about healing are being conflated on behalf of the interests of the psychopharmaceutical complex. This is propaganda and indoctrination.

But there is a huge distinction between "community participatory" and "community-driven" approaches, and I felt honored to be part of the Níix Ttáwaxt program as an example of the latter. I saw myself how the phrase "Níix Ttáwaxt" itself emerged from a language preserved against all odds within the minds and hearts of the Yakama people. To the extent this culturally nested phrase sustained its deepest meaning to this community, I could feel I was assisting with something "community-driven." When forces from outside the community sought to integrate Níix Ttáwaxt alongside practices and beliefs not originating from the Yakama people themselves, however—as in the "tribally managed" PL-638 Yakama Nation Behavioral Health Services designed by federal authorities—the result defaults back to "community participatory." Outside interests and ideologies are being served and have priority. Even "participation," i.e., control, is then being co-opted by people who are not Yakama. To my mind, this sort of shift is never truly participatory at all but merely an extension of white supremacism clothed in Native regalia.

RADICAL INDIGENISM IN NATIVE BEHAVIORAL HEALTH PROGRAM DESIGN AND PRACTICES

Cherokee sociologist Eva Marie Garroutte emphasizes "root" within the etymology of the word "radical" in applying "radical indigenism" to improving collaboration with and between Native people, including when seeking to heal intergenerational wounds brought about by colonialism and oppression:

> Radical Indigenism, as I define it, illuminates differences in assumptions about knowledge that are at the root of the dominant culture's misunderstanding and subordination of indigenous knowledge. It argues for the reassertion and rebuilding of knowledge from those roots.[4]

Despite tacit acceptance of traditional healing alongside, or more accurately, subordinate to its practices, a proper deconstruction and reformulation of the U.S. mental health system in the manner Garroutte recommends has never been undertaken in Native America. A methodology she proposes toward such goals would include

> at least three sources to which a researcher working within the perspective of Radical Indigenism may turn to discover Original Instructions on a specific subject.... [For example, (1)] in the statements of elders and others who know community lifeways from

their own long experience.... [(2)] grounded in larger bodies of teachings—stories, oral narratives, songs, dances, and other records.... [And (3) in] the ways our ancestors created forms of community life that made flesh the teachings our traditions set forth.[5]

"Original Instructions" about the mental, emotional and spiritual well-being at Yakama Nation are still held among numerous elders but won't be found within Western mental health epistemologies, biopsychiatric ideologies, or theories of psychopathology. Even the best approaches to hybridizing such teachings with culturally modified Western mental health practices (Níix Ttáwaxt being an example) are not established, particularly from a Native-centered perspective. Instead, a hegemony of Western mental health ideologies and practices remains entrenched currently and empowered to displace or even block Native pathways to well-being despite their survival being achieved at great cost.

One crucial survival factor for Indigenous cultures in North America— and everywhere else—is the restoration and preservation of traditional languages, especially when efforts to destroy them have been part of community trauma experience. Allies of Native mental and emotional well-being should consider themselves intrinsically involved simultaneously with such a project, including learning traditional values, virtues, and concepts, rather than forcing or imposing foreign, often antithetical ideas from their own language. Our community of helpers and client families sought to build Níix Ttáwaxt around the centerpiece of Yakama language virtues as articulated by my *kála*, Levina Wilkins (Kussamwhy). (See "The Twelve Virtues of Níix Ttáwaxt" at the end of this chapter.) I can testify to my own dogged effort to learn from Ichishkíin Sínwit to describe attributes of well-being at Yakama Nation. Although I'm not very good at speaking it, making the effort has meant a great deal to me and the people I've served.

In this and other ways, Radical Indigenism represents a values-oriented ethos that supports Native communities and their allies in reversing the status quo. Native perspectives about emotional, mental, and spiritual healing and well-being are placed first and Western approaches become ancillary, supportive, and optional. Still relatively unknown in mental health circles, Radical Indigenism has already exerted a positive influence on sociology, ethnic studies, and, most conspicuously, landscape architecture through proposed "Lo-TEK" (traditional ecological knowledge) solutions for climate collapse, where longstanding Indigenous practices are being rediscovered worldwide for their efficiency, utility, and ecological benefit.[6]

But any successful community journey driven by Radical Indigenism would require the alliance of non-Native providers and academics, some of whom may feel entrenched in the current system and reluctant about such a major transformation. Experience tells me, additionally, not to underestimate the resistance of Native community members themselves. In her own quest to help restore Indigenous knowledge and practices, historian and decolonization activist Waziyatawin (Angela Cavender Wilson, Wahpetunwan Dakota) has noted:

> Some of the greatest resistors to the recovery of Indigenous knowledge are our own Native people who have internalized the racism and now uncritically accept the ideologies of the dominant culture.... Because of the extent to which colonization has taken root, any efforts to restore our traditional ways would have to be matched with a strong community decolonization agenda. While developing a critical consciousness aimed at understanding precisely how colonization has affected our health and mindset, and thus how we might meaningfully challenge that oppression, we can begin to reaffirm the richness and wisdom inherent in our traditional ways.[7]

I believe one way this critical consciousness can grow is through egalitarian dialogue between Native and non-Native people working in and being served by the U.S. mental health system in Indian Country. The "talking up" or "talking down" of the past must be nullified by the careful public dismantling of domination codes long embedded within this system. The best examples I've seen for how to accomplish this lie within the superb equalizer of the traditional talking circle.

The circle represents sacredness, balance, centering, compassion, and relationship, and with the assistance of Native tradition, all people learn to share from the heart, leading to a greater opportunity for total consensus. In the mid-1970s, Lakota medicine healer John Fire Lame Deer (Lakota name: Tahca Ushte) and EuroAmerican graphic artist Richard Erdoes began a four-year collaboration toward documenting traditional teachings, among which were included John Lame Deer's explanation of the importance of the circle:

To our way of thinking the Indians' symbol is the circle, the hoop. Nature wants things to be round. The bodies of human beings and animals have no corners. With us the circle stands for the togetherness of people who sit with one another around the campfire, relatives and friends united in peace while the pipe passes from hand to hand. The camp in which every tipi had its place was also a ring. The tipi was a ring in which people sat in a circle and all the families in the village were in turn circles within a larger circle, part of the larger hoop which was the seven campfires of the Sioux, representing one nation. The nation was only a part of the universe, in itself circular and made of the earth, which is round, of the sun, which is round, of the stars, which are round. The moon, the horizon, the rainbow—circles within circles within circles, with no beginning and no end.

To us this is beautiful and fitting, symbol and reality at the same time, expressing the harmony of life and nature. Our circle is timeless, flowing: it is new life emerging from death—life winning out over death.[8]

THE POTENTIAL RELEVANCE OF THE POWER-THREAT-MEANING FRAMEWORK

The United Kingdom has been experiencing more dramatic public controversies recently about power and dominance in Western mental health ideologies than the United States. In June 2011 the British Psychological Society (BPS), representing more than 50,000 of the United Kingdom's registered psychologists, officially expressed its displeasure with the American Psychiatric Association's latest manual of diagnostic labels, the *DSM-5*:

The putative diagnoses presented in DSM-V are clearly based largely on social norms, with 'symptoms' that all rely on subjective judgements, with little confirmatory physical 'signs' or evidence of biological causation. The criteria are not value-free, but rather reflect current normative social expectations. Many researchers have pointed out that psychiatric diagnoses are plagued by problems of reliability, validity, prognostic value, and co-morbidity.[9]

BPS recommended instead

> a revision of the way mental distress is thought about, starting with recognition of the overwhelming evidence that it is on a spectrum with 'normal' experience, and that psychosocial factors such as poverty, unemployment and trauma are the most strongly-evidenced causal factors.[10]

BPS's official statement was the first major crack I've seen across a thirty-five-year career in the armor of a global biomedical ideological stranglehold on mental health policy making. Perhaps the American Psychiatric Association can no longer enjoy carte blanche in its labeling, stigmatizing, medicalizing, and drugging of an uninformed public.

In fact, six months after the BPS position statement, Division 32 of the American Psychological Association, the Society for Humanistic Psychology, followed suit with an open letter and public petition challenging the worth and validity of *DSM-5*. Division 32 then brought together an alliance of over fifty other international mental health societies and organizations, including BPS, the Danish Psychological Association, seven divisions of the American Counseling Association, the American Family Therapy Academy, and the Society of Indian Psychologists. Among many other criticisms, these petitioners objected to the draft *DSM-5*'s attempt to redefine a "mental disorder" in terms of an "underlying psychobiological dysfunction."[11]

In line with its past hegemony, however, the American Psychiatric Association strategic response to these *DSM-5* critics was mostly to ignore them. Objectionable "psychobiological dysfunction" language in the manual's early draft was quietly changed to the similar "dysfunction in psychological, biological or developmental processes" in its 2013 publication.[12]

Five years after the publication of *DSM-5*, a working group composed of BPS members, psychiatric survivors, and other contributors from various backgrounds made good on the organization's call to revise "the way mental distress is thought about." In January 2018, a critically important 414-page document was published by BPS entitled *The Power Threat Meaning Framework*[13] representing a valuable alternative to the dominant biopsychiatric paradigm. The Power Threat Meaning Framework, or PTMF, de-pathologizes and de-medicalizes the ways in which mental health professionals view troubled (or troubling) people and, more importantly, is not intended only for professionals but for everyone. The PTMF is already being applied by professionals and lay people around the world.

The PTMF offers exceptional potential for U.S. mental health providers trained in but questioning the culture of individualist Western approaches to well-being. I refer the reader to the actual online document for a more comprehensive sense of its qualities but will briefly summarize it and offer a few quotes relevant to Native America. There are numerous additional summaries, resources, and webinars available through the BPS website.

Rather than creating "symptoms" and categorizing them into "disorders" or "diseases" (as occurs in the biopsychiatric and medical models), the PTMF listens to people's stories of their own lived experiences of Power and Threat, the Meaning they attribute to the Threats, and their own Responses to Threat. Based upon a large body of research regarding threats to core human needs, "Threat Response" recognizes spiritual, cognitive, emotional, and physiological reactions not as "symptoms" but as adaptive means of coping that may no longer feel useful or helpful. The PTMF attaches the greatest significance to the idea that the experiences of each child, youth, adult, and family are understood within a wider context of culture, community, and society.[14]

Each of the overlapping domains in the PTM framework offers relevant questions:

- "What has happened to you?" (How has **Power** operated in your life?)
- "How did it affect you?" (What kind of **Threats** does this pose?)
- "What sense did you make of it?" (What is the **Meaning** of these situations and experiences to you?)
- "What did you have to do to survive?" (What kinds of **Threat Response** are you using?)[15]

In webinar sessions, Dr. Lucy Johnstone, who is lead author with Professor Mary Boyle of the PTMF, acknowledges that such questions are intended as *whole realms of inquiry and helping* that lend themselves to a wide array of community approaches to well-being. The PTMF intends to move well beyond checklists and close-ended approaches of the established system, which herds people toward labels and drugs. Instead, this approach recognizes the context and interdependence of every person and family and seeks to investigate the complex story of how power, threat, meaning, and threat response functions in their lives.

The authors of *The Power Threat Meaning Framework*, published by the British Psychological Society in 2018, charge that the dominant Western positivist epistemology contributes to "limited and misleading" depictions of "the social world," "the body," and the relations between both of these and personal psychological experience. These authors remark:

> Human beings are active agents in their lives, both determined and determining beings, rather than objects acted upon by external forces. As human agents we both conform to the reality we encounter and seek to transform it. We do this through our capacity for meaning making, and for reflecting on and learning from our experiences. Social and cultural influences do not simply provide backgrounds and constraints; they are the conditions out of which meaning, agency, feeling and action arise.[16]

From such a vantage point, the PTMF celebrates "Indigenous Psychology" in challenging "the idea of decontextualised, mechanical, universal principles and focus[ing] on understanding people in context."[17] In my own communication with lead author Dr. Johnstone, she remarked:

> We want to go further than saying 'The psychiatric model doesn't work even in its own terms' or 'We need to respect Indigenous understandings' (which could sound quite patronising.) We need to take the position that Indigenous understandings are absolutely valid reflections of reality in their own right.[18]

Again, the authors of *The Power Threat Meaning Framework* argue:

> To impose dominant Western models of social 'deviance' and distress on to other cultures is to fall into the racist assumption that our worldview is superior because it is more 'true'; a subtle but no less damaging form of colonialism than more overt forms.[19]

Thus, the PTMF at the very least represents a lens through which highly individualistic Western models and approaches to well-being might be more deeply scrutinized, deconstructed, and revised. Moreover, the authors are careful to distinguish the greater relevance to Native communities of family pathways and story in considering the PTMF variables of Power, Threat, Meaning, and Threat Response:

Narratives at the level of the social group may be seen as equally or more valuable in collectivist cultures, where the idea of engaging in one-to-one therapy may be alien and inappropriate and there might consequently be more emphasis on locating emotional distress within the contexts of extended family relationships, ties to village and social network, relationship to house and land, and so on ... These perspectives are comparatively under-emphasised in more individualistic cultures, despite the strong evidence about the central importance of relationships and community ties for emotional wellbeing in all societies.[20]

As I've tried to do herein, the PTMF authors assert that liberation psychology or any community psychology "approaches based on narrative, relational, dialogical and social justice principles"[21] must consider "the process of 'conscientisation', or developing critical consciousness about the impact of societal structures on wellbeing."[22] The PTMF openly acknowledges intergenerational and historical trauma as expressions of Power and Threat "in which entire peoples or colonised groups suffer from loss of language, traditions, genocide, and other forms of deliberate destruction of their lives and culture."[23]

The authors of *The Power Threat Meaning Framework* also acknowledge community-driven approaches as being of primary importance because they "reintroduce some of the shared communal experiences that have been neglected, while dialogical, interpretative and phenomenological approaches also acknowledge the centrality of shared meaning in human experience and behaviour."[24] In summary, within "the aims of the [PTMF] project, the implication is that patterns underpinning individual and group experiences of distress will be inseparable from their material, environmental, socio-economic and cultural contexts."[25]

Sadly, I'm forced to admit that the PTMF—or any other potentially desirable alternative—could never become part of the U.S. mental health system in Indian Country as long as the federal government and the Indian Health Service sustain authority and control directly or through tribal grant programs. Yet the PTMF represents a fascinating and articulate challenge to biopsychiatric ideology and to *DSM*– and International Classification of Diseases (ICD)–based diagnostic labeling. At the same time, it is a clear threat to highly vested interests. The PTMF brings a deeper way of understanding and allying as a helper, whether one is professional, academically credentialed, or a layperson, yet it also implies the leveling down of the status of thousands of U.S. mental health providers.

Such threats to the status quo represented by the PTMF also clarify one of its strengths: to work one's way out of further need as communities take on their own healing. To date, this has never been the stated end goal of the U.S. mental health system in Native America. As William Charley suggested to Lucullus McWhorter long ago, it will be the push and pull of Coyote's Swing that decides whether this can ever change. A Facebook post I recently spotted on the UK page "Drop the Disorder," where many PTM fans reside, summarizes the distinctions:

Medical Model—You do things "to" us
Charity Model—You do things "for" us
Community Driven Model—You do things "with" us
Sovereignty Model—Things are done "by" us

RESTORING THE CIRCLE

I was looking for new ideas and innovation when I came to Yakama Nation, but what I discovered were beautiful, even astonishing *old* ways marginalized by the U.S. mental hygiene movement. I've described my own profound encounters with the *xwyách* (sweat lodge), *káatnam* (longhouse), and Shíikash (Indian Shaker) practices and their relevance to spiritual and emotional well-being and healing among the Yakama people. These are the real "innovations" carried down through many generations. There are many more traditional practices among Original Nations, and it's a duty of any helping outsider to "seek to be taught" about them, but only if such teaching is freely offered.

The racist sentiment that traditional healing is somehow "primitive" or "second-class" must be disrupted and transcended. This sometimes implicit bias has its roots in cultural evolutionism. In their splendid summary of new revelations emerging over the last thirty or more years in their chosen fields, anthropologist David Graeber, who died in 2020, and archaeologist David Wengrow conclude in *The Dawn of Everything*[26] that the mythical and ubiquitous hunter-gatherer clans so often romanticized or impugned in cultural evolutionism as gradually displaced by agriculture and civilization *never existed*:

There was no truly 'original' state of affairs. Anyone who insists that one exists is by definition trading in myths ... Human beings had many tens of thousands of years to experiment with different ways of life, long before any of them turned their hands to agriculture. Instead we might do better to look at the overall direction of change, so as to understand how it bears upon our question: how humans came largely to lose the flexibility and freedom that seems once to have characterized our social arrangements, and ended up stuck in permanent relations of dominance and subordination.[27]

One discussion within *The Dawn of Everything* that particularly struck me as relevant to *Coyote's Swing* pertains to "Nebelivka: a prehistoric 'mega-site' in the Ukrainian forest-steppe,"[28] one of numerous archaeological sites up to 6,000 years old demonstrating "people who have figured out a way for a large population to govern and support itself without temples, palaces and military fortifications—that is, without overt displays of arrogance, self-abasement and cruelty."[29]

The supplied map shows the layout of the Nebelivka community also seen across "tens of these settlements" where "houses form such neat circular patterns that from a bird's-eye view, any mega-site resembles the inside of a tree trunk: great rings, with concentric spaces between."[30] Graeber and Wengrow feel they can "safely infer" that the governance of these many ancient settlements of 10,000 or more people was "based on the image of a circle and its properties of transformation."[31]

As John Fire Lame Deer proclaimed, and I can attest, this way survives and thrives. The sacred circle and what it has meant for human beings has not only been inherently disruptive to the hierarchies of Europe and Christianity and the divine right of kings but to the neo-feudal, corporate hierarchies of today. The circle retains the consultative means for a meeting between equals.

In a recent article, I suggested the U.S. (and global) mental health system, including my own profession, represents a *secular priesthood* still serving hierarchy:

> By *secular*, I mean we are granted a worldly, non-religious identity managed by governmental entities that reflects and enforces Western cultural norms. It would be illegal, for instance, for me to publicly promote myself as providing services of a "psychologist" without having jumped through the culturally prescribed hurdles leading to obtaining that right from the state. The state owns and

defines my role; I do not. By *priesthood*, I mean we are a mental health community of "elders" or *presbyter* permitted to administer specific esoteric, culturally nested ideologies and methods toward people who are not initiated.[32]

Sadly, my own profession's history includes many efforts to tear apart the ancient circles of humanity. But William Charley's story of Coyote's Swing still teaches lessons of transformation, even redemption, by learning from one another how to "swing back." For my part, I know as a practicing psychologist and human being that I've been able to serve people while refusing to pathologize, while seeing them as my equals—and, like me, struggling to find a fulfilling and peaceful life within a society that is mostly broken.

The massive project of remaking well-being in Native America must, therefore, emphasize making rather than breaking circles. I know this is true; we must all come together, heal, dismantle, rethink, and rebuild.

In April 2019, I was invited as a co-facilitator on a team led by writer, healer, and elder Deena Metzger[33] to participate in a large healing circle called "ReVisioning Mental Health" held in Minneapolis at PrairieCare, a psychiatric health care system in Minnesota. The circle was called by psychotherapist and social worker Lora Matz, a faculty member at the Center for Mind-Body Medicine and an amazing woman who somehow survived the very worst abuses of biopsychiatry.[34]

I arrived with more than sixty other people to this circle designed for healers from many ethnic backgrounds: African Americans, Asian Americans, Cuban Americans, EuroAmericans, Indian Americans, Indonesian Americans, Persian Americans, Sri Lankan Americans, Ukrainian Americans, and—most importantly for this gathering—Native Americans.

Our circle began by acknowledging the contested, occupied Dakota land upon which we sat together. Seemingly in response, traditional healers from the Dakota people offered special sanction and beautiful blessings. Other Native healers then presented themselves spontaneously and worked together to offer blessings from Ojibwe, Menominee, Cherokee, and Aleut traditions. Still more prayers and good thoughts emerged from among this myriad of cultures represented by the diversity of the circle participants.

When these prayers and good wishes from so many traditions and belief systems concluded, there was a pregnant pause during which everyone sat, completely silent, gazing at this globally constituted *circle* of human beings.

How rare and precious this seemed to all present. Imagine over sixty people all able to see and face one another and originating from so many parts of the world, each with their politics and social attitudes held back, falling silent and gazing about at one another after all these prayers, affirmations, blessings, stories, and loving thoughts. It was a sense of warmth and longing, and one of true safety, combined with profound expectation. I felt as if I'd waited to sit in this circle all my life.

People were invited to speak—or not—and the genuine desires of every person present emerged within our circle's climate of true counsel. Many of the providers in attendance—psychiatrists, psychologists, physicians, counselors, social workers, acupuncturists, yoga instructors, mind-body practitioners, and others—were stepping out of busy working lives and into the healing ways of Original People for the first time. Some seemed very surprised to enter an event not at all academic or intellectual but responding to their inmost unmet needs for healing and respite from systems everyone agreed are not working.

Most of what was said must stay with me within that remembered moment. I'll disclose, however, that throughout our weekend together, strangers became friends, people wept together, and many embraced over shared grief and tragedy regarding so many unmet aspirations and dysfunctional realities. We stopped worrying about the categories into which we might be lumped and held fast to the view that polarizing, political bickering was inadmissible to our process. This circle brought us back to a very ancient way of holding counsel, one practiced not only in Native America but at one time in the forest steppes of ancient Ukraine and all over Europe, Africa, Asia, and beyond. A talking stick was continually passed, and all present listened and spoke to one another with unprecedented intensity and respect.

Little attention was paid to the clock. And yet, so many expressed the feeling that time is of the essence. We were continually made aware of one another's concerns about how climate collapse, racist hatred and bigotry, and the unrelenting violence of our society are manifesting the imminent threat of extinction of our own and many other species. Numerous people present explained how this threat was foretold by their own traditions and how, therefore, our gathering was propitious and could not possibly be accidental. Instead, we concluded, many more such circles must be convened *now*.

The beautiful Menominee water ceremony brought people even closer, and big questions soon arose. What is it that we humans are truly seeking to heal *from*? Might our chronic tendency toward maltreatment of one another, our myopic beliefs, our powerlessness, and our hopelessness about proactively changing this world we share together constitute our core "dis-ease"? How is it that we who are drawn toward healing work have become trapped by systems tending to exacerbate rather than ameliorate suffering? How do we step out and restore humanity, compassion, and love in action in ourselves and within our communities? What is Real Medicine?

Nighttime dreams of participants were brought into the circle. I mentioned recurrent dreams of mountain lions I experienced throughout my time working at Yakama Nation (and periodically since). I was astonished to hear numerous others describe similar intense, recurring dreams of this same powerful animal who *protects her young*. Several others reported having premonitions and dreams of ancestors aiding the very circle in which we sat. There was much more along these lines too specific to individual people to comfortably disclose.

As in so many times in my life, I felt *led* to the ReVisioning Mental Health circle, just as I felt in my encounters with the buck, with Joshua Maiden, with my old friend Barney . . . I felt brought *toward* this gathering of loving people sharing a genuine wish to transcend all that has been imposed upon us, from inside and outside, all of which delays or impedes the urgent needs of the next seven generations.

And then we were all shut down by the worldwide calamity of the pandemic, a massive human problem that, like so many these days, can only be resolved by a unified community of nations. Again and again, I have thought of the circle in 2019 and known in my heart that there are many more good people like those out there.

On the last day of ReVisioning Mental Health, we were asked to describe what we wished to carry away with us. I consider now all the darkness and grief I've walked my reader through as I turn back to what others said in our circle that day. I so wish I could fully impart all the hope I heard, all the light and energy still glowing in the darkness right now.

And, yes, I held on to my own notes of what I wanted to say to others in the circle, and they form yet another knot on the string of my life. Here they are, read aloud as I sensed the presence of my old friend Long Standing Bear Chief, whom I felt standing right next to me:

Ni kso ko wah. *All my relatives.*

My older brother who taught me these words took me into the sweat lodge nineteen years ago. He is standing by me and whispering, "Remember what I taught you about being a good relative. Remember what I said about being a Real Human Being and bringing honor to your family and ancestors."

There is no formula to being honorable. There are only various ways to bring oneself to account each day and to determine to what degree one has behaved as a Real Human Being. I have been taught I must sustain certain sacrifices and increase others at this time to live in a manner I consider honorable.

Since I do not consider my profession to currently be honorable, I might need to do things or act in such ways so as to be a Real Human Being that don't always coincide with being perceived as a professional by my relatives caught within the same system that has hurt so many and tried to confine me too.

But I will go the same way my elder brother went before me, and I want to meet him with a clear heart and be able to tell him that I listened and learned from him and did some of the things we talked about doing together.

He is a bear, and he's sleeping now. I am dhlv:datsi gigagé, red panther, and although we are solitary beings and different, we became so close before he walked on that I call him "elder brother."

He is waiting for me with hot coffee and a fire. I will bring him tobacco for his pipe again one day, and we'll talk about all we'll try to do to help Mother Earth and her people.

THE TWELVE VIRTUES OF NÍIX TTÁWAXT

K'wyáamtimt
Honesty, Being Truthful

To be honest and truthful in talking about yourself and your opinions. To avoid any behavior that could even appear to harm the honor of yourself or your family by being dishonest.

Timnák'nik
Extending from the Heart; Compassion

To show kindness and care at all times to others whether in listening, speaking, helping, or performing a service for them. To consider the feelings of others, to avoid hurting them, and to show concern for their feelings.

Itmá'áaksha
Cautious and Careful of All Things and Others;
Restrained, Peaceful, and Responsible

To be careful in your speech and other behavior so as to avoid harming or hurting anyone, including yourself. To be responsible and accountable for your behavior. To show care for maintaining peace and harmony with all people.

Yáych'unakl
Not Afraid of Any Type of Challenge;
Courage; Heroic Perseverance

To show courage. To never give up, no matter how hard life gets. To be willing to put up with negative behaviors and pressures from others in order to do the right thing. To be a leader when others hesitate to do something positive.

Pina'tmá'áakt
Taking Care and Being Aware of One's Total Being;
Balance and Harmony;
Integrity, Honor, Nobility in Crisis

To take care of yourself and to know yourself. To constantly seek to understand yourself. Self-respect. To stay in balance with what you believe. To behave with honor and refuse to get involved in behaviors that would hurt you or others.

Tma'áakni
Respect

To maintain a spirit of harmony and cooperation with all people, including those who have differing opinions from your own. To show care and regard for preserving and protecting the cultural traditions, beliefs, and unwritten laws of Native people.

Átaw P̲xwini
Deep Thought and Feeling; Meditation and Mindfulness

To practice looking at yourself, your thoughts, and your feelings. To meditate and pray regularly. To be constantly aware of all that is around you and within you. To grow in using your mind at all times, especially when involved in getting an education.

Piná Hwaat Ku Kw'aláni
Self-Denial and Gratitude; Humility

To be humble. To be grateful just to be helpful to others. To give away all feelings of conceit or arrogance. To be the first one to apologize, to correct your behavior, and to forgive others.

Wapítat Ttáwa̲xt
Help Family Growth; Service to Others

To serve others by offering to help others in as many ways as you can think of. This might include helping elders and other family members and friends. It also includes taking part in positive community events and activities that prevent violence, helping people to heal from traumatic experiences, eliminating substance abuse and chemical dependency, promoting positive understanding and involvement in your Indian culture, modeling and encouraging education and the pursuit of life goals for others, and working to increase the unity of all people.

Pina Ch'achanwit Wawnak'sash
Dignity and Self-Preservation of Purity of the Body

Keeping the body clean and pure on a daily basis; to remain in accordance to the unwritten law. The body houses the spirit of the mind and heart. Preserving virginity until marriage. Therefore, the body must be cared for with cleanliness and purity to maintain dignity and integrity.

At'aw Pina shuukt'
Recognizing Who You Are with Love

The spirit of the elders and the knowledge of their family tree should be known by all descendants. This is proof of self-identity and recognizing the gift of life and love that was left to all the descendants of those that gave of themselves for the yet unborn.

Pinana'nak'núuwit
Taking Care of Oneself; Maintaining Good Health

Self-care will enable a person to care for their family and keep everyone else with in the family circle healthy. This is a selfish virtue, doing for oneself in order to do for others.

Thank you.
Levina Wilkins (Kussamwhy)[35]

ENDNOTES

INTRODUCTION

1. All the people described in *Coyote's Swing* are composite cases constructed out of actual events in the lives of real Native Americans I met through clinical work as a licensed psychologist in Indian Country. The composites were built using guidelines originating from Duffy, "Writing About Clients," 135–53. Additionally, in all case descriptions in this book, close adherence was maintained to Ethical Standard 4.07, "Use of Confidential Information for Didactic or Other Purposes" (effective June 1, 2003), of the American Psychological Association's *Ethical Principles of Psychologists and Code of Conduct* and the Washington State Administrative Code, WAC 246-924-363, "Protecting confidentiality of clients," Item 9: "Disguising confidential information" in "teaching, research, and other published reports."
2. I do not refer to "Fourteen Confederated Tribes," having met people from numerous bands and families recognized as part of the Yakama Nation community who are not included within the language of U.S. government documents.
3. I use the term "Blackfoot" in accord with the advice of my deceased elder and dear friend, Long Standing Bear Chief, who rejected the moniker "Blackfeet" in its application to the Piikáni people of the Blackfoot Confederacy.
4. Running Crane, "Accurate Cultural Context."
5. David Edward Walker, "WHO Owns the Language," 5–6.
6. Open Science Collaboration, "Estimating the Reproducibility."
7. Hornsey and Fielding, "Attitude Roots and Jiu Jitsu Persuasion," 459–73.
8. Vanderwerth, *Indian Oratory*, 22.
9. Kimmerer, *Braiding Sweetgrass*, 45.
10. Levina Wilkins, Yakama Nation Elder, Oral Teaching, to the author, October 11, 2010.
11. Karlberg, "Power of Discourse," 1.
12. Anonymous fifteen-year-old Yakama girl, 2004, author's collection.
13. Uebelacker, *Time Ball*, 10.
14. Ibid., 165.

15. Running Crane, "Accurate Cultural Context," 4.
16. Hathaway, "American Indian and Alaska Native People."
17. Janessa M. Graves et al., "Barriers to Telemedicine Implementation."

CHAPTER ONE

1. Evans, *Voice of the Old Wolf*, 17.
2. "Obituary for Harold Ernest Long Standing Bear Chief Gray." From Long Standing Bear Chief's obituary:

> [He served as a] high school and college instructor, as the first director of Indian Studies at the University of Montana; director of the Chippewa Cree Tribal Research Program at Rocky Boy, Mont.; Head Start director, Browning, Mont.; and educator with the Bureau of Indian Affairs, Education Department in Lame Deer, Mont. As president of Bear Chief and Associates, a consulting firm he operated with his twin brother, he provided technical assistance to many tribes, tribal programs and schools throughout the U.S. Long Standing Bear Chief spent a great deal of his career as a freelance author, historian and traditional artist. He was often sought after by people for information and knowledge regarding tribal history, traditions and laws regarding indigenous people, their governments and their rights. Long Standing Bear Chief taught his children to be proud of their Indian ancestry as well as to celebrate their diverse ethnic backgrounds.

3. Lucullus McWhorter, *Crime Against the Yakimas*.
4. Ibid., 56.
5. "What Became of Coyote," in Hines, *Ghost Voices*, 139.
6. Sometimes called "Mount Adams" by the *páshtin*.
7. Talea Anderson, "'I Want My Agency Moved Back."
8. Ibid., 182. Specifically regarding seeking local white women as allies:

> Although Native Americans seemed concerned primarily with the loss of tribal sovereignty inherent in the removal of the agency, they reframed their concerns to garner the support of particular white audiences. Leaders in the tribe sought out clubwomen as allies in the struggle with the BIA. They adopted the moralizing discourse of the clubwomen and identified their opponents as business leaders—including the BIA—who cared more about profits than the welfare of Yakama Indians.

9. Ibid., 183.
10. Krona, "World War II and Japanese Internment."
11. Heuterman, *Burning Horse*.
12. Ibid., 55.
13. Steve Ross, "Yakima Terror."
14. Associated Press, "Indians and Washington State."
15. Stewart and Bennett, *American Cultural Patterns*, 134.
16. Beyond numerous experiences I will detail with sweat lodge, longhouse, and Indian Shaker traditions, I'm thinking of a document gifted to me by my *kála* Levina Wilkins pertaining to medicinal plants and herbs on her sacred land as well as a

gift of roots to be made into tea, high in ascorbic acid, and offered by my Blackfoot friend Verna Smith when I had a bad cold.

17. Payer, *Medicine and Culture*.
18. Davis, *History of the Medical Profession*, 185.

CHAPTER TWO

1. David Edward Walker et al., "Prediction of Recovery."
2. Levine, *Resisting Illegitimate Authority*.
3. George Lee Walker, *Chronicles of Doodah*.
4. Sayer, *Ghost Dancing the Law*, 146.
5. Alan Duke, "'Billy Jack' Actor-Writer Tom Laughlin Dies at 82."
6. For a synopsis of this genealogical research, please visit my webpage "Missouri Cherokee" at http://davidedwardwalker.com/missouri-cherokee.html.
7. Jennifer Gray Reddish, "Rockin' the Rez for Bay Mills Community College"; Green, "Dream Catchers Vol. 2."

CHAPTER THREE

1. Meaning roughly "good growth to maturity" in English.
2. Three components were envisioned: a residential group home, a culture- and family-centered behavioral health program, and a fetal alcohol spectrum disorder (FASD) program.
3. Shilow, "New Youth Residential Counseling Home," 8.
4. Yakama Tribal Council, Resolution T-10-04.
5. At its peak, the Níix Ttáwaxt community advisory group had more than thirty representatives, including the Yakama Nation tribal administrator; teachers and counselors from the Toppenish, Wapato, and Mt. Adams School Districts; Yakama Nation Tribal School, Yakama Nation Youth Treatment Center, Yakama Nation Tribal Justice Services, Yakama Nation Probation Services, and EPIC Youth Services; the Region 2 administrator and program specialists from the Department of Child and Family Services of the state of Washington; and the liaison for Indian policy and programs for the state of Washington.
6. Levina Wilkins, "Nine Virtues of the Yakama Nation"; see chapter 20.
7. *Kála* is a Yakama endearment meaning adopted grandmother. Ms. Wilkins is the current manager of Yakama Nation Language Program.
8. Indian Health Service, *Indian Health Manual*.
9. Michael D. Wilson, "Reclaiming Self-Determination," 74.
10. Ward, "EPIC Turns Over"; Enterprise for Progress in the Community (EPIC).
11. Yellow Bird, "Wild Indians."
12. Garth, *Race Psychology*.
13. Hirsch, "Study of Natio-Racial Mental Differences," 239–406.

14. David Edward Walker, *Tessa's Dance*; David Edward Walker, *Signal Peak*.
15. David Edward Walker, "How the US Mental Health System"; David Edward Walker, "Lunacy, Crazy Indians"; David Edward Walker, "'A Living Burial'"; David Edward Walker, "Betrayal by Labels."

CHAPTER FOUR

1. Beavert and Hargus, *Ichishkíin Sínwit*, xxiv.
2. "Yakama" is the original treaty spelling and favored by the tribe; "Yakima," although used as a tribal spelling in the past, now refers solely to the geographic area, including the city of Yakima and the Yakima Valley.
3. Ibid.
4. Pember, "*Indian Country Today* Hiatus."
5. See, for example, Archuleta et al., *Away from Home*.
6. David Wilkins, "Dismembering Natives."
7. Anna V. Smith, "5 Obstacles for Native Voters."
8. Ta-Nehisi Coates, "First White President."
9. Tom Porter, "Trump Pocahontas Slur."
10. Reflective Democracy Campaign, "Who Leads Us?"
11. Ibid.
12. Zweigenhaft, "Diversity Among CEOs."
13. Ibid.
14. Reflective Democracy Campaign, "Who Leads Us?"
15. Schilling, "HERSTORY!"
16. National Congress of American Indians, "Every Native Vote Counts."
17. U.S. Bureau of Labor, "Labor Force Characteristics by Race and Ethnicity, 2015."
18. Ibid.
19. Woodard, "Racist Emails of Federal Judge."
20. U.S. District Court, *Wandering Medicine et al. v. McCulloch et al.*
21. Lakusiak et al., "Native Americans Still Fight."
22. Ibid.
23. Native American Rights Fund, "South Dakota Voter Registration."
24. U.S. Census Office, "American Indian and Alaska Native Heritage Month."
25. Ibid.
26. U.S. Census Office, "Annual Estimates of the Resident Population."
27. Confederated Tribes and Bands of the Yakama Nation: enacted by T-53-77; amended by T-053-94; amended by T-172-99. I am grateful to Mr. Jack Fiander, Yakama Nation tribal attorney, for providing me this information on March 9, 2021.
28. Indian Health Service, *Trends in Indian Health, 2014*, 20.
29. U.S. Department of the Interior, "2013 American Indian Population," 13–14.
30. Consider, for example, these two U.S. Board of Indian Commissioners annual report excerpts from 1899:

> The object of the general allotment act was to give homesteads to Indian families. It deals with Indians as families and as individuals. It is intended to weaken the tribal relation and ultimately to destroy it.

and:

> It is the opinion of our board that it would be wise for the Department [of the Interior] to assign a man of experience in dealing with the Indians—a man with some knowledge of ethnology, but a practical man, who would not be devoted to impracticable theories—to visit all agencies and *give his entire time to the fixing of a uniform practice in the matter of naming Indians on allotment rolls*; and where any change from the Indian name is made, to the systematic and firm association of the old name with the new, upon permanent books of record at the agency, and as far as possible, in the memory and usage of the Indians themselves. (U.S. Board of Indian Commissioners, *Thirty-First Annual Report*, 231, 234. Italics in the original.)

31. Oeser, "Avoiding Extinction," 14.
32. Haozous et al., "Blood Politics," 1–9.
33. Monet, "Linking Arms, Marching Forward."
34. Nina Shapiro, "Nooksack Tribe."
35. I'm grateful to my Cherokee friend Stan Rushworth for reminding me of this issue. In my own family history, my fifth-generation Cherokee grandmother, Elizabeth Jane Albina Alexander, refused to sign the Dawes Rolls.
36. Haozous et al., "Blood Politics," 2–3.
37. U.S. Indian Health Service, *Trends in Indian Health, 2014*, 155.
38. Ibid., 171.
39. National Congress of American Indians, "Demographics."
40. IHS calls outpatient visits "ambulatory medical visits," and the statistic includes visits to both IHS and IHS-funded, tribally operated facilities.
41. U.S. Indian Health Service, *Trends in Indian Health, 2014*, 172.
42. Ibid., 181.
43. Ibid., 158–65.
44. Ibid., 161, 175–76.
45. Ibid., 176–77.
46. Hobbs et al., "GM 12-028: Indian Health Service."
47. American Psychiatric Association, *DSM-5*; italics mine.
48. Italics mine.
49. Indian Health Service, *American Indian/Alaska Native Behavioral Health Briefing Book*, 11.
50. Ibid.
51. Ibid.

CHAPTER FIVE

1. Kroenke et al., "The PHQ-9."
2. See Indian Health Service, "Assessment and Reassessment Tools."
3. Henrich et al., "Weirdest People in the World?"
4. Virginia Mason Memorial Hospital, "2016 Community Health Needs Assessment," 45.
5. Ibid.
6. Thornton, "On Demography and Genocide," 210–16. Dr. Thornton provides reviews and brief analysis of the following books: Alvarez, *Native America and the Question*

of Genocide; Gary Clayton Anderson, *Ethnic Cleansing and the Indian*; Woolford et al., *Colonial Genocide in Indigenous North America.*
7. Ibid.
8. Ibid., 215.
9. United Nations, "Analysis Framework."
10. Italics mine.
11. United Nations, "Analysis Framework," 1–4.
12. Pember, "*Indian Country Today* Hiatus."
13. Reuben, *Facing Cancer in Indian Country*, 2.
14. Kate Brown, "People's Truth."
15. Boice et al., "Cancer Mortality Among Populations."
16. Dement et al., "Mortality of Older Construction and Craft Workers."
17. Kate Brown, *Plutopia.*
18. Kate Brown, "People's Truth."
19. Ibid.
20. Ibid.
21. Hales, *Atomic Spaces*, 204.
22. Ibid.
23. Ibid., 205.
24. Ibid., 206.
25. For a compelling history of this movement, see Ulrich, *Empty Nets.*
26. Yokel and Priddy, *Uranium and Other Chemical Contaminants.*
27. U.S. Department of Energy, "Hanford Annual Site Environmental Report," 4–28 (under "4.2.7: Radiological Dose in Perspective").
28. Reuben, *Facing Cancer in Indian Country*, 2.
29. Briggs, "Fighting Breast Cancer."
30. Farrow and McHugh, "Welcome to 'the Most Toxic Place in America.'"
31. Tolson, "Yakama Nation Fights."
32. Hoopes et al., "Regional Differences and Tribal Use," 73.
33. Reuben, *Facing Cancer in Indian Country*, 3.
34. Moore-Nall, "Legacy of Uranium Development."
35. Ibid., 21.
36. Ibid., 19–21.
37. Ibid., 17.
38. Whitney, "Native Americans Feel Invisible."
39. Dorgan, "Urgent Need to Reform," 42.
40. Ibid., 59.
41. Ibid., 66.
42. Ibid., 27.
43. Ibid., 67–68.
44. Ibid., 24.
45. Heath, *Risk Management*, 29.
46. Estimate made beginning in 2000 by IHS.
47. Ibid., 30–31.
48. Ibid., 31.
49. Fowler, *Risk Management*, 2, footnote 1.
50. U.S. Senate Committee on Indian Affairs, "Reexamining the Substandard Quality."

51. Ibid., 1.
52. Ibid., 3.
53. Ibid., 13.
54. U.S. Census Bureau, "American Indian and Alaska Native Heritage Month," 5.
55. City-Data.com, "Poverty in the US."
56. Ibid.
57. Romero-Briones, "More at Stake."
58. U.S. Department of Agriculture, "Biden-Harris Administration."
59. Bauer et al., "High Food Insecurity and Its Correlates."
60. *Food Research & Action Center. "Understanding the Connections."*
61. Gundersen, "Measuring the Extent, Depth, and Severity of Food Insecurity."
62. Jacob, "Claiming Health and Culture," 362.
63. Bauer et al., "High Food Insecurity and Its Correlates," 1346.
64. Chino et al., "Patterns of Commodity Food Use," 282.
65. Jacob, "Claiming Health and Culture," 361–80.
66. National Public Radio. "Discrimination in America," 1.
67. Ibid., 6.
68. Ibid., 26.
69. American Psychological Association, "Stress in America."
70. Johnston-Goodstar and Roholt, "'Our Kids Aren't Dropping Out,'" 40.
71. Ibid., 37.
72. Schilling, "High School Slammed."
73. State of Arizona, "House Bill 2281," 1.
74. Texas Freedom Network Education Fund, "Writing to the Standards," 23.
75. CDC, "High School YRBS."
76. Ibid.
77. National Congress of American Indians, "Policy Issues: Education."
78. Collier, "Special Education for Indigenous Students," 9.
79. Anastasiou and Kauffman, "Cultural Politics," 106.
80. Ibid.
81. Hinshaw, *Mark of Shame.*
82. Ben-Zeev et al., "DSM-V and the Stigma of Mental Illness."
83. Granello and Gibbs, "Power of Language and Labels."
84. Sieff, "Media Frames of Mental Illnesses."
85. Ben-Zeev et al., "DSM-V and the Stigma of Mental Illness."
86. Shifrer, "Stigma of a Label."
87. Author's statistical conversion to rates per 100,000 of homicide incidents reported in Yakima County Coroner, "Yakima County Coroner Annual Report," 2015, 2016, and 2017.
88. National Congress of American Indians, "Policy Insights Brief," 2.
89. Ibid., 3.
90. Ibid., 4.
91. Sweet, "Trafficking in Native Communities."
92. Farley et al., "Prostitution and Trafficking."
93. National Indigenous Women's Resource Center, "Honoring Missing and Murdered Indigenous Women."
94. Ibid.

95. Rosay, "Violence Against American Indian and Alaska Native Women and Men," 2.
96. Ibid.
97. Ibid.
98. Linton and Kim, "Traumatic Brain Injury."
99. Author's professional case files (unavailable for public perusal).
100. Brockie et al., "Relationship of Adverse Childhood Experiences," 411–21.
101. Author's professional case files (unavailable for public perusal).
102. Wong, "Dakota Access Pipeline."
103. Tolan, "North Dakota Pipeline Activists."
104. MacPherson, "North Dakota Oil Pipeline Protest."
105. Patricia Campbell, *Torture and Its Psychological Effects*.
106. Patricia Donegal, email message to author, October 30, 2017.
107. Woodard, "Police Killings No One Is Talking About."
108. Swaine et al., "Counted."
109. Ibid.
110. Ibid.
111. Koerth, "Police Violence Against Native Americans."
112. Carter, "City of Poulsbo to Pay."
113. Rosay, "Violence Against American Indian and Alaska Native Women and Men," 48.
114. Ibid.
115. Ibid., 47.

CHAPTER SIX

1. CDC, "Suicide: Facts at a Glance, 2012."
2. Sari Horwitz, "Hard Lives."
3. Ibid.
4. Rockett et al., "Suicide and Unintentional Poisoning."
5. Fitzpatrick et al., "How Bad Is It?"
6. CDC, "WISQARS Injury Data."
7. CDC, "Suicide: Facts at a Glance, 2012."
8. U.S. Department of Health and Human Services, *Mental Health*.
9. CDC, "YRBSS 1997 Middle School."
10. CDC, "High School YRBS."
11. CDC, "High School Students Who Seriously Considered Attempting Suicide."
12. Author's statistical conversion to rates per 100,000 of homicide incidents reported in Yakima County Coroner, "Yakima County Coroner Annual Report," 2015, 2016, and 2017.
13. These guidelines state, "It is appropriate to treat patients with moderate to severe major depressive disorder with medication whether or not formal psychotherapy is also used." See Agency for Health Care Policy and Research, *Depression in Primary Care*.
14. Jacobs et al., *Practice Guideline*.
15. Ibid., 62.
16. Isacsson et al., "Increased Use of Antidepressants."

17. Institute of Medicine, *Reducing Suicide.*
18. Ibid.
19. Ibid.
20. Ibid.
21. Fried and Nesse, "Depression Is Not a Consistent Syndrome."
22. Goodkind et al., "Promoting Healing and Restoring Trust."
23. Ibid., 387–88.
24. Isacsson et al., "Increased Use of Antidepressants."
25. Zahl et al., "Relationship Between Sales of SSRI."
26. Sparks, "Efficacy of Psychiatric Drugs."
27. Mora et al., "Lessons Learned from Placebo Groups."
28. Reeves et al., "Nocebo Effects."
29. Gøtzsche, *Deadly Medicines and Organised Crime,* 199.
30. Moncrieff, *Myth of the Chemical Cure,* 172.
31. Ibid., 172.
32. Greenberg, "Return of Psychosocial Relevance."
33. Kirsch, *Emperor's New Drugs.*
34. Hengartner, "Methodological Flaws."
35. Turner et al., "Selective Publication of Antidepressant Trials," 1–21.
36. Ibid., 3.
37. Robert Whitaker, *Anatomy of an Epidemic.*
38. Robert Whitaker and Cosgrove, *Psychiatry Under the Influence.*
39. Carlat, *Unhinged.*
40. Robert Whitaker and Cosgrove, *Psychiatry Under the Influence,* 180.
41. David Edward Walker, "Indian Health Service's Psychiatric."
42. Curtin et al., "Suicide Rates for Females and Males," 1–7.
43. Ibid., 6.
44. Ibid., based upon the author's own tabulation.
45. Great Lakes Inter-Tribal Council, "Suicidal Behaviors."
46. Stone et al., "Risk of Suicidality," 1–10.
47. Hengartner and Plöderl, "Newer-Generation Antidepressants."
48. Plöderl et al., "Commentary."
49. Gibbons et al., "Medications and Suicide."
50. Rodwin, "Conflicts of Interest."
51. Gibbons et al., "Early Evidence."
52. Robert Whitaker, "The Triumph of Bad Science."
53. Sparks and Duncan, "Outside the Black Box."
54. Jill E. Lavigne biography, St. John Fisher University, https://www.sjfc.edu/profiles/profile-last-name-2624-en.html.
55. U.S. Department of Veterans Affairs and U.S. Department of Defense. "VA/DoD Clinical Practice Guideline," 126–27.
56. CDC, "Reducing Military and Veteran Suicide."
57. CDC, "Disparities in Suicide."
58. Great Lakes Inter-Tribal Council, "Suicidal Behaviors," 37, 43.
59. Plöderl and Hengartner, "Antidepressant Prescription Rates."
60. Stone et al., "Risk of Suicidality," 24.
61. Great Lakes Inter-Tribal Council, "Suicidal Behaviors," 45.

62. Ibid., 42.
63. Ibid., 23.
64. Ibid. 40, 46.
65. Ibid.
66. Ibid.
67. Ibid.
68. Walls et al., "Strain, Emotion, and Suicide."
69. Szalavitz, "Native Americans"; Krisch, "Putting a Racist Myth to Bed"; Dempsey, *Firewater*. For a comprehensive history, see Frank et al., "Public Health."
70. See Szalavitz, "Native Americans," and Krisch, "Putting a Racist Myth to Bed."
71. Taylor, "Influence of Self-Efficacy."
72. Vivian M. Gonzalez and Monica C. Skewes associate the belief in the "firewater" myth with strategies to avoid alcohol consequences among American Indian and Alaska Native college students who drink. See Gonzalez and Skewes, "Association of Belief."
73. Graham, "Using Reasons for Living."
74. Strickland, "Challenges in Community."
75. Kennedy, "Community Action Research Approach."
76. Fanon, *Wretched of the Earth*, 251.
77. Duran, Guillory, and Villanueva, "Third and Fourth World Concerns," 212.
78. United Nations, "Analysis Framework."
79. Duran and Duran, *Native American Postcolonial Psychology*, 204.

CHAPTER SEVEN

1. Mohagheghzadeh et al., "Medicinal Smokes."
2. Nautiyal et al., "Medicinal Smoke."
3. All the people described in *Coyote's Swing* are composite cases constructed out of actual events in the lives of real Native Americans I met through clinical work as a licensed psychologist in Indian Country. The composites were built using guidelines originating from Duffy, "Writing About Clients."
4. Summers, *Disproportionality Rates*, 3.
5. National Indian Child Welfare Association, "What Is Disproportionality."
6. Clarren, "Right-Wing Think Tank."
7. Platoff, "5th Circuit Upholds."
8. Estus, "Court Strikes Key Provision."
9. Grimm and Darwall, "Foster Parents."
10. For an in-depth investigative report on this issue, see de Sá, "Drugging Our Kids."
11. De Sa and Savage, "California Foster Care."
12. Kelly, "Lawsuit over Psychotropics."
13. Smith and Bogado, "Immigrant Children Forcibly Injected."
14. Carey and Gebeloff, "Many People Taking Antidepressants."
15. Nielsen et al., "Dependence and Withdrawal."
16. For further practical information, the reader may wish to visit the Inner Compass Initiative website at www.theinnercompass.org.

17. See Sørensen et al., "Clinical Practice Guideline."
18. David Edward Walker, "ADHD as the New 'Feeblemindedness'"; Galves and Walker, "Debunking the Science."
19. Rockey Robbins, "Dream Catcher Meditation."
20. Author's files.
21. Anonymous IHS nurse to Mr. Tommy Thompson, November 1, 2001, author's personal collection.
22. Harris, "Debate Resumes."
23. Pfizer Incorporated, "Take This Posttraumatic Stress Disorder Quiz," 2001, author's personal collection.
24. See, for example: Johnstone, *Straight Talking*; Levine, *Surviving America's Depression*; Caplan and Cosgrove, *Bias in Psychiatric*; Levine, *Commonsense Rebellion*; Caplan, *They Say You're Crazy*; Szasz, *Ideology and Insanity*; and Laing, *Politics of Experience*.
25. Pfizer Corporation, www.pfizer.com (accessed January 15, 2018).
26. Mayes and Horwitz, "DSM-III and the Revolution"; Allsopp et al., "Heterogeneity in Psychiatric."

CHAPTER EIGHT

1. Yang and Ortega, "Bureaucratic Neglect."
2. Scott D. McDonald et al., "Validity and Diagnostic."
3. Allsopp et al., "Heterogeneity in Psychiatric," 15.
4. The operative terms and their acronyms for the citations that follow are: "structured clinical interview for DSM-III-R" (SCID; Spitzer et al., *Structured Clinical Interview*), "structured interview for PTSD measure" (SIP; Davidson et al., "Structured Interview"), and "clinician administered PTSD scale" (CAPS; Blake et al., "Development of a Clinician").
5. Meltzer-Brody et al., "Derivation of the SPAN"; Franklin et al., "Screening for Trauma."
6. Frankfurt, *On Bullshit*, 61.
7. McLaren, "Psychiatry as Bullshit."
8. Hunter and Schultz, "Brain Scan Research," 9–12.
9. Huo et al., "Neurovascular Coupling."
10. Marek et al., "Reproducible Brain-Wide Association"; Duncan et al., "Largest GWAS of PTSD."
11. Mathur et al., "Perceived Stress and Telomere Length"; Yehuda and Bierer, "Relevance of Epigenetics"; Yehuda et al., "Transgenerational Effects"; Yehuda et al., "Influences of Maternal."
12. Scorza et al., "Research Review," 124.
13. Ibid., 126.
14. Ibid.
15. Ibid., 127–28. See also the study itself: Yehuda et al., "Holocaust Exposure."
16. Ibid.
17. Yehuda, et al., "Public Reception," 1.
18. Ibid., 2.
19. MacNeill and Pérez-Edgar, "Temperament & Emotion."

20. Scorza et al., "Research Review," 129.
21. Lehrner and Yehuda, "Trauma Across Generations."
22. Brent Dean Robbins, et al., "DSM-5 Reform Efforts," 605.
23. British Psychological Society, "Statement on the Open Letter."
24. Insel, "Words Matter." See also Steingard, "Clinical Implications," 116.
25. American Psychiatric Association, *DSM-5*.
26. Insel, "Transforming Diagnosis."
27. Adam Rogers, "Star Neuroscientist."
28. Kupfer, "Chair of DSM-5 Task Force."
29. Joubert, "Are Mental Disorders Brain Disorders?"
30. American Psychiatric Association. *Diagnostic and Statistical Manual of Mental Disorders, Text Revision.*
31. Kawa and Giordano, "Brief Historicity."
32. Engstrom and Weber, "Directions of Psychiatric Research."
33. Strous et al., "Reflections on Emil Kraepelin."
34. Italics mine.
35. Beecher, "Medical Model," 10.
36. Clark, "Shock and Awe," 14.
37. Selye, *Stress of Life*.
38. Freud, "Early Studies," 27–28.
39. See Malcolm, *In the Freud Archives*.
40. van der Kolk and van Der Hart, "The Intrusive Past"; van der Kolk and Fisler, "Dissociation and the Fragmentary Nature"; Francine Shapiro, "Role of Eye Movement"; Brewin et al., "Dual Representation Theory."
41. See, for example, Bettelheim, *Freud and Man's Soul*.
42. Freud, *Question of Lay Analysis*, 61.
43. Ibid., 83.
44. Pear, "M.D.'s Make Room."
45. Boldface and italics in original.
46. Jelliffe and White, *Diseases of the Nervous System*, 904–5.
47. Beals et al., "Prevalence of Posttraumatic Stress Disorder," 93.
48. Based upon this author's analysis of Table 1 for ibid., 92.
49. U.S. Department of Veterans Affairs, "Psychological Trauma for American Indians Who Served in Vietnam."
50. LeMay, "Brief History."
51. McChesney, "Onondaga Nation Leaders."
52. Torreon, "U.S. Periods of War and Dates"; Torreon and Plagakis, "Instances of Use of United States Armed Forces Abroad."
53. See, for example, Dunbar-Ortiz, *Indigenous Peoples' History*.
54. Torreon, "U.S. Periods of War and Dates." See Duoos, "On This Day in History." According to Duoos (Leech Lake Ojibwe), the Battle of Sugar Point in 1898 came about after ongoing complaints by the Ojibwe Nation over swindling by EuroAmerican lumber companies regarding workers starting forest fires and then immediately harvesting green and semi-burned wood, claiming it was "dead." This practice nullified treaty-based compensation for logging and resulted in massive profits at the expense of the Ojibwe community. Another factor precipitating the conflict was law enforcement corruption, which consisted of years of

kickbacks and false arrests of Ojibwe people to meet the whims of white people. These circumstances led to community impoverishment, but appeals to the United States government were ignored. On October 5, 1898, the Pillager band of Ojibwe became involved in protecting an exploited inmate named Bug-O-Nay-Ge-Shig, who had escaped. This led to a standoff between a small group of band members and eighty soldiers of the 3rd U.S. Infantry. The soldiers allegedly fired upon women and children in a canoe and the Pillagers responded defensively, returning fire, which resulted in the retreat of the soldiers, with seven killed and ten wounded. It is difficult to parse the difference between what occurred in the Battle of Sugar Point as a facet of the "last Indian war" and what happened in the 1970s at Wounded Knee or in 2016 at the Dakota Access Pipeline protests.

55. Spurgeon, "Bomb Was Like the Indians," 1002.
56. Sayer, *Ghost Dancing the Law.*
57. Axe, "National Guard Deploys."
58. Andreasen, "Posttraumatic Stress Disorder."
59. Burgess and Holmstrom, "Rape Trauma Syndrome."
60. Stefan, "Protection Racket."
61. Leventhal and Krugman, "Battered-Child Syndrome."
62. Lifton, "Home from the War," 37.
63. Ibid.
64. Ibid., 447–48.
65. Ibid., 35.
66. Caplan, *They Say You're Crazy.*
67. See also Whitaker and Cosgrove, *Psychiatry Under the Influence.*
68. Caplan, *When Johnny and Jane Come Marching Home*, 87.
69. Bradley-Davino and Ruglass, "Trauma and Posttraumatic Stress."
70. Garrick et al., "America's Roads."
71. J. David Rogers et al., "Interactions Between."
72. Chengu, "How the U.S. Helped Create Al Qaida and ISIS"; Mourad, "How the US Creates Terrorism"; Thrall and Goepner, "Step Back."

CHAPTER NINE

1. Spier, *Prophet Dance*, 17.
2. Furtwangler, *Bringing Indians to the Book*, 95–96.
3. Speaks Lightning, *Indians of the Pacific States*, 55.
4. Ibid.
5. Fridlund, *Washington's Story.* Fridlund provides the following citation for this quote: "Letter from H.K.W. Perkins to Jane Prentiss, October 19, 1849, in Clifford M. Drury, *Marcus and Narcissa Whitman and the Opening of Old Oregon*, Vol. 2, Appendix 6, 393."
6. Fridlund, *Washington's Story*, 110.
7. See Hagley Museum and Library, "History of Patent Medicine."
8. Speaks Lightning, *Indians of the Pacific States*, 61.
9. Ibid.

10. Hall, "Faces of the Shasta People."
11. Fridlund, *Washington's Story*, 120.
12. Ibid., 121.
13. Speaks Lightning, *Indians of the Pacific States*, 64.
14. Ibid., 65.
15. Fridlund, *Washington's Story*, 155.
16. Speaks Lightning, *Indians of the Pacific States*, 65.
17. Josephy, *Nez Perce Indians*.
18. Fridlund, *Washington's Story*, 164.
19. Ibid., 165.
20. Speaks Lightning, *Indians of the Pacific States*, 65.
21. McWhorter and Su-el-lil, *Tragedy of the Wahk-shum*, 15.
22. Speaks Lightning, *Indians of the Pacific States*, 64.
23. Levina Wilkins, Yakama/Winátchapam elder, oral teaching with the author, November 15, 2004.
24. John Howard Smith, *Dream of the Judgment Day*, 257.
25. Speaks Lightning, *Indians of the Pacific States*, 66.
26. Ibid., 26.
27. John C. Jackson, *Little War of Destiny*, 134.
28. Levina Wilkins, Yakama/Winátchapam elder, oral teaching with the author, November 15, 2004.
29. John C. Jackson, *Little War of Destiny*, 135.
30. Andrews, "Warfield's Story."
31. John C. Jackson, *Little War of Destiny*, 135.
32. Ibid.
33. James Smith, *Away from Their Barbarous Influences*.
34. Ibid.
35. Fisher, "They Mean to Be Indian Always," 188.
36. Fisher, *Shadow Tribe*, 67.
37. Ibid., 70.
38. Columbia River Inter-Tribal Fish Commission, "Treaty with the Yakama, 1855."
39. Quoted in Fisher, *Shadow Tribe*, 158.
40. Ulrich, *Empty Nets*.
41. See *Seufert Bros. Co. v. United States*, 249 U.S. 194 (1919).
42. Ulrich, *Empty Nets*.
43. See Ulrich, *Empty Nets*.
44. Levina Wilkins, Yakama/Winátchapam elder, oral teaching with the author, November 15, 2004.
45. See, for example, the following: DeMarni Cromer et al., "Relationship of Acculturation"; Duran and Duran, *Native American Postcolonial Psychology*; Duran, Firehammer, and Gonzalez, "Liberation Psychology"; Gone, "Dialogue 2008"; Kathleen Graves et al., *Boarding School Project*; Kirmayer et al., "Rethinking Historical Trauma"; Whitbeck et al., "Conceptualizing and Measuring"; Yellow Horse Brave Heart and DeBruyn, "American Indian Holocaust."
46. Indian Health Service, *Indian Health Manual*.
47. A diagnostic label first suggested through reading Eduardo Duran and Bonnie Duran's classic, *Native American Postcolonial Psychology*.

48. Pressing "downward" from outside communities.
49. Moving across and between community members.
50. Marshall et al., "Psychology of Ongoing Threat"; Cohen Silver et al., "Nationwide Longitudinal Study"; Torabi and Seo, "National Study."
51. Zimering et al., "Posttraumatic Stress Disorder."
52. Kanno et al., "Risk and Protective Factors."
53. Ben-Zur et al., "Relationship Between Exposure."
54. Aneshensel, "Sociological Inquiry."
55. Pearlin and Bierman, "Current Issues and Future Directions," 337.
56. Whitbeck et al., "Conceptualizing and Measuring."
57. Ibid., 119.
58. Ibid., 124.
59. Ibid.
60. Ibid., 125.
61. Whitbeck et al., "Depressed Affect."
62. Ehlers et al., "Measuring Historical Trauma."
63. Levina Wilkins, Yakama/Winátchapam elder, oral teaching with the author, July 2, 2006.
64. Gone et al., "Impact of Historical Trauma."
65. Kirmayer et al., "Rethinking Historical Trauma."
66. Camerer et al., "Evaluating the Replicability."
67. Alford, "Subjectivity and the Intergenerational Transmission"; Dalla and Kennedy, "I Want to Leave."
68. Fredland et al., "Connecting Partner Violence"; Machisa et al., "Structural Pathways."
69. Ertem et al., "Intergenerational Continuity"; Newcomb and Locke, "Intergenerational Cycle."
70. Szlemko et al., "Native Americans and Alcohol."
71. Field et al., "Parental Styles"; Chaitin and Steinberg, "I Can Almost Remember."
72. Haag, "Indian Boarding School Era."
73. Ibid.
74. Kirmayer et al., "Rethinking Historical Trauma."
75. Ibid., 307.
76. Hinshaw, *Mark of Shame*; Ben-Zeev et al., "DSM-V and the Stigma of Mental Illness"; Sieff, "Media Frames of Mental Illnesses"; Celaire and McDermott, "Comparing the Psychological Effects."
77. See Levine, *Resisting Illegitimate Authority*.
78. Duran and Duran, *Native American Postcolonial Psychology*; Duran et al., "Liberation Psychology."
79. Kersting, "Suicide Prevention Efforts."
80. Yellow Horse Brave Heart, "Wakiksuyapi"; Yellow Horse Brave Heart et al., "Historical Trauma"; Yellow Horse Brave Heart and DeBruyn, "American Indian Holocaust."
81. Krystal and Niederland, *Psychic Traumatization*.
82. Duran and Duran, *Native American Postcolonial Psychology*.
83. Running Crane, "Accurate Cultural Context."
84. Compare, for example, this quote from psychoanalytic psychologist Dr. Patrick Kavanaugh, a mentor to many students at the University of Detroit, to the quote I offered from Ms. Running Crane:

Such linearized assumptions of *time* and *place* lay a deterministic foundation in analytic thinking in which past trauma psychically determines, of necessity, present symptoms. In the positivist tradition, temporal succession and spatial proximity are axiomatic assumptions in arriving at *causal explanations*: what *happens* in the present and what *will happen* in the future results largely from what *has happened* in the past. As our assumptions of a linear and sequential time are brought into question, the *non*-linear nature of *time, place, logic,* and *causality* are fore-grounded as we consider the incredible complexity of the psychoanalytic process in which experiences of the *past* and *future* might coexist, co-determine, and co-structure the *present* moment of the *future-past* . . . (Kavanaugh, "Developing Competencies"; italics in the original).

CHAPTER TEN

1. Pessah, "Violent Representations."
2. Dippold, "Wampanoag Word," 544.
3. Watts and Gutierres, "Native American-Based Cultural Model"; Moore and Coyhis, "Multicultural Wellbriety."
4. Loosely, "medicine person or healer."
5. "Sweat house."
6. See the Níix Ttáwaxt virtues in chapter 20.
7. A well-regarded resource on this history is Relander, *Drummers and Dreamers.*
8. Schuster, "Yakima Indian Traditionalism," 438.
9. Ibid., 367.
10. See the Níix Ttáwaxt virtues in chapter 20.
11. Pattison, "Exorcism and Psychotherapy," 285.
12. Ibid., 294.
13. Nelson and Slife, "Theoretical and Epistemological Foundations," 21–35.
14. Ibid., 23.
15. A brief EBSCO search of a major university library on February 26, 2018, turned up 276 professional journal articles pertaining to American Indians alongside "depression" or "posttraumatic stress" with 33 articles combining such terminology in their titles.
16. Nelson and Slife, "Theoretical and Epistemological Foundations," 23.
17. Ibid.
18. Martin, "Positivism, Quantification."
19. Steven Newcomb, *Pagans in the Promised Land,* 2.
20. Ibid., 19.
21. Albarracin et al., "There Is No Cure for Existence," 153.
22. Wyatt and Midkiff, "Biological Psychiatry," 144.
23. Indian Health Service, "American Indian/Alaska Native National Behavioral Health Strategic Plan, 2011–2015," 28.
24. Ibid., 28.
25. Engstrom and Weber, "Directions of Psychiatric Research," 347.
26. Ibid., 346.
27. As translated and quoted in Pols, "Psychological Knowledge," 118.

28. Charlotte Loppie, "Learning from the Grandmothers," 277.
29. Kavanaugh, *Stories from the Bog*, 202–3.
30. Duran, Guillory, and Villanueva, "Third and Fourth World Concerns," 212.
31. Martín-Baró, *Writings for a Liberation Psychology*, 32.
32. Ibid., 137.
33. Freire, *Pedagogy of the Oppressed*, 109.
34. Ibid., 35, from translator's note by Myra Bergman Ramos.
35. Martín-Baró, *Writings for a Liberation Psychology*.

CHAPTER ELEVEN

1. All the people described in *Coyote's Swing*, including those in this chapter, are composite cases constructed out of actual events in the lives of real Native Americans I met through clinical work as a licensed psychologist in Indian Country. The composites were built using guidelines originating from Duffy, "Writing About Clients."
2. Zaveri, "Killing of 5."
3. Sometimes called Mount Adams.
4. Morton, "Account of a Craniological Collection," 144.
5. Morton, *Crania Americana*, 5.
6. Armstrong-Fumero, "Even the Most Careless Observer," 13.
7. Morton, *Crania Americana*, 78.
8. Ibid., 173.
9. Quintyn, *Existence or Non-existence of Race?* 29.
10. Morton, *Crania Americana*, 78.
11. Umpleby, "Second-Order Science," 18.
12. Notturno, "Do We Need a Second-Order Science?".
13. Gould, *Mismeasure of Man*, 68.
14. Lewis et al., "Mismeasure of Science."
15. Murray, *Human Diversity*, 8.
16. Morgan, *Ancient Society*.
17. Gobineau, *Inequality of the Human Races*.
18. Haller, "Race and the Concept of Progress," 710.
19. Morgan, *League of the Ho-dé-no-sau-nee*, 135.
20. Just prior to the rise of the cultural evolutionists, the blood quantum concept began being used to promote intermarriage with whites as a means of "civilizing." For a time, Native families who intermingled with whites received more valuable lands, rations, privileges, etc., while "full bloods," who tended to avoid such associations, were subjected to cheating, deprivation, or relocation. The objective was to bring about less and less Indian blood quantum and thereby honor Thomas Jefferson's enjoinder: "The ultimate point of rest and happiness for them [American Indians] is to let our settlements and theirs meet and blend together, to intermix, and to become one people." (Thomas Jefferson to Benjamin Hawkins, February 18, 1803, in Ford, *Works of Thomas Jefferson*.)
21. Galton, *Inquiries into Human Faculty*, 17.

22. "I am inclined to agree with Francis Galton in believing that education and environment produce only a small effect on the mind of anyone, and that most of our qualities are innate." (Charles Darwin, quoted in Pearson, *Life, Letters and Labours*, vol. 1, xxii.)

23. One immediate result was that "mixed bloods" were now targeted themselves by American media during the eugenics movement for their potential in "polluting" white bloodlines. The popular press carried stories such as those of Tennessee mixed-blood descendants—"Wild Men Within Commuting Distance"—describing the "Jackies" or "Jackson whites": a mixture of "Indian, Negro, albino, and white blood," of whom "tales are told of promiscuous association of the sexes, of ignorance so dense that on at least two occasions women over twenty-one years of age confessed on the witness stand that they had never heard of or knew the meaning of the word God ..." (Dobbin, "Wild Men Within Commuting Distance"). In reality, this community residing in the Ramapo Mountain region in New York likely constituted refugee remnants of Tuscarora, Algonquin, and possibly Lenni Lenape tribes who fled the British in the early seventeenth century, moving northwest to join their Iroquois allies. They eventually intermarried with British and Dutch traders and Black freedmen from the plantations of the Hudson River Valley and the Catskill Mountains.

24. Galton, "Hereditary Talent and Character," 321.

25. Ibid.

26. Ibid.

27. Pearson, Life, *Letters and Labours*, vol. 2, 81.

28. Ibid., 302.

29. For more on these connections, see Ellenberger, *Discovery of the Unconscious*.

30. Ibid.

31. Jung, "Civilization in Transition," paragraph 966.

32. William James, quoted in Myers, *William James*, 412.

33. Sandall, "Sir Francis Galton."

34. Saleeby, "First Decade of Modern Eugenics," 128.

35. Eugenics Archive, *Third International Congress of Eugenics*; Selden, *Inheriting Shame*; Dowbiggin, *Keeping America Sane*; Gould, *Mismeasure of Man*.

36. Comparative analysis of prior-mentioned major psychologists promoting eugenics with former APA presidents. See American Psychological Association, "Former APA Presidents."

37. Goddard, *Feeble-Mindedness*, 565.

38. See, for example, Myers, Carey, and Szűcs, "Cognitive and Neural Correlates," 1646.

39. Guthrie, *Even the Rat Was White*, 101.

40. Lewis M. Terman, "Feeble-Minded Children in the Public Schools of California," *School and Society* 5 (February 1917): 161–65, as cited in Kamin, "Some Historical Facts," 11.

41. Ibid.

42. Hirsch, "Study of Natio-Racial Mental Differences."

43. Hirsch, *Dynamics of Juvenile Crime*, 70.

44. Hirsch, "Study of Natio-Racial Mental Differences," 331.

45. Ibid., 337.

46. Griffin, "On the Historic Location."

47. Lombardo, "Three Generations, No Imbeciles"; Supreme Court of Appeals of Virginia, *Carrie Buck v. Dr. J. H. Bell*.
48. See Lombardo, "Rape of Carrie Buck"; Lombardo, "Father of Carrie Buck's Child."
49. Laughlin, *Legal Status of Eugenical Sterilization*, 16.
50. See Cohen, *Imbeciles*.
51. Barry, "Eugenics Victims."
52. Savage, "Large Numbers of Natives."
53. Kühl, *Nazi Connection*, 22.
54. Ibid., 20.
55. Strous et al., "Reflections on Emil Kraepelin."
56. Ibid.
57. Ibid., 20. Including $325,000 from Rockefeller Foundation for a new building.
58. Ibid., 102.
59. Lemkau, *Mental Hygiene in Public Health*.
60. Ibid., 330.
61. Terman, *Measurement of Intelligence*, 91–92.
62. Lemkau, *Mental Hygiene in Public Health*, 75.
63. Author's tabulations, year to year, of CDC data from annual Summary Health Statistics Reports, including such tables as "Frequencies and age-adjusted percentages (with standard errors) of ever having been told of having a learning disability or attention deficit hyperactivity disorder for children 3–17 years of age, by selected characteristics," available at https://www.cdc.gov/nchs/nhis/SHS_1997_2012.htm.
64. Leonard, "ADHD Update."
65. See, for example: Simons, "Debunking the Latest Gene Study"; Timimi and Timimi, "Social Construction," 139–57; Horgan, "My Problem with 'Taboo'"; Joseph, "Trouble with Twin Studies"; Galves and Walker, "Debunking the Science"; Stolzer, "ADHD Epidemic"; Joseph, *Missing Gene*; Colbert, *Four False Pillars*.
66. Harry et al., *Indigenous People*.
67. Ibid., 21.
68. Hernstein and Murray, *Bell Curve*; Snyderman and Hernstein, "Intelligence Tests"; Murray, *Human Diversity*.
69. The elitist conceptual roots of the bell or normal curve are contained in this quote from Galton, *Hereditary Genius*, 34–35:

> It is an absolute fact that if we pick out of each million the one man who is naturally the ablest, and also the man who is the most stupid, and divide the remaining 999,998 men into fourteen classes, the average ability in each being separated from that of its neighbours by *equal grades*, then the numbers in each of those classes will, on the average of many millions, be as is stated in the table. The table may be applied to special, just as truly as to general ability. It would be true for every examination that brought out natural gifts, whether held in painting, in music, or in statesmanship. The proportions between the different classes would be identical in all these cases, although the classes would be made up of different individuals, according as the examination differed in its purport.

Galton's analysis presumes that the station and merit of British aristocracy is predetermined by heredity. This same presumption formed for many years the idea that an IQ score did not change over time in a given individual. It is only relatively recently that this idea has begun to be challenged via the so-called Flynn effect. (See Trahan et al., "Flynn Effect.")

70. By 1903, eugenics ideas developed by Galton and followers in Great Britain had already influenced a generation of American intellectuals, academics, and social policy makers. There is a close relationship between the emergence of the eugenics movement in the United States and the influence of a powerful and influential elite preoccupied with the perceived threat to "good breeding" posed by those considered intellectually disabled, deranged, eccentric—or culturally unacceptable. In 1910, Mrs. Mary Harriman, widow of railroad magnate E. H. Harriman, donated considerable funds to developing the Eugenics Record Office alongside the Carnegie-funded Station for Experimental Evolution at Cold Spring Harbor, Long Island, New York, so as to begin tracing this perceived threat.

71. All the people described in *Coyote's Swing*, including those in this chapter, are composite cases constructed out of actual events in the lives of real Native Americans I met through clinical work as a licensed psychologist in Indian Country. The composites were built using guidelines originating from Duffy, "Writing About Clients."

72. See Boss, *Ambiguous Loss*.

73. See Cacciatore, *Bearing the Unbearable*.

74. Lawrence, "Indian Health Service."

75. Torpy, "Native American Women," 13.

76. Ibid., 12.

77. Ibid.

78. Lawrence, "Indian Health Service," 410.

79. Ibid., 402.

80. Ibid., 403.

81. Rutecki, "Forced Sterilization."

82. Leon, "Mental Health Considerations," 54.

83. Torpy, "Native American Women," 12.

84. U.S. Food and Drug Administration, "Ortho Evra."

85. Volscho, "Racism and Disparities," 673.

86. Werneke et al., "Antidepressants and Sexual Dysfunction."

87. Bala et al., "Post-SSRI Sexual Dysfunction"; Colman, *Dictionary of Psychology*; Healy et al., "Enduring Sexual Dysfunction"; Csoka et al., "Persistent Sexual Dysfunction."

88. Nørr et al., "Use of Selective Serotonin Reuptake Inhibitors."

89. Nezvalová-Henriksen et al., "Effect of Prenatal Selective Serotonin Reuptake Inhibitor."

CHAPTER TWELVE

1. All the people described in *Coyote's Swing*, including those in this chapter, are composite cases constructed out of actual events in the lives of real Native Americans I met through clinical work as a licensed psychologist in Indian Country. The composites were built using guidelines originating from Duffy, "Writing About Clients."

2. Child, *Boarding School Seasons*, 94.
3. Lomawaima, *They Called It Prairie Light*, 47.
4. Archuleta et al., *Away from Home*, 46.
5. Child, *Boarding School Seasons*, 94.
6. See Levine, "Genocide of an Anti-Authoritarian People: Native Americans," in *Resisting Illegitimate Authority*, 89–94.
7. U.S. Bureau of Indian Affairs, *Course of Study*, 197.
8. John Bloom, "Show What an Indian Can Do," 41.
9. Ibid., 42.
10. Ibid.
11. Ibid., 40.
12. It would be sixteen more years before Jack Johnson would become the first African American heavyweight to win the title from a white man. Johnson would be accused of "barbarism" even though he was expert in many of the same techniques Corbett utilized. The hatred the flamboyant Johnson would experience from whites would be so intense that two ministers would suggest he be lynched if he kept defeating white people.
13. Bache, "Reaction Time with Reference to Race," 479, 480.
14. See "Lightner Witmer" in the bibliography. Witmer founded the first applied psychology clinic in the United States at the University of Pennsylvania when the "psychology clinic" portion of his course in "clinical psychology" was recognized by university regents as a viable community. He pioneered techniques for measuring the educational status of students from which the profession of "school psychologist" and the assessment of "learning disability" would eventually emerge. As the psychology clinic took hold at University of Pennsylvania, it became the model of the day for training clinical psychologists to provide evaluation and diagnostic services. Psychologists would not become psychotherapists for another fifty years.
15. Bache, "Reaction Time with Reference to Race," 482.
16. Cattell, "Address of the President," 148.
17. Sokal, "Unpublished Autobiography of James McKeen Cattell."
18. Schultz and Schultz, *History of Modern Psychology*, 154.
19. Klineberg, "Racial Differences," 273.
20. Ibid., 276.
21. Klineberg, *Race Differences*, 346–47.
22. Hollander, "Otto Klineberg," 125.
23. Department of the Interior, "Notice of Intent to Repatriate Cultural Items."
24. Wild, "History of Education," 190.
25. Ibid.
26. Haag, "Indian Boarding School Era."
27. Wild, "History of Education," 190.
28. Petrina, "Never-to-Be-Forgotten Investigation."
29. Many of the intelligence test scores of American Indian children in the boarding schools were computed using group-administered paper-and-pencil tests, like the National Intelligence Test (NIT), created by M. E. Haggerty, Louis Terman, Edward L. Thorndike, Guy M. Whipple, and Robert M. Yerkes, a civilian version of the Army Alpha and Beta Tests, and the Otis Intelligence Test, created by Arthur Otis, a student of Terman's who helped on the Army Alpha and Beta Tests.
30. Garth, "Study of the Foster Indian Child."

31. Richards, *Race, Racism, and Psychology.*
32. Forward to Garth, *Race Psychology,* xiv.
33. Garth, *Race Psychology,* 10–11.
34. Rowe, "Five Hundred Forty-Seven."
35. Hunter and Sommermier, "Relation of Degree of Indian Blood."
36. Fitzgerald and Ludeman, "Intelligence of Indian Children," 321.
37. Haught, "Mental Growth," 141.
38. Jamieson and Sandiford, "Mental Capacity of Southern Ontario Indians."
39. Thomson, "So Many Clever, Industrious, and Frugal Aliens."
40. Jamieson and Sandiford, "Mental Capacity of Southern Ontario Indians," 324.
41. Garth, "A Review of Race Psychology," 341.
42. Garth, *Race Psychology,* 85.
43. The remaining five studies in Garth's book appear investigative—searching for differences in color preference, for example. The fact that many of the comparisons Garth reviewed contrasted "Negro" and "Mexican" subjects illustrates the linkages of the applied psychology of his day to the "racial hierarchy" theories of cultural evolutionists.
44. Garth, *Race Psychology,* 240–41.
45. Garth, "Study of the Foster Indian Child," 709.
46. Huff, *To Live Heroically.*
47. Ibid., 5: Several states enacted laws that allowed public school administrators to exclude minority children, negating Indians from enrollment. Article X, "Schools," section 1662, of the California Political Code of 1924 stated: "The governing body of the school district shall have the power to exclude children of filthy or vicious habits, or children suffering from contagious or infectious diseases, and also to establish separate schools for Indian children and for children of Chinese, Japanese or Mongolian parentage." See Kerr, *Codes of California,* 87.
48. Garth, "Study of the Foster Indian Child," 708–9.
49. Emmerich, "Genocide or Family Planning?"
50. U.S. Department of Health and Human Services, Public Health Service, U.S. Surgeon General, *Mental Health,* chapter 4: "Mental Health Care for American Indians and Alaska Natives."
51. Garth and Barnard, "Will-Temperament of Indians," 516.
52. Garth, *Race Psychology,* 160.
53. Child, *Boarding School Seasons,* 84.
54. Ibid., 84–5.
55. Meriam et al., *Problem of Indian Administration,* 389.
56. Paskell, "Our Indian Children."
57. Forward by Senator Edward M. Kennedy, in U.S. Senate, *Indian Education: A National Tragedy.*
58. Ibid., 24.
59. Kaufman, "Flynn Effect and IQ Disparities."
60. Associated Press, "Oregon: Family Settles Lawsuit."
61. Sohappy, "Testimony."
62. St. Charles and Costantino, *Reading and the Native American Learner.*

CHAPTER THIRTEEN

1. Long Standing Bear Chief, *Ni-Kso-Ko-Wah*.
2. Marks and Shelton, "Genetic Markers Not a Valid Test.".
3. Bardill, "Tribal Enrollment and Genetic Testing."
4. Yates and Yates, *Cherokee DNA Studies*.
5. Cummings, "In Response to Trump's 'Pocahontas' Jibes."
6. For years, I have numbered the generations back to these ancestors incorrectly, and I apologize for any confusion created within past posts I may have made in blogs and other places. Please see the "Genealogy Numbering System" of the National Institute for Genealogical Studies, https://www.familysearch.org/en/wiki/Genealogy_Numbering_Systems_(National_Institute).
7. Isenberg, *White Trash*.
8. Newell, "Changing Nature of Indian Slavery," 110.
9. Treffert, "Genetic Memory."
10. A shift from Cherokee to Christianized names? Enslavement?
11. Thornton, *The Cherokees*, 58.
12. McLoughlin, *Cherokees and Missionaries*, 36.
13. Newcomb, *Pagans in the Promised Land*, 86.
14. Andrew Jackson, "Second Annual Message," 1084, 1086.
15. Sturges, *Illustrated History of McDonald County*, 229.
16. Satz, *American Indian Policy*, 53.
17. Rolater, "American Indian and the Origin," 197.
18. Sullivan, *Killing Davy Crockett*.
19. Prucha, *Documents of United States Indian Policy*, 49.
20. United States Supreme Court, *Worcester v. Georgia*.
21. Hatley, *Dividing Path*, 207.
22. Ibid., 208.
23. Miller, "Henderson, Richard."
24. Swift, "Hart, Nathaniel."
25. Hatley, *Dividing Path*, 221.
26. James Wilson, *Earth Shall Weep*.
27. Zinn, *People's History of the United States*, 40.
28. McClure, "Scots Among the Indians," 2–13.
29. Calloway, "Forgotten Links."
30. See Milner, "Irish Immigration."
31. Knapp, *Library of American History*, 200.
32. Anthony, "Execution of Joshua Tefft."
33. Simms, *The Forayers*, 46: "He was a notorious outlaw, one of the few surviving Scophilites—a banditti, which, at the opening of the revolutionary discontents in Carolina, had carried crime and terror to many a happy homestead."
34. Fauchereau Grimké, "Journal of the Campaign to the Southward," 64.
35. Hatley, *Dividing Path*, 181.
36. Ibid.
37. Ibid., 225.
38. Reynolds, *Cherokee Struggle*, 135.
39. Hatley, *Dividing Path*, 181.

40. DeLoria and Wilkins, *Tribes, Treaties, and Constitutional Tribulations*, 6.
41. West, "These Veterans Fought for Independence."
42. Cairney, *Clans and Families of Ireland and Scotland*, 10.
43. Cherokee Nation, *Laws of the Cherokee Nation*, 10.
44. Perdue, "Traditionalism in the Cherokee Nation."
45. Ibid., 163.
46. John Cooke to John Barbour, July 1, 1827, found in NARA, "Letters Received (1824–1881)." U.S. Department of the Interior, Office of Indian Affairs. Record Group (RG) 75. Washington, DC.
47. Perdue, "Traditionalism in the Cherokee Nation," 164.
48. Ibid., 166.
49. Ibid., 168.
50. Ibid., 169.
51. David Edward Walker, "Lunacy, Crazy Indians and the Witch's Hammer."
52. Italics mine.
53. Cherokee Nation, *Laws of the Cherokee Nation*, 78.
54. Ibid.
55. Donna Barlow Smouse Walker to George Lee Walker, undated letter (likely 1970), author's personal collection.
56. Ibid.
57. Ibid.
58. Ibid.
59. Huston, "Exemption of the Cherokee Indians," 135.
60. Ibid.
61. Ray, *Mental Hygiene*, 106.
62. Native History Association, "The Old Jefferson Site."
63. "Little-Known Trail of Tears Segment 'Rediscovered.'"
64. Leustig, *500 Nations*.
65. Ibid.
66. The number of deaths is controversial. The Cherokee Nation officially maintains that about 4,000 people died. American Indian Studies scholar and former Cherokee Nation councilwoman Julia Coates disputes that number: "The available evidence does not indicate the number of deaths as being that high. Today, the best estimates are that somewhere between 2,000 and 2,500 Cherokees died, either in the camps, on the march itself, or after arriving in the Indian Territory, but as a result of conditions of the march." See Coates, *Trail of Tears*, 134.
67. Sturges, *Illustrated History of McDonald County*, 21.
68. Marysville would later be renamed Pineville.
69. 1850 U.S. census data, Pineville, Missouri.
70. Navey, "1838 Indian Removal, North Carolina Regiment Volunteers."
71. Casselberry, *Revised Statutes of the State of Missouri*, 306.
72. Newton County Historical Society, *McDonald and Newton County Sections*, 32.
73. Coates, *Trail of Tears*, 134.
74. R. M. King, New Salem Minister, from a letter dated October 8, 1848, Neosho, MO, author's personal collection.
75. Thomas H. Campbell, *Good News on the Frontier*.
76. Gilbert, *Trail of Tears Across Missouri*, 98.

77. Ibid.
78. Ibid., 97–98.
79. Cobb-Greetham, "Hearth and Home."
80. Wood, *Civil War on the Lower Kansas-Missouri Border*.
81. Ibid., 96.
82. Cobb-Greetham, "Hearth and Home," 162–63.
83. Sturges, *Illustrated History of McDonald County*, 229.
84. Emily Caroline Barlow, 1969 memoirs, author's personal collection.
85. Ryan P. Smith, "Native American Slaveholders."
86. Cooper, "I'm a Descendant of the Cherokee."
87. See Minges, *Slavery in the Cherokee Nation*.
88. Perdue, *Slavery and the Evolution of Cherokee Society*, 4.
89. Ibid.
90. Jaynes, "Native Americans and African Americans," 589.
91. Perdue, *Slavery and the Evolution of Cherokee Society*, xii.
92. Minges, "Keetoowah Society."
93. Mullins, "Three Forks History."
94. Jones, "Pegg, Thomas (1806–1866)."
95. McLoughlin, *Champions of the Cherokees*.
96. Cobb-Greetham, "Hearth and Home," 160–62.
97. Emily Caroline Barlow, 1969 memoirs.
98. Ibid.
99. Gideon. *Indian Territory*, 702.
100. Donna Barlow Smouse Walker, taped interview with Edward Walker (the author's uncle), 1973, author's collection.
101. Ibid.
102. Owens, "Mapping, Naming, and the Power of Words," 211.

CHAPTER FOURTEEN

1. Wang, "Discovering Xingkaihu."
2. Graham-Harrison and Garside, "Allow No Escapes."
3. Purnell, "Thought Reform, Coercion, and Persuasion," 4.
4. McLoughlin, *Champions of the Cherokees*, 66.
5. Saunt, "Paradox of Freedom."
6. Ibid., 68.
7. Ibid., 70.
8. The end of the Civil War had little effect in emancipating these Black slaves, who were beaten and harassed into further servitude by Cherokee planter slaveholders for many years afterward. Although federal officials saw to the codification of Black freedom in treaties with Indian Territory tribes in 1866, Cherokee planters controlling leadership positions simply proclaimed such efforts an outside threat to tribal sovereignty when, in reality, they threatened a profitable existing economy serving an established aristocracy. "Cherokee Freedmen" who finally came through this ordeal, on the other hand, were perceived as an economic burden

and remained highly controversial, especially regarding whether they should be considered Cherokee citizens. Battles over their humanity versus their market worth, their inclusion versus exclusion, are embedded within generational carry into this very day.

9. Letter of W. G. Coffin, February 13, 1862, in *Report of the Commissioner of Indian Affairs for the Year 1862* (Washington, DC: Government Printing Office, 1863), 145.
10. Steen, "Home for the Insane."
11. Stratton, "Cherokee National Insane Asylum."
12. Reed, "A Nation's Charge."
13. Ibid., 126.
14. Ibid., 45–46.
15. Hurd, "Rebuilding a Nation," 88.
16. Reed, "A Nation's Charge," 137.
17. Steen, "Home for the Insane," 404.
18. Adair, *Compiled Laws of the Cherokee Nation*, Article IV: "Admission of Persons," section 9, page 245.
19. Steen, "Home for the Insane," 404.
20. Meserve, "Chief Lewis Downing."
21. Starr, *History of the Cherokee Indians*, 23.
22. Ibid.
23. Eddings, "Foreman, Stephen (1807–1881)."
24. Steen, "Home for the Insane," 404.
25. Historical Data Systems, "Regiment History."
26. Conley, *Cherokee Encyclopedia*, 45.
27. Miner, "Dennis Bushyhead," 192–206.
28. Steen, "Home for the Insane," 404.
29. Starr, *History of the Cherokee Indians*, 147.
30. Keifer, *Genealogical and Biographical Sketches*, 125.
31. Ibid.
32. Ibid., 127.
33. *Cherokee Advocate*, February 21, 1894. See also Khaled J. Bloom, "An American Tragedy."
34. Keifer, *Genealogical and Biographical Sketches*, 127.
35. Parins, *Elias Cornelius Boudinot*, 186.
36. Keifer, *Genealogical and Biographical Sketches*, 125.
37. Ibid.
38. Hambrecht and Koste, "Biographical Register of Physicians."
39. Starr, *History of the Cherokee Indians*, 510.
40. Steen, "Home for the Insane," 408.
41. Ibid.
42. Barton, *History and Influence*, 92.
43. Ibid.
44. López-Muñoz et al., "History of Barbiturates."
45. Steen, "Home for the Insane," 409.
46. Steen uses the term "patient," but I stick with "inmates" because of its interchangeability in the source text he cites. Additionally, facility problems with the asylum did necessitate moving inhabitants to the national jail in Tahlequah for months at a time on two occasions between 1880 and its closure.

47. McDonnell, "Competency Commissions."
48. Steen, "Home for the Insane," 408.
49. Ibid., 411.
50. O'Beirne, *The Indian Territory*, 405.
51. Hill, *History of the State of Oklahoma*, 282.
52. Ibid., 281.
53. Steen, "Home for the Insane," 411.
54. Ibid., 411–12.
55. To be discussed in chapter 15, "Locked Inside Hiawatha: Josephine's 'Delusions.'"
56. Steen, "Home for the Insane," 412.
57. Reed, "A Nation's Charge," 73.
58. Abbott, "Medicine for the Rosebuds," 65.
59. Mihesuah, *Cultivating the Rosebuds*.
60. Ibid., 92.
61. Ibid.
62. Steen, " Home for the Insane," 416.
63. Reed, "A Nation's Charge," 154.
64. Steen, " Home for the Insane," 413.
65. See Steen, "Home for the Insane," 415, and contrast with Berger, "Power over This Unfortunate Race," 1998. Berger indicates that Jack Spaniard was the name of a well-known Cherokee "outlaw" who was "convicted by a jury on purely circumstantial evidence after only an hour of deliberation" in 1889 and hung.

CHAPTER FIFTEEN

1. American Psychiatric Association, *DSM-5*, 20.
2. Levin, "MH Care of American Indian," 9, 20.
3. Comparative analysis of various historical sources with Hicks, "Richard S. Pearis, Sr."
4. The Tom Starr War was a series of reprisals mounted against signers of the Treaty of New Echota, who were mostly "mixed-blood" leaders, by mostly "full-blood," "Anti-Treaty" Cherokees who'd been forced off their lands and onto the Trail of Tears. In *Going Indian*, historian James Francis Hill quotes Cherokee newspaper reporter J. C. Starr's summary of the underpinnings of these years of internecine conflict, which were provided to the Indian Pioneer project of the Oklahoma Historical Society by J.C.'s son, Clarence, in 1938:

> As soon as the Anti-Treaty people landed in the Cherokee Nation they stirred up dissension and strife, out of which grew the Tom Starr War. The Anti-Treaty people were very much dissatisfied with the new country and with the Ridge Party for making the treaty, and very soon began to emphasize their displeasure by an organized attempt to kill all the leaders who had been instrumental in making it.
> The Full Bloods armed themselves and went in bands all over the country to murder any leader of the Ridge Party whom they could find. They deposed Chief John Jolly and elected John Ross Chief of the Cherokees, and then followed the declaration of war between these two powerful parties. The Anti-Treaty people went so far as to declare that they would kill every man who had signed the treaty with the United

States Government, and started blood to flowing by killing leaders of the opposite party. (Hamill, *Going Indian*, 105)

It's important to note that the violence and hatred of the Tom Starr War mounted by the Cherokee "full bloods" (traditionalists) had coalesced after years of disenfranchisement from the political processes imposed from outside Cherokee society that led directly to the Trail of Tears. In reaction to the loss of so many family members on the Trail, the longstanding "blood oath" tradition had been invoked, whereby the killing of a fellow clan member was seen as a sacred violation demanding retribution in kind. For further information, see Minges, *Slavery in the Cherokee Nation*, 17.

5. Comparative analysis, see endnote 3.
6. Ibid.
7. Starr, *History of the Cherokee Indians*, 152.
8. Hicks, "Richard Pearis, Sr.," entry 172.
9. Hicks, "Ludovic Grant."
10. Stremlau, *Sustaining the Cherokee Family*, 52.
11. Ibid., 53.
12. Hicks, "Richard Pearis, Sr.," entry 172.
13. Starr, *History of the Cherokee Indians*, 323. Death date as verified on Ancestry.com via an image of Allen Gilbert and Kiamitia Comel (West) Gilbert with her death listed as 1880 on multiple descendent family trees.
14. See also U.S. Supreme Court, "Cherokee Intermarriage Cases," which sought to provide final resolution to claims by intermarried whites to Cherokee land.
15. See Steen, "Home for the Insane," 405, 410. Steen conflates Josephine's story with that of Rachel Cornsilk, whom Adair reported as having run away in the same report. Having checked with archivist Mallory Covington of the Oklahoma Historical Society, who reviewed Adair's "Quarterly Report Asylum for the Insane & Others Ending September 30, 1887" in the society's box CHN 0067, we are assured of Steen's error.
16. Starr, *History of the Cherokee Indians*, 658.
17. U.S. Department of the Interior, "Office of the U.S. Indian Inspector."
18. Ibid.
19. Except where otherwise noted, the remainder of this account of Josephine Rider's life is based upon a reconstruction of events from original medical records pertaining to Hiawatha Asylum for Insane Indians, otherwise known as the "Canton Asylum," held as Record Group 75 (RG 75), Box 1, at the National Archives and Records Administration (hereafter cited as NARA) in Fort Worth, Texas, scanned by the author in April 2006.
20. Local newspapers reported a melee with Alma City Police on June 9, 1905, during which John Calhoun West and his entire Indian Police force were arrested and charged with assault and battery after closing seven town businesses for refusing to pay Creek taxes. John Calhoun West was the son of John W. West, who during the Tom Starr War, was given one hundred lashes by angry Anti-Treaty "full bloods" executing a "blood oath" against signers of the Treaty of New Echota that led to the Trail of Tears. See endnote 4 of this chapter for further information.
21. NARA, "William Ross to George Wright, Handwritten Note #2, April 7, 1905," Fort Worth RG 75, Box 1.
22. Burch, "Dislocated Histories."

23. Putney, "Canton Asylum for Insane Indians."
24. NARA, "Josephine Rider, Affidavit from Dr. G. F. Woodring, August 15, 1905," Fort Worth, RG 75, Box 1.
25. NARA, "Testimony by William P. Ross before Samuel Foreman, Notary Public, Cherokee Land Office, January 17, 1903." Commission of the Five Civilized Tribes.
26. "American Notes," 392.
27. "News of the Oil Field," 9.
28. NARA, "Order for Delivery of Insane Indian, Josephine Rider," Fort Worth, RG 75, Box 1.
29. Ibid.
30. Hepburn and Stratton, "Total Institutions and Inmate Self-Esteem," 237.
31. Putney, "Canton Asylum for Insane Indians," 4.
32. Ibid.
33. Riney, "Power and Powerlessness."
34. Leahy, *They Called It Madness*, 41.
35. NARA, "Josephine Rider, Monthly Reports, July–September, 1906," Fort Worth, RG 75, Box 1.

CHAPTER SIXTEEN

1. Ray, *Mental Hygiene*, 106.
2. Much gratitude to Chickasaw descendent Mike Tower for clarifying the source of his ancestor's wealth as well as her relationship to Fred Tecumseh Waite. See Tower, *Outlaw Statesman*.
3. NARA, "Irene Kerr to J. Blair Shoenfelt, January 7, 1905," Fort Worth, RG 75, Box 1.
4. Ibid.
5. Ellingson, *The Myth of the Noble Savage*.
6. NARA, "Irene Kerr to J. Blair Shoenfelt."
7. "American Girl Who Would Be Queen."
8. Ibid.
9. Ibid.
10. "Says She Is a Queen."
11. "American Girl Who Would Be Queen."
12. Ibid.
13. Ibid.
14. "Says She Is a Queen."
15. Ibid.
16. "American Girl Who Would Be Queen."
17. "Says She Is a Queen."
18. NARA, "Lunacy Cases—Questions and Answers Affidavit," Emily Waite, attested by D.W. Griffin, MD, undated, Fort Worth, RG 75, Box 1.
19. Ibid.
20. NARA, "Mrs. Perry N. Kerr to J. Blair Shoenfelt, August 3, 1904," Fort Worth, RG 75, Box 1.
21. NARA, "Affidavit of Perry N. Kerr, December 5, 1905," Fort Worth, RG 75, Box 1.

22. Ibid.
23. NARA, "S. J. Garvin to Indian Territory, Southern District, December 5, 1905," Fort Worth, RG 75, Box 1.
24. Handwritten note dated July 22, 1905, to "Dana H. Kelsey, Esq., U.S. Agent, Muskogee" on letterhead marked "Department of the Interior, United States Indian Service, Asylum for Insane Indians, Canton, S.D.," NARA, Fort Worth, RG 75, Box 1, Case 17.
25. NARA, "Lunacy Cases—Questions and Answers Affidavit," Emily Waite, attested by D. W. Griffin.
26. Ibid.
27. Ibid.
28. NARA, "Monthly Report of Emily Waite by Dr. John F. Turner, October 1, 1906," Fort Worth, RG 75, Box 1.
29. NARA, "Report from John Holst to Commissioner of Indian Affairs, August 16, 1932," RG 75, Box 4.

CHAPTER SEVENTEEN

1. Putney, "Canton Asylum for Insane Indians."
2. Ibid.
3. Ibid.
4. Tabulation based upon synthesis of data provided in Putney, "Canton Asylum for Insane Indians," and Riney, "Power and Powerlessness."
5. Putney, "Canton Asylum for Insane Indians," 12.
6. NARA, Harry Hummer to Commissioner of Indian Affairs, April 22, 1927, Kansas City, RG 75, Box 2.
7. David Edward Walker, "A Living Burial."
8. Ibid.
9. "Sane Reds Confined in Asylum."
10. Putney, "Canton Asylum for Insane Indians," 23.
11. NARA, Helen J. Groth, "Letter to Investigation Committee." Note: All spelling and other errors appear in the original.

CHAPTER EIGHTEEN

1. NARA, Harry Hummer to Commissioner of Indian Affairs, April 22, 1927, Kansas City, RG 75, Box 2.
2. Yellow Bird, "Wild Indians."
3. Find a Grave, "Robert Winans 1894–1939."
4. NARA, Harry Hummer to Commissioner of Indian Affairs.
5. Mandan Historical Society, "Alfred Burton Welch, 1874–1945," webpage, http://www.mandanhistory.org/biographiessz/abwelch.html. This biographical page notes that Welch spent much of his life in Mandan, North Dakota, was adopted by

Yankton Sioux chief John Grass, and served "overseas from December 13, 1917, to August 26, 1919. He was advanced to the rank of Major. A large number of Native American soldiers volunteered for his command." The biography "was based in part on the July 12, 2004 Dakota Datebook item compiled by the State Historical Society of North Dakota for Prairie Public Radio. The project was supported in part by a grant by the North Dakota Council on the Humanities." See also Colonel A. B. Welch's biography at https://www.welchdakotapapers.com/2012/01/welchs-biography/ for additional details including images and newspaper clippings of his service record as well as his relationship as an adopted "white chief" within the Yankton Sioux community.

6. According to a list compiled by United Tribes Technical College, "WWI Era Native American Servicemen from North Dakota Tribes."
7. Parentheses signify Hummer's questions.
8. Brackets contain my comments.
9. Matthew Brown, "Fact Check: It's True."
10. Eames, "Deadly War of Prohibition."
11. NARA, Harry Hummer to Commissioner of Indian Affairs.
12. Ibid.
13. NARA, "Occupational List, p. 3." Seattle, Washington, RG 418, E.13, Canton Documents.
14. NARA, "Letter to Dr. L.E. Culp, Dec. 11th, 1933," Washington, DC, RG75, CCF, 1907–1939.
15. Ensign, *America's Military Today*, 22.
16. Kershner and Harding, "Do Military Recruiters Belong in Schools?"
17. Black, "Respect for 'People."
18. Osha Gray Davidson, "The Forgotten Soldier."
19. Ibid.
20. U.S. Congress, "Misleading Information," 2.
21. "Lynch Calls Piestewa 'Hero' at House Hearing." This page also provides a detailed chronology of Lori Piestewa's death and its significance in Indian Country.
22. Connor and Vargyas, "Legal Implications of Gender Bias," 33.
23. Ibid., 16.
24. MacLean and Parsons, "Unequal Risk."
25. Saretzky, "Carl Campbell Brigham."
26. Trumbull and Nelson-Barber, "Ongoing Quest," 1.
27. Bailey, "Contribution to the Mental Pathology of Races."
28. Yoakum and Yerkes, *Army Mental Testing*.
29. Bailey, "Contribution to the Mental Pathology of Races," 378.
30. Ibid., 386.
31. American Psychiatric Association, *Statistical Manual for Use by Institutions for the Insane*.
32. American Psychiatric Association, *DSM-5*.
33. American Psychiatric Association, *Statistical Manual for Use by Institutions for the Insane*, 28–29.

CHAPTER NINETEEN

1. Flanagin, "Native Americans Are the Unseen Victims."
2. Bronson et al., "Veterans in Prison and Jail, 2011–12."
3. See Wentling, "Native American Veterans."
4. Minton et al., "American Indian and Alaska Natives in Local Jails, 1999–2014," Summary, https://www.bjs.gov/content/pub/pdf/aianlj9914_sum.pdf.
5. Ulmer and Bradley, "Punishment in Indian Country."
6. Ibid.
7. Flanagin, "Native Americans Are the Unseen Victims."
8. Ross, *Returning to the Teachings.*
9. Rolnick, "Locked Up," 55–56.
10. Carson, "Prisoners in 2016."
11. Minton et al., "American Indian and Alaska Natives in Local Jails, 1999–2014," https://www.bjs.gov/content/pub/pdf/aianlj9914.pdf.
12. Ibid.
13. Noonan, "Mortality in State Prisons," Table 9.
14. Noonan et al., "Mortality in Local Jails and State Prisons," Table 7.
15. Human Rights Watch, "Prisoner Abuse."
16. Human Rights Watch, "Callous and Cruel."
17. Ibid.
18. See Haney, "Psychological Effects of Solitary Confinement."
19. Human Rights Watch, "Callous and Cruel."
20. Binswanger et al., "Clinical Risk Factors for Death."
21. Leighton C. Whitaker, "Resistances to Critical Thinking."
22. Moncrieff, *Myth of the Chemical Cure.*
23. Tamburello, "Prescribed Medication Abuse," 165–69.
24. All the people described in *Coyote's Swing*, including the one in this chapter, are composite cases constructed out of actual events in the lives of real Native Americans I met through clinical work as a licensed psychologist in Indian Country. The composites were built using guidelines originating from Duffy, "Writing About Clients."

CHAPTER TWENTY

1. Indian Health Service, *American Indian/Alaska Native Behavioral Health Briefing Book*, 11.
2. Watkins and Shulman, *Toward Psychologies*, 214.
3. Substance Abuse and Mental Health Services Administration, "Mental Health Essentials."
4. Garroutte, "Defining 'Radical Indigenism,'" 170.
5. Ibid., 173.
6. See Watson, *Lo-TEK Design.*
7. Cavender Wilson, "Reclaiming Our Humanity," 72.
8. Lame Deer and Erdoes. *Lame Deer*, 112.

9. British Psychological Society, "Response to the American Psychiatric Association," 2.
10. Ibid., 3.
11. For the rationale behind this proposed change, see Stein et al., "What Is a Mental/Psychiatric Disorder?"
12. American Psychiatric Association, *DSM-5*, 20.
13. Johnstone and Boyle, *Power Threat Meaning Framework*, 45.
14. Ibid., 118. See also Johnstone and Boyle, *Straight Talking Introduction*.
15. Johnstone and Boyle, *Power Threat Meaning Framework*, 10.
16. Ibid., 45.
17. Ibid., 66.
18. Lucy Johnstone, email to author, August 5, 2018.
19. Johnstone and Boyle, *Power Threat Meaning Framework*, 71.
20. Ibid., 244.
21. Ibid., 245.
22. Ibid.
23. Ibid., 332–3.
24. Ibid., 72.
25. Ibid., 6.
26. Graeber and Wengrow, *Dawn of Everything*.
27. Ibid., 140.
28. Ibid., 289.
29. Ibid., 290.
30. Ibid., 291.
31. Ibid., 295.
32. David Edward Walker, "WHO Owns the Language," 7.
33. See www.deenametzger.net.
34. For details on Lora's remarkable story, read Matz, "Fishing for Fallen Light."
35. Used with permission.

BIBLIOGRAPHY

Abbott, Devon Irene. "Medicine for the Rosebuds: Health Care at the Cherokee Female Seminary, 1876–1909." *American Indian Culture and Research Journal* 12, no. 1 (1988): 59–71. https://doi.org/10.17953/aicr.12.1.1v646135k51mhmu2.

Adair, John L. compiler. *Compiled Laws of the Cherokee Nation: Published by Authority of the National Council.* Tahlequah, I.T.: National Advocate, 1881.

Agency for Health Care Policy and Research. *Depression in Primary Care,* vol. 2: *Treatment of Major Depression.* AHCPR Clinical Practice Guidelines, no. 5.2. Rockville, MD: Agency for Health Care Policy and Research, April 1993. https://www.ncbi.nlm.nih.gov/books/NBK52232/.

Albarracin, Dolores, Alain Ducousso-Lacaze, David Cohen, François Gonon, Pascal-Henri Keller, and Michel Minard. "There Is No Cure for Existence: On the Medicalization of Psychological Distress." *Ethical Human Psychology and Psychiatry* 17, no. 3 (January 2016). https://doi.org/10.1891/1559-4343.17.3.149.

Alford, C. Fred. "Subjectivity and the Intergenerational Transmission of Historical Trauma: Holocaust Survivors and Their Children." *Subjectivity* 8, no. 3 (September 2015): 261–82. https://doi.org/10.1057/sub.2015.10.

Allsopp, Kate, John Read, Rhiannon Corcoran, and Peter Kinderman. "Heterogeneity in Psychiatric Diagnostic Classification." *Psychiatry Research* 279 (September 2019): 15–22. https://doi.org/10.1016/j.psychres.2019.07.005.

Alvarez, Alex. *Native America and the Question of Genocide.* Lanham, MD: Rowman and Littlefield, 2014.

"American Girl Who Would Be Queen." *Norman (OK) Transcript.* October 8, 1897, 8.

"American Notes." *Petroleum Review.* June 9, 1906.

American Psychiatric Association. *Diagnostic and Statistical Manual of Mental Disorders: DSM-5.* Washington, DC: American Psychiatric Association, 2013.

———. *Diagnostic and Statistical Manual of Mental Disorders, Text Revision, DSM-IV-TR.* Washington, DC: American Psychiatric Association, 2000.

———. *Statistical Manual for Use by Institutions of the Insane.* New York: American Medico-Psychological Association, 1918.

American Psychological Association. "Former APA Presidents." Accessed August 5, 2022. http://www.apa.org/about/governance/president/former-presidents.aspx.

———. "Stress in America: The Impact of Discrimination." March 10, 2016. https://www.apa.org/news/press/releases/stress/2015/impact-of-discrimination.pdf.

Anastasiou, Dimitris, and James M. Kauffman. "Cultural Politics, Ideology, and Methodology in Disproportionality Research: A Rejoinder." *Journal of Disability Policy Studies* 30, no. 2 (2019): 105–10. https://doi.org/10.1177/1044207319863647.

Anderson, Gary Clayton. *Ethnic Cleansing and the Indian: The Crime That Should Haunt America*. Norman: University of Oklahoma Press, 2014.

Anderson, Talea. "'I Want My Agency Moved Back …, My Dear White Sisters': Discourses on Yakama Reservation Reform, 1920s–1930s." *Pacific Northwest Quarterly* 104, no. 4 (Fall 2013): 178–87.

Andreasen, Nancy C. "Posttraumatic Stress Disorder: A History and a Critique." *Annals of the New York Academy of Sciences* 1208, no. 1: Psychiatric and Neurologic Aspects of War (October 2010): 67–71. https://doi.org/10.1111/j.1749-6632.2010.05699.x.

Andrews, Clarence L. "Warfield's Story of Peo-Peo-Mox-Mox (Private Samuel Warfield's, Company H, Account)." *Washington Historical Quarterly* 25 (1934): 182–184.

Aneshensel, Carol S. "Sociological Inquiry into Mental Health: The Legacy of Leonard I. Pearlin." *Journal of Health and Social Behavior* 56, no. 2 (June 1, 2015): 166–78. https://doi.org/10.1177/0022146515583992.

Anthony, A. Craig. "The Execution of Joshua Tefft" (originally published in the *Castle Chronicle*, Winter 2001, under the title "Local Historian Examines the Execution of Joshua Tefft at Smith's Castle in 1676"), Rhode Island History Exhumed, accessed August 8, 2022, https://quahog.org/FactsFolklore/Personalities/Tefft_Joshua_Execution.

Archuleta, Margaret L., Brenda J. Child, and K. Tisianina Lomawaima, eds. *Away from Home: American Indian Boarding School Experiences*. Phoenix: Heard Museum: 2000.

Armstrong-Fumero, Fernando. "'Even the Most Careless Observer': Race and Visual Discernment in Physical Anthropology from Samuel Morton to Kennewick Man." *American Studies* 53, no. 2 (2014): 5–29. https://doi.org/10.1353/ams.2014.0100.

Associated Press. "Indians and Washington State Are at Odds Over Alcohol Ban." *New York Times*, October 10, 2000. https://www.nytimes.com/2000/10/10/us/indians-and-washington-state-are-at-odds-over-alcohol-ban.html.

———. "Oregon: Family Settles Lawsuit After Death at Indian School." *New York Times*, September 16, 2006. https://www.nytimes.com/2006/09/16/us/16brfs-001.html.

Axe, David. "National Guard Deploys Missile Launchers to Dakota Access Pipeline to 'Observe' Protestors." *Daily Beast*, January 17, 2017. https://www.thedailybeast.com/national-guard-deploys-missile-launchers-to-dakota-access-pipeline-to-observe-protestors.

Bache, R. Meade. "Reaction Time with Reference to Race." *Psychological Review* 2, no. 5 (September 1895): 475–86. https://doi.org/10.1037/h0070013.

Bailey, Pearce. "A Contribution to the Mental Pathology of Races in the United States." *Archives of Neurology and Psychiatry* 7, no. 2 (1922): 183–201. https://doi.org/10.1001/archneurpsyc.1922.02190080032004.

Bala, Areeg, Hoang Minh Tue Nguyen, and Wayne J. G. Hellstrom. "Post-SSRI Sexual Dysfunction: A Literature Review." *Sexual Medicine Reviews* 6, no. 1 (2018): 29–34. https://doi.org/10.1016/j.sxmr.2017.07.002.

Bardill, Jessica. "Tribal Enrollment and Genetic Testing." Gene Therapy Medical Treatment and Research. January 26, 2019. https://www.genetherapy.me/genetic-testing/tribal-enrollment-and-genetic-testing-genetics.php.

Barry, Ellen. "Eugenics Victims Are Heard at Last: Outrage Voiced Over State Sterilization." *Boston Globe*, August 15, 1999. http://www.bigorrin.org/archive4.htm.

Barton, Walter E. *The History and Influence of the American Psychiatric Association.* Washington, DC: American Psychiatric Press, 1987.

Bauer, Katherine W., Rachel Widome, John H. Himes, Mary Smyth, Bonnie Holy Rock, Peter J. Hannan, and Mary Story. "High Food Insecurity and Its Correlates Among Families Living on a Rural American Indian Reservation." *American Journal of Public Health* 1021, no. 7 (July 2012): 1346–52. https://doi.org/10.2105/AJPH.2011.300522.

Beals, Janette, Spero M. Manson, James H. Shore, Matthew Friedman, Marie Ashcraft, John A. Fairbank, and William E. Schlenger. "The Prevalence of Posttraumatic Stress Disorder Among American Indian Vietnam Veterans: Disparities and Context." *Journal of Traumatic Stress* 15, no. 2 (April 2002): 89–97. https://doi.org/10.1023/A:1014894506325.

Beavert, Virginia, and Sharon Hargus. *Ichishkíin Sínwit: Yakama/Yakima Sahaptin Dictionary.* Toppenish, WA: Heritage University/University of Washington Press, 2010.

Beecher, Blake. "The Medical Model, Mental Health Practitioners, and Individuals with Schizophrenia and Their Families." *Journal of Social Work Practice* 23, no. 1 (March 2009): 9–20. https://doi.org/10.1080/02650530902723282.

Ben-Zeev, Dror, Michael A. Young, and Patrick W. Corrigan. "DSM-V and the Stigma of Mental Illness." *Journal of Mental Health* 19, no. 4 (August 2010): 318–27. https://doi.org/10.3109/09638237.2010.492484.

Ben-Zur, Hasida, Sharon Gil, and Yinon Shamshins. "The Relationship Between Exposure to Terror Through the Media, Coping Strategies and Resources, and Distress and Secondary Traumatization." *International Journal of Stress Management* 19, no. 2 (May 2012): 132–50. https://doi.org/10.1037/a0027864.

Berger, Bethany R. "'Power Over this Unfortunate Race': Race, Politics and Indian Law in *United States v. Rogers.*" *William & Mary Law Review* 45, no. 5 (2004). https://scholarship.law.wm.edu/wmlr/vol45/iss5/3/.

Bettelheim, Bruno. *Freud and Man's Soul.* New York: Alfred A. Knopf, Inc., 1982.

Binswanger, Ingrid, Marc F. Stern, Traci E. Yamashita, Shane R. Mueller, Travis P. Baggett, and Patrick J. Blatchford. "Clinical Risk Factors for Death After Release from Prison in Washington State." *Addiction* 111, no. 3 (March 2016): 499–510. https://doi.org/10.1111/add.13200.

Black, Mallory. "Respect for 'People, Homelands, Culture' Motivates Native American Troops." *Tulalip News*, June 15, 2014. http://www.tulalipnews.com/wp/2014/06/15/respect-for-people-homelands-culture-motivates-native-american-troops/.

Blake, Dudley David, Frank W. Weathers, Linda M. Nagy, Danny G. Kaloupek, Fred D. Gusman, Dennis S. Charney, and Terence M. Keane. "The Development of a Clinician-Administered PTSD Scale." *Journal of Traumatic Stress* 8, no. 1 (1995): 75–90. https://doi.org/10.1007/BF02105408.

Bloom, John. "'Show What an Indian Can Do': Sports, Memory, and Ethnic Identity at Federal Indian Boarding Schools." *Journal of American Indian Education* 35, no. 3 (Spring 1996): 33–48. https://www.jstor.org/stable/24398295.

Bloom, Khaled J. "An American Tragedy of the Commons: Land and Labor in the Cherokee Nation, 1870–1900." *Agricultural History* 76, no. 3 (Summer 2002): 514–15.

Boice, John D. Jr, Michael T. Mumma, and William J. Blot. "Cancer Mortality Among Populations Residing in Counties Near the Hanford Site, 1950–2000," *Health Physics* 90, no. 5 (May 2006): 431–45. https://doi.org/10.1097/01. HP.0000183762.47244.bb.

Boss, Pauline. *Ambiguous Loss: Learning to Live with Unresolved Grief.* Cambridge, MA: Harvard University Press, 1999.

Bradley-Davino, Bekh, and Lesia Ruglass. "Trauma and Posttraumatic Stress Disorder in Economically Disadvantaged Populations." Undated briefing paper. Division 56, Trauma Psychology, American Psychological Association. https://www. apatraumadivision.org/files/58.pdf.

Brewin, Chris R., Tim Dalgleish, and Stephen Joseph. "A Dual Representation Theory of Posttraumatic Stress Disorder." *Psychological Review* 103, no. 4 (October 1996): 670–86. https://doi.org/10.1037/0033-295x.103.4.670.

Briggs, Kara. "Fighting Breast Cancer: A Native Woman's Journal; Striving to Meet Patients' Needs." *Indian Country Today,* July 21, 2005. https://indiancountrytoday. com/archive/fighting-breast-cancer-a-native-womans-journal-striving-to-meet-patients-needs.

British Psychological Society. "British Psychological Society Statement on the Open Letter to the DSM-5 Taskforce." n.d., accessed December 13, 2011. https:// dxrevisionwatch.files.wordpress.com/2011/12/pr1923_attachment_-_final_bps_ statement_on_dsm-5_12-12-2011.pdf.

———. "Response to the American Psychiatric Association: DSM-5 Development." Public letter to the American Psychiatric Association, June 2011. https://dxrevisionwatch. files.wordpress.com/2012/02/dsm-5-2011-bps-response.pdf.

Brockie, Teresa N., Gail Dana-Sacco, Gwenyth R. Wallen, Holly C. Wilcox, and Jacquelyn C. Campbell. "The Relationship of Adverse Childhood Experiences to PTSD, Depression, Poly-Drug Use and Suicide Attempt in Reservation-Based Native American Adolescents and Young Adults." *American Journal of Community Psychology* 55, nos. 3–4 (June 2015): 411–42. https://doi.org/10.1007/s10464-015-9721-3.

Bronson, Jennifer, E. Ann Carson, and Margaret Noonan. "Veterans in Prison and Jail, 2011–12." U.S. Department of Justice, Bureau of Justice Statistics. NCJ 249144, December 2015. https://www.bjs.gov/content/pub/pdf/vpj1112.pdf.

Brown, Kate. *Plutopia: Nuclear Families, Atomic Cities, and the Great Soviet and American Plutonium Disasters.* New York: Oxford University Press, 2013.

Brown, Matthew. "Fact Check: It's True, U.S. Government Poisoned Some Alcohol During Prohibition." *USA Today,* June 30, 2020. https://www.usatoday.com/story/news/ factcheck/2020/06/30/fact-check-u-s-government-poisoned-some-alcohol-during-prohibition/3283701001/.

Burch, Susan. "'Dislocated Histories': The Canton Asylum for Insane Indians." *Women, Gender, and Families of Color* 2, no. 2 (Fall 2014): 141–62. https://doi.org/10.5406/ womgenfamcol.2.2.0141.

Burgess, Ann Wolbert, and Lynda L. Holmstrom. "Rape Trauma Syndrome." *American Journal of Psychiatry* 131, no. 9 (September 1974): 981–86. https://doi. org/10.1176/ajp.131.9.981.

Cacciatore, Joanne. *Bearing the Unbearable: Love, Loss, and the Heartbreaking Path of Grief.* Somerville, MA: Wisdom Books, 2017.

Cairney, C. Thomas. *Clans and Families of Ireland and Scotland: An Ethnography of the Gael, A.D. 500–1750.* Berwyn Heights, MD: Heritage Books, 1989.

Calloway, Colin. "The Forgotten Links Between Highlanders and Native Americans." *The Scotsman,* June 2, 2016. https://www.scotsman.com/whats-on/arts-and-entertainment/forgotten-links-between-highlanders-and-native-americans-1475025.

Camerer, Colin F., Anna Dreber, Felix Holzmeister, Teck-Hua Ho, Jürgen Huber, Magnus Johannesson, Michael Kirchler, et al. "Evaluating the Replicability of Social Science Experiments in *Nature* and *Science* Between 2010 and 2015." *Nature Human Behaviour* 2, no. 9 (2018): 637–44. https://doi.org/10.1038/s41562-018-0399-z.

Campbell, Patricia. *Torture and Its Psychological Effects in Northern Ireland.* Toronto: ReMarx Publishing, 2017.

Campbell, Thomas H. *Good News on the Frontier: A History of the Cumberland Presbyterian Church.* Memphis, TN: Frontier Press, 1965.

Caplan, Paula J. *They Say You're Crazy: How the World's Most Powerful Psychiatrists Decide Who's Normal.* Reading, MA: Addison-Wesley, 1995.

———. *When Johnny and Jane Come Marching Home: How All of Us Can Help Veterans.* Cambridge: Massachusetts Institute of Technology Press, 2011.

Caplan, Paula J., and Lisa Cosgrove. *Bias in Psychiatric Diagnosis.* Lanham, MD: Jason Aronson, 2004.

Carey, Benedict, and Robert Gebeloff. "Many People Taking Antidepressants Discover They Cannot Quit." *New York Times,* April 7, 2018. https://www.nytimes.com/2018/04/07/health/antidepressants-withdrawal-prozac-cymbalta.html.

Carlat, Daniel J. *Unhinged: The Trouble with Psychiatry—A Doctor's Revelations About a Profession in Crisis.* New York: Free Press, 2010.

Carson, E. Ann. "Prisoners in 2016." U.S. Department of Justice, Office of Justice Programs, Bureau of Justice Statistics, NCJ251149, January 2018. https://www.bjs.gov/content/pub/pdf/p16.pdf.

Carter, Mike. "City of Poulsbo to Pay $2 Million to Settle Lawsuit over Fatal 2019 Police Shooting of Stonechild Chiefstick." *Seattle Times,* March 18, 2022. https://www.seattletimes.com/seattle-news/law-justice/city-of-poulsbo-to-pay-2-million-to-settle-lawsuit-over-fatal-2019-police-shooting-of-stonechild-chiefstick/.

Casselberry, Evans. *The Revised Statutes of the State of Missouri, Revised and Digested by the Thirteenth General Assembly.* St. Louis, MO: Chambers and Knapp, 1845.

Cattell, James McKeen. "Address of the President Before the American Psychological Association." *Psychological Review* 3, no. 2 (1896): 147–48.

Cavender Wilson, Angela. "Reclaiming Our Humanity: Decolonization and the Recovery of Indigenous Knowledge." In Devon Abbott Mihesuah and Angela Cavender Wilson, eds., *Indigenizing the Academy: Transforming Scholarship and Empowering Communities.* Lincoln: University of Nebraska Press, 2004.

CDC (U.S. Centers for Disease Control and Prevention). "Disparities in Suicide." Subsection: Rates are Higher Among Veterans. https://www.cdc.gov/suicide/facts/disparities-in-suicide.html.

———. "High School Students Who Seriously Considered Attempting Suicide: 2019 Results." YRBSS Explorer. Accessed 07/14/2022 https://yrbs-explorer.services.cdc.gov/#/tables?questionCode=H26&topicCode=C01&year=2019.

———. "High School YRBS: United States, 2015 Results." Youth Risk Behavior Surveillance System. https://www.cdc.gov/healthyyouth/data/yrbs/index.htm.

———. "Suicide: Facts at a Glance." 2012. https://web.archive.org/web/20150810050632/http://www.cdc.gov/ViolencePrevention/ pdf/Suicide_DataSheet-a.pdf.

———. "Reducing Military and Veteran Suicide." Testimony before the House Veteran Affairs Subcommittee on Economic Opportunity. June 15, 2022. https://www.cdc.gov/washington/testimony/2022/t20220615.htm.

———. "WISQARS [Web-Based Injury Statistics Query and Reporting System] Injury Data." Last reviewed December 2, 2021. https://www.cdc.gov/injury/wisqars/index.html.

———. "YRBSS 1997 Middle School Youth Risk Behavior Survey and 2000 Middle School Youth Risk Behavior Survey." Yakama Nation local results summary. Author's collection.

Celaire, Sarah, and Mark R. McDermott. "Comparing the Psychological Effects of Different Psychiatric Labels: Borderline, Paranoid, and Antisocial Personality Disorder; Major Depression; Anxiety Disorder; and Posttraumatic Stress Disorder." *Ethical Human Psychology and Psychiatry* 17, no. 1 (April 2015): 33–44. https://doi.org/10.1891/1559-4343.17.1.33.

Chaitin, Julia, and Shoshana Steinberg. "'I Can Almost Remember It Now': Between Personal and Collective Memories of Massive Social Trauma." *Journal of Adult Development* 21, no. 1 (March 2014): 30–42. https://doi.org/10.1007/s10804-013-9176-4.

Chengu, Garikai. "How the U.S. Helped Create Al Qaida and ISIS." *CounterPunch*, September 19, 2014. https://www.counterpunch.org/2014/09/19/how-the-us-helped-create-al-qaeda-and-isis/.

Cherokee Nation. *Laws of the Cherokee Nation: Adopted by the Council at Various Periods [1808–1835]. Printed for the Benefit of the Nation.* Tahlequah, I.T.: Cherokee Advocate Office, 1852.

Child, Brenda J. *Boarding School Seasons: American Indian Families, 1900–1940.* Lincoln: University of Nebraska Press, 2000.

Chino, Michelle, Darlene Haff, and Carolee Dodge-Francis. "Patterns of Commodity Food Use Among American Indians." *Pimatisiwin: A Journal of Aboriginal and Indigenous Community Health* 7, no. 2 (2009): 279–89. https://journalindigenouswellbeing.co.nz/volume-7-2-winter-2009/patterns-of-commodity-food-use-among-american-indians/.

City-Data.com. "Poverty in the US: Poverty Rate Data—Information About Poor and Low Income Residents, Maps, Summary Graphs and More." n.d., accessed December 10, 2018. http://www.city-data.com/poverty/#.

Clark, Natalie. "Shock and Awe: Trauma as the New Colonial Frontier." *Humanities* 5, no. 1 (February 2016). https://doi.org/10.3390/h5010014.

Clarren, Rebecca. "A Right-Wing Think Tank Is Trying to Bring Down the Indian Child Welfare Act. Why?" *Nation*, April 6, 2017. https://www.thenation.com/article/a-right-wing-think-tank-is-trying-to-bring-down-the-indian-child-welfare-act-why/.

Coates, Julia. *Trail of Tears* (Landmarks of the American Mosaic series). Santa Barbara, CA: Greenwood, 2014.

Coates, Ta-Nehisi. "The First White President." *Atlantic*, October 2017. https://www.theatlantic.com/magazine/archive/2017/10/the-first-white-president-ta-nehisi-coates/537909/.

Cobb-Greetham, Amanda. "Hearth and Home: Cherokee and Creek Women's Memories of the Civil War in Indian Territory." In Bradley R. Clampitt, ed., *The Civil War and Reconstruction in Indian Territory*. Lincoln: University of Nebraska Press, 2015, 153–72.

Cohen, Adam. *Imbeciles: The Supreme Court, American Eugenics, and the Sterilization of Carrie Buck*. New York: Penguin, 2017.

Cohen Silver, Roxane, E. Alison Holman, Daniel N. McIntosh, Michael Poulin, and Virgina Gil-Rivas. "Nationwide Longitudinal Study of Psychological Responses to September 11," *Journal of the American Medical Association* 288, no. 10 (September 11, 2002): 1235–44. https://doi.org/10.1001/jama.288.10.1235.

Colbert, Ty. *The Four False Pillars of Biopsychiatry*. Orange, CA: Kevco Publishing, 1996.

Collier, Catherine. "Special Education for Indigenous Students." *NABE Perspectives* (May-June 2012).

Colman, Andrew M. *A Dictionary of Psychology*. 3rd ed. New York: Oxford University Press, 2009.

Columbia River Inter-Tribal Fishing Commission. "Treaty with the Yakama, 1855." https://www.critfc.org/member_tribes_overview/the-confederated-tribes-and-bands-of-the-yakama-nation/treaty-with-the-yakama-1855/.

Confederated Tribes and Bands of the Yakama Nation. Resolution T-53-77; amended by T-053-94; amended by T-172-99.

Conley, Robert J. *A Cherokee Encyclopedia*. Albuquerque: University of New Mexico Press, 2007.

Connor, Katherine, and Ellen J. Vargyas. "The Legal Implications of Gender Bias in Standardized Testing." *Berkeley Women's Law Journal* 7, no. 1 (September 1992): 13–89. https://doi.org/10.15779/Z38GS2D.

Cooper, Kenneth J. "I'm a Descendant of the Cherokee Nation's Black Slaves. Tribal Citizenship Is Our Birthright." *Washington Post*, September 15, 2017. https://www.washingtonpost.com/news/post-nation/wp/2017/09/15/im-a-descendant-of-the-cherokee-nations-black-slaves-tribal-citizenship-is-our-birthright/.

Csoka, Antonei, Audrey Bahrick, and Olli-Pekka Mehtonen. "Persistent Sexual Dysfunction After Discontinuation of Selective Serotonin Reuptake Inhibitors." *Journal of Sexual Medicine* 5, no. 1 (2008): 227–33. https://doi.org/10.1111/j.1743-6109.2007.00630.x.

Cummings, William. "In Response to Trump's 'Pocahontas' Jibes, Elizabeth Warren Releases Results of DNA Test." *USA Today*, October 15, 2018. https://www.usatoday.com/story/news/politics/2018/10/15/elizabeth-warren-dna-test/1645840002/.

Curtin, Sally C., Margaret Warner, and Holly Hedegaard. "Suicide Rates for Females and Males by Race and Ethnicity: United States, 1999 and 2014." CDC National Center for Health Statistics. April 2016. https://www.cdc.gov/nchs/data/hestat/suicide/rates_1999_2014.pdf.

Dalla, Rochelle L., and Heather R. Kennedy. "'I Want to Leave—Go Far Away—I Don't Want to Get Stuck on the Res[ervation]': Developmental Outcomes of Adolescent-Aged Children of Navajo Native American Teen Mothers." *Journal of Adolescent Research* 30, no. 1 (2015): 113–39. https://doi.org/10.1177/0743558414552322.

Davidson, Jonathan R.T., Mary A. Malik, and John Travers. "Structured Interview for PTSD (SIP): Psychometric Validation for DSM-IV Criteria." *Depression and Anxiety* 5, no. 3 (1997), 127–29. https://doi.org/10.1002/(SICI)1520-6394(1997)5:3%3C127::AID-DA3%3E3.0.CO;2-B.

Davidson, Osha Gray. "The Forgotten Soldier." *Rolling Stone*, June 3, 2004. http://archive.li/9Dfas#selection-755.266-755.375.

Davis, N. S. *History of the Medical Profession from the First Settlement of the British Colonies in America, to the Year 1850*, in "Part 1—Original Communications, Chapter II, Continued," *North-Western Medical and Surgical Journal* 3, no. 3 (September 1850).

DeLoria, Vine, and David E. Wilkins. *Tribes, Treaties, and Constitutional Tribulations.* Austin: University of Texas Press, 1999.

DeMarni Cromer, Lisa, Mary E. Gray, Ludivina Vasquez, and Jennifer J. Freyd. "The Relationship of Acculturation to Historical Loss Awareness, Institutional Betrayal, and the Intergenerational Transmission of Trauma in the American Indian Experience." *Journal of Cross-Cultural Psychology* 49, no. 1 (2018): 99–114. https://doi.org/10.1177/0022022117738749.

Dement, John, Knut Ringen, Laura S. Welch, Eula Bingham, and Patricia Quinn. "Mortality of Older Construction and Craft Workers Employed at Department of Energy (DOE) Nuclear Sites." *American Journal of Industrial Medicine* 52, no. 9 (September 2009): 671–82. https://doi.org/10.1002/ajim.20729.

Dempsey, Hugh A. *Firewater: The Impact of the Whiskey Trade on the Blackfoot Nation.* Calgary, Alberta: Fifth House, 2002.

De Sá, Karen. "Drugging Our Kids." *San Jose Mercury News*, August 24, 2014. http://extras.mercurynews.com/druggedkids/.

De Sa, Karen, and Karen Savage. "California Foster Care: New Laws Signed to Restrict Psychiatric Drugs." *Woodland (CA) Daily Democrat.* October 6, 2015, updated September 7, 2018. https://www.dailydemocrat.com/2015/10/06/california-foster-care-new-laws-signed-to-restrict-psychiatric-drugs-2/.

Dippold, Steffi. "The Wampanoag Word: John Eliot's *Indian Grammar*, the Vernacular Rebellion, and the Elegancies of Native Speech." *Early American Literature* 48, no. 3 (2013): 543–75. https://doi.org/10.1353/eal.2013.0044.

Dobbin, William James. "Wild Men Within Commuting Distance." *New York Tribune*, June 12, 1921. Eugenics Archive, American Philosophical Society. http://www.eugenicsarchive.org/html/eugenics/static/images/363.html.

Dorgan, Byron L. "The Urgent Need to Reform the Indian Health Service's Aberdeen Area." Report to the Committee on Indian Affairs, 111th Congress, 2nd session, December 28, 2010. https://www.indian.senate.gov/sites/default/files/upload/files/ChairmansReportInCriticalCondition122810.pdf.

Dowbiggin, Ian Robert. *Keeping America Sane: Psychiatry and Eugenics in the United States and Canada, 1880–1940.* Ithaca, NY: Cornell University Press, 1997.

Duffy, Maureen. "Writing About Clients: Developing Composite Case Material and Its Rationale." *Counseling and Values* 54, no. 2 (April 2010):135–53. https://doi.org/10.1002/j.2161-007X.2010.tb00011.x.

Duke, Alan. "'Billy Jack' Actor-Writer Tom Laughlin Dies at 82." CNN, December 16, 2013. http://www.cnn.com/2013/12/15/showbiz/billyjack-tom-laughlin-obit/index.html.

Dunbar-Ortiz, Roxanne. *An Indigenous Peoples' History of the United States*, ReVisioning American History series. Boston: Beacon Press, 2014.

Duncan, L. E., A. Ratanatharathorn, A. E. Aiello, L. M. Almli, A. B. Amstadter, A. E. Ashley-Koch, D. G. Baker, et al. "Largest GWAS of PTSD (*N* = 20 070) Yields Genetic Overlap with Schizophrenia and Sex Differences in Heritability." *Molecular Psychiatry* 23 (2018): 666–73. https://doi.org/10.1038/mp.2017.77.

Duoos, Kayla. "On This Day in History: The Battle of Sugar Point." *Leech Lake News*, October 5, 2020. https://www.leechlakenews.com/2018/10/05/on-this-day-in-history-the-battle-of-sugar-point/.

Duran, Eduardo, and Bonnie Duran. *Native American Postcolonial Psychology.* Albany: State University of New York, 1995.

Duran, Eduardo, Judith Firehammer, and John Gonzalez. "Liberation Psychology as the Path Toward Healing Cultural Soul Wounds." *Journal of Counseling & Development* 86, no. 3 (Summer 2008): 288–92. https://doi.org/10.1002/j.1556-6678.2008. tb00511.x.

Duran, Eduardo, Bonnie Guillory, and Michael Villanueva. "Third and Fourth World Concerns: Toward a Liberation Psychology." In George Stricker, Elizabeth Davis-Russell, Edward Bourg, Eduardo Duran, W. Rodney Hammond, James McHolland, Kenneth Polite, and Billy E. Vaughn, eds., *Toward Ethnic Diversification in Psychology Education and Training* (Washington, DC: American Psychological Association, 1990), 211–217. https://doi.org/10.1037/10071-017.

Eames, Wesley. "The Deadly War of Prohibition." *Without a Trace*, October 8, 2021. https://news.trace.com/p/the-deadly-war-of-prohibition?s=r.

Eddings, Anna. "Foreman, Stephen (1807–1881)." In *Encyclopedia of Oklahoma History and Culture.* https://www.okhistory.org/publications/enc/entry.php?entry=FO021.

Ehlers, Cindy L., Ian R. Gizer, David A. Gilder, Jarrod M. Ellingson, and Rachel Yehuda. "Measuring Historical Trauma in an American Indian Community Sample: Contributions of Substance Dependence, Affective Disorder, Conduct Disorder and PTSD." *Drug and Alcohol Dependence* 133, no. 1 (November 2013): 180–87. https://doi.org/10.1016/j.drugalcdep.2013.05.011.

Ellenberger, Henri F. *The Discovery of the Unconscious: The History and Evolution of Dynamic Psychiatry.* New York: Basic Books, 1970.

Ellingson, Terry Jay. *The Myth of the Noble Savage.* Berkeley: University of California Press, 2001.

Emmerich, Lisa. "Genocide or Family Planning? Indian Health Service Policy in the 1960s and 1970s." *Inside* 28, no. 6 (1998).

Engstrom, Eric J., and Matthias M. Weber. "The Directions of Psychiatric Research by Emil Kraepelin." *History of Psychiatry* 16, no. 3 (September 2005): 345–49. https://doi.org/10.1177/0957154X05056763.

Ensign, Tod. *America's Military Today: The Challenge of Militarism.* New York: New Press, 2004.

Ertem, Ilgi Ozturk, John M. Leventhal, and Sara Dobbs. "Intergenerational Continuity of Child Physical Abuse: How Good is the Evidence?" *Lancet* 356, no. 9232 (October 2000): 814–19. https://doi.org/10.1016/S0140-6736(00)02656-8.

Estus, Joaqlin. "Court Strikes Key Provision of Indian Child Welfare Law." *Indian Country Today*, April 6, 2021. https://indiancountrytoday.com/news/court-strikes-key-provision-of-indian-child-welfare-law.

Eugenics Archive. *Third International Congress of Eugenics.* American Philosophical Society. https://eugenicsarchive.ca/discover/timeline/5172ede1eed5c60000000021.

Evans, Steven Ross. *Voice of the Old Wolf: Lucullus Virgil McWhorter and the Nez Perce Indians*. Pullman: Washington State University, 1996.

Fanon, Frantz. *The Wretched of the Earth*. Trans. Constance Farrington. New York: Grove Press, 1963.

Farley, Melissa, Sarah Deer, Jacqueline M. Golding, Nicole Matthews, Guadalupe Lopez, Christine Stark, and Eileen Hudon. "The Prostitution and Trafficking of American Indian/Alaska Native Women in Minnesota." *American Indian and Alaska Native Mental Health Research Journal* 23, no. 1 (2016): 65–104. https:// doi.org/10.5820/aian.2301.2016.65.

Farrow, Ronan, and Rich McHugh. "Welcome to 'the Most Toxic Place in America.'" NBC News, November 29, 2016. https://www.nbcnews.com/news/us-news/welcome-most-toxic-place-america-n689141.

Fauchereau Grimké, John. "Journal of the Campaign to the Southward, May 9th to July 14th, 1778." *South Carolina Historical and Genealogical Magazine* 12, no. 2 (April 1911). https://www.carolana.com/SC/eBooks/SCHGM/The_South_Carolina_Historical_and_Genealogical_Magazine_Volume_XII.pdf.

Field, Nigel P., Sophear Muong, and Vannavuth Sochanvimean. "Parental Styles in the Intergenerational Transmission of Trauma Stemming from the Khmer Rouge Regime in Cambodia." *American Journal of Orthopsychiatry* 83, no. 4 (October 2013): 483–94. https://doi.org/10.1111/ajop.12057.

Find a Grave. "Robert Winans, 1894–1939." Indian Scout Cemetery, McLean County, North Dakota, Memorial ID #141449723. https://www.findagrave.com/memorial/141449723/robert-winans.

Fisher, Andrew H. *Shadow Tribe: The Making of Columbia River Indian Identity*. Seattle: University of Washington Press, 2011.

———. "They Mean to Be Indian Always: The Origins of Columbia River Indian Identity, 1860–1885." In *The American Indian: Past and Present*. Roger L. Nichols, ed. Norman: University of Oklahoma Press, 2014.

Fitzgerald, J. A., and W. W. Ludeman. "The Intelligence of Indian Children." *Journal of Comparative Psychology* 6, no. 4 (1926): 319–28. https://doi.org/10.1037/h0071550.

Fitzpatrick, Kevin M., Casey Harris, and Grant Drawve. "How Bad Is It? Suicidality in the Middle of the COVID-19 Pandemic." *Suicide and Life-Threatening Behavior* 50, no. 6 (December 2020): 1241–49. https://doi.org/10.1111/sltb.12655.

Flanagin, Jake. "Native Americans Are the Unseen Victims of a Broken U.S. Justice System." *Quartz*, April 27, 2015. https://qz.com/392342/native-americans-are-the-unseen-victims-of-a-broken-us-justice-system/.

Food Research & Action Center. "Understanding the Connections: Food Insecurity and Obesity." October 2015. http://frac.org/wp-content/uploads/frac_brief_understanding_the_connections.pdf.

Ford, Paul Leicester, ed. *The Works of Thomas Jefferson in Twelve Volumes*. New York: G. P. Putnam, 1904–1905. http://memory.loc.gov/service/mss/mtj/mtj1/027/027_1066_1069.pdf.

Fowler, Paul R. *Risk Management & Medical Liability: A Manual for Indian Health Service and Tribal Health Care Professionals, Third Edition*. Rockville, MD: Indian Health Service, Office of Clinical and Preventive Services. August 2018. https://www.ihs.gov/riskmanagement/includes/themes/newihstheme/display_objects/documents/risk_management_manual.pdf.

Frank, John W., Roland S. Moore, and Genevieve M. Ames. "Public Health Then and Now: Historical and Cultural Roots of Drinking Problems Among American Indians." *American Journal of Public Health* 90, no. 3 (March 2000): 344–51.

Frankfurt, Harry G. *On Bullshit*. Princeton, NJ: Princeton University Press, 2005.

Franklin, C. Laurel, Thomas Sheeran, and Mark Zimmerman. "Screening for Trauma Histories, Posttraumatic Stress Disorder (PTSD), and Subthreshold PTSD in Psychiatric Outpatients." *Psychological Assessment* 14, no. 4 (2002): 467–71. https://doi.org/10.1037//1040-3590.14.4.46.

Fredland, Nina, Lene Symes, Heidi Gilroy, Rene Paulson, Angeles Nava, Judith McFarlane, and Jacquelyn Pennings. "Connecting Partner Violence to Poor Functioning for Mothers and Children: Modeling Intergenerational Outcomes." *Journal of Family Violence* 30, no. 5 (July 2015): 555–66. https://doi.org/10.1007/s10896-015-9702-1.

Freire, Paulo. *Pedagogy of the Oppressed*. New York: Continuum, 2009.

Freud, Sigmund. "Early Studies on the Psychical Mechanisms of Hysterical Phenomenon." In Ernest Jones, ed., *Sigmund Freud, Collected Papers*, vol. 1. New York: Basic Books, 1959. (Original work written with Breuer in 1892; first published in 1940 and collected by James Strachey for Hogarth Press).

———. *The Question of Lay Analysis: Conversations with an Impartial Person*, trans. and ed. James Strachey (New York: W. W. Norton, 1969).

Fridlund, Paul. *Washington's Story: The Conquest*. Puyallup, WA: P. Fridlund, 2003.

Fried, Eiko I., and Randolph M. Nesse. "Depression is Not a Consistent Syndrome: An Investigation of Unique Symptom Patterns in the STAR*D Study." *Journal of Affective Disorders* 172, (February 2015): 96–102. https://doi.org/10.1016/j.jad.2014.10.010.

Furtwangler, Albert. *Bringing Indians to the Book*. Seattle: University of Washington Press, 2011.

Galton, Sir Francis. *Hereditary Genius: An Inquiry into Its Laws and Consequences*. New York: Macmillan, 1869.

———. "Hereditary Talent and Character, 2nd Paper." *Macmillan's Magazine* 12 (1865).

———. *Inquiries into Human Faculty and its Development*. New York: J. M. Dent, 1907.

Galves, Albert, and David Walker. "Debunking the Science Behind Attention-Deficit/ Hyperactivity Disorder as a 'Brain Disorder.'" *Ethical Human Psychology and Psychiatry* 14, no. 1 (March 2012): 27–40. https://doi.org/10.1891/1559-4343.14.1.27.

Garrick, Norman, Carol Atkinson-Palombo, and Hamed Ahangari. "Why America's Roads Are So Much More Dangerous Than Europe's." *Vox*, November 30, 2016. https://www.vox.com/the-big-idea/2016/11/30/13784520/roads-deaths-increase-safety-traffic-us.

Garroutte, Eva Marie. "Defining 'Radical Indigenism' and Creating an American Indian Scholarship." In Stephen J. Pfohl, ed., *Culture, Power and History: Studies in Critical Sociology*. Boston: Brill, 2005. https://doi.org/10.1163/9789047417088_009.

Garth, Thomas R. *Race Psychology: A Study of Racial Mental Differences*. New York: McGraw-Hill, 1931.

———. "A Study of the Foster Indian Child in the White Home." *Psychological Bulletin* 32 (1935): 708–9.

Garth, Thomas R., and Mary A. Barnard. "The Will-Temperament of Indians." *Journal of Applied Psychology* 11, no. 16 (1927). https://doi.org/10.1037/h0071493.

Gibbons, Robert D., Hendricks Brown, Kwan Hur, Sue M. Marcus, Dulal K. Bhaumik, Joëlle A. Erkens, Ron M. C. Herings, and J. John Mann. "Early Evidence on the Effects of Regulators' Suicidality Warnings on SSRI Prescriptions and Suicide in Children and Adolescents." *American Journal of Psychiatry* 164, no. 9 (September 2007): 1356–63. https://doi.org/10.1176/appi.ajp.2007.07030454.

Gibbons, Robert, Kwan Hur, Jill Lavigne, Jiebiao Wang, and J. John Mann. "Medications and Suicide: High Dimensional Empirical Bayes Screening (iDEAS)." *Harvard Data Science Review* 1, no. 2 (Fall 2019). https://doi.org/10.1162/99608f92.6fdaa9de.

Gideon, D.C. *Indian Territory, Descriptive, Biographical and Genealogical: Including the Landed Estates, County Seats, Etc., Etc., with a General History of the Territory.* New York: Lewis Publishing, 1901.

Gilbert, Joan. *The Trail of Tears Across Missouri.* Columbia: University of Missouri, 1996.

Gobineau, Arthur, comte de. *The Inequality of the Human Races.* New York: Howard Fertig, 1853/1999.

Goddard, Henry Herbert. *Feeble-Mindedness: Its Causes and Consequences.* New York: Macmillan, 1914.

Gone, Joseph P., "Dialogue 2008—Introduction: Mental Health Discourse as Western Cultural Proselytization." *Ethos* 36, no. 3 (September 2008): 310–15. https://doi.org/10.1111/j.1548-1352.2008.00016.x.

Gone, Joseph P., William E. Hartmann, Andrew Pomerville, Dennis C. Wendt, Sarah H. Klem, and Rachel L. Burrage. "The Impact of Historical Trauma on Health Outcomes for Indigenous Populations in the USA and Canada: A Systematic Review." *American Psychologist* 74, no. 1 (January 2019): 20–35. https://doi.org/10.1037/amp0000338.

Gonzalez, Vivian M., and Monica C. Skewes. "Association of Belief in the 'Firewater Myth' with Strategies to Avoid Alcohol Consequences Among American Indian and Alaska Native College Students Who Drink." *Psychology of Addictive Behaviors* 32, no. 4 (2018): 401–9. https://doi.org/10.1037/adb0000367.

Goodkind, Jessica R., Kimberly Ross-Toledo, Susie John, Janie Lee Hall, Lucille Ross, Lance Freeland, Ernest Coletta, Twila Becenti-Fundark, Charlene Poola, Regina Begay-Roanhorse, and Christopher Lee. "Promoting Healing and Restoring Trust: Policy Recommendations for Improving Behavioral Health Care for American Indian/Alaska Native Adolescents." *American Journal of Community Psychology* 46, nos. 3–4 (December 2010): 386–94. https://doi.org/10.1007/s10464-010-9347-4.

Gøtzsche, Peter. *Deadly Medicines and Organised Crime: How Big Pharma has Corrupted Healthcare.* London: Radcliffe Publishing, 2013.

Gould, Stephen Jay. *The Mismeasure of Man.* New York: W. W. Norton, 1996.

Graeber, David, and David Wengrow. *The Dawn of Everything: A New History of Humanity.* New York: Farrar, Straus and Giroux, 2021.

Graham, Thomas Crofoot. "Using Reasons for Living to Connect to American Indian Healing Traditions." *Journal of Sociology and Social Welfare* 29, no. 1 (March 2002): 55–75. https://scholarworks.wmich.edu/jssw/vol29/iss1/5/.

Graham-Harrison, Emma, and Juliette Garside. "'Allow No Escapes': Leak Exposes Reality of China's Vast Prison Camp Network." *Guardian,* November 24, 2019. https://www.theguardian.com/world/2019/nov/24/china-cables-leak-no-escapes-reality-china-uighur-prison-camp.

Granello, Darcy Haag and Todd A. Gibbs. "The Power of Language and Labels: 'The Mentally Ill' Versus 'People with Mental Illnesses.'" *Journal of Counseling and Development* 94, no. 1 (January 2016): 31–40. https://doi.org/10.1002/jcad.12059.

Graves, Janessa M., Jessica L. Mackelprang, Solmaz Amiri, and Demetrius A. Abshire. "Barriers to Telemedicine Implementation in Southwest Tribal Communities During COVID-19." *Journal of Rural Health* 37, no. 1 (Winter 2021): 239–41. https://doi.org/10.1111/jrh.12479.

Graves, Kathleen, Louise Shavings, Cookie Rose, Anda Saylor, Stacy L. Smith, Cheryl Easley, and Kanaqlat (George P. Charles). *Boarding School Project: Mental Health Outcome*. Anchorage: National Resource Center for American Indian, Alaska Native, and Native Hawaiian Elders, July 2007. https://www.iam.gives/documents/resources/other_boarding-school-project.pdf.

Great Lakes Inter-Tribal Council. "Suicidal Behaviors Among American Indian/Alaska Native Populations: Indian Health Service Resource Patient Management System Suicide Reporting Form Aggregate Database Analysis, 2003–2012." Lac du Flambeau, WI: Great Lakes Inter-Tribal Epidemiology Center, 2013. https://www.glitc.org/2020/wp-content/uploads/2022/07/glitec_suicidereport_highrez.pdf.

Green, Kyle. "Dream Catchers Vol. 2—various artists," review of Blue Yonder Audio CD, "David Folks," Track 5, Disc 2, "Joshua Maiden." *Westland (MI) Observer*, February 15, 1993, 5B. http://www.westland.lib.mi.us/pdf/observers/1993-02-15.pdf.

Greenberg, Roger. "The Return of Psychosocial Relevance in a Biochemical Age." *Register Report* 40 (Spring 2014): 11–16. https://www.researchgate.net/publication/274079590_The_Return_of_Psychosocial_Relevance_in_a_Biochemical_Age.

Griffin, James B. "On the Historic Location of the Tutelo and the Mohetan in the Ohio Valley." *American Anthropologist* 44, no. 2 (April–June 1942): 275–80. https://doi.org/10.1525/aa.1942.44.2.02a00080.

Grimm, Bill, and Julian Darwall. "Foster Parents: Who Are They and What Are Their Motivations?" *National Center for Youth Law Newsletter* 26, no. 3 (September 30, 2005). https://youthlaw.org/publication/foster-parents-who-are-they-and-what-are-their-motivations/.

Gundersen, Craig. "Measuring the Extent, Depth, and Severity of Food Insecurity: An Application to American Indians in the USA." *Journal of Population Economics* 21, no. 1 (January 2008): 191–215. https://doi.org/10.1007/s00148-007-0152-9.

Guthrie, Robert V. *Even the Rat Was White: A Historical View of Psychology*. New York: Harper & Row, 1976/2004.

Haag, Ann Murray. "The Indian Boarding School Era and Its Continuing Impact on Tribal Families and the Provision of Government Services." *Tulsa Law Review* 43, no. 1 (2007): 149–68. http://digitalcommons.law.utulsa.edu/tlr/vol43/iss1/8.

Hagley Museum and Library "History of Patent Medicine." Wilmington, DE, n.d. https://www.hagley.org/research/digital-exhibits/history-patent-medicine.

Hales, Peter Bacon. *Atomic Spaces: Living on the Manhattan Project*. Champaign: University of Illinois Press, 1999.

Hall, Betty. "Faces of the Shasta People: Who We Were and Who We Are, The Shasta Nation." In Nan Hannon and R. K. Olmo, eds. *Living with the Land: The Indians of Southwest Oregon; The Proceedings of the 1989 Symposium on the Prehistory of Southwest Oregon.* Medford, OR: Southern Oregon Historical Society, 1990, 136.

Haller, John S. "Race and the Concept of Progress in Nineteenth Century American Ethnology." *American Anthropologist* 73, no. 3 (June 1971) https://www.jstor.org/stable/671764.

Hambrecht, F. T., and J. L. Koste. "Biographical Register of Physicians Who Served the Confederacy in a Medical Capacity." Unpublished database. National Museum of the Civil War, Frederick, MD, March 17, 2016.

Hamill, James Francis. *Going Indian.* Urbana: University of Illinois Press, 2006.

Haney, Craig. "The Psychological Effects of Solitary Confinement: A Systematic Critique." *Crime and Justice* 47, no. 1 (March 2018): 365–416. https://doi.org/10.1086/696041.

Haozous, Emily A., Carolyn J. Strickland, Janelle F. Palacios, and Teshia G. Arambula Solomon. "Blood Politics: Ethnic Identity, and Racial Misclassification Among American Indians and Alaska Natives." *Journal of Environmental and Public Health* 2014, article ID 321604 (February 2014). https://doi.org/10.1155/2014/321604.

Harris, Gardiner. "Debate Resumes on the Safety of Depression's Wonder Drugs." *New York Times*, August 7, 2003. https://www.nytimes.com/2003/08/07/business/debate-resumes-on-the-safety-of-depression-s-wonder-drugs.html.

Harry, Debra, Stephanie Howard, and Brett Lee Shelton. *Indigenous People, Genes, and Genetics: What Indigenous People Should Know About Biocolonialism; A Primer and Resource Guide.* Indigenous Peoples Council on Biocolonialism, May 2000. www.ipcb.org/pdf_files/ipgg.pdf.

Hathaway, Elizabeth D. "American Indian and Alaska Native People: Social Vulnerability and COVID-19." *Journal of Rural Health* 37, no. 1 (Winter 2021): 256–59. https://doi.org/10.1111/jrh.12505.

Hatley, Thomas. *The Dividing Path: Cherokees and South Carolinians Through the Era of Revolution.* New York: Oxford University Press, 1995.

Haught, B. F. "Mental Growth of the South-Western Indian." *Journal of Applied Psychology* 18, no. 1 (1934): 137–42. https://doi.org/10.1037/h0070042.

Healy, David, Joanna Le Noury, and Derelie Mangin. "Enduring Sexual Dysfunction After Treatment with Antidepressants, 5 *a*-Reductase Inhibitors and Isotretinoin: 300 Cases." *International Journal of Risk & Safety in Medicine* 29, nos. 3–4 (2018): 125–34. https://doi.org/10.3233/JRS-180744.

Heath, Stephanie W. *Risk Management and Medical Liability: A Manual for Indian Health Service & Tribal Health Care Professionals, Second Edition.* Rockville, MD: Indian Health Service, Office of Clinical and Preventive Services. April 2006. https://www.ihs.gov/riskmanagement/includes/themes/newihstheme/display_objects/documents/risk_management_manual.pdf.

Hengartner, Michael P. "Methodological Flaws, Conflicts of Interest, and Scientific Fallacies: Implications for the Evaluation of Antidepressants' Efficacy and Harm." *Frontiers in Psychiatry* 8, no. 275 (December 2017). https://doi.org/10.3389/fpsyt.2017.00275.

Hengartner, Michael P., and Martin Plöderl. "Newer-Generation Antidepressants and Suicide Risk in Randomized Controlled Trials: A Re-Analysis of the FDA Database." *Psychotherapy and Psychosomatics* 88, no. 4 (August 2019): 247–48. https://doi.org/10.1159/000501215.

Henrich, Joseph, Steven J. Heine, and Ara Norenzayan. "The Weirdest People in the World?" *Behavioral and Brain Sciences* 33, nos. 2–3 (June 2010): 61–83. https:// doi.org/10.1017/S0140525X0999152X.

Hepburn, John R., and John R. Stratton. "Total Institutions and Inmate Self-Esteem." *British Journal of Criminology* 17, no. 3 (July 1977): 237–50. https://www.jstor. org/stable/23636184.

Hernstein, Richard and Charles Murray. *The Bell Curve: Intelligence and Class Structure in American Life*. New York: Free Press, 1994.

Heuterman, Thomas H. *The Burning Horse: The Japanese-American Experience in the Yakima Valley, 1920–1942*. Cheney: Eastern Washington University Press, 1995.

Hicks, James R. "Cherokee Lineages: Register Report of Ludovic Grant." Entry 199: Rachel Smith (Mother of Narcissa Josephine Rider). https://www.genealogy. com/ftm/h/i/c/James-R-Hicks-VA/BOOK-0001/0015-0014.html.

———. "Cherokee Lineages: Register Report of Richard S. Pearis, Sr." Entry 173: Narcissa Josephine Rider. https://www.genealogy.com/ftm/h/i/c/James-R-Hicks-VA/ BOOK-0001/0022-0048.html.

Hill, Luther B. *A History of the State of Oklahoma*, vol. 2. Chicago: Lewis Publishing, 1910.

Hines, Donald. *Ghost Voices: Yakima Indian Myths, Legends, Humor and Hunting Stories*. Issaquah, WA: Great Eagle Publishing, 1992.

Hinshaw, Stephen. *The Mark of Shame: Stigma of Mental Illness and an Agenda for Change*. New York: Oxford University Press, 2007.

Hirsch, Nathaniel D. Mttron. *Dynamics of Juvenile Crime*. Cambridge, MA: Sci-Art Publishers, 1937.

———. "A Study of Natio-Racial Mental Differences." *Genetic Psychology Monographs* 1, nos. 3–4 (May and July 1926): 239–406.

Historical Data Systems. "Regiment History: United States Volunteers—Indian Troops, 3rd Regiment, Indian Home Guard." Digital transcription from official records. http://www.civilwardata.com/active/hdsquery.dll?RegimentHistory?688&U%3E.

Hobbs, Straus, Dean & Walker (law firm). "GM [General Memorandum] 12-028, Indian Health Service Proposed Fiscal Year 2013 Appropriations," February 22, 2012. https://hobbsstraus.com/general_memo/general-memorandum-12-028/.

Hollander, Edwin P. "Otto Klineberg: International Social Psychologist." In Grant J. Rich and Uwe Gielen, eds. *Pathfinders in International Psychology*. Charlotte, NC: Information Age Publishing, 2015.

Hoopes, Megan, Petersen Paneen, Eric Vinson, and Kerri Lopez. "Regional Differences and Tribal Use of American Indian/Alaska Native Cancer Data in the Pacific Northwest." *Journal of Cancer Education* 27, 1 supplement (April 2012). https:// doi.org/10.1007/s13187-012-0325-4.

Horgan, John. "My Problem with 'Taboo' Behavioral Genetics? The Science Stinks!" *Scientific American*, October 4, 2013. https://blogs.scientificamerican.com/cross-check/ my-problem-with-e2809ctabooe2809d-behavioral-genetics-the-science-stinks/.

Hornsey, Matthew J., and Kelly S. Fielding. "Attitude Roots and Jiu Jitsu Persuasion: Understanding and Overcoming the Motivated Rejection of Science." *American Psychologist* 72, no. 3 (2017): 450–73. https://doi.org/doi.org/10.1037/a0040437.

Horwitz, Sari. "The Hard Lives—and High Suicide Rate—of Native American Children on Reservations." *Washington Post*, March 9, 2014. https://www.washingtonpost. com/world/national-security/the-hard-lives--and-high-suicide-rate-of-native-american-children/2014/03/09/6e0ad9b2-9f03-11e3-b8d8-94577ff66b28_story. html?utm_term=.35de987043f2.

Huff, Delores J. *To Live Heroically: Institutional Racism and American Indian Education.* Albany: State University of New York Press, 1997.

Human Rights Watch. "Callous and Cruel: Use of Force Against Inmates with Mental Disabilities in U.S. Jails and Prisons," May 12, 2015. https://www.hrw.org/report/2015/05/12/callous-and-cruel/use-force-against-inmates-mental-disabilities-us-jails-and.

———. "Prisoner Abuse: How Different are U.S. Prisons?" May 13, 2004. https://www.hrw.org/news/2004/05/13/prisoner-abuse-how-different-are-us-prisons.

Hunter, Noel, and William Schultz. "White Paper: Brain Scan Research." *Ethical Human Psychology and Psychiatry* 18, no. 1 (2015): 9–19. https://doi.org/10.1891/1559-4343.18.1.9.

Hunter, Walter S., and Eloise Sommermier. "The Relation of Degree of Indian Blood to Score on the Otis Intelligence Test." *Journal of Comparative Psychology* 2, no. 3 (1921): 257–77. https://doi.org/10.1037/h0071783.

Huo, Bing-Xing, Jared B. Smith, and Patrick J. Drew. "Neurovascular Coupling and Decoupling in the Cortex During Voluntary Locomotion." *Journal of Neuroscience* 34, no. 33 (August 13, 2014): 10975–81. https://doi.org/10.1523/JNEUROSCI.1369-14.2014.

Hurd, Ellen Dement. "Rebuilding a Nation: Cherokee Tribal Architecture, 1839–1907." Master's thesis in architecture, University of Washington, 2019.

Huston, Robert M., ed. "Exemption of the Cherokee Indians and Africans from Insanity." In *The Medical Examiner*, vol. 1. Philadelphia: Lindsay and Blackinston, 1845.

Indian Health Service. *American Indian/Alaska Native Behavioral Health Briefing Book.* U.S. Department of Health and Human Services, Public Health Service, Division of Behavioral Health, Office of Clinical and Preventive Services. Rockville, MD: Indian Health Service, August 2011. hhttps://www.ihs.gov/newsroom/includes/themes/newihstheme/display_objects/documents/2011_Letters/AIANBHBriefingBook.pdf.

———. "American Indian/Alaska Native National Behavioral Health Strategic Plan, 2011–2015" U.S. Department of Health and Human Services, Public Health Service, Division of Behavioral Health. August 2011. https://www.nihb.org/docs/08072012/AIANNationalBHStrategicPlan.pdf.

———. "Assessment and Reassessment Tools." n.d., accessed December 10, 2018. https://www.ihs.gov/painmanagement/properpatientassessment/reassessment/.

———. *Indian Health Manual.* Part 3: Professional Services, Chapter 14: Mental Health Program. U.S. Department of Health and Human Services, Public Health Service. https://www.ihs.gov/ihm/index.cfm?module=dsp_ihm_pc_p3c14.

———. *Trends in Indian Health, 2014.* U.S. Department of Health and Human Services, Public Health Service, Office of Public Health Support, Division of Program Statistics. Rockville, MD: US Government Printing Office, 2014.

Inner Compass Initiative. Website. https://www.theinnercompass.org/.

Insel, Thomas. "Transforming Diagnosis." Director's Blog/posts from 2013 (blog), National Institute of Mental Health, April 29, 2013. http://psychrights.org/2013/130429NIMHTransformingDiagnosis.htm.

———. "Words Matter." Director's Blog/posts from 2013 (blog), National Institute of Mental Health, October 2, 2019. https://www.nyaprs.org/e-news-bulletins/2012/nimh-director-ptsd-is-an-injury-not-disorder.

Institute of Medicine. *Reducing Suicide: A National Imperative.* Washington, DC: National Academies Press, 2002. https://doi.org/10.17226/10398.

Isacsson, Göran, Charles L. Rich, Jon Jureidini, and Melissa Raven. "The Increased Use of Antidepressants Has Contributed to the Worldwide Reduction in Suicide Rates." *British Journal of Psychiatry* 196, no. 6 (June 2010): 429–33. doi: 10.1192/bjp.bp.109.076166.

Isenberg, Nancy. *White Trash: The 400-Year Untold Story of Class in America.* New York: Penguin, 2016.

Jackson, Andrew. "Second Annual Message of President Andrew Jackson (December 6, 1830)." In James Richardson, ed., *A Compilation of the Messages and Papers of the Presidents, 1789–1897,* vol. 3 (New York: Bureau of National Literature, 1897): 1084, 1086.

Jackson, John C. *A Little War of Destiny: The First Regiment of Oregon Mounted Volunteers and the Yakima Indian War of 1855–1856.* Fairfield, WA: Ye Galleon Press, 1996.

Jacob, Michelle M. "Claiming Health and Culture as Human Rights: Yakama Feminism in Daily Practice." *International Feminist Journal of Politics* 12, nos. 3–4 (November 2010): 361–80. https://doi.org/10.1080/14616742.2010.513106.

Jacobs, Douglas G., Ross J. Baldessarini, Yeates Conwell, Jan A. Fawcett, Leslie Horton, Herbert Meltzer, Cynthia R. Pfeffer, and Robert I. Simon. "Practice Guideline for the Assessment and Treatment of Patients with Suicidal Behaviors." Work Group on Suicidal Behaviors, American Psychiatric Association, 2010. https://psychiatryonline.org/pb/assets/raw/sitewide/practice_guidelines/guidelines/suicide.pdf.

Jamieson, Elmer, and Peter Sandiford. "The Mental Capacity of Southern Ontario Indians." *Journal of Educational Psychology* 19, no. 8 (1928): 536–51. https://doi.org/10.1037/h0073482.

Jaynes, Gerald D., ed. "Native Americans and African Americans." In *Encyclopedia of African American Society.* Thousand Oaks, CA: Sage, 2005.

Jelliffe, Smith Ely and William A. White. *Diseases of the Nervous System: A Text-Book of Neurology and Psychiatry.* Philadelphia: Lea & Febiger, 1917.

Johnstone, Lucy. *A Straight Talking Introduction to Psychiatric Diagnosis.* London: PCCS Books, 2014.

Johnstone, Lucy, and Mary Boyle. *A Straight Talking Introduction to the Power Threat Meaning Framework: An Alternative to Psychiatric Diagnosis.* Monmouth, UK: PCCS Books, 2020.

Johnstone, Lucy, and Mary Boyle, with John Cromby, Jacqui Dillon, David Harper, Peter Kinderman, Eleanor Longden, David Pilgrim, and John Read. *The Power Threat Meaning Framework: Overview.* Leicester, UK: British Psychological Society, 2018. https://cms.bps.org.uk/sites/default/files/2022-07/PTM%20Framework%20%28January%202018%29_0.pdf.

Johnston-Goodstar, Katie, and Ross VeLure Roholt. "'Our Kids Aren't Dropping Out; They're Being Pushed Out': Native American Students and Racial Microaggressions in Schools." *Journal of Ethnic and Cultural Diversity in Social Work* 26, nos. 1–2 (February 10, 2017): 30–47. https://doi.org/10.1080/15313204.2016.1263818.

Jones, Trevor M. "Pegg, Thomas (1806–1866)." *The Encyclopedia of Oklahoma History and Culture.* Oklahoma Historical Society, n.d. https://www.okhistory.org/publications /enc/entry.php?entry=PE008.

Joseph, Jay. *The Missing Gene: Psychiatry, Heredity and the Fruitless Search for Genes.* New York: Algora Publishing, 2006.

———. "The Trouble with Twin Studies." *Mad in America.* March 13, 2013. https://www. madinamerica.com/2013/03/the-trouble-with-twin-studies/.

Josephy, Alvin. *The Nez Perce Indians and the Opening of the Northwest.* New York: Houghton Mifflin, 1997.

Joubert, Callie. "Are Mental Disorders Brain Disorders?" *Ethical Human Psychology and Psychiatry* 17, no. 3 (May 2016): 185–201. https://doi.org/10.1891/1559-4343.17.3.185.

Jung, Carl. *The Collected Works of C. G. Jung,* vol. 10: "Civilization in Transition." Eds. Sir Herbert Read, Michael Fordham, and Gerhard Adle. Princeton, NJ: Princeton University Press, 1970.

Kamin, Leo J. "Some Historical Facts About I.Q. Testing." In *Intelligence: The Battle for the Mind.* H. J. Eysenck and Leon J. Kamin, eds. London: Macmillan, 1981.

Kanno, Hanae, Yoon Mi Kim, and Monique Constance-Huggins. "Risk and Protective Factors of Secondary Traumatic Stress in Social Workers Responding to the Great East Japan Earthquake." *Social Development Issues* 38, no. 3 (November 2016): 64–78.

Karlberg, Michael. "The Power of Discourse and the Discourse of Power: Pursuing Peace Through Discourse Intervention." *International Journal of Peace Studies* 10, no. 1 (Spring/Summer 2005): 1–25. https://www3.gmu.edu/programs/icar/ijps/ vol10_1/Karlberg_101IJPS.pdf.

Kaufman, Scott Barry. "The Flynn Effect and IQ Disparities Among Races, Ethnicities, and Nations: Are There Common Links?" IQ's Corner, website blog, August 23, 2010. http://www.iqscorner.com/2010/08/flynn-effect-and-iq-disparities-among.html.

Kavanaugh, Patrick B. "Developing Competencies in the Destruction of Psychoanalysis: Political, Pedagogical, and Practice Philosophies." *Other/Wise* (online journal of the International Forum for Psychoanalytic Education), September 15, 2010. https://ifpe.wordpress.com/2010/09/15/developing-competencies/.

———. *Stories from the Bog: On Madness, Philosophy, and Psychoanalysis.* Amsterdam: Rodopi, 2012.

Kawa, Shadia, and James Giordano. "A Brief Historicity of the Diagnostic and Statistical Manual of Mental Disorders: Issues and Implications for the Future of Psychiatric Canon and Practice." *Philosophy, Ethics, and Humanities in Medicine* 7, no. 2 (January 2012): 1–9. https://www.ncbi.nlm.nih.gov/pmc/articles/PMC3282636/ pdf/1747-5341-7-2.pdf.

Keifer, Sarah Jane Harris. *Genealogical and Biographical Sketches of the New Jersey Branch of the Harris Family in the United States.* Madison, WI: Democrat Printing, 1888.

Kelly, John. "Lawsuit over Psychotropics and Foster Youth Will Move Forward," *Imprint* (January 12, 2018). https://imprintnews.org/child-welfare-2/missouri-lawsuit-psychotropics-foster-youth-will-move-forward.

Kennedy, Kelsey. "A Community Action Research Approach to Youth Suicide Prevention at Yakama Nation." PsyD diss., Washington School of Professional Psychology, Seattle, Washington, 2012.

Kerr, James Manford. *The Codes of California: As Amended and in Force at the Close of the Forty-Third[–Forty-Fourth] Session of the Legislature.* San Francisco: Bender-Moss, 1922.

Kershner, Seth, and Scott Harding. "Do Military Recruiters Belong in Schools?" *EducationWeek*, October 27, 2015. https://www.edweek.org/ew/articles/2015/10/28/do-military-recruiters-belong-in-schools.html.

Kersting, K. "Suicide Prevention Efforts Needed, American Indian Psychologist Tells Policy-Makers." *Monitor on Psychology* 36, no. 8 (September 2005): 12. https://www.apa.org/monitor/sep05/suicide.aspx.

Kimmerer, Robin Wall. *Braiding Sweetgrass: Indigenous Wisdom, Scientific Knowledge, and the Teaching of the Plains.* Minneapolis: Milkweed Editions, 2013.

Kirmayer, Laurence J., Joseph P. Gone, and Joshua Moses. "Rethinking Historical Trauma." *Transcultural Psychiatry* 51, no. 3 (June 2014): 299–319. https://doi.org/10.1177/1363461514536358.

Kirsch, Irving. *The Emperor's New Drugs: Exploding the Antidepressant Myth.* New York: Basic Books, 2010.

Klineberg, Otto. *Race Differences.* New York: Harper & Brothers, 1935.

———. "Racial Differences in Speed and Accuracy." *Journal of Abnormal and Social Psychology* 22, no. 3 (1927): 273–77. https://doi.org/10.1037/h0074665.

Knapp, Samuel L., ed. *Library of American History: A Reprint of Standard Works; Connected by Editorial Remarks, Abounding with Copious Notes, Biographical Sketches, and Miscellaneous Matter, Intended to Give the Reader a Full View of American History, Colonial and National,* vol. 1. New York: J. C. Riker, 1839.

Koerth, Maggie. "Police Violence Against Native Americans Goes Far Beyond Standing Rock." FiveThirtyEight, December 2, 2016, updated December 5, 2016. https://fivethirtyeight.com/features/police-violence-against-native-americans-goes-far-beyond-standing-rock/.

Krisch Joshua A. "Putting a Racist Myth To Bed: American Indians Don't Drink More." *Vocativ*, March 1, 2016. http://www.vocativ.com/291393/american-indian-alcohol/index.html.

Kroenke, Kurt, Robert L. Spitzer, and Janet Williams. "The PHQ-9: Validity of a Brief Depression Severity Measure." *Journal of General Internal Medicine* 16, no. 9 (September 2001): 606–13. https://www.ihs.gov/crs/includes/themes/responsive2017/display_objects/documents/phq_9.pdf.

Krona, Rochelle. "World War II and Japanese Internment in the *Seattle Star,*" Seattle Civil Rights & Labor History Project, University of Washington, 2008, http://depts.washington.edu/civilr/news_seattle_star.htm.

Krystal, Henry, and William Niederland. *Psychic Traumatization: After-Effects in Individuals and Communities.* Boston: Little, Brown, 1971.

Kühl, Stefan. *The Nazi Connection: Eugenics, American Racism, and German National Socialism.* New York: Oxford University Press, 1994.

Kupfer, David. "Chair of DSM-5 Task Force Discusses Future of Mental Health Research." American Psychiatric Association, press release, May 3, 2013. https://www.madinamerica.com/wp-content/uploads/2013/05/Statement-from-dsm-chair-david-kupfer-md.pdf.

Laing, R. D. *The Politics of Experience.* New York: Pantheon, 1983.

Lakusiak, Mike, Erin Vogel-Fox, Courtney Columbus, and Marianna Hauglie. "Native

Americans Still Fight for Voting Equality." News21, August 20, 2016. https://votingwars.news21.com/native-americans-still-fight-for-voting-equality/.

Lame Deer, John (Fire), and Richard Erdoes. *Lame Deer, Seeker of Visions*. New York: Touchstone, 1972.

Laughlin, Harry H. *The Legal Status of Eugenical Sterilization: History and Analysis Under the Virginia Sterilization Statute, Which Led to a Decision of the Supreme Court of the United States*. Chicago: Fred J. Ringley, 1930.

Lawrence, Jane. "The Indian Health Service and the Sterilization of Native American Women." *American Indian Quarterly* 24, no. 3 (2000): 400–419. http://www.jstor.org/stable/1185911.

Leahy, Todd E. *They Called It Madness: The Canton Asylum for Insane Indians, 1899–1934*. Baltimore: PublishAmerica, 2009.

Lehrner, Amy, and Rachel Yehuda. "Trauma Across Generations and Paths to Adaptation and Resilience." *Psychological Trauma: Theory, Research, Practice, and Policy* 10, no. 1 (2018): 22–29. https://doi.org/10.1037/tra0000302.

LeMay, Konnie. "A Brief History of American Indian Military Service." *Indian Country Today*, May 28, 2012. https://indiancountrytoday.com/archive/a-brief-history-of-american-indian-military-service.

Lemkau, Paul Victor. *Mental Hygiene in Public Health*. New York: McGraw-Hill, 1949.

Leon, Robert. "Mental Health Considerations in the Indian Boarding School Program," in J. C. Cobb, ed., *Emotional Problems of Indian Students in Boarding Schools and Related Public Schools, Workshop Proceedings*. Washington, DC: Bureau of Indian Affairs, 1960, 13–17. https://files.eric.ed.gov/fulltext/ED047848.pdf.

Leonard, Elise. "ADHD Update and Focus on Learning Disabilities." Webinar via Indian Health Service at Phoenix Indian Medical Center, April 2013. https://www.ihs.gov/telebehavioral/includes/themes/newihstheme/display_objects/documents/slides/childmentalhealth/adhdlearning0413.pdf.

Leventhal, John M. and Richard D. Krugman. "'The Battered-Child Syndrome' 50 Years Later: Much Accomplished, Much Left to Do," *Journal of the American Medical Association* 308, no. 1 (July 2012): 35–36. https://doi.org/10.1001/jama.2012.6416.

Levin, Aaron, "MH Care of American Indian, Alaskan Native, and Native Hawaiian Population Has Long History, Uncertain Future." *Psychiatric News* 54, no. 13, July 1, 2019. https://doi.org/10.1176/appi.pn.2019.7a26.

Levine, Bruce E. *Commonsense Rebellion: Taking Back Your Life from Drugs, Shrinks, Corporations, and a World Gone Crazy*. New York: Continuum, 2003.

———. *Resisting Illegitimate Authority: A Thinking Person's Guide to Being an Anti-Authoritarian—Strategies, Tools, and Models*. Chico, CA: AK Press, 2018.

———. *Surviving America's Depression Epidemic: How to Find Morale, Energy, and Community in a World Gone Crazy*. White River Junction, VT: Chelsea Green Publishing, 2007.

Leustig, Jack. *500 Nations*. Season 1, Episode 6 "Removal" script. 1995. https://www.springfieldspringfield.co.uk/view_episode_scripts.php?tv-show=500-nations-1995&episode=s01e06.

Lewis, Jason E., David DeGusta, Marc R. Meyer, Janet M. Monge, Alan E. Mann, and Ralph L. Holloway. "The Mismeasure of Science: Stephen Jay Gould versus Samuel George Morton on Skulls and Bias." *PLoS Biology* 9, no. 6 (2011). https://doi.org/10.1371/journal.pbio.1001071.

Lifton, Robert Jay. *Home from the War: Vietnam Veterans Neither Victims nor Executioners.* New York: Simon & Schuster, 1973.

"Lightner Witmer and the Beginning of Clinical Psychology." University of Pennsylvania. Accessed August 6, 2022. www.psych.upenn.edu/history/witmertext.htm.

Linton, Kristen F., and Bum Jung Kim. "Traumatic Brain Injury as a Result of Violence in Native American and Black Communities Spanning from Childhood to Older Adulthood." *Brain Injury* 28, no. 8 (April 2014): 1076–108. https://doi.org/10.3 109/02699052.2014.901558.

"Little-Known Trail of Tears Segment 'Rediscovered.'" *Indian Country Today.* September 20, 2012, updated September 13, 2018. https://indiancountrytoday.com/archive/little-known-trail-of-tears-segment-rediscovered.

Lomawaima, K. Tsianina. *They Called It Prairie Light: The Story of Chiloco Indian School.* Lincoln: University of Nebraska Press, 1994.

Lombardo, Paul A. "The Father of Carrie Buck's Child." undated webinar video clip and transcript, Cold Spring Harbor Laboratory, DNA Learning Center. https://dnalc. cshl.edu/view/15235-The-father-of-Carrie-Buck-s-child-Paul-Lombardo.html.

———. "The Rape of Carrie Buck." Undated webinar video clip and transcript, Cold Spring Harbor Laboratory, DNA Learning Center. https://dnalc.cshl.edu/view/15234-The-rape-of-Carrie-Buck-Paul-Lombardo.html.

———. "Three Generations, No Imbeciles: New Light on *Buck v. Bell.*" *New York University Law Review* 60, no. 1 (April 1985): 30–62. https://pubmed.ncbi.nlm.nih. gov/11658945/.

Long Standing Bear Chief. *Ni-Kso-Ko-Wah: Blackfoot Spirituality, Traditions, Values and Beliefs.* Browning, MT: Spirit Talk Press, 1992.

López-Muñoz, Francisco, Ronaldo Ucha-Udabe, and Cecilio Alamo. "The History of Barbiturates a Century After Their Clinical Introduction." *Neuropsychiatric Disease and Treatment* 1, no. 4 (December 2005): 329–43. https://www.dovepress. com/the-history-of-barbiturates-a-century-after-their-clinical-introductio-peer-reviewed-fulltext-article-NDT.

Loppie, Charlotte. "Learning from the Grandmothers: Incorporating Indigenous Principles into Qualitative Research." *Qualitative Health Research* 17, no. 2 (February 2007). https://doi.org/10.1177/1049732306297905.

"Lynch Calls Piestewa 'Hero' at House Hearing." Indianz.com. April 25, 2007. https://www.indianz.com/News/2007/04/25/lynch_calls_pie.asp.

Machisa, Mercilene T., Nicola Christofides, and Rachel Jewkes. "Structural Pathways between Child Abuse, Poor Mental Health Outcomes and Male-Perpetrated Intimate Partner Violence (IPV)." *PLOS One* (March 17, 2016). https://doi. org/10.1371/journal.pone.0150986.

MacLean, Alair, and Nicholas L. Parsons. "Unequal Risk: Combat Occupations in the Volunteer Military," *Sociological Perspectives* 53, no. 3 (September 2010): 347–72, https://doi.org/10.1525/sop.2010.53.3.347, https://www.ncbi.nlm.nih.gov/pmc/articles/PMC3117469/pdf/nihms-302467.pdf.

MacPherson, James. "North Dakota Oil Pipeline Protest Turns Violent." *Denver Post,* September 16, 2016. http://www.denverpost.com/2016/09/06/north-dakota-oil-pipeline-protest-turns-violent/.

Malcolm, Janet A. *In the Freud Archives.* New York: New York Review Classic Books, 1983/2000.

Marek, Scott, Brenden Tervo-Clemmons, Finnegan J. Calabro, David F. Montez, Benjamin P. Kay, Alexander S. Hatoum, Meghan Rose Donohue, et al. "Reproducible Brain-wide Association Studies Require Thousands of Individuals." *Nature* 603 (March 24, 2022) 654–660. https://doi.org/10.1038/s41586-022-04492-9.

Marks, Jonathan, and Brett Lee Shelton. "Genetic Markers Not a Valid Test of Native Identity." Indigenous Peoples Council on Biocolonialism. http://www.ipcb.org/publications/briefing_papers/files/identity.html.

Marshall, Randall D., Richard A. Bryant, Lawrence Amsel, Eun Jung Suh, Joan M. Cook, and Yuval Neria. "The Psychology of Ongoing Threat: Relative Risk Appraisal, the September 11 Attacks, and Terrorism-Related Fears." *American Psychologist* 62, no. 4 (2007): 304–16. https://doi.org/10.1037/0003-066X.62.4.304.

MacNeill, Leigha A., and Koraly Pérez-Edgar. "Temperament & Emotion." In Stephen Hupp and Jeremy D. Jewell, eds., *The Encyclopedia of Child and Adolescent Development*, (Hoboken, NJ: John Wiley & Sons, Inc., 2020). https://doi.org/10.1002/9781119171492.wecad180.

Martin, Jack. "Positivism, Quantification, and the Phenomena of Psychology." *Theory and Psychology* 13, no. 1 (2003): 33–38. https://doi.org/10.1177/0959354303013001760.

Martín-Baró, Ignacio. *Writings for a Liberation Psychology*. Cambridge, MA: Harvard University Press, 1994.

Mathur, Maya B., Elissa Epel, Shelley Kind, Manisha Desai, Christine G. Parks, Dale P. Sandler, and Nayer Khazeni. "Perceived Stress and Telomere Length: A Systematic Review, Meta-Analysis, and Methodologic Considerations for Advancing the Field." *Brain, Behavior, and Immunity* 54 (May 2006): 158–69. https://doi.org/10.1016/j.bbi.2016.02.002.

Matz, Lora. "Fishing for Fallen Light." *Stillpoint*. n.d. https://stillpointmag.org/articles/fishing-for-fallen-light/.

Mayes, Rick, and Alan V. Horwitz. "DSM-III and the Revolution in the Classification of Mental Illness." *Journal of the History of the Behavioral Sciences* 41, no. 3 (Summer 2005): 249–67. https://doi.org/10.1002 /jhbs.20103.

McChesney, Charles. "Onondaga Nation Leaders Blast 'Geronimo' Codename for Bin Laden." *Syracuse Post-Standard* (May 4, 2011). https://www.syracuse.com/news/2011/05/onondaga_nation_leaders_blast.html.

McClure, J. Derrick. "The Scots Among the Indians." In Donna L. Potts and Amy D. Unsworth, eds., *Region, Nation, Frontiers: Proceedings from the 11th International Region and Nation Literature Association Conference*. Newcastle, UK: Cambridge Scholars Publishing, 2008.

McDonald, Scott D., Jean C. Beckham, Rajendra A. Morey, and Patrick S. Calhoun. "The Validity and Diagnostic Efficiency of the Davidson Trauma Scale in Military Veterans Who Have Served Since September 11th, 2001," *Journal of Anxiety Disorders* 23, no. 2 (March 2009): 247–55. https://doi.org/10.1016/j.janxdis.2008.07.007.

McDonnell, Janet. "Competency Commissions and Indian Land Policy, 1913–1920." *South Dakota History* 11, no. 1 (Winter 1980): 21–34. https://www.sdhspress.com/journal/south-dakota-history-11-1/competency-commissions-and-indian-land-policy-1913-1920.

McLaren, Niall. "Psychiatry as Bullshit." *Ethical Human Psychology and Psychiatry* 18, no. 1 (2016): 48–57. https://doi.org/10.1891/1559-4343.18.1.48.

McLoughlin, William G. *Champions of the Cherokees: Evan and John B. Jones*. Princeton, NJ: Princeton University Press, 1990.

———. *Cherokees and Missionaries, 1789–1839*. New Haven, CT: Yale University Press, 1984.

McWhorter, Lucullus V. *The Crime Against the Yakimas*. North Yakima, WA: Republic Print, 1913. https://lccn.loc.gov/13005569.

McWhorter, Lucullus V. and Su-el-lil, *Tragedy of the Wahk-shum: The Death of Andrew J. Bolon As Told by Su-el-lil, Eyewitness; Also, the Suicide of General George A. Custer, as Told by Owl Child, Eyewitness*. Issaquah, WA: Great Eagle Publishing, 1994.

Meltzer-Brody, Samantha, E. Churchill and Jonathan R.T. Davidson. "Derivation of the SPAN, a Brief Diagnostic Screening Test for Post-Traumatic Stress Disorder." *Psychiatry Research* 88, no. 1 (October 1999) 63–70. https://doi.org/10.1016/s0165-1781(99)00070-0.

Meriam, Lewis, et al. *The Problem of Indian Administration: Report of a Survey Made at the Request of Honorable Hubert Work, Secretary of the Interior, and Submitted to Him, February 21, 1928*. Baltimore: Johns Hopkins Press, 1928. https://narf.org/nill/documents/merriam/b_meriam_letter.pdf.

Meserve, John Bartlett. "Chief Lewis Downing and Chief Charles Thompson (Oochalata)." *Chronicles of Oklahoma* 16, no. 3 (September 1938): 322–32.

Metzger, Deena. www.deenametzger.net.

Mihesuah, Devon A. *Cultivating the Rosebuds: The Education of Women at the Cherokee Female Seminary, 1851–1909*. Chicago: University of Illinois Press, 1998.

Miller, Mark F. "Henderson, Richard." NCpedia (State Library of North Carolina), 1988. https://www.ncpedia.org/biography/henderson-richard.

Milner, Paul. "Irish Immigration to North America: Before, During, and After the Famine." Accessed June 15, 2018. http://broadcast.lds.org/elearning/FHD/Community/en/Community/Paul_Milner/Irish_Migration_to_NA-2011.pdf.

Miner, H. Craig. "Dennis Bushyhead." in R. David Edmunds, ed., *American Indian Leaders: Studies in Diversity*. Lincoln: University of Nebraska Press, 1980.

Minges, Patrick N. "The Keetoowah Society and the Avocation of Religious Nationalism in the Cherokee Nation, 1855–1867." Dissertation, Union Theological Seminary in the City of New York, US Data Repository, US GenNet, Inc. (1998). www.usdata.org/us/minges/keetoodi.html.

———. *Slavery in the Cherokee Nation: The Keetoowah Society and the Defining of a People, 1855–1867*. New York: Routledge, 2003.

Minton, Todd D., Susan Brumbaugh, and Harley Rohlof. "American Indian and Alaska Natives in Local Jails, 1999–2014." U.S. Department of Justice, Office of Justice Programs, Bureau of Justice Statistics. NCJ 250652, September 2017. https://www.bjs.gov/content/pub/pdf/aianlj9914.pdf.

Mohagheghzadeha Abdolali, Pouya Faridi, Mohammadreza Shams-Ardakani, and Younes Ghasemi. "Medicinal Smokes." *Journal of Ethnopharmacology* 108, no. 2 (November 2006): 161–84. https://doi.org/10.1016/j.jep.2006.09.005.

Moncrieff, Joanna. *The Myth of the Chemical Cure: A Critique of Psychiatric Drug Treatment*. New York: Macmillan, 2007.

Monet, Jenni. "Linking Arms, Marching Forward: Cherokee Nation Accepts Ruling on Freedmen." *Indian Country Today*. September 1, 2017. https://indiancountrytoday.com/archive/cherokee-nation-accepts-ruling-freedmen.

Moore, David, and Don Coyhis. "The Multicultural Wellbriety Peer Recovery Support Program: Two Decades of Community-Based Recovery." *Alcoholism Treatment Quarterly* 28, no. 3 (July 2010): 273–92. https://doi.org/10.1080/07347324.20 10.488530.

Moore-Nall, Anita. "The Legacy of Uranium Development on or Near Indian Reservations and Health Implications Rekindling Public Awareness." *Geosciences* 5, no. 1 (February 3, 2015): 15–29. http://www.mdpi.com/2076-3263/5/1/15/htm.

Mora, Meike Shedden, Yvonne Nestoriuc, and Winfried Rief. "Lessons Learned from Placebo Groups in Antidepressant Trials." *Philosophical Transactions: Biological Sciences* 366, no. 1572 (June 27, 2011): 1879–88. https://doi.org/10.1098/rstb.2010.0394.

Morgan, Lewis Henry. *Ancient Society; or, Researches in the Lines of Human Progress from Savagery Through Barbarism to Civilization.* New York: Holt & Co, 1877.

———. *League of the Ho-dé-no-sau-nee or Iroquois.* New York: Dodd & Mead & Co, 1901.

Morton, Samuel George. "Account of a Craniological Collection, with remarks on the Classification of some Families of the Human Race." *Edinburgh New Philosophical Journal: Exhibiting a View of the Progressive Discoveries and Improvements in the Sciences and the Arts* 47, no. 93 (July 1849).

———. *Crania Americana; or, A Comparative View of the Skulls of Various Aboriginal Nations of North and South America: To Which is Prefixed an Essay on the Varieties of the Human Species.* Philadelphia: John Pennington, 1839.

Mourad, Suleiman A. "How the US Creates Terrorism." *Jacobin.* May 4, 2017. https://www.jacobinmag.com/2017/05/islamophobia-isis-al-qaeda-juan-cole.

Mullins, Jonita. "Three Forks History: Ross Was Arrested and Exiled from Indian Territory." *Muskogee Phoenix.* October 21, 2017. https://www.muskogeephoenix.com/news/three-forks-history-ross-was-arrested-and-exiled-from-indian/article_3bd97812-e0e1-52a5-bcbc-0fbce7a5ad27.html.

Murray, Charles. *Human Diversity: The Biology of Gender, Race, and Class.* New York: Twelve, 2020.

Myers, Gerald E. *William James: His Life and Thought.* New Haven, CT: Yale University Press, 1986.

Myers, Timothy, Emma Carey, and Dénes Szűcs. "Cognitive and Neural Correlates of Mathematical Giftedness in Adults and Children: A Review." *Frontiers in Psychology* 25, no. 8 (October 2017). https://doi.org/10.3389/fpsyg.2017.01646.

NARA (National Archives and Records Administration). Various items; see notes for details.

National Congress of American Indians. "Demographics." Updated June 1, 2020. http://www.ncai.org/about-tribes/demographics#R2.

———. "Every Native Vote Counts." n.d. http://www.ncai.org/initiatives/campaigns/NCAI_NativeVoteInfographic.pdf.

———. "Policy Insights Brief: Statistics on Violence Against Native Women." NCAI Policy Research Center. February 2013. http://www.ncai.org/attachments/PolicyPaper_tWAjznFslemhAffZgNGzHUqIWMRPkCDjpFtxeKEUVKjubxfpGYK_Policy%20Insights%20Brief_VAWA_020613.pdf.

———. "Policy Issues: Education." http://www.ncai.org/policy-issues/education-health-human-services/education.

National Indian Child Welfare Association. "What Is Disproportionality in Child Welfare?" 2017. https://www.nicwa.org/wp-content/uploads/2017/09 /Disproportionality-Table.pdf.

National Indigenous Women's Resource Center. "Honoring Missing and Murdered Indigenous Women." Webinar. May 5, 2017. https://www.niwrc.org/resources/ honoring-missing-and-murdered-indigenous-women.

National Public Radio. "Discrimination in America: Experiences and Views of Native Americans." With the Robert Wood Johnson Foundation and Harvard University T.H. Chan School of Public Health. November 2017. https://cdn1.sph.harvard. edu/wp-content/uploads/sites/94/2017/11/NPR-RWJF-HSPH-Discrimination -Native-Americans-Final-Report.pdf.

Native American Rights Fund. "South Dakota Voter Registration." Accessed 09/15/2022. https://www.narf.org/cases/south-dakota-voter-registration/.

Native History Association. "The Old Jefferson Site." Updated January 24, 2014, accessed June 15, 2018. http://www.nativehistoryassociation.org/old_jefferson.php.

Nautiyala, Chandra Shekhar, Puneet Singh Chauhana, and Yeshwant Laxman Nene. "Medicinal Smoke Reduces Airborne Bacteria." *Journal of Ethnopharmacology* 114, no. 3 (December 2007): 446–51. https://doi.org/10.1016/j.jep.2007.08.038.

Navey Jr., William R. "1838 Indian Removal, North Carolina Regiment Volunteers." North Carolina U.S. GENWEB Archives. http://files.usgwarchives.net/nc/statewide/ military/indian.txt.

Nelson, James M., and Brent D. Slife. "Theoretical and Epistemological Foundations." In Lisa J. Miller. ed., *Oxford Handbook of Psychology and Spirituality.* Oxford Library of Psychology. New York: Oxford University Press, 2012. https://doi. org/10.1093/oxfordhb/9780199729920.013.0002.

Newcomb, Michael D., and Thomas F. Locke. "Intergenerational Cycle of Maltreatment: A Popular Concept Obscured by Methodological Limitations." *Child Abuse & Neglect* 25, no. 9 (September 2001): 1219–40.

Newcomb, Steven. *Pagans in the Promised Land: Decoding the Doctrine of Christian Discovery.* Golden, CO: Fulcrum, 2008.

Newell, Margaret E. "The Changing Nature of Indian Slavery in New England, 1670–1720." in Colin G. Calloway and Neil Salisbury, eds., *Reinterpreting New England Indians and the Colonial Experience.* Boston: Colonial Society of Massachusetts, 2003. 106–36.

"News of the Oil Field." *Bartlesville (I.T.) Weekly Examiner* 9, no. 15 (June 20, 1903): 9, https://gateway.okhistory.org/ark:/67531/metadc143478/hits/?q=ross.

Newton County Historical Society. *McDonald and Newton County Sections of Goodspeed's Newton, Lawrence, Barry and McDonald Counties History.* Neosho, MO: Newton County Historical Society, 1888/1982.

Nezvalová-Henriksen, Kateřina, Olav Spigset, Ragnhild Eek Brandlistuen, Eivind Ystrom, Gideon Koren, and Hedvig Nordeng. "Effect of Prenatal Selective Serotonin Reuptake Inhibitor (SSRI) Exposure on Birthweight and Gestational Age: A Sibling-Controlled Cohort Study." *International Journal of Epidemiology* 45 (May 2016): 2018–29. https://doi.org/10.1093/ije/dyw049.

Nielsen, Margrethe, Ebba Holme Hansen, and Peter C. Gøtzsche. "Dependence and Withdrawal Reactions to Benzodiazepines and Selective Serotonin Reuptake Inhibitors. How Did the Health Authorities React?" *International Journal of*

Risk & Safety in Medicine 25, no. 3 (2013): 155–68. https://doi.org/10.3233/JRS-130594.

Noonan, Margaret E. "Mortality in State Prisons, 2001–2014—Statistical Tables." U.S. Department of Justice, Office of Justice Programs, Bureau of Justice Statistics. NCJ250150, December 2016, https://www.bjs.gov/content/pub/pdf/msp0114st.pdf.

Noonan, Margaret, Harley Rohloff, and Scott Ginder. "Mortality in Local Jails and State Prisons, 2000–2013—Statistical Tables." U.S. Department of Justice, Office of Justice Programs, Bureau of Justice Statistics. NCJ248756. August 2015. https://www.bjs.gov/content/pub/pdf/mljsp0013st.pdf.

Nørr, L., Bennedsen, B., Fedder, J., & Larsen, E.R. "Use of Selective Serotonin Reuptake Inhibitors Reduces Fertility in Men." *Andrology* 4, no. 3 (2016): 389–94. https://doi.org/10.1111/andr.12184.

Notturno, Mark Amadeus. "Do We Need a Second Order Science?" *Constructivist Foundations* 10, no. 1 (2014): 23–26.

O'Beirne, H. F. and E. S. *The Indian Territory: Its Chiefs, Legislators, and Leading Men.* St. Louis: C.B. Woodward Company, 1892.

"Obituary for Harold Ernest Long Standing Bear Chief Gray." September 28, 2010. *Great Falls (MT) Tribune.* http://www.legacy.com/obituaries/greatfallstribune/obituary.aspx?pid=145702059.

Oeser, Michael. "Avoiding Extinction, Preserving Culture: Sustainable, Sovereignty-Centered Tribal Citizenship Requirements." *North Dakota Law Review* 91, no. 1 (2015): 1–36. https://commons.und.edu/ndlr/vol91/iss1/1/.

Open Science Collaboration. "Estimating the Reproducibility of Psychological Science." *Science* 349: 6251. August 28, 2015. https://doi.org/10.1126/science.aac4716.

Owens, Louis. "Mapping, Naming, and the Power of Words." In *Mixedblood Messages: Literature, Film, Family, Place.* Norman: University of Oklahoma Press, 1998.

Parins, James W. *Elias Cornelius Boudinot: A Life on the Cherokee Border.* Lincoln, NE: University of Nebraska Press, 2006.

Paskell, Anthony. "Our Indian Children: What is Their Future?" *Monday Morning Magazine*, Birch Island Indian Day School, January 1968.

Pattison, E. Mansell. "Exorcism and Psychotherapy: A Case of Collaboration." In Richard H. Cox, ed., *Religious Systems and Psychotherapy.* Springfield, IL: Charles C. Thomas, 1973.

Payer, Lynn. *Medicine and Culture.* New York: Owl Books, 1996.

Pear, Robert. "M.D.'s Make Room for Others in Ranks of Psychoanalysts." *New York Times.* August 19, 1992. http://www.nytimes.com/1992/08/19/health/md-s-make-room-for-others-in-ranks-of-psychoanalysts.html?pagewanted=all.

Pearlin, Leonard I., and Alex Bierman. "Current Issues and Future Directions in Research into the Stress Process." In *Handbook of the Sociology of Mental Health*, 2nd ed. Carol S. Aneshensel, Jo C. Phelan, and Alex Bierman, eds. Dordrecht, Netherlands: Springer, 2013. https://doi.org/10.1007/978-94-007-4276-5_16.

Pearson, Karl. *The Life, Letters and Labours of Sir Francis Galton.* Volume 1 and 2. Cambridge, UK: Cambridge University Press, 1918, 1924.

Pember, Mary Annette. "*Indian Country Today* Hiatus Is a Blow to Nuanced Coverage of Indigenous Peoples." *Columbia Journalism Review.* September 6, 2017. https://www.cjr.org/united_states_project/indian-country-today-hiatus.php.

Perdue, Theda. *Slavery and the Evolution of Cherokee Society, 1540–1866.* Knoxville: University of Tennessee Press, 1979.

———. "Traditionalism in the Cherokee Nation: Resistance to the Constitution of 1827." *Georgia Historical Society Quarterly* 66, no. 2 (1982): 159–70. https://www.jstor.org/stable/40580890.

Pessah, Tom. "Violent Representations: Hostile Indians and Civilized Wars in Nineteenth-Century USA." *Ethnic and Racial Studies* 37, no. 9 (2014): 1628–45. https://doi.org/10.1080/01419870.2013.767918.

Petrina, Stephen. "The 'Never-To-Be-Forgotten Investigation': Luella W. Cole, Sidney L. Pressey, and Mental Surveying in Indiana, 1917–1921." *History of Psychology* 4, no. 3 (August 2001): 245–71. https://doi.org/10.1037//1093-4510.4.3.245.

Pfizer Incorporated. "Take this Posttraumatic Stress Disorder Quiz." 2001, author's personal collection.

Platoff, Emma. "5th Circuit Upholds Indian Child Welfare Act as Constitutional, Reversing Lower Court." *Texas Tribune,* August 12, 2019. https://www.texastribune.org/2019/08/10/5th-circuit-upholds-indian-child-welfare-act-constitutional-texas/.

Plöderl, Martin and Michael Hengartner. "Antidepressant Prescription Rates and Suicide Attempt Rates from 2004 to 2016 in a Nationally Representative Sample of Adolescents in the USA." *Epidemiology and Psychiatric Sciences* 28, no. 5 (2019): 589–91. https://doi.org/10.1017/S2045796018000136.

Plöderl, Martin, Michael P. Hengartner, Tom Bschor, and Jakob André Kaminski. "Commentary to 'Antidepressants and Suicidality:' A Re-Analysis of the Re-Analysis." *Journal of Affective Disorders* 273 (August 1, 2020): 252–53. https://doi.org/10.1016/j.jad.2020.04.025.

Pols, Hans. "Psychological Knowledge in a Colonial Context: Theories on the Nature of the 'Native Mind' in the Former Dutch East Indies." *History of Psychology* 10, no. 2 (May 2007): 111–31. https://doi.org/10.1037/1093-4510.10.2.111.

Porter, Tom. "Trump Pocahontas Slur: The President Has a Long History of Insulting Native Americans." *Newsweek,* November 28, 2017. http://www.newsweek.com/trump-pocahontas-slur-president-has-long-history-insulting-native-americans-724204.

Prucha, Francis Paul. *Documents of United States Indian Policy,* 3rd ed. Lincoln: University of Nebraska Press, 2000.

Purnell, Sandra E. "Thought Reform, Coercion, and Persuasion: A Phenomenological Analysis." *Freedom of Speech Newsletter* 4, no. 2 (February 1978).

Putney, Diane. "Canton Asylum for Insane Indians: 1902–1934." *South Dakota History* 14 (1984): 1–30. https://www.sdhspress.com/journal/south-dakota-history-14-1/the-canton-asylum-for-insane-indians-1902-1934/vol-14-no-1-the-canton-asylum-for-insane-indians-1902-1934.pdf.

Quintyn, Conrad B. *The Existence or Non-Existence of Race?: Forensic Anthropology, Population Admixture, and the Future of Racial Classification in the U.S.* Amherst, NY: Teneo Press, 2010.

Ray, Isaac. *Mental Hygiene.* Boston: Ticknor and Fields, 1863.

Reddish, Jennifer Gray. "Rockin' the Rez for Bay Mills Community College." *Tribal College Journal of American Indian Higher Education* 4, no. 2. May 15, 1992. http://www.tribalcollege journal.org/rockin-rez-bay-mills-community-college/.

Reed, Julie L. "A Nation's Charge: Cherokee Social Services, 1835–1907." PhD diss., University of North Carolina at Chapel Hill, 2011. https://cdr.lib.unc.edu/concern/dissertations/t435gf39d.

Reeves, Roy R., Mark E. Ladner, Roy H. Hart, and Randy S. Burke. "Nocebo Effects With Antidepressant Clinical Drug Trial Placebos." *General Hospital Psychiatry* 29, no. 3 (May–June 2007): 275–277. https://doi.org/10.1016/j.genhosppsych.2007.01.010.

Reflexive Democracy Campaign. "Who Leads Us?" New Organizing Institute: 2014. https://wholeads.us/research/who-leads-us-findings/.

Relander, Click. *Drummers and Dreamers.* Seattle: Northwest Interpretive Association, 1986.

Reuben, Suzanne H. *Facing Cancer in Indian Country: The Yakama Nation and Pacific Northwest Tribes.* President's Cancer Panel: 2002 Annual Report. Bethesda, MD: U.S. Department of Health and Human Services, December 2003. https://deainfo.nci.nih.gov/advisory/pcp/archive/pcp02rpt/YakamaBook.pdf.

Reynolds, William R. *The Cherokee Struggle to Maintain Identity in the 17th and 18th Centuries.* Jefferson, NC: McFarland, 2015.

Richards, Graham. *Race, Racism, and Psychology: Toward a Reflexive History.* New York: Routledge, 1997.

Riney, Scott. "Power and Powerlessness: The People of the Canton Asylum for Insane Indians." *South Dakota History* 27, no. 1–2 (1997): 41–64.

Robbins, Brent Dean, Sarah R. Kamens, and David N. Elkins. "DSM-5 Reform Efforts by the Society for Humanistic Psychology." *Journal of Humanistic Psychology* 57, no. 6 (2017): 602–24. https://doi.org/0.1177/0022167817698617.

Robbins, Rockey. "The Dream Catcher Meditation: A Therapeutic Technique Used with American Indian Adolescents." *American Indian and Alaska Native Mental Health Research* 10, no. 1 (2001): 51–65. https://doi.org/10.5820/aian.1001.2001.51.

Rockett, Ian, Gerry Hobbs, Diego De Leo, Steven Stack, James L. Frost, Alan M. Ducatman, Nestor Kapusta, and Rheeda L. Walker. "Suicide and Unintentional Poisoning Mortality Trends in the United States, 1987–2006: Two Unrelated Phenomena?" *BMC Public Health* 10: 705 (November 2010). https://doi.org/10.1186/1471-2458-10-705.

Rodwin, Marc A. "Conflicts of Interest, Institutional Corruption, and Pharma: An Agenda for Reform." *Journal of Law, Medicine, and Ethics* 40, no. 3 (2012): 511–22. https://doi.org/10.1111/j.1748-720X.2012.00683.x.

Rogers, Adam. "Star Neuroscientist Tom Insel Leaves the Google-Spawned Verily for ... a Startup?" *Wired*, May 11, 2017. https://www.wired.com/2017/05/star-neuroscientist-tom-insel-leaves-google-spawned-verily-startup/?mbid=social_twitter_onsiteshare.

Rogers, J. David, G. Paul Kemp, H. J. Bosworth, Jr, and Raymond B. Seed. "Interactions Between the US Army Corps of Engineers and the Orleans Levee Board Preceding the Drainage Canal Wall Failures and Catastrophic Flooding of New Orleans in 2005." *Water Policy* 17, no. 4 (August 2015): 707–23. https://doi.org/10.2166/wp.2015.077.

Rolater, Fred S. "The American Indian and the Origin of the Second American Party System." *Wisconsin Magazine of History* 76, no. 3 (Spring 1993): 180–203. https://content.wisconsinhistory.org/digital/collection/wmh/id/48235/rec/119.

Rolnick, Addie C. "Locked Up: Fear, Racism, Prison Economies and the Incarceration of Native Youth." *American Indian Culture and Research Journal* 40, no. 1 (2016): 55–92. https://doi.org/10.17953/aicrj.40.1.rolnick.

Romero-Briones, A-dae. "More At Stake Than Just Household SNAP Cuts." *Indian Country Today.* September 3, 2017. https://indiancountrytoday.com/archive/ stake-just-household-snap-cuts.

Rosay, André B. "Violence Against American Indian and Alaska Native Women and Men." https://www.ncjrs.gov/pdffiles1/nij/249822.pdf.

Ross, Rupert. *Returning to the Teachings: Exploring Aboriginal Justice.* Toronto: Penguin, 2006.

Ross, Steve. "The Yakima Terror," *Slate.* August 4, 2017. http://www.slate.com/articles/ news_and_politics/history/2017/08/ninety_years_ago_in_washington_a_ wave_o_anti_immigrant_sentiment_resulted.html.

Rowe, E. C. "Five Hundred Forty-Seven White and Two Hundred Sixty-Eight Indian Children Tested by the Binet-Simon Tests," *Pedagogical Seminary* 21 (1914): 454–68. https://doi.org/10.1080/08919402.1914.10532701.

Running Crane, Wendy. "Accurate Cultural Context for Indigenous Research: Emphasizing the Blackfeet." Chapter in unpublished manuscript. Joseph Stone and Robert Wise, eds., unpublished book on Indigenous historical trauma, 2012.

Rutecki, Gregory W. "Forced Sterilization of Native Americans: Later Twentieth Century Physician Cooperation with National Eugenic Policies?" *Ethics and Medicine* 27, no. 1 (Spring 2011): 33–42.

Saleeby, Caleb W. "The First Decade of Modern Eugenics." *Sociological Review* a7, no. 2 (1914), https://doi.org/10.1111/j.1467-954X.1914.tb02375.x.

Sandall, Roger. "Sir Francis Galton and the Roots of Eugenics." *Society* 45, no. 2 (March 2008): 170–76. https://doi.org/10.1007/s12115-008-9058-8.

"Sane Reds Confined in Asylum." *Helena (MT) Independent.* October 15, 1933.

Saretsky, Gary D. "Carl Campbell Brigham, the Native Intelligence Hypothesis, and the Scholastic Aptitude Test." Educational Testing Service, Princeton, NJ, Report No. ETS-RM-82-4, December 1982, https://archive.org/details/ERIC_ED237516/ mode/2up.

Satz, Ronald N. *American Indian Policy in the Jacksonian Era.* Norman: University of Oklahoma Press, 1975.

Saunt, Claudio. "The Paradox of Freedom: Tribal Sovereignty and Emancipation During the Reconstruction of Indian Territory." *Journal of Southern History* 70, no. 1 (February 2004): 63–94. https://doi.org/10.2307/27648312.

Savage, B. "Large Numbers of Natives Were Sterilized." *Alberta Native News* (June 1998).

Sayer, John William. *Ghost Dancing the Law: The Wounded Knee Trials.* Cambridge, MA: Harvard University Press, 1997.

"Says She Is a Queen." *Shreveport (LA) Progress.* October 23, 1897, 7.

Schilling, Vincent. "HERSTORY! Deb Haaland, Sharice Davids in Congress and Peggy Flanagan as Lt. Gov." *Indian Country Today* (November 7, 2018).

———. "High School Slammed for Its Mocking and Shocking 'Trail of Tears' Banner." *Indian Country Today*, November 19, 2013. https://indiancountrytoday.com/ archive/high-school-slammed-for-its-mocking-and-shocking-trail-of-tears- banner.

Schultz, Duane P., and Sydney Ellen Schultz. *A History of Modern Psychology.* Boston, MA: Cengage Learning, 2015.

Schuster, Helen Hersh. "Yakima Indian Traditionalism: A Study in Continuity and Change." PhD diss., University of Washington, December 19, 1974, 75–28. Ann Arbor, MI: Xerox University Microfilms, 1975.

Scorza, Pamela, Cristiane S. Duarte, Alison E. Hipwell, Jonathan Posner, Ana Ortin, Glorisa Canino, Catherine Monk, on behalf of Program Collaborators for Environmental Influences on Child Health Outcomes. "Research Review: Intergenerational Transmission of Disadvantage: Epigenetics and Parents' Childhoods as the First Exposure." *Journal of Child Psychology and Psychiatry* 60, no. 2 (2019): 119–132. https://doi.org/10.1111/jcpp.12877.

Selden, Steven. *Inheriting Shame: The Story of Eugenics and Racism in America.* New York: Teachers College Press, 1999.

Selye, Hans. *The Stress of Life.* New York: McGraw-Hill, 1956.

Shapiro, Francine. "The Role of Eye Movement Desensitization and Reprocessing (EMDR) Therapy in Medicine: Addressing the Psychological and Physical Symptoms Stemming from Adverse Life Experiences." *The Permanente Journal* 18, no. 1 (Winter 2014): 71–77. https://doi.org/0.7812/TPP/13-098.

Shapiro, Nina. "Nooksack Tribe Boots Out 300 Members, Faces Showdown with Feds." *Seattle Times*, November 23, 2016. http://www.seattletimes.com/seattle-news/northwest/nooksack-tribe-disenrolling-hundreds-in-high-stakes-showdown-with-feds/.

Shifrer, Dara. "Stigma of a Label: Educational Expectations for High School Students Labeled with Learning Disabilities." *Journal of Health and Social Behavior* 54, no. 4 (2013): 462–80. https://doi.org/10.1177/0022146513503346.

Shilow, Tiffany O. "New Youth Residential Counseling Home Takes Yakama Language, Teachings to Heart." *Yakama Nation Review*, October 1, 2004.

Sieff, Elaine. "Media Frames of Mental Illnesses: The Potential Impact of Negative Frames." *Journal of Mental Health* 12, Issue 3 (2003): 259–69. https://doi.org/10.1080/09 63823031000118249.

Simms, William Gilmore. *The Forayers, or The Raid of the Dog Days.* Fayetteville: University of Arkansas Press, 1855/2003.

Simons, Peter. "Debunking the Latest Gene Study." *Mad in America*, April 12, 2018. https://www.madinamerica.com/2018/04/debunking-the-latest-gene-study/.

Smith, Anna V. "5 Obstacles for Native Voters in the November Midterms." *High Country News*, October 16, 2018. https://www.hcn.org/articles/tribal-affairs-5-obstacles-for-native-voters-in-the-november-election.

Smith, James. *Away from Their Barbarous Influences: The Yakama Boarding School at Fort Simcoe.* Toppenish, WA: Yakama Nation Museum, 1993.

Smith, John Howard. *A Dream of the Judgment Day: American Millennialism and Apocalypticism, 1620–1890.* New York: Oxford University Press, 2021.

Smith, Matt and Aura Bogado. "Immigrant Children Forcibly Injected With Drugs at Texas Shelter, Lawsuit Claims." *Texas Tribune.* June 20, 2018 https://www.texastribune.org/2018/06/20/immigrant-children-forcibly-injected-drugs-lawsuit-claims/.

Smith, Ryan P. "How Native American Slaveholders Complicate the Trail of Tears Narrative." *Smithsonian*, March 6, 2018. https://www.smithsonianmag.com/smithsonian-institution/how-native-american-slaveholders-complicate-trail-tears-narrative-180968339/.

Snyderman, Mark, and Richard J. Hernstein. "Intelligence Tests and the Immigration Act of 1924." *American Psychologist* 38, no. 9 (1983): 986–95 https://doi.org/10.1037/0003-066X.38.9.986.

Sohappy, Corinna. "Testimony of Corinna Sohappy Before the United States Senate Finance Committee." September 21, 2004. https://www.finance.senate.gov/imo/media/doc/092104cstest.pdf.

Sokal, Michael M. "The Unpublished Autobiography of James McKeen Cattell." *American Psychologist* 26, no. 7 (July 1971): 626–35. https://doi.org/10.1037/h0032048.

Sørensen, Anders, Karsten Juhl Jørgensen and Klaus Munkholm. "Clinical Practice Guideline Recommendations on Tapering and Discontinuing Antidepressants for Depression: A Systematic Review." *Therapeutic Advances in Psychopharmacology* 12 (2022): 1–16. https://doi.org/10.1177/20451253211067656.

Sparks, Jacqueline A. "White Paper: Efficacy of Psychiatric Drugs." *Ethical Human Psychology and Psychiatry* 18, no. 1 (2016): 20–28. https://doi.org/10.1891/1559-4343.18.1.20.

Sparks, Jacqueline A., and Barry L. Duncan. "Outside the Black Box: Re-assessing Pediatric Antidepressant Prescription." *Journal of the Canadian Academy of Child & Adolescent Psychiatry* 22, no. 3 (August 2013): 240–46. https://www.cacap-acpea.org/wp-content/uploads/Black-Box-Sparks-1.pdf.

Speaks Lightning. *Indians of the Pacific States: A Winter Count of the Indian Nations of Washington, Oregon, and California.* Browning, MT: Spirit Talk Press, 1998.

Spier, Leslie. *The Prophet Dance of the Northwest and its Derivatives: The Source of the Ghost Dance.* Menasha, WI: George Banta, 1935.

Spitzer, R. I., J. B. W. Williams, M. L. Gibbons, and M. B. First. *Structured Clinical Interview for DSM-III-R.* Washington, DC: American Psychiatric Press, Inc., 1990.

Spurgeon, Sara. "'The Bomb was Like the Indians': Trickster Mimetics and Native Sovereignty in Martin Cruz Smith's *The Indians Won*." *American Quarterly* 66, no. 4 (December 2014). https://www.academia.edu/17872415/_The_Bomb_was_like_the_Indians_Trickster_Mimetics_and_Native_Sovereignty_in_Martin_Cruz_Smiths_The_Indians_Won.

Starr, Emmet. *History of the Cherokee Indians and Their Legends and Folklore.* Oklahoma City, OK: Warden Company, 1921.

State of Arizona, House of Representatives, 49th Legislature, 2nd Reg Session. "House Bill 2281." 2010. https://www.azleg.gov/legtext/49leg/2r/bills/hb2281s.pdf.

St. Charles, Joe, and Magda Costantino. *Reading and the Native American Learner: Research Report.* ED 451 026, RC 022 919. Olympia, WA: Washington Office of Superintendent of Public Instruction, Office of Indian Education, June 2000. https://files.eric.ed.gov/fulltext/ED451026.pdf.

Steen, Carl T. "The Home for the Insane, Deaf, Dumb and Blind of the Cherokee Nation." *Chronicle of Oklahoma* 21, no. 4 (December 1943): 402–19. https://gateway.okhistory.org/ark:/67531/metadc1827456/.

Stefan, Susan. "Protection Racket: Rape Trauma Syndrome, Psychiatric Labeling, and Law." *Northwestern University, School of Law Review* 88, no. 4 (1993): 1272–1319.

Stein, D. J., K. A. Phillips, D. Bolton, K. W. M. Fulford, J. Z. Sadler, and K. S. Kendler, "What Is a Mental/Psychiatric Disorder? From DSM-IV to DSM-V." *Psychological Medicine* 40, no. 11 (January 2010): 1759–65. https://doi.org/10.1017/S0033291709992261.

Steingard, Sandra. "Clinical Implications of the Drug-Centered Approach," in Sandra Steingard, ed., *Critical Psychiatry: Controversies and Clinical Implication*. New York: Springer, 2018.

Stewart, Edward C., and Milton J. Bennett. *American Cultural Patterns: A Cross-Cultural Pattern*. Boston: Intercultural Press, 2005.

Stolzer, Jeanne. "The ADHD Epidemic in America." *Ethical Human Psychology and Psychiatry* 9, no. 2 (June 2007): 37–44. https://doi.org/10.1891/152315007782021204.

Stone, Marc, Thomas Laughren, M. Lisa Jones, Mark Levenson, P. Chris Holland, Alice Hughes, Tarek A Hammad, Robert Temple, and George Rochester. "Risk of Suicidality in Clinical Trials of Antidepressants in Adults: Analysis of Proprietary Data Submitted to U.S. Food and Drug Administration." *British Medical Journal*, 339:b2880 (August 2009). https://doi.org/10.1136/bmj.b2880.

Stratton, Ray "The Cherokee National Insane Asylum." *Bulletin of the Menninger Clinic* 47, no. 3 (1983): 266–68.

Stremlau, Rose. *Sustaining the Cherokee Family: Kinship and the Allotment of an Indigenous Nation*. Chapel Hill: University of North Carolina Press, 2011.

Strickland, C. June. "Challenges in Community-Based Participatory Research Implementation: Experiences in Cancer Prevention with Pacific Northwest American Indian Tribes" *Cancer Control* 13, no. 3 (July 2006): 230–36. https://doi.org/10.1177/107327480601300312.

Strous, Rael D., Annette A. Opler, and Lewis A. Opler. "Reflections on 'Emil Kraepelin: Icon and Reality.'" *American Journal of Psychiatry* 173, no. 3 (March 2016): 300–301. https://doi.org/10.1176/appi.ajp.2016.15111414.

Sturges, J.A. *Illustrated History of McDonald County, Missouri: From the Earliest Settlement to the Present Time*. Pineville, MO: NP, 1897.

Substance Abuse and Mental Health Services Administration (SAMHSA). "Mental Health Essentials in Native Communities: A Guide for Grantees." May 2018. https://www.samhsa.gov/sites/default/files/sites/default/files/tttac-cy4-mental-health-fact-sheet-508-compliant.pdf.

Sullivan, Roy. *Killing Davy Crockett*. Bloomington, IN: AuthorHouse, 2017.

Summers, Alicia. *Disproportionality Rates for Children of Color in Foster Care (FY 2014): Technical Assistance Bulletin*. Reno, NV: National Council of Juvenile and Family Court Judges, 2016. http://www.ncjfcj.org/sites/default/files/NCJFCJ%20 2014%20Disproportionality%20TAB%20Final.pdf.

Supreme Court of Appeals of Virginia. *Carrie Buck v. Dr. J. H. Bell, Superintendent for State Colony for Epileptics and Feeble-Minded*. No. 1700, September Term 1925, 40–42.

Swaine, Jon, Oliver Laughland, Jamiles Lartey and Ciara McCarthy. "The Counted: People Killed by Police in the U.S." online database maintained by the *Guardian*. https://www.theguardian.com/us-news/ng-interactive/2015/jun/01/the-counted-police-killings-us-database.

Sweet, Victoria. "Trafficking in Native Communities." *Indian Country Today*, May 24, 2015. https://indiancountrytoday.com/archive/trafficking-in-native-communitie.

Swift, Vance E. "Hart, Nathaniel." NCpedia (State Library of North Carolina), 1988. https://www.ncpedia.org/biography/hart-nathaniel.

Szalavitz, Maia. "No, Native Americans Aren't Genetically More Susceptible to Alcoholism." *The Verge* (October 2, 2015). https://www.theverge.com/2015/10/2/9428659/firewater-racist-myth-alcoholism-native-americans.

Szasz, Thomas. *Ideology and Insanity: Essays on the Psychiatric Dehumanization of Man.* Syracuse, NY: Syracuse University Press, 1991.

Szlemko, William J., James W. Wood, and Pamela Jumper Thurman. "Native Americans and Alcohol: Past, Present, and Future." *Journal of General Psychology* 133, no. 4 (October 2006): 435–51.

Tamburello, Anthony. "Prescribed Medication Abuse: Limitless Creativity." Chapter 31 in *Oxford Textbook of Correctional Psychiatry*, edited by Robert L. Trestman, Kenneth L. Appelbaum, and Jeffrey L. Metzner. New York: Oxford University Press, 2015.

Taylor, Matthew J. "The Influence of Self-Efficacy on Alcohol Use Among American Indians." *Cultural Diversity and Ethnic Minority Psychology* 6, no. 2 (May 2000): 152–167. https://doi.org/10.1037//1099-9809.6.2.152.

Terman, Lewis. *The Measurement of Intelligence: An Explanation of and a Complete Guide for the Use of the Stanford Revision and Extension of the Binet-Simon Intelligence Scale.* Boston: Houghton Mifflin, 1916.

Texas Freedom Network Education Fund. "Writing to the Standards: Reviews of Proposed Social Studies Textbooks for Texas Public Schools." September 2014. http://tfn. org/cms/assets/uploads/2015/11/FINAL_executivesummary.pdf.

Thomson, Gerald. "'So Many Clever, Industrious, and Frugal Aliens': Peter Sandiford, Intelligence Testing, and Anti-Asian Sentiment in Vancouver Schools between 1920 and 1939." *BC Studies* 197 (Spring 2018), 67–100. https://doi.org/10.14288/bcs. v0i197.189756.

Thornton, Russell. *The Cherokees: A Population History.* Lincoln: University of Nebraska Press, 1992.

——— "On Demography and Genocide." *Reviews in American History* 44, no. 2 (June 2016).

Thrall, A. Trevor, and Erik Goepner. "Step Back: Lessons for U.S. Foreign Policy from the Failed War on Terror." *Policy Analysis* 814 (June 2017). https://object.cato.org/ sites/cato.org/files/pubs/pdf/pa-814.pdf.

Timimi, Sami, and Lewis Timimi. "The Social Construction of Attention Deficit Hyperactivity Disorder." In *The Palgrave Handbook of Child Mental Health.* London: Palgrave Macmillan, 2015. https://doi.org/10.1057/9781137428318_8.

Tolan, Sandy. "North Dakota Pipeline Activists Say Arrested Protesters Were Kept in Dog Kennels." *Los Angeles Times* (October 28, 2016). http://www.latimes.com/nation/ la-na-north-dakota-pipeline-20161028-story.html.

Tolson, Michelle. "Yakama Nation Fights for Nuclear Waste Cleanup at Hanford Site." *Earth Island Journal.* May 21, 2014. http://www.earthisland.org/journal/index. php/elist/eListRead/yakama_nation_fights_for_nuclear_waste_cleanup_at_ hanford_site/.

Torabi, Mohammad R., and Dong-Chul Seo. "National Study of Behavioral and Life Changes Since September 11." *Health Education and Behavior* 31, no. 2 (April 2004): 179–92. https://doi.org/10.1177/1090198103259183.

Torpy, Sally J. "Native American Women and Coerced Sterilization: On the Trail of Tears in the 1970s." *American Indian Culture and Research Journal* 24, no. 2 (2000): 1–22. https://doi.org/10.17953/aicr.24.2.7646013460646042.

Torreon, Barbara Salazar. "U.S. Periods of War and Dates of Recent Conflicts." Congressional Research Service. Version 31, updated June 5, 2020. https://fas.org/sgp/ crs/natsec/RS21405.pdf.

Torreon, Barbara Salazar, and Sofia Plagakis. "Instances of Use of United States Armed Forces Abroad, 1798–2017." Congressional Research Service, March 8, 2022. https://fas.org/sgp/crs/natsec/R42738.pdf.

Tower, Mike. *The Outlaw Statesman: The Life and Times of Fred Tecumseh Waite.* Bloomington, IN: AuthorHouse, 2007.

Trahan, Lisa, Karla K. Stuebing, Merril K. Hiscock, and Jack M. Fletcher. "The Flynn Effect: A Meta-Analysis." *Psychological Bulletin* 140, no. 5 (September 2014): 1332–60. https://doi.org/10.1037/a0037173.

Treffert, David. "Genetic Memory: How We Know Things We Never Learned." *Scientific American* blog post (January 28, 2015). https://blogs.scientificamerican.com/ guest-blog/genetic-memory-how-we-know-things-we-never-learned/.

Trumbull, Elise, and Sharon Nelson-Barber. "The Ongoing Quest for Culturally-Responsive Assessment for Indigenous Students in the U.S." *Frontiers in Education* 4: 40 (2019). https://doi.org/10.3389/feduc.2019.00040.

Turner, Erick H., Andrea Cipriani, Toshi A. Furukawa, Georgia Salanti, and Ymkje Anna de Vries. "Selective Publication of Antidepressant Trials and Its Influence on Apparent Efficacy: Updated Comparisons and Meta-Analyses of Newer Versus Older Trials." *PLOS Medicine* 10, no. 1 (January 2022). https://doi.org/10.1371/ journal.pmed.1003886.

Uebelacker, Morris L. *Time Ball: A Story of the Yakima People and the Land.* Yakima, WA: Yakima Nation, 1984.

Ulmer, Jeffrey T., and Mindy S. Bradley. "Punishment in Indian Country: Ironies of Federal Punishment of Native Americans." *Justice Quarterly* 35, no. 5 (July 2018): 751–81. https://doi.org/10.1080/07418825.2017.1341540.

Ulrich, Roberta. *Empty Nets: Indians, Dams, and the Columbia River, Second Edition, Culture and Environment in the Pacific West.* Corvallis: Oregon State University Press, 2007.

Umpleby, Stuart. "Second-Order Science: Logic, Strategies, Methods." *Constructivist Foundations* 10, no. 1 (November 15, 2014). https://constructivist.info/10/1/016. umpleby.

United Nations. "Analysis Framework." Office of the Special Adviser on the Prevention of Genocide. n.d. Accessed December 10, 2018. http://www.un.org/ar/preventgenocide /adviser/pdf/osapg_analysis_framework.pdf.

United Tribes Technical College. "WWI Era Native American Servicemen from North Dakota Tribes." n.d. https://bloximages.chicago2.vip.townnews.com/ bismarcktribune.com/content/tncms/assets/v3/editorial/9/2b/92b93d52-373d-5f5c-ba07-da5af84139c2/598cfff19ff22.pdf.

U.S. Board of Indian Commissioners. *Thirty-First Annual Report of the Board of Indian Commissioners to the Secretary of the Interior.* Washington, DC: U.S. Government Printing Office, 1899. http://images.library.wisc.edu/History/EFacs/CommRep/ AnnRep99p2/reference/history.annrep99p2.i0006.pdf.

U.S. Bureau of Indian Affairs. *Course of Study for the Indian Schools of the United States: Industrial and Literary.* Washington, DC: U.S. Government Printing Office, 1901. https://hdl.handle.net/2027/uiug.30112004348220.

U.S. Bureau of Labor. "Labor Force Characteristics by Race and Ethnicity, 2015." September 2016. https://www.bls.gov/opub/reports/race-and-ethnicity/2015/ home.htm.

U.S. Census Bureau. "American Indian and Alaska Native Heritage Month: November 2016." Profile America Facts for Features: CB16-FF.22. November 2016. https://www.census.gov/content/dam/Census/newsroom/facts-for-features/2016/cb26-ff22_aian.pdf.

———. "Annual Estimates of the Resident Population by Sex, Age, Race, and Hispanic Origin for the United States: April 1, 2010 to July 1, 2019." Table NC-EST2019-ASR6H. https://www2.census.gov/programs-surveys/popest/tables/2010-2019/national/asrh/nc-est2019-asr5h.xlsx.

U.S. Congress, "Misleading Information from the Battlefield: The Tillman and Lynch Episodes." U.S. House of Representatives, Union Calendar No. 555, Report 110-858 (Washington, DC: U.S. Government Printing Office, 2008), accessed August 20, 2022, https://www.congress.gov/110/crpt/hrpt858/CRPT-110hrpt858.pdf.

U.S. Department of Agriculture. "Biden-Harris Administration's Actions to Reduce Food Insecurity Amid the COVID-19 Crisis." Press release, March 3, 2021. https://www.usda.gov/media/press-releases/2021/03/03/biden-harris-administrations-actions-reduce-food-insecurity-amid.

U.S. Department of Energy. "Hanford Annual Site Environmental Report for Calendar Year 2018." Rev. 0. September 2019, https://hmis.hanford.gov/files.cfm/DOE-RL-2019-33_Rev0_public.pdf.

U.S. Department of Health and Human Services. *Mental Health: Culture, Race, and Ethnicity.* Public Health Service, U.S. Surgeon General. Washington DC: U.S. Government Printing Office, 2001. https://www.ncbi.nlm.nih.gov/books/NBK44243/.

U.S. Department of the Interior. "2013 American Indian Population and Labor Force Report." January 16, 2014. https://www.bia.gov/sites/bia.gov/files/assets/public/pdf/idc1-024782.pdf.

———. "Notice of Intent to Repatriate Cultural Items: Northwest Museum, Whitman College, Walla Walla, WA." National Park Service. *Federal Register* 73, no. 57 (August 13, 2008): 47235–36. https://www.gpo.gov/fdsys/pkg/FR-2008-08-13/pdf/E8-18677.pdf.

———. "Office of the U.S. Indian Inspector for Indian Territory. 1898–1907." Organization Authority Record. https://catalog.archives.gov/id/10560285?organization NaId=10453496.

U.S. Department of Veterans Affairs. "Psychological Trauma for American Indians Who Served in Vietnam." National Center for PTSD. https://www.ptsd.va.gov/professional/treat/type/vietnam_american_indians.asp.

U.S. Department of Veterans Affairs and U.S. Department of Defense. "VA/DoD Clinical Practice Guideline for the Assessment and Management of Patients at Risk for Suicide." Washington, DC. 2019. https://www.healthquality.va.gov/guidelines/MH/srb/VADoDSuicideRiskFullCPGFinal5088919.pdf.

U.S. District Court. *Wandering Medicine et al. v. McCulloch et al.* District of Montana, Billings Division. "Order Denying 3 Plaintiffs' Motion for Preliminary Injunction," Signed by Judge Richard F. Cebull, November 6, 2012. https://law.justia.com/cases/federal/district-courts/montana/mtdce/1:2012cv00135/42299/79/.

U.S. Food and Drug Administration. "Ortho Evra (Norelgestromin/Ethinyl Estradiol) Information." FDA (website) https://www.fda.gov/drugs/drugsafety/postmarketdrugsafetyinformationforpatientsandproviders/ucm110402.htm.

U.S. Senate. *Indian Education: A National Tragedy—A National Challenge.* Special Subcommittee on Indian Education. Washington: U.S. Government Printing Office, 1969. https://narf.org/nill/resources/education/reports/kennedy/toc.html.

———. "Reexamining the Substandard Quality of Indian Health Care in the Great Plains." Committee on Indian Affairs. 114th Congress, Second Session. Washington, DC: U.S. Government Printing Office, 2016. https://www.indian.senate.gov/sites/default/files/documents/CHRG-114shrg21662.pdf.

U.S. Supreme Court. "Cherokee Intermarriage Cases, 203 U.S. 76 (1906)." *United States Supreme Court Reports, Vol. 51.* Rochester, NY: Lawyer's Cooperative Publishing Company, 1921. https://supreme.justia.com/cases/federal/us/203/76/.

———. *Worcester v. Georgia.* 31 U.S. 515. January term, 1832. Accessed August 10, 2022. https://www.loc.gov/item/usrep031515/.

van der Kolk, Bessel A. and Rita Fisler. "Dissociation and the Fragmentary Nature of Traumatic Memories: Overview and Exploratory Study." *Journal of Traumatic Stress* 8, no. 4 (October 1995): 505–25. https://doi.org/10.1002/jts.2490080402.

van der Kolk, Bessel, and Onno Van Der Hart. "The Intrusive Past: The Flexibility of Memory and the Engraving of Trauma." *American Imago* 48, no. 4 (1991): 425–54.

Vanderwerth, W. C., compiler. *Indian Oratory: Famous Speeches by Noted Indian Chieftains.* Norman: University of Oklahoma Press, 1982.

Virginia Mason Memorial Hospital, Yakima, WA. "2016 Community Needs Assessment." https://www.yakimamemorial.org/pdf/about/community-hna-2016.pdf.

Volscho, Thomas W. "Racism and Disparities in Women's Use of the Depo-Provera Injection in the Contemporary USA." *Critical Sociology* 37, no. 5 (2011): 673–88. https://doi.org/10.1177/0896920510380948.

Walker, David Edward. "ADHD as the New 'Feeblemindedness' of American Indian Children." in Gwynned Lloyd, Joan Stead, and David Cohen, eds., *Critical New Perspectives on ADHD.* New York: Routledge, 2006, 66–82.

———. "Betrayal by Labels: The Feebleminded, ADHD Native Child." *Indian Country Today,* January 21, 2016. updated September 13, 2018. https://indiancountrymedianetwork.com/.culture/health-wellness/betrayal-by-labels-the-feebleminded-adhd-native-child/.

———. "How the US Mental Health System Makes Natives Sick and Suicidal." *Indian Country Today,* June 18, 2015. https://indiancountrymedianetwork.com/culture/health-wellness/how-the-us-mental-health-system-makes-natives-sick-and-suicidal/.

———. "The Indian Health Service's Psychiatric Drug Habit & the 'Heavy Influence of Biomedical Models.'" *Mad In America* (November 6, 2014). https://www.madinamerica.com/2014/11/indian-health-services-psychiatric-drug-habit-heavy-influence-biomedical-models/.

———. "'A Living Burial': Inside the Hiawatha Asylum for Insane Indians." *Indian Country Today,* November 9, 2015, updated September 13, 2018. https://indiancountrymedianetwork.com/culture/health-wellness/a-living-burial-inside-the-hiawatha-asylum-for-insane-indians/.

———. "Lunacy, Crazy Indians and the Witch's Hammer: Mental Health Care as Oppression." *Indian Country Today,* August 13, 2015. updated September 13, 2018. https://indiancountrytoday.com/archive/lunacy-crazy-indians-and-the-witchs-hammer-mental-health-care-as-oppression.

————. *Signal Peak.* Seattle: Thoughtful Publishing, 2013.

————. *Tessa's Dance.* Seattle: Thoughtful Publishing, 2011.

————. "WHO Owns the Language: 'Domination Code' in the Mental Health GAP Action Program." *Ethical Human Psychology and Psychiatry* 24, no. 1 (Spring 2022): 5–25. https://doi.org/10.1891/EHPP-2021-0008.

Walker, David Edward, Virginia Blankenship, Jeffrey A. Ditty, and Kevin Lynch. "Prediction of Recovery in Closed Head Injured Adults: An Analysis of the MMPI, the Adaptive Behavior Scale, and a 'Quality of Life' Rating Scale." *Journal of Clinical Psychology* 43, no. 6 (November 1987): 699–707.

Walker, George Lee. *The Chronicles of Doodah.* New York: Houghton-Mifflin, 1985.

Walls, Melissa L., Constance L. Chapple, and Kurt D. Johnson. "Strain, Emotion, and Suicide Among American Indian Youth." *Deviant Behavior* 28, no. 3 (2007): 219–46. https://doi.org/10.1080/01639620701233100.

Wang, Willie. "Discovering Xingkaihu: Political Inmates in a PRC Labor Camp." *East Asia* 25, no. 3 (2008): 267–92.

Ward, Leah Beth. "EPIC Turns Over Head Start Programs to Another Provider." *Yakima Herald-Republic,* April 15, 2013. http://www.yakimaherald.com/news/local/epic-turns-over-head-start-programs-to-another-provider/article_c43e7d4f-eeba-5d7e-9b03-cad3ba64d778.html.

Watkins, Mary, and Helene Shulman. *Toward Psychologies of Liberation.* New York: Palgrave Macmillan, 2008.

Watson, Julia. *Lo-TEK Design by Radical Indigenism.* Cologne, Germany: Taschen, 2021.

Watts, Linda K. and Sara E. Gutierres. "A Native American-Based Cultural Model of Substance Dependency and Recovery." *Human Organization* 56, no. 1 (Spring 1997): 9–18. https://doi.org/10.17730/humo.56.1.482676010686tq51.

Wentling, Nikki. "Native American Veterans Finally Get Audience with Congress." *Stars and Stripes.* November 1, 2019. https://www.stripes.com/theaters/us/native-american-veterans-finally-get-audience-with-congress-1.605544.

Werneke, U., S. Northey S., and D. Bhugra. "Antidepressants and Sexual Dysfunction," *Acta Psychiatrica Scandinavica* 114 (2006): 384–97. https://doi.org/10.1111/j.1600-0447.2006.00890.x.

West, Mike, "These Veterans Fought for Independence," *The Murfreesboro Post* (June 29, 2007). http://rutherfordtnhistory.org/veterans-fought-independence/.

Whitaker, Leighton C. "Resistances to Critical Thinking About Brain Shrinking 1955–2015." *Ethical Human Psychology and Psychiatry* 17, no. 2 (2015): 86–99. https://doi.org/10.1891/1559-4343.17.2.86.

Whitaker, Robert. *Anatomy of an Epidemic: Magic Bullets, Psychiatric Drugs, and the Astonishing Rise of Mental Illness in America.* Danvers, MA: Broadway Books, 2011.

————. "The Triumph of Bad Science." *Mad in America,* July 11, 2012. https://www.madinamerica.com/2012/07/the-triumph-of-bad-science/.

Whitaker, Robert, and Lisa Cosgrove. *Psychiatry Under the Influence: Institutional Corruption, Social Injury, and Prescriptions for Reform.* New York: Palgrave Macmillan, 2015.

Whitbeck, Les B., Gary W. Adams, Dan R. Hoyt, and Xiaojin Chen. "Conceptualizing and Measuring Historical Trauma Among American Indian People." *American Journal of Community Psychology* 33, nos. 3–4 (June 2004): 119–30. https://doi.org/10.1023/b:ajcp.0000027000.77357.31.

Whitbeck, Les B., Melissa L. Walls, Kurt D. Johnson, Allan D. Morrisseau, and Cindy M. McDougall. "Depressed Affect and Historical Loss Among North American Indigenous Adolescents." *American Indian and Alaska Native Mental Health Research* 16, no. 3 (2009): 16–41. https://doi.org/10.5820/aian.1603.2009.16.

Whitney, Eric. "Native Americans Feel Invisible in U.S. Health Care System." National Public Radio, *Morning Edition*, December 12, 2017. https://www.npr.org/sections/health-shots/2017/12/12/569910574/native-americans-feel-invisible-in-u-s-health-care-system.

Wild, George Posey. "History of Education of the Plains Indians of Southwestern Oklahoma Since the Civil War." PhD diss. Proquest Dissertations & Theses, 1941.

Wilkins, David. "Dismembering Natives: The Violence Done by Citizenship Fights." *Indian Country Today*, May 16, 2014. https://indiancountrytoday.com/archive/dismembering-natives-the-violence-done-by-citizenship-fights.

Wilkins, Levina. "Nine Virtues of the Yakama Nation." *Democracy & Education* 17, no. 2 (2008): 29–32. https://www.cwu.edu/teaching-learning/sites/cts.cwu.edu.teaching-learning/files/documents/9_virtues_yakama_nation.pdf.

Wilson, James. *The Earth Shall Weep: A History of Native America.* New York: Grove/Atlantic, 2007.

Wilson, Michael D. "Reclaiming Self-Determination for the Indian Self-Determination and Education Assistance Act of 1975." *International Journal of Qualitative Studies in Education* 25, no. 7 (2012): 905–12. https://doi.org/10.1080/09518398.2012.720734.

Wilson, Reid. "Native Americans Warn of Voter Suppression in Western States." *The Hill.* April 22, 2022. https://thehill.com/homenews/state-watch/3459240-native-americans-warn-of-voter-suppression-in-western-states/.

Wong, Julia Carrie. "Dakota Access Pipeline: 300 Protesters Injured After Police Use Water Cannons." *Guardian*, November 21, 2016. https://www.theguardian.com/us-news/2016/nov/21/dakota-access-pipeline-water-cannon-police-standing-rock-protest.

Wood, Larry E. *The Civil War on the Lower Kansas-Missouri Border.* Joplin, MO: Hickory Press, 2016.

Woodard, Stephanie. "The Police Killings No One Is Talking About." *In These Times*, October 17, 2016. https://inthesetimes.com/article/the-police-killings-no-one-is-talking-about.

———. "Racist Emails of Federal Judge; Why Native Advocates Want to See Them." *Indian Country Today*, January 20, 2014. updated September 13, 2018. https://indiancountrytoday.com/archive/racist-emails-of-federal-judge-why-native-advocates-want-to-see-them.

Woolford, Andrew, Jeff Benvenuto, and Alexander Laban Hinton, eds. *Colonial Genocide in Indigenous North America.* Durham, NC: Duke University Press, 2014.

Wyatt, W. Joseph and Donna M. Midkiff. "Biological Psychiatry: A Practice in Search of a Science." *Behavior and Social Issues* 15, no. 2 (Fall 2006): 132–51. https://doi.org/10.5210/bsi.v15i2.372.

Yakima County Coroner. "Yakima County Coroner Annual Report." 2015, 2016, 2017. http://www.yakimacounty.us/1867/Annual-Reports.

Yang, Jessica L., and Debora Ortega. "Bureaucratic Neglect and Oppression in Child Welfare: Historical Precedent and Implications for Current Practice." *Child and Adolescent Social Work Journal* 33, no. 6 (December 2016): 513–21. https://doi. org/10.1007/s10560-016-0446-4.

Yates, Donald N., and Teresa A. Yates. *Cherokee DNA Studies: Real People Who Proved the Geneticists Wrong*. Phoenix, AZ: Panther's Lodge, 2014.

Yehuda, Rachel, and Linda M. Bierer. "The Relevance of Epigenetics to PTSD: Implications for the DSM-V." *Journal of Traumatic Stress* 22, no. 5 (2009): 427–34. https://doi.org/10.1002/jts.20448.

Yehuda, Rachel, Nikolaos P. Daskalakis, Linda M. Bierer, Heather N. Bader, Torsten Klengel, Florian Holsboer, Elisabeth B. Binder, "Holocaust Exposure Induced Intergenerational Effects on FKBP5 Methylation," *Biological Psychiatry* 80, no. 5. (2016): 372–380. https://doi.org/10.1016/j.biopsych.2015.08.005.

Yehuda, Rachel, Nikolaos P. Daskalakis, Amy Lehrner, Frank Desarnaud, Heather N. Bader, Iouri Makotkine, Janine D. Flory, Linda M. Bierer, and Michael J Meaney. "Influences of Maternal and Paternal PTSD on Epigenetic Regulation of the Glucocorticoid Receptor Gene in Holocaust Survivor Offspring." *American Journal of Psychiatry* 171, no. 8 (August 2014): 872–80. https://doi.org/10.1176/appi.ajp.2014.13121571.

Yehuda, Rachel, Stephanie Mulherin Engel, Sarah R. Brand, Jonathan Seckl, Sue M. Marcus, and Gertrud S. Berkowitz. "Transgenerational Effects of Posttraumatic Stress Disorder in Babies of Mothers Exposed to the World Trade Center Attacks During Pregnancy." *Journal of Clinical Endocrinology & Metabolism* 90, no. 7 (July 2005): 4115–18. https://doi.org/10.1210/jc.2005-0550.

Yehuda, Rachel, Amy Lehrner, and Linda M. Bierer. "The Public Reception of Putative Epigenetic Mechanisms in the Transgenerational Effects of Trauma." *Environmental Epigenetics* 4, no. 2 (March 2018). https://doi.org/10.1093/eep/dvy018.

Yellow Bird, Pemina. "Wild Indians: Native Perspectives on the Hiawatha Asylum for Insane Indians." n. d. https://power2u.org/wp-content/uploads/2017/01/NativePerspectivesPeminaYellowBird.pdf.

Yellow Horse Brave Heart, Maria. "*Wakiksuyapi*: Carrying the Historical Trauma of the Lakota." *Tulane Studies in Social Welfare* 21–22 (January 2000): 245–66.

Yellow Horse Brave Heart, Maria, and Lemyra M. DeBruyn. "The American Indian Holocaust: Healing Historical Unresolved Grief." *American Indian and Alaska Native Mental Health Journal* 8, no. 2 (1998): 60–82. https://doi.org/10.5820/aian.0802.1998.60.

Yellow Horse Brave Heart, Maria, Josephine Chase, Jennifer Elkins, and Deborah B. Altschul. "Historical Trauma Among Indigenous Peoples of the Americas: Concepts, Research, and Clinical Considerations." *Journal of Psychoactive Drugs* 43, no. 4 (October–December 2011): 282–90. https://doi.org/10.1080/02791072.2011.628913.

Yoakum, Clarence Stone, and Robert M. Yerkes. *Army Mental Testing*. New York: Henry Holt, 1927.

Yokel, Jerry, and Mike Priddy, *Uranium and Other Chemical Contaminants Entering the Columbia River from the South Columbia Basin Irrigation Outfalls: A Cooperative Study by the Washington State Departments of Ecology and Health*. November 2010. Publication no. 10-05-019. https://fortress.wa.gov/ecy/publications/documents/1005019.pdf.

Zahl, Per-Henrik, Diego De Leo, Øivind Ekeberg, Heidi Hjelmeland, and Gudrun Dieserud. "The Relationship Between Sales of SSRI, TCA and Suicide Rates in the Nordic Countries." *BMC Psychiatry* 10 (August 2010). https://doi. org/10.1186/1471-244X-10-62.

Zaveri, Mihir. "Killing of 5 on Indian Reservation Underscores Challenge with Violent Crime." *New York Times*, June 12, 2019. https://www.nytimes.com/2019/06/12/ us/yakama-indian-reservation-killings.html.

Zimering, Rose, Suzy B. Gulliver, Jeffrey Knight, James Munroe, Terence M. Keane. "Posttraumatic Stress Disorder in Disaster Relief Workers Following Direct and Indirect Trauma Exposure to Ground Zero." *Journal of Traumatic Stress* 19, no. 4 (August 2006): 553–57. https://doi.org/10.1002/jts.20143.

Zinn, Howard. *A People's History of the United States, 1492–Present.* New York: Routledge, 1980.

Zweigenhaft, Richard. "Diversity Among CEOs and Corporate Directors: Has the Heyday Come and Gone?" American Sociological Association, New York City, August 12, 2013. From website transcription, "Who Rules America," administered by G. William Domhoff, Department of Sociology, University of California at Santa Cruz. http://www2.ucsc.edu/whorulesamerica/power/diversity_among_ceos.htm.

INDEX

References to illustrations are in italic type.

Alexander, Elizabeth Jane Albina
(Missouri Cherokee, author's
ancestor), 224, 226, 308n35
"Alvin" (composite case), 187–90
American Indian Movement (AIM), 28,
118, 183
American Medico-Psychological
Association *See* American Psychiatric
Association
American Psychiatric Association, 50–51,
74–75, 104, 159, 241, 242, 288–89;
Association of Medical Superintendents
of American Institutions for the
Insane, 220, 236; American Medico-
Psychological Association, 271
American Psychological Association, 65,
176, 178, 192, 289
Armed Forces Qualification Test
(AFQT) *See* Tests and surveys
Armed Services Vocational Aptitude
Battery (ASVAB). *See* Tests and
surveys
Army Alpha and Beta tests. *See* Tests and
surveys
Attention Deficit Hyperactivity
Disorder (ADHD), 67, 90, 94–95,
104, 109, 143, 328n65; and Native
"feeblemindedness," 181, 316n18

Bache, Richard Meade (U.S. race
psychologist), 192
Bailey, Colonel Pearce (U.S. military
neurologist), 271
Battle of Sugar Point (Ojibwe uprising),
391n54

Bell curve (Gaussian distribution), 182;
and classist underpinnings, 329n69
Binet, Alfred (French psychologist),
176–77, 179, 199
Biomedical model, 37–38, 52, 79, 84, 160,
180–81, 289; bioreductionism, 140,
156, 159, 162, 164; biopsychiatric,
84, 108, 140, 160, 181, 284, 286, 290;
and "Decade of the Brain," 159, 162;
and "domination code," 159–60, 181,
284, 287; and brain-wide association
studies, 109
Blood quantum. *See* Native American,
identity factors
Boarding schools, American Indian, 4,
39, 44, 69, 83, 139, 141, 184, 187–206;
and boxing, 190–92; Chemawa
Indian School (Salem, OR), 95,
205–6, *206*; "child snatching," 196;
Flandreau Indian School (Flandreau,
SD), 188, 203; Fort Simcoe Boarding
School (White Swan, WA), 131, *197*;
Haskell Indian School (United States
Indian Industrial Training School,
Lawrence, KS), 187–88, 199;
Methodist Mission Boarding School
(Yakima Indian Christian School,
White Swan, WA), 4; "outing programs,"
203; psychological testing, 191–205;
and regimen, 131, 195–96; Santee
Normal Training School (Santee,
NE), 199; St. Mary's Mission School
(Springfield, SD), 199; student
defiance, 187–88, 197, 203, 206;
Tulalip Indian School, *196*